Teaching in an Age of Ideology

Teaching in an Age of Ideology

Edited by John von Heyking and Lee Trepanier

LEXINGTON BOOKS
Lanham • Boulder • New York • Toronto • Plymouth, UK

Published by Lexington Books
A wholly owned subsidiary of The Rowman & Littlefield Publishing Group, Inc.
4501 Forbes Boulevard, Suite 200, Lanham, Maryland 20706
www.rowman.com

10 Thornbury Road, Plymouth PL6 7PP, United Kingdom

British Library Cataloguing in Publication Information Available

Library of Congress Cataloging-in-Publication Data

Teaching in an age of ideology / edited by John von Heyking and Lee Trepanier.
    p. cm.
  Includes bibliographical references.
  ISBN 978-0-7391-7359-6 (cloth : alk. paper)—ISBN 978-0-7391-7360-2 (ebook) 1.
Political science—Study and teaching. 2. Philosophers. 3. College teachers. I. Heyking,
John von. II. Trepanier, Lee, 1972–
  JA86.T38 2012
  320.071—dc23

                                                              2012027981

♾™ The paper used in this publication meets the minimum requirements of American
National Standard for Information Sciences—Permanence of Paper for Printed Library
Materials, ANSI/NISO Z39.48-1992.

Printed in the United States of America

To our teachers,

and for our students

Table of Contents

Introduction

Teaching Political Philosophy: Thinking in Action
John von Heyking and
Lee Trepanier

Michael Henry, in his contribution to this volume, reports on the experience of James Rhodes, whose life changed when, as an undergraduate at the University of Notre Dame, he walked into the classroom of Gerhart Niemeyer:

> Like Socrates [Niemeyer] exerted such a magnetic attraction on those of kindred spirit that many can still vividly recall the first encounter with him as a sudden, electrifying realization of being in the mind-expanding and life-changing presence of an extraordinary man. James Rhodes, for instance, reports that his life changed forever when as a chemistry major he "wandered into" Niemeyer's course in Political Theory in 1959 and found a professor "thinking, luminously, about the ultimate questions of human existence," something he had never encountered before. He abandoned chemistry because, as he put it '…I realized soon that I wanted to spend all my years doing what he did, in the way he did it.'[1]

The experience of meeting a teacher who expands one's mind and changes one's life is common to all the great thinkers discussed in this book. Indeed, the capacity to instill such transformation is central to the art of teaching, as recognized by teachers and students going back to Plato's discovery of his "elder friend," Socrates and to the turning-around of the soul (*periagoge*) that Plato describes as the essence of education.

Which is that education is a quest shared by persons, with the entirety of their personalities engaged. Unlike Socrates, the thinkers discussed in this volume were scholars and, as such, each left behind a considerable amount of written work detailing their ideas concerning political order and disorder, wisdom and ignorance, virtue and vice, and liberal education. But the focus of this volume is as much on their activities as teachers as on their writings. Socrates left behind no writings. Plato's (and Xenophon's) account of Socrates presents him, though, as a teacher and, when read dramatically, one is reminded that learning is not merely a matter of receiving doctrine (which would be the viewpoint of the sophists), but is also an embodied experience whereby the teacher's presence is perhaps equally important as the ideas that he or she is communicating. Of course, none of the contributors express the sort of dramatic (or salacious) excitement that an Alcibiades expresses for Socrates. Though at least one thinker examined in this volume, Stanley Rosen, compares with Plato insofar as both came to their respective teachers first as poets, and then ended up studying philosophy.

This volume considers the political philosopher in action, namely, as a teacher. The critique of ideology, in one form or another, forms the focus of the writings among most political philosophers of the twentieth century, which distinguishes these thinkers from Socrates, as ideology is a particularly modern phenomenon. We shall not here attempt to provide a definition for it; each contributor defines it in accordance to the way his or her political thinker understood it. Even so, each thinker considered in this volume analyzed ideology, denounced it, criticized it, and attempted to find ways of transcending it in the form of a more authentic way of thinking. While many of the thinkers considered here were active in the twentieth-century, their resistance, as teachers, to the ideologies they confronted illuminates our current experience. For example, the criticism of Marxism or historicism by Eric Voegelin or Leo Strauss illuminates our own efforts as teachers to assist students confront cognate ideologies, including political correctness, Islamism, conspiricism, virulent anti-Americanism, and technicism (or technology) and scientism. Indeed, for many thinkers under review, including Edmund Husserl, Hannah Arendt, and Leo Strauss, technology and scientism are at the core of modern ideology. Ideology, then, seems to represent a distortion of political philosophy, which each these thinkers attempted to recover.

Together, but a way of being in the world or a way of life. While intellectual biography offers one mode of considering the action of political philosophy, considering their activity of teaching is another. This volume of essays considers their activity of political philosophy as exhibited in their teaching as well as how, in their writings, they understood ideology and political philosophy.

Contributors to this volume each consider a number of questions in their presentation of each thinker as teacher. What is the nature of liberal education? What is the nature of ideology? To what extent, or how, can liberal education be pursued in an age of ideology? To what extent is the modern university a place of learning? What are the obstacles to liberal education in the modern university? How does the thinker embody liberal education? How did he/she get students to learn? What is teaching? What is learning?

This volume is divided into three main sections. Section One, "Thinking and Teaching Against Ideology" considers the teaching efforts of a variety of political thinkers and philosophers, including Edmund Husserl, Hannah Arendt, Raymond Aron, and Bernard Lonergan. On the surface, these thinkers share little in common. Indeed, neither Husserl nor Lonergan are usually considered political thinkers. Even so, the essays on these thinkers demonstrate a common understanding of the art of teaching in an ideological age and the challenges of transcending ideology into philosophical thinking.

In her essay, "Edmund Husserl: Transcending Ideology," Molly Flynn sets the tone for the volume by providing a careful analysis of Husserl's critique of ideology in the form of historicism, as well as in the form of scientism which for him, as for several other thinkers treated in this volume, forms of the core of the "crisis" of modern intellectual and political life. While Husserl was not a political thinker in the sense of offering a political philosophy that studies political forms, virtues, justice, and so forth, Flynn argues that by teaching his students how to think, he understood himself as contributing to a re-founding of European culture, and in that sense he was a political thinker in a grander sense. Flynn shows that Husserl was hardly a charismatic teacher, but that his lack of charisma had in fact pedagogic value because his students "were convinced by a man's thoughts, not by a man." Like an ironic Socrates whom Kierkegaard notes "must magnanimously will to annihilate himself,"[2] Husserl served as midwife to his students who learned to think for themselves. As Flynn reports,

> being a disciple of Husserl could not mean being a mere follower. By disappearing behind the thought, by displaying sincerity and dedication to the truth, Husserl at his best drew out of his students a desire to be like him in crucial virtues without impressing on his students the desire to become another him or to act as his dummy.

Husserl's influence on subsequent thinkers who were more ostensibly political cannot be overestimated. It is difficult to imagine Leo Strauss's critique of historicism without the precedent of Husserl, and Eric Voegelin acknowledges his own intellectual debt, in developing his understanding of consciousness, to Husserl. Hannah Arendt, in her *Human Condition*, picks up Husserl's critique of modern scientism, with its Galilean roots, as one of the main sources of modern ideology. The mathematicization of reality is a form of will to power over reality, it is a mode of making, not of thinking. Thus, in her essay, "How Thinking Saves Us," Leah Bradshaw considers Arendt's understanding of the activity of thinking as an antidote to ideology whereby (quoting Jerome Kohn), Arendt "was reviving the Greek distinction between *theoria* and *theoremata*, between the activity of thinking and its outcome in 'true' theorems." This distinction is crucial for her understanding of totalitarianism and ideology: "the ideal subject of a totalitarian state is not the committed party loyalist, but 'people for whom the distinction between fact and fiction (i.e., the reality of experience) and the distinction between true and false (i.e., the standards of thought) no longer exist." Bradshaw suggests that modern life today is too mediated and confused by technology, which makes it fertile ground for new ideologies. Thus, Arendt tried to retrieve that sense of experience in the activity of thinking. Like many other thinkers in this volume, Socrates serves as a prime example for thinking (as opposed to philosophy), which "means not being out of harmony with myself." Socrates exemplifies the "two in one" activity of thinking of an individual who lives in the world and is responsible for herself and for her world (like one of Arendt's mentor's, Karl Jaspers, and unlike her other mentor, Martin Heidegger). And the "two in one" character of thinking means, ultimately, that one must be friends with oneself; one must take responsibility for one's life and for one's actions.

Responsibility for political thinking is at the core of Raymond Aron's thinking and teaching. As Bryan-Paul Frost explains in his contribution, "Raymond Aron's Pedagogical Constitution and the Pursuit of Liberal Education," a humiliating experience Aron suffered in his early academic career, in 1932, made a profound mark upon him. An undersecretary in the French Foreign Ministry, Joseph Paganon had invited Aron to deliver some remarks on the rising tensions with Germany and he had been critical of the French Prime Minister's handling of the situation. However, Aron's remarks seem to have been too abstract and theoretical for the politician to gain any benefit. Paganon bluntly asked Aron: "what would you do if you were in his place?" Paganon's query, which was simple enough, caught Aron flat footed because until then Aron had approached political thinking in the "literary" way typically conducted by most ideologues, of offering critique but without attention to the prudential concern that political knowledge is about what should be done. This concern for practice, and taking responsibility for one's prudential decisions, forms the hallmark of Aron's brand of liberalism and his critique of ideology. Frost shows how Aron combined the wisdom of Aristotle and Machiavelli to transcend ideology. First, Aristotle's perspective allows the thinker to understand all competing political demands and that "no claim (or party) in politics is either completely wrong or right, and that no side has a perfectly just cause...: politics is not about good versus evil but about choosing between 'the preferable and the detestable.'" Next, Machiavelli's perspective is not altogether dissimilar in that it offers the government's perspective "of what it could most reasonably expect to accomplish under the prevailing circumstances." Most ideologues reverse the order and importance of these two perspectives and end up promoting some utopian evil: they end up refusing to think politically. Frost uses the example of Aron's response to the crisis of French universities in 1968 to show Aron the teacher in action, which consisted largely of reminding his compatriots of the mission of the university and why it is not the same as the radical egalitarianism, which the students demanded.

In his essay, "Bernard Lonergan: Towards a Pedagogy of Political Thinking," Lance Grigg addresses how responsibility for thinking is central to Lonergan. With his "transcendent method," Lonergan teaches us to be fully conscious of what we are doing when we are thinking. "What am I doing when I am thinking," is the central question for the method, which issues four basic imperatives: be attentive, be intelligent, be reasonable, and be responsible. Not surprisingly, the ideologue fails to think authentically because it discourages the formation of political questions and insights following them. For Lonergan, "ideological thinking suffers from an oversight of insight," which restricts the scope of thinking. Conversely, insight "comes as release to the tension of inquiry... and comes suddenly and unexpectedly." While Lonergan did not develop a systematic political philosophy, his focus on the activity of thinking, as well as his own practice of teaching within the setting of the Catholic church, provides insight into political thinking. For Lonergan, thinking depends on the capacity to develop "well-phrased questions" that arise with direct attention to the setting or community in which the thinker's action takes place. As with Aristotle, political thinking is prudential and rooted in one's regime, which conditions the sorts of political questions one must ask. This setting is crucial also to understand Lonergan as teacher, who somehow managed to teach students to think during his years at the Gregorianum in Rome, with classes as large as 650 students and with oftentimes overbearing oversight of his insight by his superiors.

Section Two consists of essays on Eric Voegelin and teachers influenced by him, Gerhart Niemeyer, Ellis Sandoz, and John Hallowell. This group does not so much consist of a school as opposed to a set of scholars animated by a set of concerns voiced primarily by Plato and Christianity.

In "The Art of the *Periagoge*: Eric Voegelin as Teacher," John von Heyking examines the centrality of the turning around of the soul (*periagoge*) for Voegelin by considering Voegelin's assessment of ideology, both in its soft forms (positivism) and hard forms (i.e., Marxism, Gnosticism, pneumopathology), and how Voegelin regarded, Socratically, education as the enlargement of common sense, not as displacement, as ideology has it. The task of education in age of ideology consists in the effort to regain reality, which requires the cultivation of pretheoretical virtues, and so consists in a reorientation and bringing-to-consciousness of one's philosophical eros. Education consists of becoming conscious of man's restless quest for order. Because this is both a personal and a political activity, the essay concludes with a consideration of Voegelin's effort in his "Hitler and the Germans" lectures to refound the German spiritual community.

In "Gerhart Niemeyer as Educator: The Defense of Western Culture in an Ideological Age," Michael Henry reflects on the profound impact Niemeyer had on his students, mostly at the University of Notre Dame. His "defense of western culture" consisted in cultivating "sons" (though not disciples) who "would pass on the heritage of the wisdom of tradition and the love of truth 'in God.'" He regarded the student-teacher relationship as a "species of friendship," though one in which the student was required to meet very high standards of thought and scholarship. "Ontology was at root of everything for Niemeyer" because the good life consists in the proper ordering of our entire selves to the whole amplitude of reality, whereas ideology has its roots in modernity's rebellion and commitment to "substitute realities." Education therefore is the cultivation of the "existential virtues," which in Niemeyer's approach includes reflections on the role of the Catholic university in society, where "the pursuit of truth and the transmission of knowledge are systematically kept open to the presupposition of a divine creation and the reliance on divine salvation."[3]

In "Ellis Sandoz as Master Teacher: Consistent in belief, Steadfast in Purpose," Charles Embry considers Ellis Sandoz's influence on a wide array of students...Embry describes the turning around of the soul (periagoge) that Sandoz instilled in numerous students, and that Sandoz himself experienced under the master teacher, Eric Voegelin:

> In the past of many teachers and political philosophers there stands an existential encounter with another philosopher and teacher, in many cases a master teacher, whose character, insight, erudition, intellect, and presence inspires the student to become who he is already. In other words, the future teacher in the present student is evoked from the encounter with the master teacher. In a sense this existential encounter gives form to the pre-existing, inchoate, unformed teacher, identifying the vocation that student and future teacher is destined to follow. This existential encounter is sometimes so "drastic" that it effects a change in the student, a change that challenges and/or inspires that student to fulfill his potential both as a teacher and as a human being.

Evoking "what is already present" is the key to periagoge, of which Sandoz was master artist. As with Voegelin, education is an enlargement of common sense, whereas the Socratic "look and see if this is not the case," is spoken frequently because it invites students to look at "what is already present" within their own souls. Sandoz's focus in political thought pushes him further into the soul of American republicanism. He teaches human beings and American citizens, and encourages "the development of a civic consciousness that grounds liberal democratic political systems in 'self-evident truths.'"

Rounding out this section is Timothy Hoye's "John H. Hallowell: Principled Pragmatist." Hallowell's "principled pragmatism" rested on a Christian humanism that was also a "classical realism" according to which there is a "meaningful reality," "cosmos, not a chaos," that human beings are endowed with the dim capacity to understand it, that "being and goodness belong together," and that abiding by these principles makes life in society possible. Hallowell had personal experience in a tyranny that failed to abide by them, namely pre-Nazi Germany. After his undergraduate studies, Hallowell went to the University of Heidelberg to study with Karl Jaspers (a teacher of Hannah Arendt noted above). While there, he noticed the effects of totalitarian ideology among the students: "speaking in whispers huddled over a coffee table, for example, mindful that the children in the house were rewarded at school for sharing what their parents discussed at home; watching indigenous, German students stop coming to lectures by Jaspers... because SS agents in the hall outside of class periodically looking in and writing down names." For Hallowell, the ideological undercurrents of modernity had corroded our sense of the moral foundations of democracy, of which the collapse of Weimar Germany is the most vivid example. Throughout his career he sought to resist "decadent liberalism" by promoting an "integral liberalism" that is characterized by 1) rule of law, 2) belief in natural order that sustains society and individual, and 3) belief in natural rights which the state not only cannot deny but must protect.

Section Three considers Leo Strauss and two scholars working in the natural rights tradition he set forth, Stanley Rosen and Harvey Mansfield.

In "Liberal Education, Philosophy, and Politics: Leo Strauss as Teacher," Michael Zuckert describes Strauss's "two-fold intention" of education, the one being aimed at cultivating political life, and the other aimed at cultivating the activity of philosophy. Zuckert focuses on two essays by Strauss on liberal education to focus on the question: the one addresses liberal education in light of politics, whereby liberal education cultivates gentlemen (the Aristotelian intention), and the other essay addresses liberal education in light of philosophy (the Platonic intention), whereby liberal education (i.e., the study of great texts) prepares the way for philosophy. Regarding politics, liberal education resists the tastes and mores of mass culture and gives citizens a sense of the good and beautiful; regarding philosophy, liberal education resists historicism and technicism and introduces potential philosophers to the perennial questions of political order. Addressing Strauss as a teacher at the University of Chicago, Zuckert shows how Strauss emphasized the latter intention: "nearly every course began with a demonstration of the self-contradictory character of the historicist position, as prerequisite to opening the minds of his students to the possibility of that bold and even presumptuous act of judging that constitutes the step into philosophy." He goes on to describe Strauss's pedagogy of close readings of texts, and how Strauss the teacher rarely offered his own interpretations of texts because "he modeled for students the idea that one had to understand a thinker properly before one could judge him."

In "Stanley Rosen as an Educator," Nalim Ranasinghe explains the centrality for Rosen of common sense for philosophy. His extensive studies of nihilism and modern philosophers document the gap between thought and common sense, which Rosen's Platonism always strove to keep together. This insistence on common sense is what makes Rosen a great teacher, who never "'hermenutered' his students and left them incapable of reading for themselves." Indeed, his insistence on common sense drives Rosen's criticism of his Leo Strauss, his teacher, and his esoteric readings of texts. Esotericism, Rosen thinks, is irrelevant for the modern age. The crisis of nihilism and ideology makes today's students "unlettered, thoughtless and thoroughly exoteric." "By contrast, Rosen's account of the essential connection between Reason and the Good provides a richly comprehensive erotic Platonism that is agreeable to the generous heart and fevered temperament of modernity."

In "Teaching Not Differently, But Further Than the Parties," Travis D. Smith describes the liberal education that students at Harvard receive from Harvey Mansfield, though Smith also extends his analysis to show how Mansfield is a public intellectual who teaches America about self-government. If Rosen emphasizes the Platonic intention of Strauss, it seems Mansfield emphasizes the Aristotelian. Mansfield shares the concern of Strauss and many others presented in this volume with modernity's flattening of the human soul, and its political expression in technology, or rational control. Responsibility is the focus of Mansfield's liberal education, as responsibility is what rational control and the shallow egalitarianism brought about by modernity attacks. Smith details the various ways Mansfield, through close readings of the texts of political philosophy, teaches responsibility: "To combat the prevailing ideologies of modernity, part of Mansfield's teaching is to tenaciously affirm the truth of various 'facts' that problematize the wishful thinking characteristic of his opponents. It is irresponsible not to take the facts into account and try to engineer the impossible, or succumb to utter defeatism or destructive nihilism just because perfection is unattainable. A genuinely philosophical or scientific theory of politics takes into account the whole of human nature, including an acknowledgment of its limitations. A responsible political regime likewise respects the limits that nature imposes, bounding the realm of the possible, cognizant that 'law cannot control nature.'" Responsibility, of course, requires the willingness to take risks, in thought and in action. Smith explains how Mansfield's pedagogy echoes his political teaching of responsibility, where rule seems invisible to the citizen/student: "His supervisory authority is left ambiguous in its particulars but ever-present in the backdrop, leaving it to the imagination of any student to guess at where they stand, supposing that he worries about them at all. Training graduate students to rely on themselves, he trusts that they will figure out what they need to, and if they cannot or will not, that's on them. Practicing political theory requires courage, self-assertion, self-examination, resilience, and risk-taking."

This collection celebrates the works of extraordinary individual thinkers who have tried to comprehend and to improve their political communities by turning the souls of their students away from ideology and towards their understanding of the truth. Although each of these thinkers approached the question of teaching differently, they all embodied the experience of a teacher's presence in the education of his or her students. Thus, the theoretical contributions of their scholarship remain not only in print but in the lives and practice of their students.

By no means is this volume comprehensive in its covering of the major political philosophers and thinkers of the twentieth century: it is merely a start of what we hope becomes a larger conversation about teaching and truth in an age of ideology. We also realize that written exposition will always fall short of the actual experience when the student encounters the teacher in periagoge. Our hope then is that this volume will be a record, albeit an imperfect one, of outstanding teachers who boldly sought to evoke wonder and to pass down truth to their students.

Before we conclude, we also want to thank our teachers who have influenced us in this project as well as people who have assisted us in its completion.

Specifically, we would like to thank James Harrison, director of the Southern Utah University Tanner Center, who hosted a symposium on this topic in 2011 which allowed some of the participants to present their ideas for critique and criticism; Donald J. Bachand, Provost at Saginaw Valley State University for his support; and Ann Garcia, the university's technical writer. On a personal note, we would like to acknowledge the love and support of our families: MiJung, Sonya, Geoff, Evie, Audrey, and Sebastian. As our teachers have showed us the importance of truth, our families have demonstrated the need for love.

Notes

1. Michael Henry, "Gerhart Niemeyer as Educator: The Defense of Western Culture in an Ideological Age," this volume.
2. Søren Kierkegaard, *Works of Love*, trans., Howard and Edna Hong, (Princeton: Princeton University Press, 1995), 276.
3. "Gerhart Niemeyer as Educator: The Defense of Western Culture in an Ideological Age," in this volume, citing Gehart Niemeyer, "The New Need for a Catholic University," in *Within and Above Ourselves: Essays in Political Analysis*, (Wilmington: The Intercollegiate Studies Institute, 1996), 250.

SECTION I:

THINKING AND TEACHING
AGAINST IDEOLOGY

Chapter 1

Edmund Husserl:
Transcending Ideology
Molly Brigid Flynn, Assumption College

Husserl was a German mathematician-turned-philosopher, born in Moravia—
now part of the Czech Republic, then part of the Austro-Hungarian Empire—
into a Jewish household. His breakthrough work, *The Logical Investigations* of
1900–1901, started the phenomenological movement, which tremendously influenced European thought in the twentieth century and which continues today
in Europe, America, and beyond.

After reading the New Testament, Husserl converted as a young man to a
rather non-doctrinal Christianity. He was a patriotic German and lost a son in
World War I. He was known for living a stoical, respectable, and even bourgeois
life at home and in universities: writing, lecturing, and talking. In 1933, his son
Gerhard, a philosopher of law, lost his job at the same time that the emeritus
Husserl was denied privileges at his university, because of their Jewish ethnici-
ty. His most famous student and his successor in the chair at the University of
Freiburg became Rector there and was just one of many National Socialists
called upon to enforce such ordinances. In 1938 Husserl died naturally before he
might have died violently—as Edith Stein, another of his students, did at
Auschwitz in 1942. In 1939, his wife and his incredible mass of papers were
smuggled safely to Belgium.

After the *Logical Investigations,* Husserl published several more, and indeed better, books and essays and lectures, treating philosophically, e.g., logic,
perception, our experience of other people, knowledge, time, human rational and
spiritual life, and the "lifeworld" of straightforward human experience. He was a

committed critic of the irrationalism of radical subjectivistic skepticisms, historicism, psychologism, and any theory that attempts to convince human persons
that they are incapable of reason and knowledge. For Husserl, the human mind
finds its fulfillment in truth, insight, evidence; that is, authentic thought is
knowledge of true being. Still, Husserl avoids a naïve rationalism, identifying
this fulfillment as an infinite task, with relative and temporary victories. While a
defender of the human ability to know and of philosophy as a science, he also
saw clearly that absolute knowledge is only approached by humans and that
philosophy is always re-beginning.

He wrote much more than he published. His posthumously published
works, lectures, letters, and personal research manuscripts show that he had a
philosophical breadth and a keenness for detail and deep problems that belong to
but a handful of philosophers in history. There is practically no philosophical
theme—from essences to cultural ontology to ethics—that he did not write about
rather intensely. Except, perhaps, for political life.

He was not a political philosopher. He was an apolitical philosopher. Still, I
think, Husserl's apolitical philosophy has some deep, if indirect, political implications.

The marching banner for phenomenologists has been "To the things themselves!" and phenomenologists feel most at home describing objects as they
show up to us. Husserl's philosophy attempts to recover the objectivity of reality
without succumbing to a crude objectivism. It recognizes that the objects we
experience have essences that structure how we can experience them, and it is as
interested in the subjective life in which we experience things as it is in the
things experienced. Phenomenology resists the objectification of persons, rational subjects who experience and know the world, into mere things; at the
same time, it resists the anti-realism that would deny either the objectivity of
worldly things or the special and distinct type of "transcendental" being that
each human person has.

This unjustly cursory summary of the man's life and conclusions must suffice as an introduction to this chapter and an invitation to the reader for a closer
look. This essay offers an Husserlian account of ideology and suggests, with
some appeal to "the things themselves" (the facts of his life), how Husserl the
teacher succeeded and perhaps failed in an time of ideological illusions and
tragedies.

Husserl's Apolitical Philosophy

> *Transcendental philosophy, a very useless art, does not aid the lords and mas-
> ters of this world, the politicians, engineers, industrialists.*[1]

Husserl wrote to his son Gerhard (July 5, 1935) that his philosophy is "wholly
unpolitical."[2] Except for a few scattered remarks, he is at his most political when
he speaks between the World Wars about the cultural "crisis" and growing irra-

tionalism of European life. The crisis, that is, was in his lights not primarily political. The obvious, terrifying, and tragic political events of this period of European history seem to have appeared to him as symptoms of a deeper disease of spirit and values: a disorder in our beliefs about reason, personhood, and truth. Namely, he believed that human beings as rational animals live under absolute norms of truth. To be genuinely human persons, to live up to our personhood, we must seek to live up to truth, where truth is not just theoretical but also evaluative and practical—it is a matter of how and what we think, but also of how and what we feel, value, and do. The crisis of values he identified and fought against in his later years arose, he thought, from a terrible rejection of reason. A narrow rationalism, identified usually with Enlightenment thought, is one form of this: "The European crisis has its roots in a misguided rationalism."[3] This rationalism had symptoms (e.g., naturalism, consumerism, a rebirth of egoistic nationalism, Nazism) in other cultural and political phenomena, which should be seen, at least partly, as misguided responses to or fallouts of this rejection of reason's central role in human life.

He thought that, to address this deeper crisis, what European life needed most was a rediscovery of reason in its properly broad and rich sense. And this was the task especially of philosophy and the philosophy of the other sciences. Husserl therefore emphasized (in a way many of his readers find embarrassing) the beginnings of philosophy in ancient Greece; the *telos* of European culture as the development of this love of truth with its concern for self-critique and evidence; the need for Europe to rededicate itself to this idea; and our vocation to share it with the rest of humanity. He feared that our response to the failure of modern rationalism would be a "fall into hostility toward spirit and into barbarity," but he hoped that we might instead overcome what a narrow rationalism has led us into, namely, a reductive, naïve objectivism, with its cynical dismissal of ethical and rational norms: the choice was between "the downfall of Europe in its estrangement from its own rational sense of life" and "the rebirth of Europe from the spirit of philosophy."[4]

In speaking of this crisis, Husserl urged a return to the Greek spirit, especially in its rejection of sophistry. He paints Socrates as defending the ethical life against the sophists who had, "through their subjectivism, confused and corrupted general moral convictions."[5] Socrates did not just defend the pre-sophistic status quo, of course, but responded to sophistry by trying to raise humanity to a new level, insisting on the need for human beings to live out a radical, self-critiquing search for justification and insight in ethical life. Husserl paints Plato as further defending this radical Socratic dedication to ethical truth and self-responsibility by responding to the sophistic "anti-scientific skepticism"; namely, Plato did this by developing philosophy as a science, as theoretical knowledge, and by developing an understanding of how "the communal life" or "man writ large" defends "the rational individual life."[6] In these ways, philosophy becomes in some sense the foundation for a reasonable and genuinely human life, individually and communally.[7]

When concluding the 1910 "Philosophy as a Rigorous Science," after refuting the skeptical pseudoscientific reductions of reason by naturalism, psychologism, and historicism, Husserl turns to discuss worldviews and philosophy. He rejects what we might call worldviewism, the claim linked especially to historicism that one's reason is determined by one's or the epoch's view of the world. But he does not deny that worldview is something influential over the way we think, and even a positive something, since in its best sense it is wise. He then discusses worldview philosophy, which is the attempt by thinkers to give a worldview grand theoretical clarity and depth. We need wisdom in the world, good practical judgment shaped by experience and informed by a sense of the puzzles of human life and the cosmos. The attempts to deepen and make consistent such thought are worthwhile.

Here Husserl recognizes a service played by such thought, he just denies that it is philosophy in the proper, scientific sense. He implies that, though such thought may be more urgent, it is "from certain points of view" less important than true philosophy.[8] To try to turn worldview reflection into philosophy in his radical and proper sense is to give in to our age's "fanaticism" about science, and would manage only to sacrifice real philosophizing for a proliferation of worldview-filled wise men.[9] Here belongs Husserl's comment to his student Aron Gurwitsch: "There are philosophers aplenty. Someone must do the dirty work—that is me and you."[10] Worldview philosophy must take positions without radical ground, whereas philosophy must work slowly, from the ground up, seeking truth with justification and understanding. "For the sake of time, we must not sacrifice eternity."[11] Even those thinkers who have given history its highest worldviews, he comments, did so because they were aiming for philosophy as knowledge.

In 1919, an admiring and critical young thinker, Arnold Metzger, who later became his personal assistant, wrote to Husserl and included several writings, including *Phänomenologie der Revolution*, which was a "critique of philosophies which become ideologies defending a bankrupt social order" and a "quest for genuine ideals of humanity which can serve as a basis for social rebirth."[12] Husserl responded in a long letter urging the young man to study with him. He encouraged Metzger while deeply and sharply disagreeing with him: "I cannot help doubting and even definitely rejecting much of what you say."[13] Husserl praised Metzger's idealism and "ethical maximalism," his desire to renew mankind by reminding it of true ideals, and his "critical examination" of Marxism, naturalism, positivism, and any other attempt to rob human life of worthy ideals, but Husserl also marks some deep disagreements.[14]

In addition to trying to correct Metzger's interpretation of his transcendental turn, Husserl insisted on a kind of practical difference between them. Husserl was clearly moved by the young man's dedication to ideals and to the imperative of improving culture and politics. In fact, in the letter Husserl identifies the point of his whole life and philosophy as, in a sense, serving this improvement of humanity, and he denies that scientific truth is the fulfillment of human life. Still, Husserl backs off of politics and of any direct political use of philosophy.

He says, contrasting Metzger to himself, "you are a man of action by vocation and preference." Though driven by the same radical ethical and philosophical concerns as Husserl, Metzger's theoretically informed political striving needs more, and better, philosophy *first*: "then comes the demanding task already attributed to you, the study of human realities and their philosophical guidance."

> This is not my task; I am not called to lead humanity in striving for happy life. I had to acknowledge this in the sorrowful course of my war years: my *daimonion* warned me. I live consciously and by choice purely as a scientific philosopher (I have written no books concerning the war, since I regarded that as a pretentious philosophical ostentation). Not that I consider truth and science the highest values. Quite the contrary, "Intellect is the servant of the will," and so also I am the servant of those who shape our practical life, of the leaders of humanity.—Naturally, you will not want to accept this apportioning of functions as valid. You are young, and full of the overflowing consciousness of your strength; you still believe that you can and must attempt both functions. But as long as God preserves you in the Socratic dedication and in the radicalism of truthful life, your *daimonion* will speak to you at the right time.[15]

Husserl then adds a warning, because genuine philosophy is harder than it seems.

The will is subject to the norms of truth, namely, the true good, and seeking truth in its fullness is an ethical task, but Husserl suggests here that scientific truth is not sufficient for good practical decisions, and that the scientific life should not be confused with the active life of political leadership.

In his 1923-24 articles for the Japanese journal *Kaizo*, Husserl expresses the need for a reorientation of culture and values. He makes two points in the first of these articles, "Renewal: Its Problem and Method," key to understanding his approach to philosophy, politics, and ideology.

First, he distinguishes between the type of rationalization of the universe done by the natural sciences, which explain by appealing to causes, and the rationalization to be done with the help of the spiritual sciences, which can explain by pointing toward norms according to which humans as free and rational animals should motivate themselves. Because human thought is subject to norms, and not merely the play thing of (psychological, economic, political, historical, etc.) forces, the human sciences must not ape the natural sciences in methods or aims. Real cultural renewal, a movement toward a more genuinely human life, requires scientific philosophy of the human person, community, and reason.

Scientific philosophy must help us understand the essential structures of human life and the world, but it must also articulate the normative ideals of reason, and in this way lead humanity toward a higher life. Though sometimes Husserl is too naïve in his statement of this kingly role of philosophers, we should perhaps understand his vision as something like this: natural scientists seem to be in our time admired as the paradigm of reason and as the articulators of the ideals of the rational life, and Husserl believes this role should be filled by those who are dedicated to reason in its radicalness, breadth, and normative power—philosophers. As he says later, the "prosperity" of positive sciences has blinded us and has "meant an indifferent turning-away from the questions which are decisive for a genuine humanity. Merely fact-minded sciences make merely fact-minded people."[16] Husserl's is simultaneously a call to culture at large to reorient itself toward a fuller sense of reason and also a call to philosophers to do so, and thereby to serve culture, not by doing something other than philosophy, but precisely by being better philosophers.[17]

Though the first point from the "Renewal" essay worth emphasis here is that scientific philosophy is needed in order to move toward a truly human, reasonable life, individually and communally, the second is that scientific philosophy is limited in its ability to help us live in practical reason. Though at other times he seems to overstate the effectiveness of a philosophical renewal for a cultural renewal, here Husserl clearly indicates that a proper philosophy is needed, but not enough. Whereas "the merely empirical sciences of man...cannot offer us what we need in our striving for renewal," the proper "helper" of this renewal is an actual understanding of what human spirituality—in its individual, social, political, and cultural dimensions—essentially is, can be, and should seek to be.[18] A scientific philosophy of human life provides "preparatory theoretical work" for the reasonable renewal of culture.[19] And again, reflecting on the failure of philosophy so far to provide an understanding of the essential structures and norms of human life, Husserl asks,

> What should we do? Should we again proceed, as in political matters when, for instance, as citizens we prepare to vote? Are we supposed to judge only according to instinct and inclination, according to assumption we tend to overlook? Actions like these may be perfectly justified if the day comes on which such a decision is required, and with it the action is completed. But in our case there is a concern for a temporal infinity and for the eternal in the temporal—the future of mankind, the genesis of a true humanity—for which we still feel ourselves responsible.[20]

The task of the philosopher is in certain respects more important but less urgent in addressing the cultural crisis. It is more kingly, but less forceful. It reaches in more deeply but cuts less directly than politics. It invests for centuries, but does not solve the pressing practical problems of today and tomorrow.

Some have accused Husserl of presenting an ultimately anarchist political philosophy, because when he describes the ideal human community—the "genuine humanity" for which his philosophy feels responsible—it is not a political community. The question remains[21] how various types of political community could help or hinder the development toward such a perfect "community of love," an ideal and infinitely distant, multi- and super-national human life. Still, this ideal is in itself not political. That is just to say, for Husserl, human being would find its highest earthly culmination in a truly ethical, reasonable, and love-infused personal and communally shared life; government is not the point or the fulfillment, but a servant of this life, and how it can serve this life seems to be mostly a matter of prudence. This prudence can and should be informed by scientific philosophy's elucidation of the essential structures of human life and community, and should be inspired by the norms of reason and ethics that philosophy can help articulate. Still, he implies, philosophy seems neither called nor able to supplant this prudence, the wisdom needed to serve human fulfillment politically in the human space that must remain under of this ideal.

Husserl did not confront political ideologies directly. This came partly from a decision to protect what was most important in his work. This seems to me a wise tactical move. Philosophies are too often either expropriated or attacked by political movements. The best political thought to come out of his students has partly arisen from the conviction that there is a reality to human beings deeper than politics and a calling of human beings far beyond politics. Zdzisław Krasnodębski comments, for example, that it was the very apolitical nature of phenomenology that attracted philosophers behind the Iron Curtain to it, since in a totalitarian situation being unpolitical is a most powerful and subversive political statement.[22] Naturally—but ironically, from the point of view of politics—this conviction seems necessary for a decent politics. Politics has nothing to serve apart from itself unless we preserve and honor nonpolitical human goods. In philosophy it is a mistake and in practical politics it is a mishandling of our situation to make too much of politics.

The "apportioning of functions" Husserl wrote about to Metzger seems to follow from an important insight, an insight that gives political reason an incomplete but real independence from the philosophical task of securing scientific knowledge about essential structures of human life, valid but far off ideals, and universal *a priori* truths. It is an insight that respects non-philosophical knowledge and authority. It therefore protects the world of human living from experts with a "scientific" theory, aping the natural sciences, about how the human world "really" works.

Husserl's most important insight in political philosophy seems to be a distinction between politics and philosophy. This seems to me a crucial point. It is not an error *from within* chemistry to think that chemistry can solve all human problems. It is not the effect of a psychological defect that some psychologists think that human beliefs are all explained psychologically. These are philosophical errors. It is a *political* mistake, in addition to a philosophical error, terrible and too common, to elevate politics to the point of life or political thought to the highest human knowledge, to think that politics can solve all human problems or that our beliefs are all determined politically. It does not complete a political philosophy, but it is a good start, to distinguish between politics and philosophy. Likewise, it is a philosophical mistake to presume philosophy replaces rather than elucidates, elevates, and protects non-philosophical life. Though we should wish that this great thinker reflected more on the structures of political life, we should be grateful for what he has left us and thankful that he at least did not make these mistakes.

Ideologism

*And what of the rationality of that irrationalism which is so much vaunted and
expected of us? Does it not have to convince us, if we are expected to listen to
it, with rational considerations and reasons? Is its irrationality not finally rather a narrow-minded and bad rationality?*[23]

In "Science as a Vocation," Max Weber argues that values should be left out of
a teacher's lessons. The student turns to the teacher not as a partisan prophet, a
worldview preacher, or a lifecoach, but to teach *what is known* about some subject. It is wrong to transform the lectern into a pulpit or platform.

Science is a matter of facts, known truths, whereas values for Weber are not
a matter of reason—or of unreason. They are not knowable, but result from personal decision, from one's ultimate position to life. To disagree with Weber, one
must disagree somehow with the way he characterizes facts and values. It is a
naïve distinction, and the cynical rejection of it claims that the facts are as much
up for grabs and in need of a personal decision as values. If we think following
Weber, but reject his distinction in this cynical way, then what he fears most
comes to pass more than ever. Facts would be putty in the hands of a worldview,
and teachers would not be able to be anything other than prophets or activists.

In short, the particular danger to teaching and learning that I wish to discuss
with Husserl's help is ideologism. This is its danger: it transforms teaching and
learning from a truth-approaching activity to a prejudice-, preference-, and
worldview-infecting process. Ideologism is the claim that all people have an
ideology: all people are adherents of some system of fundamental beliefs that (1)
determines their other beliefs, in the sense that it (2) is the interpretive framework by which they understand any thing or state of affairs, and thus that (3) is
not susceptible of evidence (because it is the interpretive framework for all possible evidence).

Grand ideologies are no longer stylish, but ideologism is quite popular. Its
presence in a student's mind blocks true learning, and because it gives a prose-
cutorial immunity to any person's ideology of choice, it invites a teacher to become an agitator.

In order to recover teaching and learning as truth-relevant activities, we
must destroy this ism of isms. Husserl's "Philosophy as a Rigorous Science" is
directed at various doctrines (naturalism, psychologism, historicism, worldviewism) that reject the person's ability to get to truth, so we start there.

Husserl attacks intellectual ideologies, always in defense of the ability of
mind to transcend itself. Psychologism claims that beliefs are caught in a system
of causally determining psychological laws. Naturalism claims that all things—
including beliefs and values—are nature in the sense asserted by modern natural
science, quantified matter governed by exact laws. Historicism claims that beliefs are produced by historical milieu. This pattern appears in many varieties.
Also common is the sociologistic version, claiming that beliefs are determined
by social or socioeconomic status. There is also a sexist version, a genderist ver-

sion, a racist version, a psychoanalytic version, and so on. The common factor is the assignment of causes where reasons are supposed to be capable of operating. For some reason, since Husserl's time until now, these anti-intellectual ideologies have been *très chic* among intellectuals.

Husserl's disproof of such skeptical claims is to show that they are self-defeating, "counter-sense." In each case, the belief asserting the causal claim that all beliefs are caused by such and such should also be caused by such and such, in which case the assertion must lack reasons. Husserl likes to remind us here of basic logic rules. Such truths would not afford our insight (and we could not think at all) if all beliefs were determined as dominos in some pattern of events. A "radical subjective skepticism" about logic is absurd because it denies to logical principles their role as ideals presiding over thought, and even (often enough, *especially*) the people attempting to deny them appeal to ideals of reason, and must.

In urging others to render tribute to whatever reduction you fancy, you must pay them in reasons, but any appeal you make to principles for consistent thinking robs your conclusion of its currency and meaning. To argue for the despotism of force over thought, one must pay homage to the sovereignty of reason and the liberty of the mind.

Any reason-giving *for* these claims begs the question *against* such claims that mind is not open to reasons. The man who asserts, in communication, such a proposition is performing the intellectual version of mutually assured destruction, though he doesn't know it.

But equally, any reason-giving *against* these claims begs the question. The best we can do to disprove such a claim is point out to ourselves and to anyone else around that this man's position (proposition) destroys his own position (ground) as truth-claimer and reason-giver. We then want to *appreciate*—and I mean, not just *notice*, but also *wonder at* and *be thankful for*—the fact that mind is open to evidence.

These isms have a common factor—the claim that ideas are not ideas but something else. Husserl's accusation of self-refutation against them is decisive, but a negative and not a positive victory. His entire philosophical career, the key moves he makes in establishing the phenomenological movement, is the positive response, because it elucidates the openness of the mind to the world and thereby helps us see the absurdity in denying that the mind is the mind, and not something else.

Husserl makes several basic moves that help us reopen the space of reason in an age of cynical skepticism:

(a) By its nature, the mind is essentially open and receptive to other things. This is his celebrated doctrine of intentionality, a small thing with deep implications. We are not aware merely of our own creations, our images or concepts. We are aware of things other than ourselves.

(b) He urges us to return to the things themselves for their truths. Against systems of *a priori* hypothesizing, against "top down" thinking that imagines it can tell us how things must be in abstraction from our encounters with them, Husserl insists that thought finds its *telos* and becomes authentic in the insightful presence of the objects about which we think.

(c) He reasserts the rights of the world of human experience. Because, even pre-philosophically, mind encounters things, he defends the everyday reason operative in pretheoretical life. The mind's encounter with the world is not invented by philosophy. Intentionality, mind's openness to and interest in the things themselves, didn't go comatose in the modern era, even though many philosophers stopped believing in it. This is the major reason moderns discount the commonly assumed world and the reason operative in it. In contrast, Husserl insists that, while *episteme* [science] is higher than *doxa* [opinion], the higher levels build on and cannot replace the lower level.

Teaching is supposed to be a guiding of students to learn, and learning means gaining and deepening one's understanding of the world, oneself, and beyond. What are the conditions of the possibility of authentic teaching? That there is a truth about things and that we can encounter things in their truth. That the realm of things themselves shows up to us, teachers and students, in common, so that we can talk about it. That the student doesn't start from nowhere, but starts with prior, valid though less perfect, contact with the truth of things.

Husserl is a teacher who leads us to see that these theses are not ungrounded, merely hopeful hypotheses. They follow from the nature of our situation—that we find ourselves *together, minded, and in the world.*

An Husserlian Contribution to Political Philosophy: Naturalism and other Ideologies

"We must also allow relative evidences. Otherwise we dissolve life."[24]

Husserl also teaches us how to understand those systems of assertions that would deny our situation. One of his most important, and original, analyses is of the naturalistic attitude. I shall argue that this analysis should be extended by analogy to help us understand ideology generally. About naturalism, he makes two main claims:

(1) Everyday prephilosophical intentionality (Husserl's "natural" attitude or "personalistic" attitude) does its job too well, though of course fallibly: it sees the world, but it is invisible to itself, it lacks self-knowledge. The natural*istic* attitude attempts to abstract from all subject-relative characteristics of the world—for example, values, culture, prejudices, sensations. In an attempt to overcome the weaknesses of common human subjectivity, it digs in deeper on self-forgetfulness. It is hyperaware of how the activities of consciousness skew others' beliefs, but it is more thoroughly unaware of its own fallibility because it pretends to have escaped subjectivity. The naturalistic attitude may acquire an expansionist disdain for everyday experience and dismiss its accomplishments.

When it does so, it claims to uncover the "true" world beneath the world of experience, and to dismiss as false subjective construction the world as experienced and understood by common human sensibility, thought, and culture.

(2) The naturalistic attitude operates on the assumption that physical things are ideally mathematical and perfectly determined by laws we can formalize mathematically. We never in fact come across ideally flat planes, perfect spheres, or falling objects immune to incidental friction. In fact we know that concrete things cannot fulfill these geometrical ideals. But Galileo's theories about freefalling objects speak as though the boards and balls of his experiment instantiate this ideal realm and obey perfectly laws formulated in its terms.

In sum, the naturalistic attitude involves us in two abstractions: it abstracts away the human involvement in the world and abstracts away the non-ideal concreteness and irregularities of things. Theorists adopting the naturalistic attitude commit the fallacy of misplaced concreteness, and undermine their own ground, if they assert that this method captures wholly the one true world and provides an etiology of the merely subjective experiences of prescientific life.

When these abstractions are applied to ideas and the life of reason, theorizing persons taking up the naturalistic attitude cut off their legs—or, more aptly, close up their eyes and ears and minds: since the naturalistic attitude abstracts from human meaning and subjective experience, it cannot make sense of these as what they are. It is by making this reifying, self-referential move of trying to causally explain acts of reason, which must after all include scientific theorizing, that natural science warps itself into a self-refuting naturalistic dogmatism. It is the reification of mind and its ideas and laws that results in the ideological character of naturalism and of other ideologies.

Naturalism is the ideological evil twin of natural science, and is only one example. Ideology is usually about more properly human things: about politics, culture, religion, morality, etc. But other ideologies approach these phenomena with analogous dual abstractions. (1) Ideology dismisses pre-theoretical ideas about how the human world works. It tries to explain the human things of ethics and politics in formulas, imagining that it has discovered a telescope that sees around, and no longer through, normal human eyes. (2) Ideology speaks as though people fulfilled a theoretical ideal. Not only are we pushed into being merely instances of an ideal type governed by simplified laws, so that our irregularities are smoothed away to fit into the theory, but also usually ideologies abstract away some particular necessary feature of human nature (for example, that we must know and care about certain people more than others, or that not all goods can be measured monetarily, or that persons bear responsibility for their actions and products despite the social structures they find themselves within).

I suggest these are the essential features of ideology. That ideologues are closed to counter-evidence is the first property flowing from this essence. Someone in the grip of an ideology cannot appreciate and weigh evidence contrary to their overall theory because they start by rejecting the validity of normal evidence and believe their fundamental theory about what is "really" going on morally or politically explains the origin of the appearances, the false consciousness, of those who do not accept their system.

This is analogous to the way a conspiracy theory works. A conspiracy theory involves two allegations: the primary crime and the cover-up. A conspiracy theory becomes a closed system, not open to public reason and disproof, when any evidence that does not support the primary accusation is taken to support the cover-up allegation. This creates an unchallengeable interpretive framework. Ideologies can work as complete explanations and closed interpretative frameworks only because they discount the evidence offered in common to human beings. In order to permanently and rationally trump the conflicting, imperfect, and unclear opinions that dominate the human realm, ideologies begin by discounting the concrete world of pre-theoretical life.

It is not just coincidence that ideologies share this structure with naturalism of rejecting the obvious, experienced world and constructing a new and neater one. Ideologies take on this structure because they ape naturalism. This seems to be because the natural sciences provide in our culture the model of how to theorize. And like naturalism, ideologies generally must start with the notion that the real world is not the one available to common human opinion and with the correlate notion that *human opinion too must be explained by this real world* that their story maps by identifying its basic objects and laws. It is fundamental to naturalism and to other ideologies to deny that our basic experiences are truthful, however inadequate, and to claim, instead, that they are things, causes and effects, explainable like things. But the real world they map is in truth a theoretically constructed world, and it must be an absurd one to the extent that they deny that pre-theoretical evidence grounds and can correct the account. After all, if the real world were not given, however imperfectly, in basic human experience, no amount of our theorizing could get us there. And if the mind and its reasoning were drained of their veracity and unmasked as merely thingly effects of something else, as this type of theorizing presumes, no amount of reason-giving and evidence-finding could move us toward the truth.

Ideology originally was to be the "scientific" psychological explanation of human ideas. Ideologies, in the pejorative contemporary sense, always involve a moment of the pseudoscientific reification and explanation of our beliefs. They attempt to dismiss normal human experience, to deprive it of its validity, in order to put some idealized system in its place. The response to ideology must be a true study of ideas, one that lets ideas be ideas rather than turning them into things to be explained away and controlled.

Aurel Kolnai writes that Husserl's *Experience and Judgment* "propounds a grandiose vista of absolute anti-Cartesianism: the discovery, as original as it is epoch-making, but Aristotelian in spirit, that our valid and strict 'scientific' or 'philosophical' knowledge proceeds, not from a 'minimum' knowledge of certain and evident truth, but from our inexplicit world knowledge in all its wealth, manifoldness and implication of order."[25] Husserl often says that philosophy must be a presuppositionless science and that it, as first philosophy, provides foundations for the rest of human knowledge, everyday as well as scientific.

But, as Kolnai saw clearly, phenomenology fulfills this Cartesian-sounding mission in an unCartesian way. It provides a foundation for knowledge by reflecting upon and understanding it, such that it can defend this nonphilosophical knowledge while also deepening and elevating it. And this is true of empirical as well as moral and practical knowledge. This is why Husserl can present his philosophy as reasserting the rights of *doxa*, opinion. "Essentially the path of knowledge is to ascend from *doxa* to *epistēmē*—it is simply that even concerning this ultimate goal, the origin and specific rights of the lower stages should not be forgotten."[26]

Kolnai points especially to sections seven to ten of *Experience and Judgment*.[27] While not giving up on the claim that *episteme* really does go beyond everyday *doxa*, Husserl insists that knowledge builds upon it and cannot therefore reject the realm of opinion. Naturalism and scientistic human sciences seem to claim that they discover the true, exact, and causally explained world behind the merely false show of the subjectively distorted realm that naïve humans live in. Husserl argues that they substitute a creation of their minds for the true world. As an unavoidable fact, science is accomplished by scientists, and scientists are people, too: the conclusions of scientists need to build upon rather than reject this world that appears to humans in common, and scientists must return to this realm to verify and give meaning to their conclusions. Particular ideologies, I suggest, have a parallel form to naturalism: they do not claim merely to discover true features of the world, but they claim to discover the true world according to which our appearances prior to their theory are false, and to explain how these appearances themselves are generated by the unapparent world they purport to know.

Ideologism is unlike other ideologies in an important respect. It is motivated by the multiplicity of such theories asserting a hidden real world, and in response it asserts a subjectivistic skepticism—according to their theory, we are *all* caught in such systems of false appearances. Thus ideologism seems to suggest, unlike other ideologies, that there is no true world either hidden but scientifically knowable or available in common. There is just a multiplicity of opinions. But by calling the variety of ideologies the ultimate reality, which ideology-studies can uncover, ideologism takes on the shape of other ideologies. Since theorists committed to ideologism claim that by adopting an ideology a person's other opinions are determined, they in their study of ideologies provide a dehumanizing explanation of people's appearances, beliefs, and reasonings—just as other ideologies claim to do.

The defenders of ideologism sometimes argue for this theory by observing that human observations are never of raw data. We never experience a pristinely objective intuition of the facts. When we see something we interpret the data with the help of pre-established opinions and concepts. Thus, as I have been told, for example, what one see as a tree, another may see as a nymph; what you see as an act of kindness, I may see as a passive-aggressive attempt to keep me subjugated. The move that Kolnai represents as anti-Cartesian brilliance in *Ex-*

perience and Judgment might be taken as evidence of this claim. Husserl emphasizes that our basic experience of things in the world, the experience upon
which the sciences build, involves never pure and clear, self-evident data, but
givens that we accept from an "external horizon" of the assumed world, a horizon by which we anticipate things to be a certain way, more or less of a certain
type and style. And every particular thing also has, according to Husserl's analysis of perception, an "internal horizon," a set of expectations on our part that the
given object has certain features we do not yet directly encounter. Given these
rich and unarticulated assumptions, every given is *interpreted* by us, and not just
experienced self-evidently.

Husserl's analysis of our perceptions allows us to admit that subjective history and belief color our experiences. Still, we should not conclude with a subjectivistic skepticism, since as Husserl's analysis also shows, the world and its
objects are still *given* and with their own integrity. Even when some person sees
a tree as potential lumber and another sees it as the body of a tree spirit, there is
still a basic encounter with reality they share. The world of our past experience
is the source of these anticipations, and often enough what the world gives us
fails to fulfill our expectations. We experience such failures, too. The world is
not putty in the hands of our assumptions.

Husserl argues in "The Origin of Geometry" that geometry comes from taking the shaped things of our concrete surrounding world and imaginatively push-
ing them toward ideal "limit shapes." Geometry then progresses as a tradition,
taught by one generation to the next and added to. The "developed capacity" to
recognize the ground of geometry in our surrounding world is not passed on in
geometry textbooks. This ground may even be forgotten, although it can always
be retraced. Authentic thinking about abstract objects requires the "actually developed capacity for reactivating the primal beginnings" of our abstractions,
recognizing how they are built intellectually out of materials from the experienced world.[28] This capacity must be personally developed and cannot be hand-
ed over in a formula—but it can be apprenticed.

Ideologies not only forget but *deny* their origins. They cut off the branch
they are sitting on. They poison the spring we all drink from. They refuse our
right to return to the true world to insightfully cash in their propositions. To respond to ideologies, we need this "developed capacity" for concreteness.

Ideologism alleges that we are all ideologues. It is the bad faith *tu quoque*
response of those who want a free pass to profess their worldview. Ideologism
unmasks naturalism as just another ideology, and unmasks the facts as just as
arbitrary as values and everything else naturalism tells us belongs to the merely
subjective false show that is the human world. But this whole style of thinking is
a mistake.

In fact, neither worldviews nor human values float free. Even the worst are
ultimately rooted in and are about the world we view and our life in it.

People too often turn away from aspects of the world that do not fit their
system, and—as Weber says—a good teacher reminds students of "inconvenient
facts" that do not flatter their party opinions.[29] Husserl shows us a truth that is

inconvenient for ideologists: human persons cannot avoid the question of truth and the norm of evidence, even when it comes to worldviews and values.

Teaching in the age of abstractions requires remembering our ground, that we find ourselves together, minded, and in the world—and then apprenticing and nurturing the capacity for concreteness.

Husserl as Teacher

> *"It is a discomforting, challenging, and troublesome philosophy that has no use for partisans and discipleship, that above all sends everyone off on the path of one's own reflective thought."*[30]

In the classroom, Husserl seems to have been an uncharismatic teacher wrapped up in his thoughts. Many students who would become significant thinkers in their own rights attended his classes, but the excitement that drew students to the phenomenological movement came from the content of his thought more than from his personality. The effect it had on Jean-Paul Sartre, though not a direct student of Husserl's, illustrates what inspired many of his students. Raymond Aron told Sartre, as they were Frenchly discussing philosophy over drinks, that phenomenology allows one to philosophize about concrete human experience and about the things of real human life—even this wine bottle. It was love at first sight.

Modern philosophy, especially neo-Kantianism, still dominated. The modern philosophical dogma of the separation of the subject from the object, with the problem of knowledge that results, was overcome by Husserl's recovery of intentionality, his rejection of psychologism, and his reaffirmation of the human connection with the world. An energizing concreteness and realism invited students to illuminate descriptively human experience of our world. The phenomenological groups that sprung up in German universities show how the *Logical Investigations* opened the windows and rejuvenated creative minds. It is this overcoming of modernity that prompted Kolnai, a passing student who would not call himself a phenomenologist, to say that Husserl was perhaps the greatest philosopher since Aristotle and to suggest, "the future historiography of ideas…will set it down as a common place that with Husserl commences the non-Cartesian Age in European thought."[31]

Many of the early phenomenologists rejected Husserl's later development, especially the epoché and transcendental idealism, precisely because his recovery of realism had convinced them so deeply. One of these early phenomenologists, Edith Stein worked with Husserl closely as an assistant soon after this transcendental turn. In her words, "All of us had the same question on our minds.…The *Logical Investigations* had caused a sensation primarily because it appeared to be a radical departure from critical idealism which had a Kantian and neo-Kantian stamp.…Knowledge again appeared as reception, deriving its laws from objects not, as criticism has it, from determination which imposes laws on the objects. All the young phenomenologists were confirmed realists. However, the *Ideas* included some expressions which sounded as though the Master wished to return to idealism."[32]

That many early students rejected his next big move shows, perhaps, that his lack of charisma had pedagogic value: they were taught not cowed; they were convinced by a man's thoughts, not by a man. I think they misunderstood Husserl in rejecting transcendental reflection, but the point is that these "realist phenomenologists" saw in this turn a relapse into pre-phenomenological thinking, into the ideology of modern philosophy. Husserl rejected also a naïve objectivism, one that refused to take subjectivity seriously, and even if modern philosophy had emphasized subjectivity at the expense of objectivity and thus made a mess of both, Husserl was convinced that objectivism was as real a danger as subjectivism, since both block our understanding of the human encounter with the world. We must not make the world into a misadventure of the subject, but neither may we make the person just another element of the world.

Though Husserl as a teacher did not come across as terribly engaged with his students, it was according to himself in a teaching moment that he became truly philosophical. Lev Shestov had written several articles critical of Husserl, and in response Husserl had sent a request ahead of his arrival at a 1928 conference in Amsterdam that Shestov stay a few days longer so that they might meet and talk. He immediately addressed Shestov personally and generously, "with sincerity, enthusiasm, and inspiration."[33] First he defended himself: "You have turned me into a stone statue, raised me onto a lofty pedestal, and then with hammer-blows you have shattered this statue to bits. But am I really so lapidary?"[34] This first defense is interesting. He resisted being turned into an inflexible and impersonal set of theories. If we approach fellow thinkers like that we may attack them or follow them, but we may not learn from them. Husserl encouraged his students to read the history of philosophy, but not to read it as historically done and gone.

It is possible that he failed to always approach other thinkers the way he wished to be approached. But this view of himself gives a clue about Husserl as a thinker and teacher. While presenting himself as the founder a movement and a leader into a new epoch of philosophy, he also insisted he was—and he truly was—always a beginner and a re-beginner. He felt an intense, personal responsibility to himself, his students, and fellow thinkers to be honest and radical in his defense of our search for knowledge.

Describing himself thirty years prior, he then said to Shestov, "To my own indescribable horror, I convinced myself that if contemporary philosophy has said the last word about the nature of knowledge, then we have no knowledge."[35] At this thought we should wonder, why teach? If all we teachers do is reinforce the modern or contemporary theories of non-knowledge, of locked mind-cabinets without keyholes or worldviews without windows on the world or ungroundable perception-permeating conceptual schemes, we are neither teaching knowledge nor encouraging and drawing out our students so they may discover knowledge on their own. Husserl then confessed to Shestov a personal moment of radical philosophical motivation:

> Once, when I was giving a lecture at the university, expounding ideas I had taken over from our contemporaries, I suddenly felt like I had nothing to say, that I was standing before my students with empty hands and an empty soul. And then I resolved both for myself and for my students to submit the existing theories of knowledge to that severe and unrelenting criticism which has aroused the indignation of so many people.

This moment, he reported to Shestov, was the "origin of my *Logical Investigations*."[36]

His sense of philosophical responsibility, for himself as a thinker and as a teacher with influence over others, gave rise to what Husserl would become as a thinker and a teacher.

Descriptions of him while teaching formally and while talking with students, which he did often, indicate paradoxically that Husserl was both unengaged with his audience and intensely engaging. He would often speak almost as though speaking to himself. He monologued; he did not lead discussions or elicit participation. Even worse, his intense involvement with the objects of his thought seemed sometimes to distract him from the presence of other people. But, if we may flaunt current pedagogical nostrums, in doing so he still managed to teach, and perhaps teach better for it. We can guess that two things came across, often enough engagingly and even inspirationally: first, on the object side, that the topics of his thought are interesting, and second, on the subject side, that we should be, like him, intensely honest philosophically, searching for the truths of being and facing our responsibilities as thinkers. The result seems to have been many students who wanted to get to the truth of things and who felt not only free but obliged to disagree with "the Master."

In 1966, Aron Gurwitsch eloquently described the effect Husserl had on him as a student:

> When the author made his first acquaintance with Husserl's philosophy about forty years ago, he was overwhelmed by the spirit of uncompromising integrity and radical philosophical responsibility, by the total devotedness which made the man disappear behind his work. Soon the young beginner came to realize the fruitfulness both of what Husserl had actually accomplished and of what he had initiated, the promise of further fruitful work....It was the style of Husserl's philosophizing, painstaking analytical work on concrete problems and phenomena rather than the opening up of large vistas, that made the young student take the decision to devote his life and work to the continuation and expansion of Husserl's phenomenology—in a word, to remain a disciple forever, faithful to Husserl's spirit and general orientation, but at the same time prepared to depart from particular theories if compelled to do so by the nature of the problems and the logic of the theoretical situation.[37]

Being a disciple of Husserl could not mean being a mere follower. By disappearing behind the thought, by displaying sincerity and dedication to the truth, Husserl at his best drew out of his students a desire to be like him in crucial virtues without impressing on his students the desire to become another him or to act as his dummy.

From the point of view of someone interested in research on Husserl, it is frustrating that this thinker was so detail oriented, always working from the ground up, and repeatedly rethinking everything, even and especially the beginnings. But of course these are some of Husserl's philosophical virtues. They manifest his sense of the responsibility that fallible human thinking has to the truth of being. Toward the end of his life, he commented to a former student, Adelgrundis Jaegerschmid, that philosophy must rededicate itself to the essential thing, "to truth." "The question about ultimate being, concerning truth, must be the object of every philosophy. *That is my life's work.*"[38] But this dedication to philosophy as a science, as knowledge of being and of the subjectivity that knows it, means also humility: "One must have the courage to admit and say that something that one still considered true yesterday, but that one sees to be an error today, is such an error. There is nothing absolute here."[39] The absolute truth that philosophy must seek to be itself—and especially the most important truth, about the absolute—is an infinite task, but this means philosophy is always on the way, always incomplete and beginning again.

I think Husserl is right in this characterization of philosophy, but it requires a lot of us.

Sometimes a student is looking for the absolute truth, especially about the most pressing practical questions of personal and communal life. When such a student meets a genius, it is easy to hold on too tightly, to be convinced too quickly that one has happened upon and can now possess the ultimate key that unlocks the meaning of it all. The impulse to genuine philosophy might then collapse into enrapture by a grand worldview or neat, all-explaining ideological system, and many who lack Husserl's indefatigable philosophical conscience and daunting work ethic were, and are, more satisfied with that. Though Husserl said, as quoted above, that his life's work was reorienting philosophy to its true *telos* of the truth of being, this is why Husserl also characterizes his "task for the world," as showing "people through phenomenology a new modality of their responsibility in order to free them of their vanities and their ego."[40]

Husserl had his vanities, too. These included a belief that he had a mission from God to re-found philosophy—this time in its fullness—and a desire to have a group of students who would fulfill his work for him faithfully.

He influenced many, but his lack of continuers troubled him. Especially beginning in the late 1920s, others, raising existential and anthropological issues more starkly, stole his thunder. More than a few students rejected central parts of his philosophy. A few students even betrayed him personally. (His most influential student, Martin Heidegger, in letters from the 1920s brags of attacking his work while teaching and even of "wringing his neck," writing in 1923 to fellow thinkers in the phenomenological milieu about the "old man": "He lives off his mission as the 'Founder of Phenomenology,' but nobody knows what that means."[41]) Though he had many more students who were grateful to him and remained friends with him, even those students dedicated to him personally and philosophically were too independent minded to fulfill Husserl's mission for him. Husserl wrote to former student Roman Ingarden in 1927, "it often weighs heavily on my soul that others in the circle of phenomenologists do not see this necessity" of the paths his thought had taken: "instead, they all prefer to follow their own way."[42]

While sick in the fall of 1937, in conversation with Jaegerschmid, he wished to have succeeded in freeing himself from vanity, "including the professional vanity without which a young person cannot work: the honor and admiration of my students."[43] Part of this fault of Husserl's reminds us of the natural allure of admiration. But for Husserl it was more complex. Ingarden described the situation beautifully:

> The range of problems with which he occupied himself, problems which in their essence are entirely original and new, is enormous. Their solution, however, if they were all to be treated with the same exactness and intuitive vision, was undoubtedly beyond the spiritual powers of one man. But Husserl could not treat them in any other way, guided as he was by his great sense of responsibility, and his ethical approach to his whole philosophical activity. The task to which he devoted his life, and with the development of his personality was bound up, was—frankly speaking—impossible. No one could really help him with it. He often spoke of a generation of "selfless" researchers, who would devote themselves completely to the solution of the problems he had outlined. But of course that was just an illusion. Should such researchers be really "selfless," they would be only simulacra of men, and not human beings of flesh and blood. As such they could never solve any of his problems. And should they be really human, it would be simply impossible for them in the Husserlian spirit.[44]

In 1935, toward the end of his life and while being increasingly marginalized socially and intellectually within Germany, and even prevented from travelling abroad to conferences because, as ethnically Jewish, he was seen by the regime as not a proper representative of Germany, Husserl lamented to Jaegerschmid: "except for [Eugen] Fink, for the past four years I have not had one student to whom I could speak my mind....Now that I am seventy—I am seventy-six—I have no circle of students or the possibility to lecture, I lack the school that would want to take my thought further and publish them."[45] Still, later in conversations with her, he seems to remember that he is not the only person with the philosophical vocation requiring taking one's own path, saying to Jaegerschmid, his student and confidant: "Promise me never to say anything just because others have said it."[46]

Part vanity and part self-consolation in the face of his inability to fulfill the impossible responsibility of a philosopher, this conceit—and its disappointment—stayed with Husserl, it seems, till the end, or at least close to it. Jaegerschmid reports, that "from Maundy Thursday on"—less than a fortnight before his death on April 26, 1938—"he did not speak one more word about his philosophical work, which had occupied him throughout the previous months. Just how much his entire life was subject to the mission of a higher power was revealed only as he was dying. Now he felt finally discharged and released from his task."[47]

Conclusions

"In the path of true science, this path is endless. Accordingly, phenomenology demands that the phenomenologist foreswear the ideal of a philosophical system and yet as a humble worker in community with others, live for a perennial philosophy."[48]

While restoring the validity of the experienced world, Husserl rehabilitates human reason as capable of and fulfilled in truth. His attacks on truth-obscuring dogmas can be understood as reminding reason of its work when it has been distracted and dejected by ideologies. For many thinkers, his call back to the things themselves was rejuvenating fresh air, opening the windows of the modern mind.

His claim to make philosophy a science must not be misunderstood. This science, like all others, is accomplished by human beings, is never perfect, and must be done with the help of others, both contemporary coworkers and those long dead. About himself, Husserl wrote, "If he has been obliged, on practical grounds, to lower the ideal of the philosopher to that of a downright beginner, he has at least in his old age reached for himself the complete certainty that he should thus call himself a beginner."[49]

Also struggling to become genuine beginners, those he influenced went in all directions doing their own thing. At the end, he says, "I seek not to instruct, but to lead, to point out and describe what I see. I claim no other right than that of speaking according to my best lights, principally before myself but in the same manner also before others, as one who has lives in all its seriousness the fate of a philosophical existence."[50] Yet he was disappointed that he lacked phenomenological heirs, faithful students who might carry out the "infinite tasks" of philosophy as he wanted. His lack of followers must not be taken as a failure. With Husserl's help, we can insightfully understand and reject ideologies. We then can appreciate the great and varied work lying before our fallible reason and be thankful that good teachers are not gurus. The quality of a teacher cannot be judged by his students' mistakes when they have failed to follow him faithfully, but it can be judged if his students have merely followed him faithfully.

Though unpolitical, Husserl's life's work can be seen as profoundly anti-ideological. One of his students, Jan Patočka, had another student, Czech dissident Václav Havel, who wrote bravely of ideology: "To wandering humankind it offers an immediately available home: all one has to do is accept it, and suddenly everything becomes clear once more, life takes on new meaning, and all mysteries, unanswered questions, anxiety, and loneliness vanish. Of course, one pays dearly for this low-rent home: the price is abdication of one's own reason, conscience, and responsibility." It is most of all in defense of reason, conscience, and responsibility that Husserl's philosophy is animated, and we see Husserl's reverberations in Havel's claim that "the human predisposition to truth" is ultimately what is at issue in our response to ideology.[51]

We might conclude by pointing to Patočka's dissident death in Prague and to Wojtyła's courageous crusade to build a church in Kraków as evidence that Husserl's influence bore heroic fruit in the struggles against ideology and totalitarianism, which must also be struggles for the integrity of the person as reasonable, responsible, and called to live in truth. But giving him this credit would be a stretch, and self-defeating. Honesty would then force us to debit him for the many ideological failings of those he influenced. Instead, each thinker must take responsibility for himself, and it is a mark of Husserl's success as a teacher and leader that his students and admirers went in their many own directions.

Notes

1. Edmund Husserl. "Kant and the Idea of Transcendental Philosophy." Trans. T.E. Klein and W.E. Pohl. *Southwestern Journal of Philosophy* 5 (Fall 1974), 9–56: 53.

2. Edmund Husserl. 1994. *Briefwechsel*. Edited by Karl Schuhmann. The Hague, Netherlands: Kluwer Academic Publishers. Vol. IX, 244.

3. Edmund Husserl. 1973. *The Crisis of European Sciences and Transcendental Phenomenology: An Introduction to Phenomenological Philosophy*. Edited and translated by David Carr. Evanston, IL: Northwestern University Press, 290.

4. Husserl, *Crisis*, 299.

5. Edmund Husserl. "The Idea of a Philosophical Culture: Its First Germination in Greek Philosophy," New Yearbook for Phenomenology and Phenomenological Philosophy III (2003): 285–93. Translated by Marcus Brainard, 289.

6. Husserl, "The Idea of a Philosophical Culture," 289–292.

7. Husserl, "The Idea of a Philosophical Culture," 292.

8. Edmund Husserl, "Philosophy as a Rigorous Science," in Peter McCormick and Frederick A. Elliston, (ed.), *Husserl: Shorter Works*, 166–197. Translated by Quentin Lauer, p. 191.

9. Husserl, "Philosophy as a Rigorous Science," p. 194.

10. Quoted in *The Collected Works of Aron Gurwitsch (1901–1973): Vol. I: Constitutive Phenomenology in Historical Perspective*. Edited by Jorge Garcia-Gómez. Dordrecht, The Netherlands: Springer, 2009, p. 45.

11. Husserl, "Philosophy as a Rigorous Science," 193.

12. Erazim Kohák, "Husserl's Letter to Arnold Metzger" in McCormick and Elliston, (ed.), *Husserl: Shorter Works*, p. 358.

13. Edmund Husserl, Letter to Arnold Metzger, Sept 4, 1919; translated by Erazim Kohák, in McCormick and Elliston, (ed.), *Husserl: Shorter Works*, 360–64; p. 362.

14. Husserl, Letter to Arnold Metzger, 362.

15. Husserl, Letter to Arnold Metzger, 361.

16. Husserl, *Crisis*, 6.

17. His student Aron Gurwitsch puts the Husserlian position as follows: "Philosophy is concerned with human welfare and has to promote it. It cannot do so except by contributing knowledge and by criticizing knowledge already acquired. In other words, philosophy has to become knowledge in the sense of episteme, not satisfied so long as it has to carry along implications and presuppositions not yet cleared up, seeking to expand itself to all fields of being. This task, perhaps, is an infinite one; at any rate it does require the cooperation of generations. But for the sake of the supreme practical interests of mankind—if not for theoretical needs—this task must be tackled. We may be sure that the more we proceed in its realization, the more reasonable life will become, the more it will become *human* life. Hence, I think, we ought to persist on the path opened by Husserl, regardless of the higher or lower esteem we will enjoy as philosophic personalities because we are mere disciples," (in "Review of Jean Héring's 'La Phénoménologie d'Edmund Husserl *il y a trente ans*,'" *Philosophy and Phenomenological Research* 1 (1940), 515.

18. Edmund Husserl, "Renewal: Its Problem and Method," translated by Jeffner Allen, in McCormick and Elliston, (ed.), *Husserl: Shorter Works*, 326–37; 329.

19. Husserl, "Renewal: Its Problem and Method," 327.

20. Husserl, "Renewal: Its Problem and Method," 331.

21. See Edmund Husserl "Erneuerung und Wissenschaft," in Thomas Nenon and Hans Rainder Sepp (eds.), *Aufsätze und Vorträge (1922–1937)*, Dordrecht, The Netherlands: Kluwer, 1989; 58–59.

22. Krasnodębski, "Longing for Community: Phenomenological Philosophy of Politics and the Dilemmas of European Culture," *International Sociology* 8, no. 3 (Sept. 1993), 339–53. Even Husserl's student Jan Patočka, who died in 1977 at 70 after an 11 hour police interrogation for his involvement with the dissident movement in Czechoslovakia, had tried to live a rather unpolitical, philosophical life.

23. Husserl, *Crisis*, 16

24. Quoted in Adelgrundis Jaegerschmid, "Conversations with Edmund Husserl, 1931–1938," translated by Marcus Brainard, *The New Yearbook for Phenomenology and Phenomenological Philosophy* I (2001), 331–50: 342.

25. Aurel Kolnai, *Political Memoirs*, edited by Francesca Murphy; New York, NY: Lexington Books, 1999; 127.

26. Edmund Husserl, *Experience and Judgment: Investigations in a Genealogy of Logic*. Evanston, IL: Northwestern University Press, 1995; 46.

27. See "The Sovereignty of the Object," in Daniel J. Mahoney (ed.), *Privilege and Liberty and Other Essays*. New York, NY: Lexington Books, 1999.

28. Husserl, *Crisis*, 366.

29. Max Weber, *The Vocation Lectures*, Trans. Rodney Stone, Ed. David Owen and Tracy B. Strong, Indianapolis, IN: Hackett, 2004; 22.

30. Quoted in Ronald Bruzina, *Edmund Husserl and Eugen Fink: Beginnings and Ends in Phenomenology, 1928–1938*. New Haven, CT: Yale University Press, 2004; 521–22.

31. Kolnai, *Political Memoirs*, 137, 127.

32. Quoted in Alasdair Macintyre, *Edith Stein: A Philosophical Prologue, 1913–1922*. New York, NY: Rowan and Littlefield, 2006; 66.

33. Leon Shestov, "In Memory of a Great Philosopher: Edmund Husserl," *Philosophy and Phenomenological Research* 22, no. 4 (Jn 1962), 449–71: 451.

34. Shestov, "In Memory of a Great Philosopher," 450.

35. Shestov, "In Memory of a Great Philosopher," 451.

36. Shestov, "In Memory of a Great Philosopher," 451.

37. Quoted in Lester Embree, "Biographical Sketch of Aron Gurwitsch," in Garcia-Gómez (ed.), *The Collected Works of Aron Gurwitsch (1901–1973): Vol. I*; 42.

38. Jaegerschmid, "Conversations with Edmund Husserl," 336.

39. Jaegerschmid, "Conversations with Edmund Husserl," 337.

40. Jaegerschmid, "Conversations with Edmund Husserl," 346.

41. Martin Heidegger, Letter to Karl Löwith (May 8, 1923) and Letter to and Karl Jaspers (July 14, 1923), in Theodore Kisiel and Thomas Sheehan, *Becoming Heidegger: On the Trail of His Early Occasional Writings, 1910–1927*. Evanston, IL: Northwestern University Press, 2007; 372–73.

42. Edmund Husserl, Letter to Roman Ingarden (Dec. 26, 1927), in 384.

43. Jaegerschmid, "Conversations with Edmund Husserl," 346.

44. Roman Ingarden, "Edith Stein on her Activity as an Assistant to Edmund Husserl," *Philosophy and Phenomenological Research* 23, no. 2 (Dec. 1962), 155–75; 159–60

45. Jaegerschmid, "Conversations with Edmund Husserl," 338.

46. Jaegerschmid, "Conversations with Edmund Husserl," 346.

47. Jaegerschmid, "Conversations with Edmund Husserl," 349.

48. Edmund Husserl, "Phenomenology," in McCormack and Elliston (ed.), *Husserl, Shorter Works*, 21–35; 35.

49. Edmund Husserl, "Author's Preface to the English Edition of Ideas I," in McCormack and Elliston (ed.), *Husserl, Shorter Works*, 43–53; 52.

50. Husserl, *Crisis*, 18.

51. Václav Havel, "The Power of the Powerless," in Paul Wilson, (ed.), *Open Letters: Selected Writings, 1965–1990*, 125–214; 129, 148.

Chapter 2

Hannah Arendt: How Thinking Saves Us
Leah Bradshaw, Brock University

It has been said often of Hannah Arendt that she had no "disciples." Despite the fact that Arendt is widely regarded as one of the most influential thinkers of the twentieth century, and that her substantial body of work continues to spawn a wealth of secondary literature, there is no singular Arendtian school of thought. On the contrary, her many admirers disagree in important ways on Arendt's prescriptions for political and philosophical engagement. Arendt herself remarked that she had no desire to produce acolytes;[1] rather, she hoped that her students would go out into the world with open and inquisitive minds, and she was comfortable with the realization that this openness could result in a wide range of policy positions on political questions. In a conversation between Elisabeth Young-Bruehl and Jerome Kohn, two of Arendt's most distinguished students, the two friends recall that Arendt's first words to them in a 1968 seminar at the New School for Social Research were: "No theories! Forget all theories! We want to be confronted with direct experience." She distinguished "thinking" from "theory," and in so doing, according to Jerome Kohn, "she was reviving the ancient Greek distinction between *theoria* and *theoremata*, between the activity of thinking and its outcome in 'true' theorems."[2]

Arendt's greatest concern for her students and her readers, I suggest, was that whatever their opinions on current political matters, they should avoid ideological thinking. which was for her a particularly insidious mutation of *theoramata*. Ideological reasoning she described as a specifically modern corruption, one that is attached to a deeper modern turn to science, and its predilection for making as opposed to understanding, commanding the future as opposed to taking account of the present. "Ideologies," she wrote, "are never interested in the miracle of being."[3] Instead, they are "historical," in the sense that they are intent upon conferring upon lived experience a preconceived narrative, into which all lived reality (including the "miraculous") can be fitted. "To an ideology, history does not appear in the light of an idea (which would imply that history is seen *sub specie* of some ideal eternity which itself is beyond historical motion) but as something which can be calculated by it."[4]

The antidotes to ideological corruption that Arendt pursued are twofold. One, we have her constant reminder that we ought to approach the human world as it is given to us in its fundamental plurality. We live among others; we learn from them, we are affirmed by them. As Arendt wrote in *The Human Condition*: "No human life, not even the life of the hermit in nature's wilderness, is possible without a world which directly or indirectly testifies to the presence of other human beings....All human activities are conditioned by the fact that men live together, but it is only action that cannot even be imagined outside the society of men."[5] People acting and speaking together have the capacity to create new ways of being in the world, ways that are themselves constitutive of meaning and a testimony to freedom.

There is a second antidote to ideology that is somewhat at variance with the first, and that is the retreat of "thinking." In the conclusion of *The Human Condition*, Arendt's bold defense of action and plurality, she enigmatically comments that the greatest vulnerability in the modern world may lie with thinking, not acting. "If no other test but the experience of being active, no other measure but the extent of sheer activity were to be applied to the various activities within the *vita activa*, it might well be that thinking as such would surpass them all."[6] Arendt would turn to an exploration of thinking as the final project of her life, and she asked there a pointed question that had preoccupied her since her reporting upon the trial of the Nazi war criminal Adolph Eichmann:[7] "Might the problem of good and evil, our faculty for telling right from wrong, be connected with our faculty for thought?"[8] This emphasis upon thinking seems to pose something of a tension with her emphasis upon action and plurality in *The Human Condition*, because thinking is something I do alone, in silence. From the perspective of thinking, Arendt wrote, the active way of life is "laborious," the contemplative way is sheer quietness; the active one goes on in public, the contemplative one in "the desert;" the active one is devoted to "the necessity of one's neighbour," the contemplative one to the "vision of God." The thinking person is of the world, but Arendt was surely correct to identify thinking as in some profound way an "unworldly" experience. The "soundless dialogue" that I carry on with myself in the activity of thinking Arendt traces to the origins of Western philosophy: "thinking aims at and ends in contemplation, and contemplation is not an activity but a passivity; it is the point where mental activity comes to rest."[9]

My discussion of Hannah Arendt, conceived within the mandate of this volume on great political thinkers as great teachers, will focus specifically upon

Arendt's understanding of the difference between philosophical thinking and ideological thinking against the backdrop of Arendt's lifelong commitment to things political, plural and active. I believe that the articulation of this distinction is Arendt's greatest legacy for her students (among whom I include the readers of her work); certainly it is the case for me that it is only after encountering Arendt's work, and struggling to understand the lessons she relayed to us regarding twentieth-century forms of domination, and twentieth century derailments of thinking, that I came to understand fully the importance of this distinction. From Hannah Arendt I learned to think. I shall provide a brief summary of the trajectory of Arendt's intellectual biography, highlighting some of the profound influences upon her thinking, and her most important contributions to political thought. I will return toward the conclusion of my chapter with the emphasis upon ideology, "worldliness" and philosophical thinking.

Hannah Arendt was a Jew, born in 1906, lived her childhood in a prosperous, secular middle class household in Konigsberg, Germany with her mother, her stepfather and her half siblings (her father died of syphilis when she was seven), and came to maturity at the time that the Nazis were ascending to power. She was by all accounts a brilliant student, inclined to write poetry, and she began her studies in philosophy at Marburg University at the age of eighteen. Infamously, as we know, at this young age, Arendt became the lover of Martin Heidegger, the charismatic philosopher whom many regard as the contemporary Western world's greatest philosopher. In Heidegger's classes, in which the philosopher was working through the central tenets of *Being and Time*, Arendt wrote much later that "thinking and aliveness became one."[10] Arendt and Heidegger wrote letters and poems to one another; the effect of this clandestine love affair upon Arendt was formative and deep.[11] Heidegger was married, with young children, to a woman who was anti-Semitic and the affair did not last. Heidegger ended the affair when Arendt was midway through her doctoral studies, and she was relocated to Heidelberg where she completed her thesis on the subject of love in the work of St. Augustine under the tutelage of Karl Jaspers. Clearly, these two great German philosophers—Martin Heidegger and Karl Jaspers—were the principal philosophic mentors in Arendt's early life, but she was to take from her association with the two of them divergent "lessons" on thought and love that I see as metaphors of her dualistic stances on life.

For Arendt, Karl Jaspers was the exemplary public philosopher. In a laudation she wrote for him upon his receipt of the German Book Trade's Peace Prize, she remarked that Jaspers had "never shared the general prejudice of cultivated people that the bright light of publicity makes all things flat and shallow, that only mediocrity shows up well in it, and that therefore the philosopher must keep his distance from it."[12] Significantly for Arendt, Jaspers became a prominent intellectual figure in Germany after 1933, during which time he "remained firm in the midst of catastrophe." Nazism held no appeal for him, even in its inception, and in his resistance to it, Arendt commented that Jaspers represented "what was left of humanitas in Germany."[13] Arendt cites Jaspers as having pro-

nounced that "the individual by himself cannot be reasonable," and she emphasizes that Jaspers neither enjoyed the solitude that was thrust upon him by the
circumstances of the Nazi regime, nor did he think "very highly" of it. Jaspers
saw his enforced solitude in a climate of political repression as a lacunae, a period of darkness in which he had a responsibility to fight for the light of an open
public realm. "Inviolable, unswayable, untemptable": these are the words that
Arendt used to describe her teacher.

The essay on Jaspers is one of the few places where Arendt engages in biographical narrative in order to explain someone. She speaks of Jaspers' childhood, with parents who were "high spirited and strong-minded Frisian peasant-
ry," and she lavishes praise on Jaspers' marriage to his Jewish wife, a marriage
that she regarded as a model of a "public space." These two partners never succumbed to the "illusion that the ties binding them have made them one," and
between them they created a world that became a "model for the whole realm of
human affairs."[14] In a separate essay on Jaspers, Arendt writes glowingly about
Jaspers' endorsement of a world federation of states (a commitment that owes its
origins to Kant), in which independent sovereign states will freely accede to
international laws governing their actions. She saw this political commitment of
Jaspers as perfectly consistent with the way in which he lived his private life.
Individuals and states cannot stand alone, but need the intercourse and exchange
with others in order to fulfill the commitment to freedom and plurality. The prospects for mankind, as Jaspers conceived them, lay not in Hegel's world history,
"where the world spirit uses and consumes country after country, people after
people, in the stages of its gradual realization," but in the embrace of communi-
cative thought in politically created and preserved spaces of freedom. In Arendt's praise for Jaspers, we find one of her strongest endorsements of the public
life. Singling out Jaspers as one of a series of "men in dark times" whom Arendt
chose to profile in her book of the same name, Arendt wrote that the "illumination" that emanated from Jaspers in a very dark time in Germany in the 1930s
and 1940s came not from his "theories and concepts" but from the "uncertain,
flickering and weak light" that persisted in his life.

The comparison of Karl Jaspers to Martin Heidegger, Arendt's other great
teacher, is striking. There are no biographical sketches of Heidegger in Arendt's
written work. There is no recounting in her publicly disseminated work of the
love affair between them. Arendt's accounts of Heidegger's contribution to
Western thought are mixed. Notoriously, Heidegger joined the Nazi party in
1933, he accepted the rectorship of the University of Freiburg under the administration of the Nazi regime, and he published a preface to his philosophical
work *Being and Time* in which he exalted the Nazi party as the future of Germany. Heidegger never renounced publically his Nazi affiliations, and he continued
to publish *Being and Time* with the original preface long after the horrifying
policies of the Third Reich were well known. After the war, and the defeat of the
Nazis, Heidegger retreated into the reading and writing of philosophy, never
uttering publically a reference to his foray into politics. Hannah Arendt, who had
emigrated, first to France, subsequently to the United States, did not see

Heidegger after the abrupt conclusion of their love affair until she was in her forties and she arranged a meeting with Heidegger in Germany. They established a reconnection and a correspondence, and Arendt was instrumental in the translation and distribution of Heidegger's work in the English-speaking world.

Everything we know from what Arendt has written about Heidegger suggests that she regarded him as the quintessential "philosopher." In *Men in Dark Times*, her tribute to illuminating lives of exceptional integrity, she writes about Heidegger in the introduction, not in the company of those she honours in this book, but as a counterexample. According to Heidegger, she writes, there is no escape from the "incomprehensible triviality of this common everyday world except by withdrawal from it into that solitude which philosophers since Parmenides and Plato have opposed to the political realm."[15] The "philosophical relevance" of Heidegger's claim, Arendt comments, is "undeniable," but then she proceeds to praise a catalogue of individuals whose refusal to withdraw in dark times is precisely their mark of integrity. In Arendt's posthumously published *The Life of the Mind*, she writes extensively about Heidegger's ideas, but the only mention of his involvement with the Nazi regime is a sympathetic one. She makes reference to an "interruption" in Heidegger's writing, an interruption that "coincided with the catastrophic defeat of Nazi Germany and [Heidegger's] own serious difficulties with the academic community and the occupation authorities immediately thereafter."[16]

What are we to make of this? I can only think that Arendt's almost complete silence on Heidegger's political engagement with the Nazis is part of her broader defense of philosophical contemplation, and her conviction that indeed, philosophical contemplation is a withdrawal. Philosophers like Heidegger, Arendt thought, are pursuers of truth, not justice, and are bad at political judgment because they take their bearings not from the world of plurality and action, but from that which is constant, eternal and possibly divine. In her essay on truth and politics (published in the 1960s, in the aftermath of the controversy over Arendt's book on the Eichmann trial), Arendt wrote that "the story of the conflict between truth and politics is an old and complicated one, and nothing would be gained by simplification or moral denunciation."[17] I also think that Arendt's turn to the investigation of the life of the mind toward the final stages of her life, was an attempt to think through the fundamental tension she felt between the "active" and public life, and the "passive" and contemplative life. From the introduction to *The Life of the Mind*, we read: "What interested me in the *Vita Activa* was that the contrary notion of complete quietness in the *Vita Contemplativa* was so overwhelming that compared with this stillness all other differences between the various activities in the *Vita Activa* disappeared."[18] In a lengthy investigation of Heidegger's philosophy in "Willing" (Volume II of *The Life of the Mind*), Arendt concludes that despite the transitions in Heidegger's thought throughout his life, and against those who would designate an "early" and a "late" Heidegger, there is a consistent antipathy in Heidegger to action, the world and plurality. She pronounces that for Heidegger, "to act is to go

astray."[19] What *stands out* for Arendt is the singularity, and the singular brilliance, of Heidegger's mind.

She wrote that the solitude of the philosopher is one of the outstanding existential modes of "truth-telling," and when it is adopted as a way of life (as was
the case with Heidegger), even if this life is never lived in total isolation and
independence, it "forfeits his position if he tries to interfere directly in human
affairs and to speak the language of persuasion or violence."[20] I find no evidence
in any of Arendt's work that she ever thought about Heidegger as anything but a
philosophic "truthteller." This does not mean that Heidegger always told the
truth about *himself.* In correspondence with Karl Jaspers, Arendt wrote that she
found in Heidegger a mixture of "vanity and deceitfulness" noting that he "lies
notoriously always and everywhere, and whenever he can."[21] But she put this
down to a failure of character, not one of thought. He made bad judgments in
politics, for a time he may have forfeited his title to philosopher because of his
entry into the politics of persuasion, but he regained his ground. Hannah Arendt
wrote on the occasion of Heidegger's eightieth birthday, in the *New York Times
Book Review* that it matters not where the winds of the century carried Martin
Heidegger. His thoughts remain a powerful assessment of modernity. [22]

About the love affair with Heidegger, Arendt is completely silent. She is
almost as silent about the topic of erotic love in general. (Arendt wrote a doctoral thesis on the notion of love in St. Augustine, but that work is really an exposition of the Christian understanding of caritas.)[23] In an exceptional passage in *The
Human Condition*, Arendt writes about passionate love, and the parallels between what she says there about love, and what she says about true philosophy,
are uncanny. Love, she writes, is one of the rarest occurrences in a human life,
but it possesses an "unequalled power of self-revelation and an unequalled clarity of vision for the disclosure of who, precisely because it is unconcerned to the
point of total unworldliness with what the loved person may be…love, by reason
of its passion, destroys the in-between which relates us to and separates us from
others."[24] The only happy ending to a great love affair, according to Arendt, is
the birth of a child, because while the child ends the "unworldliness" of the experience, the child "returns the lovers to the world from which their love had
expelled them." Arendt pronounces: "Love, by its very nature, is unworldly, and
it is for this reason, rather than its rarity that it is not only apolitical, but antipolitical, perhaps the most powerful of all antipolitical forces."[25] It seems that
Heidegger, for Arendt, sustained throughout her life as the exemplary lover, as
well as the exemplary philosopher.[26] Indeed, they may have been inseparable for
her.

If there is any ambivalence on the part of Hannah Arendt toward Heidegger,
it is on moral grounds, not philosophical ones. In 1953 (almost thirty years after
her love affair with him) in an entry in her personal journal, she wrote an essay
titled "Heidegger the Fox."[27] She tells a fable that "once upon a time there was a
fox who was so lacking in slyness that he not only kept getting caught in traps
but couldn't tell the difference between a trap and a non-trap." After a sequence
of getting caught in traps, Arendt writes that the fox decided to build himself a

burrow/trap of his own. Oddly enough, the fox subsequently became annoyed because no one sought him out, so he decorated his trap "beautifully" in order to attract visitors. The "visitors" came in droves. In this trap cut to his "own measurement," the fox could declare: "so many are visiting me in my trap that I have become the best of all foxes." Hannah Arendt concludes in remarking: "There is some truth in that too. Nobody knows the nature of traps better than one who sits in a trap his whole life long." There is both dismay and forgiveness in Arendt's tale. Lacking the courage to venture into the glare of the public realm, Heidegger seduced people into his lair of thinking. Lacking too in the fortitude that is required of solipsism, he longed for admirers. But despite Arendt's indictment of Heidegger on these grounds, she did not impart her criticisms to his philosophy. Morality and philosophy are two distinct "callings."

How different are Arendt's portraits of the two towering figures in her early education. Jaspers was a model of "worldliness," both in his partnership with his wife, and in the broader political context: a "citizen of the world" who embodied for Arendt everything that she admired about a life actively engaged with others. Heidegger was a model of "unworldliness," both as a lover and as a philosopher: a ruthless pursuer of truth, a contemplative and a solitary someone who moved toward singularity (both in love and thought) rather than dwelled in plurality. Arendt's respective portraits of these two men encapsulate her dualistic commitments. In the remainder of the chapter, I want to map out some of the chronology of Arendt's life and scholarship in an effort to show how she tried to reconcile these.

Hannah Arendt arrived by boat in New York City in 1941, at the age of thirty-five. By this time, she had been married twice, the first time in Germany to a fellow student, Gunther Stern, and the second time to Heinrich Blucher, a Communist activist whom she met in Paris in 1936. Arendt had left Germany for Paris in 1933 after being detained by police for questioning in connection with her research into anti-Semitism. Her second exodus, from Paris to New York, was precipitated by the Vichy occupation, and was facilitated by Arendt's first husband, who was already in New York in 1941. Arendt and Blucher were to remain married for the rest of their lives, and by all accounts this union was one modeled on the partnership between Karl Jaspers and his wife. Blucher was boisterous, worldly, intellectually engaged (but not formally educated), and the poet Randall Jarrell described the marriage as a "dual monarchy: a wholly equal but deeply united couple, standing up passionately to each other for their ideas and concealing none of them, but always attentive about providing little pleasures and signs of love."[28] The start of their life together in the United States was precarious; Arendt's taciturn mother had accompanied them in their emigration from France, and the threesome lived in cramped conditions in a rooming house for almost ten years, patching together a livelihood out of part time work, some of it in letters, much of it in physical labour. At the end of that first decade, despite the difficult circumstances, Arendt published *The Origins of Totalitarian-*

ism, her formidable and controversial account of the historical and philosophical roots of Nazism and Bolshevism.

From the early 1950s on, Hannah Arendt was a celebrated, if sometimes vilified, figure in the English-speaking world of philosophers, political thinkers, and journalists. She became part of the intellectual circles of New York, especially that of *The Partisan Review,* and published widely in magazines such as *The New Yorker* and *Commentary.* She taught at The New School for Social Research, also briefly at the University of Chicago (where she was a colleague of Leo Strauss). In 1958 Arendt published *The Human Condition,* her bold and imaginative defense of the *vita activa,* and its triad of labour, work and action. In 1961, she was asked by *The New Yorker* to cover the trial of the Nazi war criminal Adolph Eichmann in Jerusalem, and the series of articles she produced for that magazine were eventually collated into her book *Eichmann in Jerusalem,* with the subtitle "A Report on the Banality of Evil" that would become Arendt's most famous legacy. Interspersed among these major works—*Origins, Human Condition* and *Eichmann*—Arendt published prolifically essays on a wide range of topics, including violence, revolution, racial integration, republicanism, the Pentagon Papers, and the student movement. She was actively engaged with politics in the United States, and became a citizen of that country in 1951. In the late 1960s, Arendt turned away from reflections upon politics and "worldly matters," and began her projected three-volume study of *The Life of the Mind.* She completed only two of the three—"Thinking" and "Willing"— and the editing and publishing of these we owe to Mary McCarthy, Arendt's great friend and literary executor, because Arendt died before the series was completed. We have a sense of what she would have put into the third volume— "Judging"—from her lectures on Kant's political philosophy, compiled and edited with commentary by Ronald Beiner.[29]

What strikes me as I summarize so briefly Hannah Arendt's life and writings, is the range and the depth of her experiences and her thoughts. She was a refugee, twice; she lived both in obscurity and in the limelight; she loved a number of men, in different ways; and she left behind a body of work that traverses politics and philosophy. She published her thoughts on most of the controversial matters of her time, often to severe criticism. For example, when efforts were made to integrate white and black Americans by bussing children between schools so as to achieve a more equitable mix of races in education, Arendt published a scathing attack on the proposition. One can see in her rationale, the core arguments of *The Human Condition.* There, Arendt had drawn a clear line between political and social "space," and had defined political space as the publicly demarcated realm of artifice, in which one can expect, indeed demand, that people engage in exchange of ideas under created conditions of equality. Social "space," on the other hand, she relegated to the private realm, in which people forge ties of intimacy and friendship, often based upon commonality (perhaps familial, perhaps racial or ethnic, or even experiential). Arendt felt it was fundamentally errant to compel children, whose sense of stability and security comes foremostly from their private and social world, to act as agents of *political* equality. She did not think that young children should be the front lines of a political push for greater equality; she did not think that bussing would achieve its intended outcome, and in retrospect, she was right.

The most notorious of her "transgressions" for some, was her depiction of the chief architect of the "final solution" for the Jews under the Third Reich as banal.[30] Arendt viewed Eichmann as the incarnation of a novel form of evil, made possible by the bureaucratic, technological and ideological structure of the totalitarian state. Eichmann's kind of evil, for her, lacked intention. Classical accounts of evil could not explain him. "When I speak of the banality of evil," Arendt wrote, "I do so only on the strictly factual level, pointing to a phenomenon which stared one in the face at the trial. Eichmann was not Iago or Macbeth, and nothing would have been further from his mind than to determine with Richard III 'to prove a villain.' Except for an extraordinary diligence in looking out for his personal advancement, he had no motives at all...He merely, to put the matter colloquially, never realized what he was doing."[31]

I want to investigate further in this chapter the "thoughtlessness" of Eichmann as that was portrayed by Hannah Arendt, and how this led into her final (and I believe most important work) on the life of the mind. But before that, I want to take readers back to Arendt's first important published work in the United States, *The Origins of Totalitarianism*, to look more closely at ideology, and the dangers that Arendt associated with this particular kind of thought, indeed a kind of over-thinking.

As I began this chapter, I wrote that I believe Hannah Arendt's greatest contribution to us is her example of how we ought to think. Her instruction in this begins with her penetrating attack on ideology, stated most forcefully in *The Origins of Totalitarianism*. Ideological reasoning, Arendt concluded, was the end result of thought unhinged from its natural home in the world of common sense and experience, and its equally natural attachment to the suprasensible. The totalitarian regimes under Hitler and Stalin served as instances for her, in which we witnessed the catastrophic consequences of ideology in power. In her characterization of these regimes, we come to understand that their success depended upon *both* the suspension of the conditions of plurality and freedom that Arendt deemed critical to politics, *and* the denial that there is any extra-historical standard to which we owe a loyalty. There is a fundamental difference, she wrote, between the totalitarian state and other forms of domination, because it tries to do away with the *consensus iuris* that is at the base of all political consent. The totalitarian state "can do without the *consensus iuris* because it promises to release the fulfillment of law from all action and will of men; and it promises justice on earth because it claims to make mankind itself the embodiment of the law."[32] From classical times in the West, Arendt reminds us that Nature or Divinity has been the source for authority. Positive laws, if they are to have substance, must refer to a basis of "natural" law that can serve as the anchor of our political constitutions, and can stand as a recourse to which one can turn for the redress of political wrongdoing. (A modern variation on this can be found in the exploration of "conscience"; how could one make a claim based on "conscience" if one had no authority to which one could turn to justify one's stance, except the laws under which one lives in a community?) Arendt writes: "Nature or Divinity as the source of authority for positive laws were thought of as permanent and eternal; positive laws were changing and changeable according to circumstances, but they possessed a relative permanence as compared with the much more rapidly changing actions of men; and they derived their permanence from the eternal presence of their source of authority."[33] What totalitarian regimes do, in their embrace of ideology, is collapse any distinction between natural and positive law. All laws become laws of movement.

Underlying Arendt's indictment of the ideological thrust of totalitarian states is a much deeper analysis of the modes of thinking that have propelled these regimes. In *Origins,* she points out the affinity between Marx and Darwin, two towering figures in the modern firmament that are not often placed in the same camp. Darwin, Arendt impresses upon us, introduced the idea that natural movement is linear, moving cumulatively and progressively through time, in such a way that nature appears to have been subsumed in history. For Marx, as we know, all of history is the history of class struggle, supposedly reaching its apotheosis in the classless communist state. For both Darwin and Marx, and their claim to science, history plays out a truth that is made manifest in the meaning that we as human beings confer upon it. "The 'natural' law of the survival of the fittest is just as much a historical law and could be used as such by racism as Marx's law of the survival of the most progressive class."[34]

Totalitarian regimes have in common their allegiance to ideological modes of reasoning. Totalitarian rulers are not classical tyrants, holding on to personal power so as to increase their wealth, their territory or their individual glory. They see themselves as the agents of history, as messianic leaders transforming the world in accordance with a preconceived idea. Without the curb of natural law, and without even the obligation to respond to the *consensus iuris* of the body politic, there is absolutely nothing that can persuasively alter the objectives of an ideological ruler. "The rulers themselves do not claim to be just or wise, but only to execute historical or natural laws; they do not apply laws, but execute a movement in accordance with its inherent law. Terror is lawfulness, if law is the law of movement of some suprahuman force, Nature or History."[35] Terror is the handmaiden of ideology, because it requires coercion, surveillance, and an enormous amount of control to insist that a whole state, perhaps even a world, conforms to the madness of ideology. Sadly, as a reading of Arendt's account of totalitarianism reminds us, this madness prevailed for such a time that it wounded Western civilization and killed millions of people. Arendt remained convinced that totalitarianism, with its combination of ideology and terror, was a unique presence in the history of Western civilization. Even its methods of incarceration and murder testify to this uniqueness. Carnage, rape, brutality, imprisonment and enslavement have always been with us. Incarceration and incineration for the sake of realizing an ideological goal, backed up by bad science, have not.

Totalitarian regimes did not consume the world in the end. Although a combination of ideology and terror attempts to control conditions in such a way that "every action aims at the acceleration of the movement of nature or history," it proved impossible to encircle every single human being under totalitarian rule (and certainly outside it) with the "iron band" required to sustain the project. Arendt famously declared that every single human being born into the world is the beginning of freedom; every new human being brings with her or him the possibility of thought, action and political reform. She cites Augustine: "initium ut esset homo creates est—that a beginning be made man was created."[36]

Totalitarianism may have been defeated, and the constitutional and democratic practices introduced into the post-Nazi and post-Communist regimes may have ensured that state orchestrated terror cannot prevail. But ideological thinking is still with us, grounded in the overwhelming confidence that we seem to have in science and technology. Anyone who holds to deterministic theories of unfolding essence—biological determinists, globalization enthusiasts, environmentalists—is an ideologue. Arendt had written that the ideal subject of a totalitarian state is not the committed party loyalist, but "people for whom the distinction between fact and fiction (i.e., the reality of experience) and the distinction between true and false (i.e., the standards of thought) no longer exist."[37] So here we have implicit the two "antidotes" to ideology that are embedded in all of Arendt's work: 1) make certain that we are taking our bearings from real experience, and not from a preconceived allegedly scientific account of what our experience *ought* to be; 2) think about what we are doing when we think, and about how we can know the difference between the true and the false. The first prescription, I suggest, is particularly difficult to follow, given that we live in such a technological milieu. A lot of experience, especially for the young, is mediated through technology. Is a romance conducted on Facebook a real experience? Is the arrival in an international chain hotel in a distant part of the world from one's home, via rapid air travel, a real experience? When I buy clothes for low prices, that have been manufactured across the world in factories by young girls earning less than subsistence wages, am I contributing to a globally integrated economy, or am I just indulging in greed and indifference? Experience for most people is too confusing now, too mediated, to be much of a deterrent to ideological thinking. In fact, the confusion of experience is likely to exacerbate it.[38] Political engagement among the young is very, very low and even though we have secured constitutional and representative forms of government throughout the Western world, much of what passes for political participation is the advancement on the part of individuals of special interests, or ideological platforms. The emphasis that Arendt put upon conditions of plurality, openness, deliberative democracy, and "worldliness" seems to me of less and less significance as the technological society marches on. This leaves us with the imperative of thinking.

How can thinking save us? We have seen that while Hannah Arendt wrote extensively and critically about the "unthinking" of ideology and bureaucracy, and its devastating consequences for politics, she did not believe that *philosophical thinking* can be a buffer against these modern political and moral travesties. Heidegger, for Arendt the archetypal philosopher, faltered badly in his judgments in the world. Arendt always defended Heidegger as a philosopher, but derided him as a moral and political actor. She wanted to account for a kind of thinking that has real connection to moral and political action, but without becoming handmaiden to it. Arendt's final project, in *The Life of the Mind*, gives us a guide to a kind of thinking that embraces the retreat from the world that is requisite for reflection, and still takes its bearings from the world. "Seen from the world of appearances," Arendt wrote, "the thinking ego always lives in hiding, *lathe biosas.* And our question, What makes us think? is actually inquiring about ways and means to bring it out of hiding, to tease it, as it were, into manifestation."[39] Arendt called this "worldly" manner of thinking the "two in one," the conversation that I have with myself, when I am alone and I am attempting to reconcile things in my mind, and make sense of my life.

Arendt's model for thinking the "two in one" is Socrates: "an example of a thinker who was not professional, who in his person unified two apparently contradictory passions, for thinking and acting—not in the sense of being eager to apply his thoughts or to establish theoretical standards for action but in the much more relevant sense of being equally at home in both spheres and able to move from one sphere to the other with the greatest apparent ease." [40] Socrates according to Arendt, was a "gadfly, electric ray and midwife," neither a philosopher (since he taught nothing and had "nothing to teach") nor a sophist. What Socrates was capable of, was examining and reexamining ordinary opinions, subjecting them to careful criticism. The only moral imperative to issue from his thought, but one that forges the link between thought and world, is the axiom: it is better to suffer an injustice than to commit one. And the reason why this is an imperative that can accrue from thinking, is because thought's object is a kind of "desirous love" for things that are *real,* like beauty, wisdom and justice. If we think upon the *real,* we come to understand that ugliness and evil are deficiencies. They can only be thought as the *absence* of good. "That is why Socrates believed that no one could do evil voluntarily—because of, as we would say, its ontological status: it consists in an absence, in something that is not."[41]

Thinking, in the Socratic mode, means not being out of harmony with myself. Arendt thus imparts a pluralistic characterization to the activity of thinking, in contrast to the singularity that she attributes to "philosophy." "Nothing perhaps indicates more strongly that man exists *essentially* in the plural than that his solitude actualizes merely being conscious of himself . . . it is this *duality* of myself with myself that makes thinking a true activity, in which I am both the one who asks and the one who answers."[42] For Socrates, if I want to *think,* I had better make sure that "the two who carry on the dialogue be in good shape." The one person from whom I can never get away, is myself, and who would want to live with an evildoer? "It is better to suffer wrong than to do wrong, because you remain the friend of the sufferer; who would want to be the friend of and have to live together with a murderer?" Thinking is not conscience, but it releases conscience in such a way that can have enormous consequences in the world. "Conscience is the anticipation of the fellow who awaits you if and when you come home."[43]

I suggested earlier in the chapter that Karl Jaspers and Martin Heidegger stand as the two poles of mentorship in Arendt's education but I do not mean to imply by that statement that Arendt is a derivative thinker. Her contributions to modern political thought are original and important. Still, in her teaching on thinking, she is closer to Jaspers than to Heidegger. Despite her respect for the brilliance of Heidegger's philosophy, she felt that it was important to tie thinking to matters of the world. Hannah Arendt did not want to be called a philosopher. In an amusing exchange with Gunter Gaus for West German Television in 1964, Arendt interrupted Gaus's introduction to insist, "I do not belong among the circle of philosophers." To Gaus's objection "I consider you to be a philosopher!" Arendt responded, "well, I can't help that."[44] In her depiction of thinking, Arendt draws a parallel between her formulation of the "two in one" inner dialogue that she attributes to Socrates, and Jaspers' derision of loneliness. "Loneliness comes about when I am alone without being able to split up into the two-in-one, without being able to keep myself company, when, as Jaspers used to say, 'I am in default of myself' (*ich bleibe mir aus*) or, to put it differently, when I am one and without company."[45]

I believe that Arendt's understanding of thinking is profound and compelling. Her grounding of thinking in the inner duality of the "conversation with myself" makes it possible for a human being to retain a sense of self under the most arduous of conditions, and it promises the hope of moral and political responsibility for we contemporary individuals who inhabit a world without strong and sure metaphysical anchors. Arendt once called her kind of thinking "thinking without a bannister." It is a characterization that challenges the thoughtlessness of an Eichmann, the ideological seduction of a Darwin or a Marx, and the solitude and singularity of a Heidegger. It is tied to the real and substantive existence of beauty, justice and good. In conclusion I would say that this is what Hannah Arendt has to teach us: above all else, make sure that I *think* about what I am doing, and that means that I must be friends with myself, and understand that to be friends with myself I must think upon the just, the beautiful and the good. Thinking so defined is not the prerogative of the philosophers, or the few, but "an ever-present possibility for everybody."

Notes

1. Hannah Arendt, from Melvyn Hill, *The Recovery of the Public World* (New York, St. Martin's Press, 1979).

2. "A Conversation Between Elisabeth Young-Bruehl and Jerome Kohn," originally recorded as "On Truth, Lies, Politics and Media in Dialogue With Hannah Arendt," Goethe Institute, Washington, DC, November 28–29, 2006. Subsequently published in *Social Research*, 2007.

3. Hannah Arendt, *The Origins of Totalitarianism* (New York, Harcourt Brace and World, 1951) 469.

4. Arendt, *Origins*, 469.

5. Hannah Arendt, *The Human Condition* (Chicago and London, University of Chicago Press, 1958) 22.

6. Arendt, *Human Condition*, 325.

7. Hannah Arendt, *Eichmann in Jerusalem: A Report on the Banality of Evil* (New York, Penguin, 1963).

8. Hannah Arendt, "Thinking": Volume I, *The Life of the Mind* (New York and London, Harcourt Brace Jovanovich, 1971) 5.

9. Arendt, "Thinking," 6.

10. Derwent May, *Hannah Arendt: The Remarkable Thinker Who Shed a New Light on the Crises of the Twentieth Century* (New York, Penguin, 1986) 23.

11. For a somewhat controversial account of the relationship between Arendt and Heidegger, see Elzbieta Ettinger, *Hannah Arendt, Martin Heidegger* (New Haven and London, Yale University Press, 1995).

12. Hannah Arendt, "Karl Jaspers: A Laudatio," *Men in Dark Times* (New York and London, Harcourt Brace Jovanovich, 1955) 74.

13. Arendt, "Jaspers," 76.

14. Arendt, "Jaspers," 78.

15. Arendt, "Preface," *Men in Dark Times*, ix.

16. Arendt, "Willing": Volume II of *The Life of the Mind*, 188.

17. Hannah Arendt, "Truth and Politics," *Between Past and Future* (New York, Viking, 1968) 229.

18. Arendt, "Thinking," 7.

19. Hannah Arendt, "Willing," 194.

20. Arendt, "Truth and Politics," 570.

21. Letter from Hannah Arendt to Karl Jaspers, September 29, 1949. *Hannah Arendt and Karl Jaspers Correspondence, 1926–1969,* ed. Lotte Kohler and Hans Sanes, trans. Robert Kimber and Rita Kimber (New York, Harcourt Brace Jovanovich, 1992) 142.

22. Hannah Arendt, "Martin Heidegger at Eighty," *New York Review of Books*, 17 (October 21, 1971) 50–54.

23. Arendt's doctoral thesis was published as *Love and Saint Augustine*, ed. Joanna Vecchiarelli Scott and Judith Chelius Stark (Chicago, University of Chicago Press, 1996).

24. Arendt, *The Human Condition*, 242.

25. Arendt, *The Human Condition*, 242.

26. I think here of course of Socrates in the *Symposium* and his discussion of Diotima's ascendance toward the greatest eros: the erotic love of individuals is surpassed by the love of the beautiful and the good. The love of ideas is higher than the love of real people. Heidegger may have embodied the "unworldly" eros of carnal lover and philosopher for Hannah Arendt.

27. Hannah Arendt, "Heidegger the Fox," ed. Peter Baehr. *The Portable Hannah Arendt* (New York, Penguin, 2000) 543–544.

28. Cited in May, *Hannah Arendt*, 74–75.

29. Hannah Arendt, *Lectures on Kant's Political Philosophy*, ed. Ronald Beiner (Chicago, University of Chicago Press, 1982).

30. Deborah Lipstadt has reinvigorated the controversy over Arendt's interpretation of Eichmann recently with the publication of a new book, *The Eichmann Trial* (Schocken Books, 2011) Lipstadt takes issue specifically with the portrait of Eichmann as an "unthinking" bureaucrat, and she finds Arendt's account of the trial consistent with what she identifies as Arendt's self-loathing as a Jew. Lipstadt's analysis of the Eichmann trial is far narrower and less philosophically penetrating, than Arendt's.

31. Arendt, *Eichmann in Jerusalem*, 287. Italics Arendt's.

32. Arendt, *Origins*, 462.

33. Arendt, *Origins,* 463.

34. Arendt, *Origins*, 463.

35. Arendt, *Origins*, 465.

36. Arendt, *Origins*, 479.

37. Arendt, *Origins*, 474.

38. For an excellent account of the way in which technology has impacted liberal democracy, and especially debilitated the capacity for deliberative democracy and public "space," see Jodi Dean, *Publicity's Secret: How Technoculture Capitalizes on Democracy* (Ithaca and London, Cornell University Press, 2002).

39. Arendt, "Thinking," 167.

40. Arendt, "Thinking," 167.

41. Arendt, "Thinking," 179.

42. Arendt, "Thinking," 185.

43. Arendt, "Thinking," 191.

44. K. Haddad, "Hearing Hannah: Listening to German Language Recordings of Hannah Arendt from the 1950s and 60s," *Logos* (7:2).

45. Arendt, "Thinking," 185.

Chapter 3

Raymond Aron's Pedagogical Constitution
and Pursuit of Liberal Education

Bryan-Paul Frost, University of Louisiana at Lafayette

By the time of his death in 1983, Raymond Aron was widely considered to be "not just a great professor, but the greatest professor in the French university."[1] Very few today would deny that he richly deserved this accolade; and equally few during his lifetime would have been able to predict him ever attaining it.

I

Even a cursory glance at Aron's prodigious intellectual output would indicate that he easily merited this distinction. He was the author of tens of books, hundreds of articles, and thousands of newspaper and magazine editorials on subjects the totality of which few individuals could claim familiarity, let alone competence. Whether it was sociology or political science, international relations or economics, ideology or ethics, history or current events, Aron displayed a breadth of learning that befuddled his critics and bedazzled his admirers. But even more impressive than his prolific scholarship was the fact that (we can now affirm with the assistance and assurance of hindsight) on every major issue of the twentieth century Aron simply got it *right*—and often far earlier than many of his contemporaries. He correctly divined Hitler's diabolical nature and the belligerent path National Socialism would inevitably take; he was never seduced by the messianic pretensions of Karl Marx and communism; and he correctly pierced through the tortuous logic and outlandish propaganda of Stalin and the former Soviet Union. Although he was a French patriot through and through, he never wavered in his commitment to German integration and the Atlantic alliance; he was an early advocate of Algerian independence, albeit from a conservative (rather than leftist) perspective; and he possessed a healthy but not uncritical appreciation of the greatness of Charles de Gaulle (he was never hypnotized by the General's princely mystique), and he was willing to criticize the President when he felt it necessary, as perhaps he most famously did on the issue of Israel and the Jews.[2] Suffice it to say that getting even a few of these issues right would have been an achievement in the tumultuous twentieth century; that he got these and so many others correct as well is a rare accomplishment indeed. For that sizable (but often silent) segment of the French population that never took Parisian intellectuals and their debates all that seriously, and that loosely identified itself politically as conservative, centrist, moderate, or independent, Aron was a trusted analyst and interpreter, and he often clarified, or gave expression to, the opinions of those who did not have the time (or inclination) to angrily protest in the streets whenever the government did something with which they disagreed. Aron's educative legacy continues to live on through such associations and institutions as the *Société des Amis de Raymond Aron* and the *Centre de Recherches Politiques Raymond Aron* at the École des Hautes Études en Sciences Sociales in Paris. New editions of his works continue to be published (in the United States, notably through Transaction Publishers), and the scholarship on all aspects of his thought shows no sign of diminishing.[3]

But despite these accomplishments, Aron was not always popular with his fellow professors and intellectuals, and his writings were often misinterpreted, maligned—or perhaps worst of all for an academic—simply dismissed and ignored. Several reasons account for this neglect. In the first place, Aron was not a flashy individual: he never created an "—ism" and he repeatedly denied that there was a distinctly "Aronian" school of thought. Consequently, not only was he outflanked in popularity by those of his generation such as Jean-Paul Sartre, Simone de Beauvoir, Maurice-Merleau Pony, and Louis Althusser, but his sober and prudential judgments were considered *passé* by those who were entranced by such fashionable movements as existentialism, deconstructionism, structuralism, neo-Marxism, feminism, post-modernism, and the like. In the second place, Aron was often accused of lacking passion and commitment. In the words of François Mauriac, Aron displayed an "icy clarity" that simply repelled those who believed that the essence of existence was in commitment to something (what that commitment was to, and whether there was philosophical clarity to that commitment, were seemingly secondary concerns). It is no surprise to learn, therefore, that a popular saying during his lifetime was that "it was better to be wrong with Sartre than right with Aron"—a sentiment that Aron found both distasteful and irresponsible. But perhaps most importantly, third, Aron was considered a man of the Right—a classical, conservative-minded liberal both politically and economically when all things Right and Liberal were suspect or pilloried in so much of "progressive" society.[4] In other words, for many students and intellectuals, one had to be very *wary* of Aron. This sentiment is wonderfully captured (ironically enough) by Jean-Louis Missika and Dominique Wolton, two individuals who helped to establish Aron's great popularity throughout France near the end of his life.

> For those of us who during the 1970s gradually detached ourselves from Marxist claims of monopoly on the idea of progress and of arrogating to themselves the privilege of deciding who is on the Right and who on the Left, the discovery of Raymond Aron's thought was a distinct pleasure. Obviously, it was not unknown to us, for we had studied it at the university, but it had been catalogued as "reactionary." It was less understood as such than so perceived through an ideological filter and the Right-Left cleavage. In short, it was intelligent, but rightist? This attitude permitted one to recognize the quality of his analyses and at the same time to be wary of them. (*TP* 5)[5]

In short, Raymond Aron was "not one of ours" (*TP* 6). Despite this early sentiment, Missika and Wolton became more and more impressed with his thought, so much so that they decided to do a series of television interviews with him in 1980. These interviews (subsequently followed in 1981 by the publication of a more complete transcript of the interviews) proved quite successful in France as a whole—which was now able to see and appreciate his life-long achievement as a civic educator *par excellence*—and this helped to set the stage for the equally successful publication and reception of his *Memoirs* in the last year of his life.[6] At long last, Raymond Aron became, and deservedly remains, "fashionable" (*TP* 267).

What this essay seeks to accomplish is to limn Aron's underlying educational philosophy, i.e., not so much to describe what Aron specifically thought on any particular subject (there are many fine studies on almost all aspects of his corpus as a whole), but the more foundational question as to what he saw as the necessary and sufficient conditions for the existence of higher education in a modern, commercial republic. More specifically, the essays seeks to address the following set of questions as discussed in the "Introduction" to this volume. First, how did Aron become both liberally educated and a liberal educator in an age of ideology? Second, to what extent is the modern university a place of learning? And finally, third, what are the obstacles to liberal education in the modern university? Now it must be emphasized at the outset that despite Aron's voluminous writings, he did not consecrate any single work to these questions *per se* (but cf. *M* 233; *ER* 167). While he makes mention of education in a number of his writings, one must approach his overall educational philosophy or pedagogy in a *negative* way—in his *response* to the events of May 1968.[7] But perhaps this is not so surprising. Although Aron was a persistent critic of the French educational system as a whole, May 1968 presented a situation in which the very pillars and pursuit of higher education were in jeopardy, or at the very least were so in danger of being eviscerated in the name of "democratic," "social," and "progressive" reforms that it would remain "higher education" in name only. Aron would have none of this. The very existence of the university was at stake (not to mention the government and country as a whole), and Aron simply tore the veil off the illusions and pretenses of the student protestors (although we will see that they were not the most thorough-going target of his criticisms). In doing so, however, he also revealed what he saw as the core philosophical or pedagogical principles that must be acknowledged, preserved, and pursued if the university is going to remain an institution of free learning and inquiry rather than one of political indoctrination. In order to uncover and situate this criticism and analysis, we must first begin with a description of Aron's philosophical upbringing in order to see in more detail how he approached this as well as other issues of such national import.

II

Born into a secularized Jewish, bourgeois family from Lorraine in 1905, Aron entered the prestigious *grande école,* the École Normale Supérieure (ENS), in 1924. In 1928, he was awarded first place in the highly competitive *agrégation* (which is essentially a high-level and highly coveted teaching diploma), and a decade later he successfully defended his dissertation, *Introduction to the Philosophy of History*, before a skeptical jury, breaking as he did with the reigning neo-Kantian, historical positivism of his professors. By this time, Aron had already published two books on German sociology and historical philosophy, effectively introducing thinkers like Max Weber to a wider French, academic audience.[8] His own philosophy of history was pessimistic—even relativistic—arguing as he did that there were a plurality of possible historical interpretations, and that there could never be one over-arching explanation of the past (especially of the Marxist variety). Despite his professors' skepticism, it was close to universally acknowledged at this time that Aron was clearly on the path to becoming the most promising philosophical student and teacher of his generation.

Aron's early academic career is marked by two characteristics that he forever carried with him, and which presaged the great educator he was ultimately to become: a healthy combination of humility and ambition. Listen to his remarks upon entering the ENS for the first time—and this from the student who was to receive top honors in four short years: "My first impression of the ENS, I confess at the risk of appearing foolish, was wonder. Even today, if I were asked why, I would answer with complete sincerity and naïveté: I have never met so many intelligent men assembled in such a small space" (*M* 20). Or again, although Aron knew he was a very promising and gifted student, he possessed an acute awareness of how he measured up to the genuinely great thinkers of the past. He admitted that studying Kant for one year "cured me once and for all of vanity (at least in the deep sense)," and he believed that "nothing can replace, even for those who are not committed to philosophical labors, the deciphering of a difficult text" (*M* 14, 26; *TP* 252–53). Aron understood that while he was a gifted scholar, he was not the intellectual equal to a genuinely great philosopher. What these remarks suggest is that Aron possessed a truly unique pedagogical approach, especially if one recalls the unprecedented creative zeal of so many French intellectuals in the postwar era. On the one hand, Aron was more than able (and willing) to see through the philosophical pretensions of those who claimed to possess an all-encompassing sort of knowledge. He could never accept that one thinker, no matter how great, could effectively have all the answers, especially when it came to knowledge of the past and claims about the future. But on the other hand, Aron was equally aware of his own limitations such that he did not erect his own edifice to replace the one whose deficiencies he had just revealed. By arguing for the plurality of historical interpretations, Aron was able to guard against the all-too-intellectual temptation to offer his own comprehensive system in its place. One sees these two characteristics of ambition and humility on full display as Aron recalls the lectures he gave at the Sorbonne from 1955–58 (often referred to as the Sorbonne Trilogy) comparing the Western and Soviet Blocs economically, socially, and politically.[9]

> A number of students, Marxists or *marxisants*, were waiting to trip me up. I arrived [at the Sorbonne] with the reputation of a man of the right and a journalist; I had to tame the Marxists, to convince them of my knowledge, make myself recognized by all as a fully competent teacher. In *Dix-huit Leçons* [*18 Lectures*], I more than once was less than candid about my judgement of the Soviet Union. To demonstrate my objectivity, I had to grant to the regime to which I was opposed the benefit of the doubt, to show it some indulgence. I sincerely believe that I achieved my aim. We should not forget that Khrushchev's speech to the Twentieth Congress dates from 1956, the year of my first course. The facts that I pointed to in my courses were confirmed by the general secretary of the Communist Party of the Soviet Union. (*M* 236)

Aron always displayed a sober (but not debilitating) degree of skepticism, whether towards his own ideas or those of others, both inside and outside the classroom.

Despite Aron's success at the ENS and in defending his dissertation, what ultimately proved to be most decisive in his formation as a future educator was his teaching sojourn to Germany in the early 1930s (first at the University of Cologne from 1930–31, and then in Berlin from 1931–33). For the first time, Aron had to confront the political in its rawest and most virulent form, something his previous formal education had prepared him for very little. With the collapse of the Weimar regime and the rise of Hitler and National Socialism, Aron could no longer affirm and rely on the historical optimism of his professors and others, who somehow remained assured that the future would inevitably secure the blessings of science and reason. From now on, Aron would have to think politically. He needed new conceptual tools if he was to understand what was occurring. Indeed, as he later recounted, he needed a decidedly less "philo-sophical" and more "political" trajectory as a student and educator altogether.

Aron explains this change in perspective through two episodes in chapter 3 of the *Memoirs*, "The Discover of Germany" (which he had originally consid-ered entitling "The Discovery of Germany and of Politics"). In the first episode, Aron recounts an epiphany he had on the banks of the Rhine that lastingly shaped the questions he would ask and the comportment he would exhibit throughout his life.

> I gradually grasped my two tasks: to understand or know my time as honestly as possible, without ever losing awareness of the limits of my knowledge; to detach myself from immediate events without, even so, accepting the role of spectator. Later, when I became a commentator in the daily press, my tendency to look at events from a distance, to present the world as it was, not the ways of changing it, constantly irritated many of my readers. (*M* 39–40)

In the second episode, Aron reveals the particular way in which he would frame and thereafter answer those questions of "history in the making." In 1932, Aron was introduced to an undersecretary in the French Foreign Ministry, Joseph Pa-ganon, and was asked to speak about his growing anxiety over political devel-opments in Germany, especially the "threat of war" that Hitler's ascension to power would surely pose to all of Europe.

> When my speech had ended, he answered me, by turns ridiculous and to the point. "Meditation is essential. Whenever I find a few moments of free time, I meditate. So I am grateful to you for having given me so many subjects for meditation. The prime minister, minister of foreign affairs, possesses excep-tional authority, he is a man out of the ordinary. The moment is ripe for all ini-tiatives. But you, who have spoken so well about Germany and the dangers ap-pearing on the horizon, *what would you do if you were in his place?*" (emphasis added)

Aron continues:

> I do not remember my answer; I am sure that it was embarrassed, unless I kept silent. What should I have said?
>   This lesson from a diplomat to a future commentator bore fruit. Fifteen years later, in the offices of *Combat*, I asked Albert Ollivier, who had criticized the government in an editorial: "What would you do in its place?" He an-swered, more or less: "That's not my problem; it has to find what to do, I have to criticize." As often as possible, I have tried to carry out my role as a com-mentator in an entirely different spirit, to suggest to governments what they should or could do. (*M* 41–42)

Although Aron does not use the following categories, we might reconceptu-alize these two episodes in the following way: Aron was rare among French intellectuals for combining in equal measure an Aristotelian (or citizen's) perspective with a Machiavellian (or ruler's) perspective. Similar to Aristotle, Aron sought to understand as clearly and objectively as possible the competing claims of those in the political arena, not in order to traduce his opponents but rather to instill a needed dose of moderation into the likely heated debates. Aron understood that no claim (or party) in politics is either *completely* wrong or right, and that no side has a *perfectly* just cause: as he was wont to remind others, politics is not about good versus evil but about choosing between "the preferable and the detestable," and this goes a long way in explaining his remarkably judicious and tolerant remarks on the Vichy regime and Germany during and after that especially volatile time (*TP* 242). The citizen's perspective ensured that Aron was most interested in analyzing the situation correctly, and not in imposing a solution and demanding the capitulation of his opponents. But similar to Machiavelli, Aron was willing to offer advice to a prince, or at the very least, when offering such advice, to incorporate as sincere an appreciation as possible of the government's own perspective and of what it could most reasonably expect to accomplish under the prevailing circumstances. Objective analysis does not at all preclude giving advice—indeed, for an editorialist in Aron's unique position it even required it, but always with the understanding that the solutions advocated must be within the realm of genuine political possibility, and thus must take account of the totality of pressures the government is under as well as the competing claims of the partisans involved. This does not mean that Aron was little more than a tepid compromiser—far from it. As was mentioned above, he often took very unpopular and even extreme positions when the issues and times demanded it. Instead, it suggests that political prescriptions that ignore or forego the government's point of view are, at the very best, somewhat hollow and even puerile, and at the very worst, deceitful and possibly dangerous. A tempered Machiavellianism coupled with a thoughtful Aristotelianism often yields sound political judgment.

It must be emphasized, however, that although Aron combined both an Aristotelian and Machiavellian perspective, it was the former perspective that was prior both in time and importance: concrete, impartial analysis of the situation was required before any reasonable decision could be made. Aron gently scolded many of his fellow leftist intellectuals (and certainly some of the most famous or infamous) of so often doing precisely the opposite, and it is for this reason that they got some many issues terribly wrong. By reversing the order of Aristotle and *then* Machiavelli, many intellectuals ended up "justify[ing] the unjustifiable" (most notably the Soviet Union and other incarnations of totalitarianism), all in the name of protecting and promoting some utopian ideal that defied all logic (*M* 457). In other words, "they refuse[d] to think politically." In Aron's estimation, this failure meant two things.

> First, they prefer ideology, that is, a rather literary image of a desirable society, rather than to study the functioning of a given economy, of a liberal economy,

of a parliamentary system, and so forth.

And then there is a second element, perhaps more basic: the refusal to answer the question someone once asked me: "If you were in the minister's position, what would you do?"....They rarely ask [this question]. They think that
kind of question is for the experts, the technocrats. They are worried, anguished
by the fact that there is evil in our system (evil exists in all systems); they thirst
for the solution that would provide the "universalizable" society. (*TP* 154–55)[10]

To return to the language of Machiavelli, French intellectuals were more often
interested in creating "imaginary republics and principalities" (what Aron called
"construct[ing] cathedrals of concepts with the courage of imagination" [*M*
456]) rather than studying the "effectual truth" of the matter, something that
Aron (like Machiavelli) explicitly warned against! By allowing their untem-
pered, creative ambition to win out over their sober, measured humility, leftist
intellectuals ended up understanding neither Machiavelli or Aristotle. In sum,
the above discussion should help to explain why Aron described himself, and
was often described as, the "committed observer" (*TP* 257). He was that rare
individual who at one and the same time could be a non-partisan advocate or an
engaged witness (terms that most people today would consider to be an oxymoron). These were the foundational hallmarks of Aron's pedagogical constitution.

III

Aron fled to London during the war and quickly became one of the leading writers (and in essence the de-facto editor) of *La France libre*, an extremely influential periodical of French independence. Returning to Paris afterwards, he briefly
joined André Malraux's Ministry of Information, the only official political position he ever held. Although Aron was offered the opportunity to continue his
interrupted professorial career, he decided against it, and instead opted to become a journalist for *Le Figaro* and thereafter a member of the newly formed
Gaullist party the RPF (*Rassemblement du Peuple Français*). As Aron admitted,
he had caught the "political virus," and he wanted to part of the rebuilding of
France after its crushing and humiliating defeat as well as of warding off the
growing specter of communism (*TP* 94). Only some ten years later (1955) did he
decide to return to the university, although he never abandoned his role as an
editorialist. Aron therefore pursued two different careers and in fact lived two
different lives—but they were two *separate* lives. He knew very well the difference between teaching about politics (in which he sometimes used, and to great
advantage, various Marxist concepts [see, e.g., *TP* 5]) and teaching politically
(*ER* 56–57, 187–91).[11] While the previous section might have intimated that
Aron was a very political teacher, his stated position is precisely the opposite:
after admitting that "we learned nothing or almost nothing about the world in
which we lived" while he was in school, he speculates whether it is not better to
keep high schools insulated from political life altogether.

Sometimes I even wonder whether the isolation of lycées from the outside
world didn't have more advantages than disadvantages. A teacher likes to provide an example of detachment, he represents an arbiter, a witness, he judges
according to the truth. As soon as he discusses politics, he has difficulty in raising himself, even when he attempts to do so, to that serenity he demonstrates
with ease when he translates or interprets Caesar's commentaries on the Gallic
wars. (*M* 20)

Of course, there are those who will dispute this claim and argue that his journalism compromised his teaching—and inherently so, for it is impossible for an
editorialist to keep his advocacy out of the classroom. Strictly speaking, this is
true: an editorialist who is committed to the political positions sketched out
above will certainly teach courses differently from a committed Marxist, Maoist,
or Castroist. Nevertheless, Missika and Wolton once again capture an important
truth about Aron when they describe the interaction of these two careers.

Raymond Aron is not simply an intellectual who has dabbled in journalism. An
intellectual dabbling in journalism generally chooses the subjects and the occasions on which he wishes to comment and take a position. Aron, however, has
imposed upon himself the discipline of commenting regularly upon events,
without choosing the causes to defend or the moments in which to defend them.
This resolve to pursue two careers at once over the last thirty-five years forces
upon him something much more than discipline and a rigorous organization of
his time. It makes it necessary to live with two different processes of thought,
generally mutually exclusive, and thus pursued in a permanent state of tension.
This alternating between two logical processes, two ways of looking at things
(commenting upon an event and overall interpretation), leads to a world view
more sensitive to the uncertainty and fragility of events than to the search for
final causes. Perhaps we should perceive in this choice both the will toward
personal transcendence and the mark of historic relativism. In any case, this
constraint of regular confrontation with economic and political events has
probably helped preserve Raymond Aron from the intoxication of ideology.
Such confrontation makes it impossible to choose only the facts that support a
theory—he must treat everything. (*TP* 11–12)

In reality, Aron's journalism complemented and even aided his teaching—but
only because he kept his journalism and teaching, his advocacy and analysis,
strictly separated.

When he returned to the "old Sorbonne" (he would later teach at the École
Practique des Haute Études and the Collège de France), Aron began a critical
appraisal of the French university system that greeted him (*M* 229). Not surprisingly, Aron starts off in an admittedly pedestrian way: resources. "What struck
me most [when I returned] was the dinginess of the building and the institution.
The chairs, in the tiny offices next to the lecture halls, could have come from the
flea market. The rooms were gray, dirty, sad. I could not help recalling American and English universities, of which I had some experience. In my eyes, the

poverty of the building illustrated the decrepitude of the system" (*M* 232). Putting aside the question of whether American and English universities today enjoy such a riches of resources(!), Aron's observation became more poignant as the number of students multiplied over the course of the next decade, with the public universities admitting far more students than they could reasonably accommodate. In the French system, all students who earn the *baccalauréat* (roughly equivalent to a high school diploma) can enter the university system; by contrast, France's elite *grandes écoles* have a competitive admission process. While open admission to the public universities might satisfy France's desire for a democratic and egalitarian educational system, it was equally true that the government was wasting vast resources on what Aron called "pseudo-students, [namely those] who achieve no degrees and derive little profit from their hesitant efforts" (*M* 234). Ultimately, the state would either have to increase funding to the universities or adopt some sort of selective admissions process. It ended up doing neither. To put it bluntly, if the state is going to claim that it supports higher education, it has to put its money where its mouth is (*ER* 20, 41ff., 60ff., 151).

Compounding this problem of resources was the increasingly uncertain employment prospects for those who did manage to complete their degrees: even those who (like Aron) had successfully completed the *agrégation* were suffering from a scarcity of jobs. Not only must there be an equilibrium between students and resources, but there must also be some rough correspondence between a particular course of study and future employment opportunities. Aron was deeply cognizant of the *economic* dimensions of higher education and the modern university, and he often argued that what France needed first and foremost were more scientists and engineers. If there were limited career paths in what we might loosely call theoretical disciplines such as philosophy or sociology, then teachers, universities, and the government have a responsibility to make students aware of these unpleasant facts far in advance: indeed, they may have to regulate or restrict those who wish to matriculate in these areas to the best and the brightest alone (*ER* 42ff., 64ff., 141, 151, 186). Aron might not go as far as Tocqueville in this regard, who states in *Democracy in America* (vol. 2, pt. 1, ch. 15) that studying classical Greek and Latin literature can be safely confined to a few good universities so that the majority of individuals can turn their attention to receiving an education in science, commerce, and industry. But similar to Tocqueville's spirit, Aron understood quite clearly that a modern, commercial republic needs modern, commercial citizens if it is going to prosper (albeit hopefully well-rounded ones). At all events, the public university cannot make false promises: it must not only reflect the nature of political society and its needs in the future, but it must also back up that support with the appropriate resources.[12]

The lack of adequate resources and career opportunities also had a deleterious effect on the relationship between students and teachers, unintentionally fostering an unhealthy and even adversarial relationship between them. After all, if the university will not employ selective admissions *before* students are admitted to the university, then professors will be forced to employ one *after* they arrive. Professors will be required to lecture to large numbers of students, the majority of whom they do not know and will never meet; many students will simply drop out because they were not qualified to attend to begin with; and for those who do make it through to the end of the year, professors will be forced to fail large numbers of students given the university's limited resources. With some process of selective admission, by contrast, this adversarial relation would be reversed: the university needs admit only those it thinks worthy of it, and thus professors are eager for and expecting students to succeed (rather than seeking excuses to fail them). This unhealthy relationship between students and teachers was made even worse by the extraordinary power and lack of accountability that many professors enjoyed but which Aron deplored. "The concentration of power rather than of talents scandalized me long before the students took to the streets [in May 1968]." Professors who were so inclined could exercise an "excessive and sometimes stifling" degree of influence over the choice and direction of a student's research, and the power that they exercised (and often exercised quite "vigorously") was literally unchecked by any other person or agency. In respect to their own teaching and research, professors only had to follow their own "conscience"; and while Aron admits there were some very fine professors, courses, and research agendas, he makes perfectly clear that this was not always the case. Thus, while professors would be personally familiar with students who were writing dissertations under their supervision, the others were more or less left to "fend for themselves," without any sort of guidance or "precise goal." It is no wonder that when Aron left the Sorbonne in 1968, he felt the school was at the "end of its tether" (*M* 232–34; *ER* 41ff., 60ff.).

IV

We might say that all of Aron's major criticisms of the public university system revolved around the theme of accountability: of the state for matching resources, enrollment, and career prospects; of teachers for exemplifying the highest standards of their profession; and of students for diligently fulfilling the requirements of their course of study. This must be understood in order to appreciate Aron's almost blanket condemnation of May 1968. For it is all too easy to view him as simply a curmudgeon who was either too old or too conservative or both to fathom the putative salutary revolutionary activities that were occurring throughout France: tellingly, the chapter in his *Memoirs* on this event is entitled "He Has Not Understood Us." The Spirit of '68 continues to have an almost hypnotic effect upon so many leftist intellectuals and even the public at large, not unlike the hagiography that surrounds the 1960s in the United States (see *TP* 207–20). Why did Aron reject an event that promised to reform the university wholesale?

To begin once again at the most prosaic level, Aron always doubted that genuine reform could occur in a revolutionary environment. With passions running fever-pitch, it was unlikely that genuinely thoughtful proposals would be adopted, let alone be heard and seriously considered. In the festival, carnival-like atmosphere that often prevailed at the time, the university was now being used as a political organization or tool—indeed, it was becoming a veritable political arena, but without all of those necessary accouterments that accompany decent (i.e., non-revolutionary) politics, such a elections, representation, deliber-ation, and checks and balances.[13] If reforms were to be instituted they had to take place through properly legitimate political channels and not through a self-appointed oligarchy claiming to be the only authentic voice of the students, teachers, and university as a whole. "France had to be put back to work and to have a government again before reconstruction, particularly of the university, could be placed on the agenda" (*M* 316). Stability is the condition and hallmark of the university, and academic classes cannot be used as avenues for activism. Even as higher education is subject to legitimate political change, the institution itself must remain outside of the political fray, lest it forever change its nature. As Thucydides taught Aron so well, and as he knew from his own experience, revolutions—even psychodramas like this one—do not cause moderates and centrists to rush into the streets and clamor for reasonable and meaningful change (*ER* xvii, 10, 20–21, 34, 126, 164ff.).

But granting for a moment that the university could reform itself under this set of conditions, what precisely was being offered in the name of such reform? In other words, what sort of educational accountability was May 1968 likely to bring? This was not at all clear. In the first place, Aron repeatedly observed that there was no concrete, identifiable program for change among the heterogeneous groups participating in the events. Instead, students and others gathered together at various venues and endlessly "talked and talked and talked"; and while many parents and teachers believed that this activity in and of itself was both trans-formative and educational, Aron shook his head in consternation (*ER* 5, 17, 19–20, 24; *M* 321–22). In the second place, many of the demands the students were making were completely contradictory. The protesters displayed what we might call a vague "againstism": they were against the "government," the "system," "hierarchy," "lack of opportunities," and ultimately "consumer society" as a whole (*ER* 4, 7, 30, 76, 100, 105, 136, 179, 186; *M* 321). But it was precisely consumer society and all the rest that allowed the students the opportunity to pursue higher education in the first place: students would drive their parents' car to rallies only to denounce that very middle-class lifestyle that had been un-known by the previous generation![14] But most importantly, third, those individ-uals who did have a reform agenda in mind were calling for some form of great-er "democratization," the outcome of which would have involved greater student involvement in key aspects of university decision-making (*M* 320–26). Now Aron was never against greater student involvement *per se*, and he tried to do this in his own classes. For example, he required students to give oral presenta-tions, but he soon abandoned this as students were more interested in his "cri-tique" than in the presentation of one of their peers (*M* 236). Or again, he invited

students to become more involved in departmental matters, but only on the condition that final authority rested with the professors (*ER* 59, 181). But involvement was one thing; control was something entirely different, and it is here that
Aron drew the line. As he wrote in an editorial at the time:

> 1. *It is unthinkable that the students should in any way participate in the elec-
> tion of teachers.*
> 2. *It is unthinkable that the students should in any way fulfil the function of ex-
> aminers.*
> 3. *It is unthinkable that those who represent teachers in the combined teacher-
> student committees should be elected by general assemblies which include stu-
> dents and delegates of the administrative staff....*
> The only chance of salvaging anything of the liberal tradition, of the intellectu-
> al and moral values for which the University remains accountable before histo-
> ry, is to reject any deal on the three simple and fundamental principles I have
> just quoted. (*ER* 175–76, emphasis in the original)

Although few protesters seemed to realize it, the May 1968 method of student
accountability would have rendered the university into a co-ed dormitory.

The above remarks help to reveal one of Aron's foundational pillars: the
necessity of hierarchy. Aron was fully aware that in any educational environment some students will surpass their teachers, and some teachers will fall below their students. But May 1968 tried to make this exception the rule: throughout the French university system (Aron's criticisms notwithstanding), teachers
merited their positions, and students needed instruction. By giving the students a
larger voice in everything from the hiring of professors to the overseeing of examinations, the inevitable result would have been the appointment and promo-
tion of professors based solely on their political beliefs. Academic diplomas
would then become utterly worthless. The university absolutely requires for its
existence a voluntary respect and discipline on the part of the students towards
the authority of their professors, and if this is compromised, so too is the very
character of education (*ER* 4, 34, 54–55, 58–59, 75–76, 129, 181). The university is not an equal and democratic institution, and to make it so would echo
Aron's warnings above about the dangers of politicization. Perhaps this is why
he saved his harshest criticisms for the actions of "adults" in May 1968 (his
comments about Sartre are particularly revealing) (*M* 320–28). Aron understood
(but did not always agree with) what the students desired and yearned for; but
the cravenness of the adults during this time made him livid, especially his fellow colleagues. Suddenly, professors who did not even know the names of their
students were participating in sit-ins, denouncing the centralization of power,
and clamoring for greater student involvement. If one of the causes or symptoms
of student unrest in the 1960s was a general "weakening of adult authority,"
certainly many Parisian intellectuals helped to weaken it even further (*M* 324,
317).

Although student violence seems to me to be a threat to the continued survival
of universities throughout the western hemisphere, my hostility is directed
much more against the adults than against the young, against teachers rather
than taught, against my ex-colleagues rather than against my ex-students. Nowhere else did teachers take part, as a far from negligible number of French
teachers did, in the students' revolutionary action. They shared in the setting up
of illegal *ad hoc* assemblies and institutions, and openly or tacitly supported the
action of a trade union which refused to regard the government as a valid nego-
tiating body. They were civil servants, but they unconcernedly broke the law
and claimed to be acting collectively with the aim of overthrowing the Gaullist
Government. Not even the most left-wing teachers at Berkeley or Columbia
went as far in their contempt for authority, for common sense, or for the law. In
my view the faults of the French University are not enough to justify conduct
unworthy of those whose job it is to teach. (*ER* xvii)

Aron may indeed have been a curmudgeon, but only because he understood, and
therefore treasured, genuinely liberal education. He gave voice to those other
curmudgeons in France who looked upon May 1968 as the undoing of all that
had been accomplished since "the catastrophe of 1940." As he indicated in the
many letters written to him during this time, "At last, someone had finally had
the courage to break the conspiracy of silence" (*ER* xv, 2).

V

In the polarizing climate of the Cold War, Aron's career was one that attempted
to maintain the distinction between "*teaching* and *indoctrination*"—between
"*exposing* all the various doctrines as objectively as possible, and setting out the
arguments for and against them, and *imposing* one single doctrine and rejecting
all the others" (*ER* 56–57, 188, emphasis in the original). Aron was aware that
this was an ideal, and difficult to put into practice (his near non-appointment at
the Sorbonne was an indication of that). But, nevertheless, it was an ideal, a
principle—a standard to which one could appeal—and he claimed that the pre-
1968 university did its best to preserve "a distinction between learning and politics," however imperfectly (*ER* 187). But the ideological agitators of 1968 wanted to scrap this ideal wholesale in order to transform the university into a political institution that preached some version of the "great God Marx and all his
prophets" (*ER* 182). Let us allow Aron to have the last word on the necessary
conditions of higher education in an age of ideology:

The teaching of sociology cannot avoid a certain degree of partiality by what it
says and does not say, and by the manner in which it says it. But no one acting
in good faith could fail to see the difference between two sorts of practice—on
the one hand the presentation of facts and doctrines without dogma and without
excluding anything, and on the other the imposition of one doctrine, say Marxism, and the rejection of all other doctrines as bourgeois or reactionary—*or, al-*

ternatively, outlawing Marx and Marxism.

In French universities until May 1968, the teaching was of the former type. Even in the socialist countries of Eastern Europe there are signs here and there of a return to the norms of the liberal University.

Some of the May revolutionaries, initially the students, and later some of the teachers, embarked on the course which leads to teaching of the second type. (*ER* 188, emphasis added)

Notes

1. This is according to François Furet, himself considered to have been one of the greatest historians of the French Revolution in the twentieth century. See "La rencontre d'une idée et d'une vie," in *Raymond Aron 1905–1983: Textes, études, et témoignages* (Paris: Julliard, 1985), 52, a compilation of articles published in the Aron-inspired journal *Commentaire*, nos. 28–29 (February 1985).

2. See Raymond Aron, *De Gaulle, Israel and the Jews*, trans. John Sturrock (London: André Deutsch, 1969).

3. For a bibliography of Aron's writings, see Perrine Simon, *Raymond Aron: bibliographie* (Paris: Julliard, 1986) as well as Robert Colquhoun, *Raymond Aron*, 2 vols. (London: SAGE Publications, 1986), the latter of which contains a substantial index of the secondary literature on Aron. It should be noted that neither of these works contain references to Aron's voluminous number of editorials in such publications as *Combat* (1946–47), *Le Figaro* (1947–77), and *L'Express* (1977–83). Throughout this essay, I have utilized, and made reference to, the English translations of Aron's work whenever possible so as to increase the accessibility of the essay to a non-French speaking audience.

4. In this context, it is important to remember, in the words of Pierre Manent (*Le Monde*, December 3, 2005), that France remains "effectively the only country where 'liberal' has become an insult." Despite this reputation, it is undeniable that Aron's conservative-minded liberalism (along with that of André Malraux) helped to save "the honor of French intellectuals" after the war. See Nicolas Baverez and Pierre Manent, "Raymond Aron: Political Liberalism, Civic Passion, and Impartial Judgement," *Society* 41 (March/April 2004), 19.

5. Raymond Aron, *Thinking Politically: A Liberal in the Age of Ideology*, trans. James and Marie McIntosh, intro. Daniel J. Mahoney and Brian C. Anderson (New Brunswick, NJ: Transaction Publishers, 1997), hereafter cited in the text as *TP*. It was originally published as *Le Spectateur engagé* (*The Committed Observer*) (Paris: Julliard, 1981).

6. Raymond Aron, *Memoirs: Fifty Years of Political Reflection*, trans. George Holoch (New York: Holmes and Meier, 1990), hereafter cited in the text as *M*. This is an abridged translation of *Mémoires: 50 ans de réflexion politique* (Paris: Julliard, 1983), recently reissued with additional material (Paris: Robert Laffont, 2010).

7. The principal text here is *The Elusive Revolution: Anatomy of a Student Revolt*, trans. Gordon Clough (New York: Praeger Publishers, 1969), hereafter cited as *ER*.

8. See Raymond Aron, *Essai sur une théorie de l'histoire dans l'Allemagne contemporaine: La philosophie critique de l'histoire* (Paris: Vrin, 1938); *German Sociology*,

trans. Mary Bottomore and Thomas Bottomore (Glencoe, IL.: Free Press, 1957); and *Introduction to the Philosophy of History: An Essay on the Limits of Historical Objectivity*, trans. George J. Irwin (Boston: Beacon Press, 1961).

9. Raymond Aron, *18 Lectures on Industrial Society*, trans. Mary K. Bottomore (London: Weidenfeld & Nicolson, 1967); *La Lutte de classes: Nouvelles leçons sur les sociétés industrielles* (Paris: Gallimard, 1964); and *Democracy and Totalitarianism*, trans. Valence Ionescu (New York: Praeger, 1969).

10. Aron's language here echoes that of Alexis de Tocqueville a century earlier, who also complained that too many intellectuals "carry the spirit of a salon over into literature, and that of literature into politics. What I call the literary spirit in politics consists in looking for what is ingenious and new rather than for what is true, being fonder of what makes an interesting picture than what serves a purpose, being very appreciative of good acting and fine speaking without reference to the play's results, and, finally, judging by impressions rather than reasons." Tocqueville hastens to add, however, that "this peculiarity is not confined to Academicians. To tell the truth, the whole nation shares it a little, and the French public as a whole often takes a literary man's view of politics." See *Recollections: The French Revolution of 1848*, eds. J. P. Mayer and A. P. Kerr, trans. George Lawrence (New Brunswick, NJ: Transaction Publishers, 1987), 67.

11. The inability by other professors to make this critical distinction almost resulted in Aron not being elected to the Sorbonne. Because he had recently published *The Opium of the Intellectuals*, trans. Terence Kilmartin (New York: W. W. Norton & Co., 1962), where he effectively undermined the Marxist idolatry of history as well as such treasured concepts as "Left," "Revolution," and "Proletariat," Aron was not supported by communist and many other left-leaning professors. Although he ultimately prevailed, the distinguished historian H. I. Marrou had to remind the faculty that they were not necessarily voting for the author of *Opium* but of *Introduction to the Philosophy of History*. It should be mentioned that Marrou also had to remind them that they had recently appointed a communist as well (*M* 230–31).

12. For all of Aron's comments on the topic of resources, very little is said about the salaries of professors. In fact, when he does mention this issue, it is almost always from the perspective of those who did not earn the coveted *agrégation*. According to Aron, these individuals often "suffered from their permanently inferior status": they were forever denied the career advantages (both remunerative, social, and otherwise) that came to the *agrégés*, even when they did the same work and might be more capable at doing it (*M* 56). The emphasis placed on this diploma over all others created a "heterogeneous teaching body, with duties and rewards determined not by present merit, but by examinations taken before entering the career" (*M* 233). Aron readily admitted that the *agrégation* was neither better nor worse than other methods of selection, and that those who deserved it generally earned it (*M* 25). Nonetheless, such a rigid system hardly corresponded to the meritocracy the university aspired to be: success or failure on a single test should not determine the entirety of one's future prospects. In this respect, the system in the United States compares favorably to France's, where all teachers are civil servants, and are thus centrally regulated by Ministry of National Education. In the decentralized system of the United States, educators who are dissatisfied with their career prospects or salary are free to move elsewhere, something which is really not possible in France (cf. *ER* xiii–xiv, 41ff., 68).

13. Although Aron famously called the events of May 1968 a "psychodrama," it was nevertheless a drama all the same, and one that nearly brought down de Gaulle's government. Despite all the impressive accomplishments France had achieved since the end

of the war, the protests by students and others showed how truly fragile the Fifth Republic was, and much of Aron's analysis in *The Elusive Revolution* focuses on the causes of this fragility.

14. This hypocrisy is vividly brought forth when Aron recounts what one of his colleagues at the Faculty of Science in Lille, M. Savard, more or less told his students in May: "You are all, even the poorest amongst you, a privileged group, for you all still have the chance of escaping from the fate of the proletariat, the lot of the worm. Your comrades in the factories no longer have this chance, supposing that they ever had it. Whether the society is capitalist or socialist, it is in large measure at the expense of society that you pursue your studies. The young worker who labours on the building site or toils in the din of the workshop pays taxes so that you may rise above him in the social scale. It is true that your academic merit justifies your privileges. But you would have had a more receptive audience if instead of shouting 'We have our rights,' you had said: 'We are fortunate.'" Aron wryly remarks: "Overstatements perhaps, but many students from bourgeois backgrounds would nevertheless do well to ponder them" (*ER* 150).

Chapter 4

Bernard Lonergan:
Toward a Pedagogy of Political Thinking
Lance M. Grigg, University of Lethbridge

Introduction

What is a political insight? What does it mean to teach *for* or *about* political thinking? What am I doing when I'm thinking politically? Is there such a thing as political thinking pedagogy? These are the many "further questions" a society needs to ask if it is at all serious about nurturing a culture of political thinking. Education can play a significant role in this enculturation process, focusing on pedagogy that teaches for an authentic, political thinking that grounds responsible citizenship. Hence, powerful teaching is not restricted to a specific location. It finds teachable moments in all sorts of situations, ranging from formal classroom debates to conversations in coffee shops.

In one sense, this chapter is intended to be such a moment. It works toward developing a pedagogy of political thinking, and is written from a perspective far adrift from mainstream political discourse. It draws upon insights from the North American, philosopher and economist, Bernard Lonergan who wasn't a professional political philosopher. His main areas of research were metaphysics, economics and epistemology of math and science.

Oddly, Lonergan's philosophy can be deceptively simple. Like a fractal equation or the four main elements of DNA, the building blocks of his thought are basic, yet they have a surprising complexity that expresses itself in development and exposition. Hence, it is important to keep that insight in mind when reading a piece of reasoning applying his thought to related areas of inquiry.

This chapter extrapolates insights from his philosophy to navigate the murky waters of political thinking. It outlines the implications of such an exploration for liberal education in an era of ideology, and develops an approach to teaching and learning that values self-consciousness. Importantly, the chapter makes references to Lonergan-the-teacher, remarking on how that lived experience was instrumental in shaping his notions of authority, power, justice and political thought. Given the edition's shared focus on teaching, the tone throughout the chapter is often facilitative and conversational.

Moreover, it is the first part in a series of essays applying Lonergan's thought to current topics in education. Being an educationalist and not a political scientist or philosopher, I hope my readers are not unfamiliar with the principle of charitable disagreement.

A good place to start would be Lonergan engaged in a "teachable moment." Lonergan always felt that good teaching creates situations wherein students have the opportunity to catch themselves in the act of thinking. But as any history professor knows, teaching *about* history is far less demanding than teaching *for* historical thinking.

One afternoon while giving a lecture on his philosophy of insight, a rather disgruntled, graduate student interrupted Lonergan: "I still don't get it. What is an insight?" As the story goes, he pondered the question for a minute, went to the blackboard, and began filling it with differential equations. After a few minutes he stopped, turned to the student, and said, "There, I think that explains it nicely." Needless to say, the expression on the young man's face suggested things weren't all that clear.

Noting his blank expression, Lonergan returned to the blackboard, and showed how each equation emerged from the one preceding it. Occasionally, he'd stop and do a comprehension check to see if the student was following him. If so, Lonergan would continue, explicitly focusing on the mathematical insights that grounded the progression from one equation to the next. After a few minutes, he asked if the demonstration was helping. Nodding, the student replied, "Yes. I think so. I'm not sure I get all the math but having an insight sure feels good."

Although the above conversation may not have unfolded exactly the way it's outlined, the spirit of it is definitely historical. Why? Simply, Lonergan's philosophical project is fundamentally, pedagogical. As both a philosopher and a teacher, he was a consummate facilitator. He used examples from mathematics, science, philosophy, theology and economics as tools for empowering students with the ability to know themselves, and experience the self-constituting power of that knowing. His text, *Insight* is in effect, an 875 page exhortation to know thyself. Lonergan often referred to it as his "little book," claiming its first few chapters are a five-finger exercise in self-knowing.[1]

Because Lonergan's thought is dense and voluminous, some have claimed it is obscure and unduly abstract. For example, Lonergan often used his own critiques of Western philosophy, theology and economics in his teaching. Needless to say, many of the concepts he addressed were difficult in themselves let alone his criticisms of them. Consequently, he would listen to his students complain about the material. In reply, he would say, "Knowledge makes a bloody entrance." I can think of no better aphorism when applying the thought of Bernard Lonergan to the complex world of political thinking, ideology and education.

Who Was Bernard Lonergan?

Bernard Lonergan was a philosopher, economist and theologian. He was born on December 17, 1904, in Buckingham, Quebec. At the age of 18, he joined the Jesuits. After spending four years at the Jesuit house in Guelph, Ontario, Lonergan studied mathematics and philosophy at Heythrop College and the University of London from 1926–1930. As well, Lonergan studied at the Gregorian in Rome from 1933–1939. He returned to Canada in 1940 where he taught at the Collège de l'Immaculée Conception in Montreal, Quebec.

Much of Lonergan's academic career was spent teaching and writing. He was a professor at the Gregorian University, Rome (1953–65), at Harvard (1971–72) and at Boston College (1975–83). The University of Toronto Press is publishing Lonergan's writing in its *Collected Works Series*. To date, there are 16 volumes published with another nine currently in press. Lonergan died in Pickering, Ontario on November 26, 1984.

What Am I Doing When I'm Thinking Politically?

Biographical Note
As a Jesuit, Lonergan personally experienced what one could call weak-sense political thinking.[2] During his formation, he had to spend time in regency; a customary three years of teaching in a Jesuit college or university. He was to spend his time at Loyola College in Montreal from 1930–1933. Because he had already spent a year in England, Lonergan could have gone to study theology in Rome after two years in Montreal. But due to clashes over sleeping schedules with the vice-chancellor of his college, Lonergan's request for an early departure was denied. Apparently, he was staying up too late reading Plato, economics and various mathematicians. His disregard for protocol did not bode well with his superiors.

Nonetheless, Lonergan bowed to authority, and accepted the postponement, doing so with painful reservation. It, however, made him question his vocation, chosen area of study and future academic life. Surprisingly, soon afterwards, there arose an opportunity for Lonergan to go to Rome sooner than expected. The Jesuit authorities, however, wanted to first question him about his orthodoxy. By this time, Lonergan had a reputation. In any case, when asked, he told them, "I am orthodox, but I think a lot." Lonergan left for Rome shortly afterwards but this suspicion of blind obedience and a deep respect for unrestricted questioning never left him.[3]

The Political in Context: A Brief Overview of Lonergan's Thought

As mentioned earlier, Lonergan was not a professional, political philosopher. Instead of addressing topics such as sovereignty, representation, regimes, forms of government, participatory democracy or the polity, he spent his time on problems in mathematics, theology, economics and philosophy of science. His deep interest in the political questions of the day, however, never wavered. He tirelessly sought ways of developing structures that promote social progress and discourage its decline. He was deeply concerned about the dialectic of power and authority in a society, and highlighted how economics contributes to a polity's understanding of just, self-governance. In the next few pages, a brief overview of Lonergan's thought is given followed by further elaboration and application of those insights to the areas of political thinking and political thinking pedagogy.

It's worth noting at the outset that readers of Lonergan are often frustrated by his interdisciplinarity. For example, in order to address social justice issues during the Depression, and critique Social Credit politics, Lonergan constructed a macroeconomics grounded in circulation analysis. As well, he deconstructed relativity and quantum theory to make room for theological method. He used elements from Piaget's psychology to demonstrate how constructivism works in the formation of mathematical insights. In Howard Gardner's language, Lonergan had a synthetic mind.

For the most part, Lonergan's project is motivated by three questions: (1) What am I doing when I am knowing? (2) Why is that knowing? and (3) What do I know when I do it?[4] His answer to the first question is a cognitional theory, to the second, an epistemology and the third, a metaphysics. Consistent with the pedagogical intent of his work, Lonergan argues that by posing these questions to ourselves, and doing a phenomenology of how we answer them, we are constructing philosophical foundations.

Significantly, he exhorts us to perform this inquiry in the act of doing so. This focus on attending to one's experience of thinking-in-action gives one the opportunity of taking hold of or in Lonergan's words, self-appropriating one's way of knowing. In turn, this self-appropriation offers a method for understanding the complex relationships that exist among disparate disciplines, themselves products of human knowing.[5] Not unlike the iterations involved in fractal mathematics, Lonergan's philosophy unfolds with infinite boundaries. He puts it succinctly:

Thoroughly understand what it is to understand, and not only will you understand the broad lines of all there is to understand but also you will possess a fixed base, an invariant pattern, opening upon all further developments of understanding.[6]

Questions, therefore, become the operator engaging human understanding in its pursuit of self-knowledge, reality and value. For Lonergan, inquiry begins with questions, and ends in knowledge that in turn, raises deeper questions. They stimulate further inquiry, direct and sustain its focus, facilitate the formation of subsequent insights, and in a political context, work to prevent ideological thinking from pre-determining both political questions and the answers to them.

As well, questions foster a positive attitude towards discovery. Pedagogically, this is significant. Without well-phrased questions, political inquiry would be specious at best. In turn, political thinking pedagogy would be reduced to giving someone a lesson in civics. Learning itself would become regurgitation of facts, and the *critical* in critical thinking would come to mean silent acceptance; the ideological antithesis of Lonergan's philosophical enterprise. Liberal education would be similarly disadvantaged.

Next, Lonergan's cognitional theory is foundational to all his work. As mentioned earlier, it is a response to his question, *what am I doing when I am knowing?* Summarily, it is a phenomenology of authentic, human knowing. Its origins are in questions whose terminus is knowledge and action that become the ground of further questions. Specifically, it is grounded in an attentiveness to the mental acts of sensing, imagining, remembering, questioning, grasping insights, formulating, weighing evidence, judging, deliberating, evaluating and deciding.[7] For Lonergan, knowing is authentic to the degree it arises out of a sustained performance of these mental acts. While one can arbitrarily and capriciously inhibit a mental act specific to thinking, Lonergan cautions against it. To stop the dynamic flow of thinking at any point in cognitional process would constitute inauthenticity. Restricting the range of experience, the number of questions to be asked or concepts to be critically considered would be, from Lonergan's point of view, a flight from insight and authenticity.[8] Accordingly, authentic knowing is highly distrustful of a relativism that accedes simplistic solutions to complex problems, a hegemony that distorts historical judgments to enhance political membership or a static conceptualism that is uncritical of its own development in space and time.

Hence, Lonergan envisages authentic knowing as a dynamic structure that is both context-sensitive and generalizable. This insight will prove very useful when answering the question, *what am I doing when I'm thinking politically.* Lonergan envisages authentic knowing as a recurrent and related set of mental *activities* that (1) begins with a sense of wonder about the universe, (2) poses questions to our experience of that universe, (3) seeks intelligent insights into its meaning and nature, (4) makes reasoned judgments about the quality of those insights, (5) decides on responsible courses of action arising from those judgments, (6) demands we act on those decisions with integrity, and (7) returns to a sense of wonder from which all questions arise. Unlike a Cartesian *cogito*, Lonergan's authentic knower is not a disembodied intellect. She remains concretely engaged in the act of thinking about the universe of being, and her rightful place within it.[9]

For Lonergan, consciousness is a differentiated unity that is intimately linked to this perspective on human knowing.[10] It is differentiated to the degree that human consciousness is multilayered, and a unity insofar as one experiences this differentiation as one consciousness. As such, consciousness is an awareness immanent in and through inter-dependent, cognitional acts.[11] Hence, by attending to the diversity of cognitional activity in its recurrent operations, the knower or thinker becomes increasingly present to herself.[12] In short, deepening one's awareness of cognitional activity is constitutive of self-consciousness. The story involving Lonergan's graduate student is an example of teaching for a heightening of self-consciousness by focusing on the learner's own thinking-in-action.

It's important to note that for Lonergan, self-consciousness is not a matter of taking some sort of inner look. Rather, it involves catching oneself in the act of sensing, understanding, judging, deciding and ultimately, loving. A sustained attentiveness to one's own cognitional activity enlarges awareness of consciousness as this differentiated unity.

Intentionality is another fundamental and powerful concept for Lonergan. He views it as an orientation of consciousness directed to the universe of being. He saw consciousness as an immanent awareness in cognitional acts. By attending to those mental acts, one can uncover this directionality of consciousness. In turn, one can clarify how they function, and inter-relate. For example, mental acts are relational and directional; they are always *of* or *about* something. By seeing we see what is to be seen, by understanding we seek intelligibility in what we see, having insights into both the world around us as well as ourselves trying to make sense of it. In judging, we seek the true, and move to verify the truth-value of our insights. By deciding, we intend value and make decisions about what should be done about our judgments.[13]

In a political context, the good of order is the value intended at the level of consciousness associated with deciding. At this level, one intends the good when making responsible decisions.[14] Being politically conscious, therefore, would entail making decisions directed towards the preservation and deepening of the good of order. It manifests itself in a care and concern for (1) responsible forms of government, (2) a balanced understanding of the relationship between authority and power, and (3) a just economic system that ensures the consistent circulation of goods and services so that every citizen can have his basic needs met. In other words, consciousness intends being at every level, from experience to actions grounded in decisions.

Lonergan understood this intentional or directional orientation of consciousness as being unrestricted,[15] and it becomes the source of intellectual, moral and religious self-transcendence.[16] For example, Lonergan would suggest that the intentionality of consciousness could empower the political thinker with the capacity to transcend personal opinion on political matters. Hence, although fallible in nature, she can make objective judgments about the nature and morality of a political theory, judgment or decision. Allowing this insight to iterate so to speak, Lonergan developed what he called a generalized empirical method (hereafter GEM) and broadly applied it to the natural, social and human sciences.[17]

Accordingly, Lonergan is often called a critical realist. Influenced by Aristotelian and Thomistic philosophy, he believed that we could make true judgments of fact and value. Lonergan is a *critical* realist to the degree he grounds knowing and valuing in a critique of the human mind. Unlike Kant, however, Lonergan understands concepts as *a posteriori* and not *a priori*.[18] They are generated from our experience of the universe, the insights that arise from our efforts to understand that experience, and the judgments we make about the reliability of those insights. Lonergan believed that attending to this performance of concept formation avoids a static *a priorism* basic to many forms of conceptualism.[19] As well, it avoids an historicism that relativizes the significance of insights to their origins.

The Dynamic Structure of Political Thinking
Returning to the earlier question of *what am I doing when I'm thinking politically*, a preliminary note is in order. Although Lonergan uses the language of human knowing, for the purposes of this discussion, terms referring to knowing and thinking will be used interchangeably. Consistent with Lonergan's central focus, human knowing is essentially, thinking-in-action. Thinking itself, is a series of mental acts and processes that comprise knowing the universe of being, and ourselves making meaning within it. Ongoing efforts to know that universe are in effect, "thinking events." Political thinking, therefore, can be thought of as a set of incomplete knowing or cognitive events that strive to both construct and discover political meaning.

An important assumption underpinning this association of knowing and thinking is that thinking occurs largely because human knowledge is fallible. As such, it is by definition, open to constant revision. Moreover, *thinking* terminology is the commonly accepted discourse in educational research on teaching and learning; critical thinking, historical thinking, creative thinking, economic thinking, etc.

Notably, Lonergan was leery of phenomenology's emphasis on visual metaphors when talking about human thinking or knowing. He understood it to be much more than just *taking a look*. Thinking is a complex mental activity with a diversity of parts operating inter-dependently. For example, observing is a necessary but not sufficient condition for the possibility of political thinking. Other features of human thinking are needed in order to make sound political judgments and decisions. Hence, Lonergan was critical of reductionism in any form: neurophysiological, linguistic, materialistic, etc.

For Lonergan, attending to the complexity of one's mental acts is possible by virtue of his notion of the *subject as subject*.[20] For example, if one were to try and look at oneself thinking, one would be a subject looking at an object; namely oneself. But the human subject can look but never see herself as an object in this way. The more she searches, the greater is her frustration in finding nothing. Consequently, it's a mistake to view the subject as an object by taking some sort of inward look. Rather, by attending to the subject-as-subject in the concrete activity of thinking, fundamental features of human thinking are discernible.

In turn, when trying to understand the nature of political thinking, Lonergan would counsel us not to begin with a political concept or theory. Rather, the starting point for inquiry into political thinking is the political thinker in the act of thinking politically. With a sidelong bow to Aristotle,[21] one begins by posing the question, *what am I doing when I'm thinking politically?* For the political thinker, the product of such an inquiry will be none other than the unfolding, dynamic structure of political thinking itself, grounding subsequent political insights, concepts, theories, judgments and actions. Thinking politically, there-fore, begins by attending to one's own cognitional performativity within a polit-ical context. Such a context can be sitting in a political science lecture, reading a treatise on political philosophy or voting in a federal election.

If students catch themselves in the act of thinking politically, a number of features basic to that type of thinking emerge.[22] First, they notice it is structured. Lonergan understood the structure of human thinking not as a fixed entity but as a relational unity or whole wherein each active component co-exists among oth-ers. This co-existence is essential for the performance and survival of its related parts:

Each part is what it is in virtue of its functional relations to other parts; there is no part that is not determined by the exigencies of other parts; and the whole possesses a certain inevitability in its unity, so that the removal of any part would destroy the whole, and the addition of any further part would be ludi-crous. Such a whole is a structure.[23]

Suffice it to say, thinking is an integrated and inter-dependent unity whose diversity of functions allows for it to be "self-maintaining,[24] self-assembling, (and) self-constituting."[25]

As mentioned earlier, Lonergan often used examples from science in his teaching. Biology featured prominently in his demonstrations of how a structure can be self-constituting.[26] For example, human anatomy has structured itself in such a way that it is what it is by virtue of its ability to be self-structuring, and it survives and evolves accordingly. The circulation of blood is a different biologi-cal activity from respiration and digestion, yet each needs the other to function properly. They exist if and only if they co-exist. Similarly, the interdependence of seeing, hearing, smelling, imagining, understanding, reflecting and judging, constitutes human thinking itself due to their self-constituting inter-dependence.

Drawing upon Lonergan's notion of structure, one could argue that the con-ditions necessary for the possibility of political thinking are similar. Political thinking occurs within a dynamic structure beginning with a well phrased, polit-ical question that in turn, engages subsequent, integrated thinking moments. For example, applying Lonergan, a political concept can be understood as a proposi-tional response to a political question arising within a specific political experience prompting the posing of that question. As such, because the historical and linguistic context conditions the occurrence of political concepts, they remain vulnerable to active, probative questioning by virtue of the dynamic, self-constituting nature of human thought. A political theory that asserts its concepts are fixed and invariant may be inattentive to the dynamic nature of concept formation operating within a broader more fluid, cognitional context.

Political Thinking and the Interdependence of Experiencing, Understanding, Judging and Deciding

According to Lonergan's cognitional theory, thinking structures itself around the inter-related activities of experiencing, understanding and judging.[27] Although deciding what should be done about one's judgments is a necessary political activity, for Lonergan, decisions follow upon the heels of judgments that establish facticity. Hence, political decision-making is subsequent to and a sublimation of political judgments.[28] One could claim the ongoing iteration of these mental acts comprises the breadth of human knowledge it creates.

Political knowledge may be similarly constituted. Political thinking can produce knowledge by virtue of its open-ended structure. It is open on account of its primary dependence on experience. Lonergan argues it is structured because all knowing or thinking naturally moves in a pre-selected pattern beyond experiencing into a desire to intelligently understand the meaning of our experiences; itself a natural, unrestricted curiosity. In turn, we experience the need to reasonably judge whether or not we've understood the nature of our experiences correctly. We make judgments because an emergent, critical rationality moves us to reflect upon the quality of our understanding. In this context, we experience a desire to judge whether our political insights have any credibility. In short, the dynamic of authentic thinking moves from experiencing through to judging. With those judgments in hand, we experience the natural drive to deliberate upon appropriate courses of action and the plans needed to carry them out.

Importantly, Lonergan saw teaching as a way of nurturing an ownership of one's thinking. His students often spoke of the personal impact he had on their thinking:

I learned to attend to my own judgments. I understood that a judgment occurs at the end of a whole process. And it doesn't occur frequently…each student (is) to appropriate his own knowledge. You cannot appropriate another person's knowledge…People tend to jump instantly from insight to judgment. I remember Lonergan using the word "concept" cautiously. He considered a concept as something quite rigid, fixed for a long time.[29]

It is interesting to see how Lonergan's suspicion of conceptualism trickled down to his students. One might say they saw concepts and judgments as moments of rest waiting upon further questioning rather than as static, permanent fixtures invulnerable to criticism. Another of his students remarked on how Lonergan's teaching focused on developing a personal awareness of how one experiences concept-formation: "In fact, he (Lonergan) invited us to do what he tries to do in the first five chapters of *Insight*. Have you go through an experience of getting an insight, understanding what you're doing."[30]

Facilitating this experience was crucial for Lonergan as a teacher and a philosopher. He wanted his students to engage their own unrestricted desire to know; a wonder about why things happen, that poses questions for inquiry and terminates in reasoned judgment and responsible decision-making.[31] By doing so, Lonergan was able to deepen his students consciousness of their own cognitional activity, giving them a philosophical basis for thinking in a variety of contexts. Although Lonergan never explored the issue of transferability, potentially, it could be a fruitful area of political inquiry.

Generally, what does this kind of thinking look like? Specifically, within the inter-dependence of experiencing-understanding-judging-deciding what does it mean to think politically? Firstly, through an experience of sense-data (hearing, seeing, smelling, tasting, touching) or the data of consciousness (feelings, images, thoughts) one may daydream or ask questions. Although daydreaming is enjoyable, when needing to make a reasonable, political judgment, it's inadequate to the task at hand. For example, when analyzing a political theory or voting to elect a president, responsible readers and citizens operate within a pattern of intellectual experience that is focused, demonstrating a desire to make sound judgments.

In order to do so, however, these individuals have prior tasks to perform. For example, they need to know specifics about the political theory in question: socio-historical backgrounds, authorial histories, structure of the theory itself, etc. Similarly, responsible voting needs relevant information about each candidate. Hence, each task requires attentive listening, reading and observing. Doing so creates open spaces wherein one hears and sees things that pique interest and arouse concern. Without such spaces, relevant data remains distant and obscure. In this context, political thinking engages the data of sense and consciousness because it has a desire for precision and accuracy so that it may know correctly.

So, for Lonergan, this desire to know occurs within a discernible intellectual pattern of experience: a desire to correctly know what is the case and why.[32] Whether or not one is interpreting a political theory or casting a vote, this unrestricted desire remains the same. Hence, responsible readers and citizens pose questions to their experience; asking related questions about relevant texts, credentials, feasibility of campaign promises, etc.

In other words, when it comes to reading a political piece of reasoning or voting in an election, authentic political thinking begins its inquiry by posing a *question for intelligence*. Lonergan posits the occurrence of questions for intelligence at the level of understanding. They take the form: *What is it? Why is it? How often does it occur? Who is it?* In response to questions for intelligence, direct insights grasp intelligibilities in perceived or imagined data: correlations, laws, etc. Those insights are then formulated into hypotheses and concepts using the appropriate format: words, symbols, numbers, etc. Lonergan uses examples from mathematics, natural science and common sense to illustrate this movement from experience and questions for intelligence to direct insights and their linguistic and symbolic expressions.[33]

As a student himself, Lonergan was not unaware of the daunting challenges such an approach has for thinking and teaching *for* thinking. In his preface to *Insight*, he says:

> I am led to think...of the teachers and writers who have left their mark upon me in the course of twenty-eight years that have lapsed since I was introduced to philosophy. But so prolonged has been my search, so much of it has been a dark struggle with my own flight from understanding, so many have been the half-lights and detours in my slow development...[34]

The movement from experience to judgment is often wrought with difficulty: poorly phrased questions leading to dead ends, outdated concepts prematurely restricting inquiry, and communities discouraging unorthodox interpretations of texts. But as Lonergan acknowledges, it is also the case that a good teacher can liberate a student's unrestricted desire to know from these strictures, and facilitate the discovery of new insights that transform and re-direct entire fields of study.

Still, Lonergan was quite the realist when it came to the rewards and challenges of teaching in this way. He personally encountered the eternal need for educational reform during his years at the Gregorianum in Rome. He often spoke of "having to teach under impossible conditions" and doing "practical chores that you have to do if you are teaching a class of 650 people...a period in which the situation was hopelessly antiquated."[35]

During the 1961–62 academic year, he was teaching courses in Christology and The Trinity. Since they were taught in Latin, preparing lectures was often time consuming and tedious. According to both Lonergan and many of his students, these and related conditions were less than conducive to what one would call "active learning." Still, Lonergan was capable of teaching difficult material in a manner that made a significant impact on his students. Richard Liddy comments:

> Those of us who were his (Lonergan's) students in Rome in the 50s and 60s knew him as a rather un-prepossessing Jesuit teacher who spoke with a pronounced Canadian accent and had a certain grandfatherly mein...His presentation of the Trinitarian life gave us a glimmer of how our lives are caught up in the mystery of infinite love. He taught us that somehow our own thinking and acting is a participation in the life of the Father, the eternally spoken Word and the spirit proceeding as love from grasped meaning.[36]

So despite the less than ideal teaching conditions, Lonergan's pedagogy of self-appropriation remained influential. His students saw themselves in the genesis and development of their efforts to understand the philosophies and theologies they were studying. Although site-based conditions in Rome didn't exactly nurture a culture of inquiry-based teaching and learning, Lonergan's philosophy seemed to fill in some pedagogical gaps.

Not surprisingly, Lonergan's project wasn't met with universal approval. His critics were diligent, some fearful of the direction his philosophy, theology and teaching were taking. One of his students acknowledged the difficulties Lonergan experienced on this front:

> ...Lonergan highlighted the problems of the development of doctrine. His was a liberating perspective. I believe that he might well have suffered the accusation of heresy by the hierarchy. As a matter of fact, he was taxed with heresy by a Spanish theologian...Lonergan defended himself vigorously.[37]

Whether or not the Vatican would have actually accused Lonergan of heresy, one student has this to say: "The dominant mentality of the Vatican did not seem to me to involve an openness to historical development."[38] Hence, it isn't surprising that Lonergan's ideas would be met with suspicion or that he would need to defend himself with vigor. Despite these levels of intellectual engagement, Lonergan felt a sense of alienation from the intellectual climate of the day. Phil McShane, a long-term friend, comments: "He (Lonergan) knew he was way ahead. He had a desperate need for community."[39] Lonergan's focus on the primacy of insight-formation in philosophical and theological inquiry definitely went against the cultural and "official" grain so to speak.

So why would Lonergan's focus cause such a stir? Before we can answer that, we need ask a prior question: what is an insight? Lonergan claims insight: (1) comes as release to the tension of inquiry, (2) comes suddenly and unexpectedly, (3) is a function not of outer circumstances but inner conditions, (4) pivots between the concrete and the abstract, and (5) passes into the habitual texture of one's mind.[40] Fortunately, unlike Archimedes, few political scientists run naked through the streets shouting *Eureka* when they have an insight. Still, they too have a "drive to know, to understand, to see why, to discover the reason, to find the cause, to explain."[41] Hence, insights are thinking moments that perceive and organize intelligibilities in the data of sense and consciousness. *A posteriori*, they find conceptual expression in a broad range of languages and symbols.

But in Lonergan's words, the dynamic structure of human knowing is a natural heuristic that seeks the best available answers to well-phrased questions. Hence, one needs to assess the quality of one's insights. Consequently, at the level of judging, one asks questions for reflection such as *Is it so? Is it probably so?* These questions are a product of and a stimulant for subsequent, critical reflection. They operate upon answers given to questions for intelligence, and can only be answered *Yes* or *No*. If one answers *Yes*, one judges the insight to be correct/probably correct at the time. Authentic, political thinking, therefore, realizes the need for a sustained effort to continually judge the quality of political insights and the subsequent concepts constructed at the level of understanding.[42]

For example, with a sidelong bow to the educational context of the chapter, let us do some civics education, and return to our responsible voter in the act of voting. Although less dramatic than a deconstruction of the history of political philosophy, it does begin with a very concrete activity of deep concern for the polity: choosing a political leader.

After she attends to the relevant data, poses a question for intelligence (*Who should I vote for?*) has a direct insight into the data of her experience, formulates a hypothesis as to who is the best candidate, our voter still needs to know if her preferred candidate is warranted. Hence, she asks, *Is this person truly the best candidate?* In turn, she marshals out the available evidence, weighs it, has a reflective insight, and makes her judgment. She may respond with a resounding *Yes*, in which case she goes to the ballot box, and casts her vote accordingly. In the transition from understanding to judging, she has moved from possibility to actuality, from the best possible candidate to the best actual one. This judgment will vary according to the level of her cognitive, self-awareness and the quality of thinking and data gone into making the decision. It's important to note that the weighing of evidence remains context-sensitive and subject-specific; political scientists don't use particle accelerators when confirming their hypotheses or disconfirming a political theory.

Given Lonergan's call to attend to our own cognitional performativity, what are the mechanics of this verification process when thinking politically? Generally, Lonergan suggests judgments arise from *reflective insights* that recognize evidence as sufficient for a proposition to be either modally or absolutely true. Recalling an earlier point, those insights do not occur in a vacuum; they are conditioned by the person having them, and the presence of specific, sets of evidence.

But as Lonergan asks, what constitutes sufficient evidence? When do I have sufficient grounds for assenting to a political theory or believing a politician's campaign promises? Consistent with Lonergan's directive to attend to what one is doing when one is thinking, evidence is deemed sufficient for a claim when that claim is grasped as virtually unconditioned.[43] By "virtually," Lonergan means "almost certainly." The virtually unconditioned has conditions but they are grasped as being present. The geometer and political scientist know that judgments involve data that is relevant or irrelevant. For example, the definition of a circle is true given the fulfillment of certain conditions. As well, the judgment that a political theory is better than another is true only under certain conditions. Importantly, those conditions judged to be sufficient are not field invariant; the conditions sufficient for a geometrical proof are different from those required by a political theorist. Nonetheless, in response to a question for reflection, both the political scientist and the mathematician have reflective insights that grasp the presence of fulfilling conditions, allowing them to make their prospective judgments.

Hence, using Lonergan, we can observe that making political judgments is a very concrete and personal affair. For example, whenever we want to know whether or not a certain candidate is the one to vote for or if a specific political theory is warranted, we begin by asking a question for reflection, *Is it so?* Within our own, personal sphere of care and concern, we identify the relevant evidence, weigh it, and experience a reflective insight that grasps the presence of sufficient evidence to make a sound, political judgment. Although their form is generic, reflective insights occur in specific contexts, and remain open to the self correcting-process of learning.[44] Naturally, one reflects on what should be done with a reasoned judgment, decides what is to be done, and acts upon that decision with integrity. Specifically, in a political context, a visual of Lonergan's cognitional theory would have these features:

JUDGING

Reflecting upon the products of our understanding, we

- pose questions for reflection:
  *Is it so? Is it probably so?
  Is this the best political candidate, theory, etc.?*
- marshal and weigh evidence
- have reflective insights
- make judgments that remain open to the self-correcting process of learning

DECIDING

Needing to know what should be done about our reasoned judgments, we

- deliberate upon what we are going to *do* with our judgments
- ask questions for deliberation:
  What should/am I going to do about it?
- identify responsible courses of action that promote the good of order

UNDERSTANDING

Herein we,

use our imagination to pose questions for intelligence:
*What is it? Why is it?
How often does it occur?
Who should I vote for?/Why should I vote for them?
What political theory is best at this time? Why?*

have direct insights into the data of our experience (sense or consciousness)

hypothesize an explanation or interpretation arising from that insight

formulate the insight into an hypothesis/explanation/interpretation in a context-specific expression

conceptualize it (where appropriate)

Our desire for *criticality* in our expressions moves us beyond this level to assess the quality of our understanding

EXPERIENCING

At this stage or level, we

- see, hear, touch, taste, smell, feel, perceive the relevant political experiences

Generalized Empirical Method and Transcendental Method
There is an intimate connection between Lonergan's cognitional theory and his notion of method, and this is significant for political thinking pedagogy. His generalized empirical method is an extended reply to the question, *What am I doing when I am knowing?* As mentioned earlier on, drawing upon the success of natural science, GEM expands its focus on empirical data to include the data of consciousness: feelings, images, sensations, memories, etc.

In short, Lonergan generalizes empirical method to include metacognitives. For example, one can ask the question *what am I doing when I am knowing* and formulate an interpretation or hypothesis answering that question by using the data of consciousness. As well, one can confirm or disconfirm that interpretation or hypothesis by attending to the evidence provided by that data. Allowing the dynamic of consciousness full sway, one can discern what occurs when one decides what should be done about one's judgments. Recalling an earlier discussion, this data emerges through an attentiveness to one's thinking in act. It is not associated with taking some sort of inner look.

Lonergan's transcendental method (hereafter TM) is also a transposition of his cognitional theory. Lonergan's TM is a set of recurrent and related operations that yield cumulative and progressive results.[45] It is transcendental because it transcends specific times, places, subjects and fields of study. As well, it's pattern of operations remains invariant across cultures.[46]

TM comprises four basic transcendental imperatives: *Be attentive, Be intelligent, Be reasonable* and *Be responsible.* They correspond to specific features of human thinking. For example, if thinking needs the data experience, one should be attentive to a breadth of experience prior to making efforts to understand that experience. In turn, TM maintains that one should be intelligent in envisaging a range of possible explanations and interpretations of one's experience prior to claiming one has understood it correctly. Next, since the unrestricted desire to know what is true moves one to ask whether or not specific theories, interpretations and concepts have any merit, one should be reasonable in judging their warrant and assertibility. Lastly, after making a reasonable judgment, we need to be responsible in deciding what should be done about it, and act on that decision with integrity.[47]

Lonergan sees sustained fidelity to these transcendental imperatives as the source of authenticity and objectivity. In short, objectivity becomes the fruit of an authentic subjectivity.[48] By them, we achieve cognitive and moral self-transcendence. Moreover, the authentic human inquirer is consciously aware of her innate, unrestricted desire to know and an emergent, unrestricted capacity for being-in-love. As such, her openness to transcendent mystery manifests itself in a love of oneself, one's community and, ultimately, being itself. As such, she is aware of self, community and transcendent mystery as a gift.[49]

TM has four basic functions: normative, critical, systematic, and foundational.[50] It has a normative function because if any method is to produce true statements about the world, it must be attentive, intelligent, reasonable and responsible. As well, it has a critical function because all knowledge is the product of reasonable judgment that grasps propositions as virtually unconditioned, and pronounces that something is or is not the case. TM is systematic in the sense that there exists a set of basic operations and relations: "in the measure that transcendental method is objectified, there are determined a set of basic terms and relations, namely the terms that refer to cognitional process, and the relations that link these operations to one another."[51] In this sense, TM is systematic and as such, foundational.

Re-Visiting the Question

So, what is political thinking? Given the previous discussion, a number of observations are in order. First, authentic, political thinking is a highly structured cognitional activity involving distinct yet inter-related parts that survive and evolve through their inter-dependence.

Political thinking occurs in specific, experiential contexts, and is moved by an unrestricted desire to know. It is engaged by a political question that seeks intelligibility in the data of sense and consciousness. The intentionality of human consciousness moves the political thinker to pose a question for intelligence, and inquiry into the data occurs. In turn, a direct insight into relevant data is experienced, and expressed in theories, concepts, hypotheses, explanations, etc.

Allowing the dynamic of consciousness to operate freely, expressed insights are subjected to critical reflection. As such the political thinker poses a question for reflection, has a reflective insight, and pronounces her political judgment. In turn, a political decision is made ensuring the good of order, and a plan of action is developed, and eventually carried out. It is important to note the intentionality of political thinking is intimately linked to content. Applying Lonergan, we can add that political thinking isn't some abstract, pure form of thought independent of political content. Moreover, political thinking occurs in the context of a community, and its political thinking is objective to the degree its members are authentic subjects. Lonergan is not unaware of the danger an inauthentic community poses by producing inauthentic political thinkers.[52] Ideological thinking flourishes in such traditions.

By contrast, authentic political thinking involves a sustained effort to be attentive, intelligent, reasonable and responsible. By doing so, the political thinker becomes an authentic subject capable of making objective, political judgments. Those judgments, however, are fallible and open to the self-correcting process of learning. In short, the political thinker is well aware of Lonergan's dictum, *concepts have dates.*

Political Thinking Pedagogy, Liberal Education and Ideology

Political Thinking Pedagogy Re-Constructed

A political thinking pedagogy grounded in Lonergan's thought, would have a number of highly distinguishable characteristics. It would contain elements of both progressivism and student-centeredness. It would focus on creating an educational culture that accommodates interactive models of instruction, inquiry-based curricula and democratic classrooms. Moreover, pedagogical content knowledge would attend to the relevant political questions, and view political theories and concepts as fallible constructions. Their status as socio-historical constructions grounded in an authentic human subject, however, would not reduce their relevance to a specific set of historical conditions. In short, political concepts and theories can remain open to the self-correcting process of learning without falling under the knife of historical relativism.

As well, traditional models of education would not fare well in such a political thinking pedagogy. Teaching and learning for political thinking would be understood very differently from current, popular approaches to civics instruction. Learning about a political system or ideology within such a pedagogy would begin with the student's experience of that system, and only afterwards, engage her understanding of and reflection upon it through the mediation of well-posed, political questions. In turn, it would be the educator's responsibility to re-direct the student's attention towards her own political thinking in the act of doing so wherever possible.

Leadership practices would not remain unaffected as well. They would focus on capacity-building and professional development rather than compliance to the will of administration; power would be grounded in authentic authority. Moreover, an administrator would explicitly attend to her staff's ongoing self-appropriation of their own political thinking to ensure the best decisions are put forward. In doing so, she would need to nurture her staff so that they become an authentic community that continually makes responsible policies grounded in reasonable judgments.

Generally, teaching itself would be transformed. It would be envisaged as both didactic and transformative. It would be didactic to the extent an educator imparts her knowledge of curricula, and transformative insofar as she explicitly facilitates her students' self-appropriation of their own authentic, political thinking in the act of learning that curricula. This focus on personal appropriation of cognitional activity in context transforms the student from a passive recipient into a critical consumer of information. As such, she develops a self-consciousness that is attentive to herself in the act of doing political thinking; from an unrestricted desire to know that moves her to pose political questions, to have insights, and decide upon responsible courses of action grounded in her own political judgments.

Importantly, directed, Neo-Socratic questioning features prominently in political thinking pedagogy. As a teaching strategy, Neo-Socratic questioning is considered to be essential for critical thinking.[53] In this context, well-phrased political questions are foundational when teaching for critical thinking and deeper learning. Rather than being preliminaries to the regurgitation of facts found in a textbook, thoughtfully crafted questions become the engine of political insight-formation. But this is a difficult task as Lonergan himself suggests: "The questions of children are simply endless. The problem is to teach them that the answers to questions are not as easy as they think, and to do so without discouraging and stopping the flow of questions."[54] Given his experience with teachers and superiors, his focus on unrestricted questioning and the diligence needed to find the best answers is not surprising.

Liberal education is also given a slightly nuanced perspective. It becomes a creative source of *directional* energy that remains unsatisfied with facile solutions to complex issues. Within this approach to political thinking pedagogy, liberal education explicitly attends to the student's self-appropriation of her own cognitional activity in the act of doing liberal education. For example, when exploring questions of autonomy and paternalism in political theory, a liberal education student is directed to be attentive to her own mechanism of meaning construction while reading the relevant materials on the topic. This bi-directional focus explicitly attends to both knowledge production and pre-existent knowledge. As such, content is not reduced to process, and liberal education does not fall prey to the fallacy of psychologism or mere instrumentalism.

This approach to liberal education contextualizes insights without relativizing them. For example, by locating political judgments in a broader context that includes cognitive performativity, liberal education encourages sensitivity to the multiple factors that influence concept-formation within specific disciplines. As such, socio-historical and psychological factors are attended to without being summarily dismissed because they are spatio-temporal. The liberal education student who has self-appropriated her own dynamic consciousness is aware that knowledge itself has been constructed by subjects-as-subjects with varying degrees of authenticity. Hence, there is a respect for tradition without the static traditionalism; a willingness to bring multiple perspective into a political discussion without the accompanying perspectivism.

Authentic, political thinking pedagogy, therefore, would focus on the freedom of students to ask any number of questions within its purview. At liberty to question prevailing notions of justice, order, power, governance and authority, the student would be dynamically oriented towards finding ways of improving human living; of furthering the political, economic and social good of order in her community.

Accordingly, liberal and conservative approaches to politics do not become the final arbiter in a political debate. Rather than beginning with liberal or conservative concepts, as a self-appropriated, political thinker, the student begins the inquiry process with her own political thinking in action. That is her *a priori.*

Political concepts arise *a posteriori* from the exigency of the student's own political thinking.

Political Thinking Pedagogy and Ideological Thinking

By contrast, ideological thinking cares little for such a self-correcting, self-appropriated dynamic. It arbitrarily restricts the scope of thinking, and creates structures that resist the formation of unpopular, political questions. For Lonergan, this restriction and resistance usually occurs when there is a perceived threat to the power and authority of the governing regime holding the dominant ideology. Lonergan doesn't go into lengths about how ideological thinking works. His focus is on how group and individual bias distorts truth, causing feelings of frustration, resentment, bitterness and hatred among classes and groups.[55] Ideological thinking seems to thrive on a blind obedience that discourages the formation of political questions and the insights following from them. To use Lonergan's language, ideological thinking suffers from an *oversight of insight*.[56]

But, what is ideological thinking? Drawing upon insight from Mannhiem,[57] Gramsci[58] and Friere,[59] one could argue that an ideology gives a group its identity by narrowly interpreting its past for the purpose of making policies in the present that direct its future. It does this by nurturing a way of thinking that serves to preserve and enhance the interests of the ideology itself.[60] Hence, any program of action uncritically interprets the group's present situation in light of equally unreflective insights into its past.

How can a re-constructed notion of political thinking pedagogy critique the limitations of an ideology and the biased perspective of the ideologue? To begin, the ideologue is encouraged to appropriate the self-constituting dynamic of her own political thinking. From that vantage point, she critiques the basic questions, assumptions, concepts, theories and judgments grounding the ideology. As such, she (1) attends to experiences relevant to the ideology (2) intelligently envisages a range of possible alternatives to the ideology's explanation of those experiences, (3) reasonably judges whether or not the ideology in question is the best possible account, and (4) decides what should be done about it, and constructs policies supporting or rejecting the ideology. By doing so, the political thinker can achieve a fallible yet authentic position on the warrant of an ideology. Given the critical, normative and systematic features of Lonergan's TM, the foundations of ideological thinking remain in desperate need of revision.

Naturally, the ideologue will reject such an approach for a number of reasons. Firstly, the ideology's limited range of acceptable questions cannot facilitate the formation of insights necessary to critique the ideology itself. As such, the ideology never develops that reflexivity political theories need in order to evolve. More importantly, the policies created developed out of judgments arising from insights in response to the ideologue's poor and biased questions will inevitably, fail. Lonergan adds, "For insights can be implemented only if people have open minds. Problems can be manifest. Insights that solve them may be available. But the insights will not be grasped and implemented by biased minds."[61] This failure is due to an inability to address a concrete situation in a manner that is displeasing to the ideologue herself.

This displeasure arises from the constraints on questioning imposed upon the ideologue by the dominant ideology. Because she lacks the self-appropriation of her own political thinking, the natural dynamism moving her from experience to deciding is radically limited in scope. This creates a vacuum for the ideology to operate at will. The result is what Lonergan calls the longer cycle of decline.[62] However, by being attentive, intelligent, reasonable and responsible, the political judgments of an authentic few can offset this cycle of decline.[63]

Conclusions

The chapter began by asking a few questions about political thinking and political thinking pedagogy. Given the context of this book, it felt using the philosophy of Bernard Lonergan to address them was warranted because of the primacy he gives to cognitive performativity. This performativity is relational, privileging neither subjectivism nor objectivism. It resides in the middle ground between the political thinker and the political concept, theory or event she is thinking about. In short, the dynamism of authentic, political thinking-in- action grounds the nature and quality of political questions, insights, judgments and decisions.

In turn, a political thinking pedagogy focuses on the self-appropriation of political thinking. It applies Lonergan's transcendental method in the classroom to empower the student with the freedom to critique the narrow and selective hermeneutic of ideological thinking. Such an approach to teaching and learning has a transformative role: creating a citizenry of authentic political thinkers.

Liberal education too is afforded a central place. The role of the liberal educator is to facilitate and nurture student self-appropriation for the purpose of preserving and enhancing the common good of order. As liberally educated students are empowered to resist the bias of ideological thinking and its consequent cycles of decline.

Notably, the chapter is entitled, Toward a Pedagogy of Political Thinking: *Pt. 1*. This is purposeful. It is a foray into areas that Bernard Lonergan himself never ventured: political thinking and political thinking pedagogy. He wrote on a number of related areas yet seemed to leave this one alone. This chapter tries to bring his insights into dialogue with the challenging field of political thinking. Much remains to be done, and hopefully, a Pt. 2 is just on the horizon.

Notes

1. Bernard, J.F. Lonergan, *Insight: A Study of Human Understanding, 5th* ed, *Collected Works of Bernard Lonergan. Vol. 3,* ed. Frederick E. Crowe (Toronto: University of Toronto Press, 1992), p. 197.

2. Researchers in the critical thinking movement make the distinction between weak and strong-sense critical thinking. Weak-sense critical thinking is highly egoistic, sociocentric and unwilling to subject personal beliefs and values to the self-correcting process of learning. See Paul, R. W. & Elder, *Critical Thinking: Tools for Taking Charge of Your learning and your life. Pearson* (Boston: Pearson, 2011).

3. Pierre Lambert and Phil McShane, *Bernard Lonergan: His life and Ideas* (Vancouver, Axial Publishing, 2010) 31.

4. Bernard, J.F. Lonergan, *Method in Theology.* (NY, NY, Herder and Herder), 25.

5. Bernard J.F. Lonergan, "Self-Appropriation" in *The Lonergan Reader*, eds. Morelli, E. and and Morelli, E. (Toronto: University of Toronto Press), 354.

6. Bernard, J.F. Lonergan, *Insight: A Study of Human Understanding, 5th* ed, *Collected Works of Bernard Lonergan. Vol. 3,* ed. Frederick E. Crowe (Toronto: University of Toronto Press, 1992), 22.

7. *Insight*, pp. 297-300; Bernard J.F. Lonergan, *Method in Theology*, (New York: Herder and Herder, 1972) 6-9.

8. *Insight*, pp. 5-6, 223-227.

9. *Insight*, pp. 234-242.

10. *Method in Theology*, 8-9, 139.

11. *Method in Theology*, 6-9.

12. *Insight*, 344-352.

13. *Method in Theology*, 34-35.

14. *Method in Theology*, 47-57.

15. *Insight*, 378-381.

16. *Method in Theology*, 38, 45, 114, 121-122, 241, 338.

17. *Insight.* 96.

18. Giovanni B. Sala, *Lonergan and Kant*, (Toronto: University of Toronto Press, 1994), 114-123.

19. *Insight,* 716-718.

20. Bernard J. F. Lonergan, *Phenomenology and Logic: The Boston College Lectures on Mathematical Logic and Existentialism*, vol. 18, *Collected Works of Bernard Lonergan*, ed. Philip J. McShane (Toronto: University of Toronto Press, 2001), 213-215, 310-317.

21. For a clear discussion on Aristotle and Lonergan, see, Robert Fitterer, *Love and Objectivity in Virtue Ethics: Aristotle, Lonergan and Nussbaum on Emotions and Moral Insight.* (Toronto: University of Toronto Press, 2008).

22. For a current discussion of pedagogy for active engagement in a democracy see: Mary Lee Webeck, "Enlightened Political Engagement Deep in the Heart of Texas: Teaching for Democracy and Developing Digital Documentaries," *Action in Teacher Education*, 28, (2) 73-85 (2006).

23. Bernard J. F. Lonergan, "Cognitional Structure," in *Collection,* (Herder and Herder: New York, 1967) 222.

24. At this point, many parallels can be made between general systems theory and Lonerganism. F. Capra and others argue that the new scientific view of reality is based on a consciousness of the essential interrelatedness and interdependence of all phenomena.

For Capra, systems are internally dynamic, self-constituting, self-renewing and self-organizing. If any part of the whole is absent or malfunctioning, the whole cannot exist. Lonergan's theory of knowing is quite similar in these regards.

25. *Collection*, 222.

26. *Insight*, pp. 280-281, 290.

27. *Method in Theology*, 6-9.

28. *Insight*, pp. 479-882.

29. Pierre Lambert and Philip McShane, *Bernard Lonergan: His Life and Leading Ideas*, (Vancouver; Axial Publishing, 2010) 91.

30. *Bernard Lonergan: His Life and Leading Ideas*, 89.

31. In regards to feelings, he distinguishes between non-intentional states (such as fatigue, irritability, bad humor which have causes) and intentional responses that answer to what is intended, apprehended or represented. These later feelings relate us to objects and they give intentional consciousness its mass, momentum, drive, power without which, our knowing and deciding would be paper thin. *Method in Theology*, 31.

32. *Insight*, 209-210.

33. *Insight*. 27-33.

34. *Insight*, 9.

35. *Bernard Lonergan: His Life and Leading Ideas*. 70.

36. *Bernard Lonergan: His Life and Leading Ideas* 72.

37. *Bernard Lonergan: His Life and Ideas*, 71.

38. *Bernard Lonergan: His Life and Leading Ideas,* 71.

39. *Bernard Lonergan: His Life and Leading Ideas* 73.

40. *Insight,* 4.

41. *Insight*, 4.

42. *Insight*, 105-106, 296-299.

43. *Insight,* 280.

44. Bernard, J.F. Lonergan, *Understanding and Being, Collected Works of Bernard Lonergan. Vol. 56,* eds. Morelli, E. and Morelli, M. (Toronto: University of Toronto Press, 1990), 111.

45. *Method in Theology*, 4.

46. *Method in Theology, 13-26.*

47. *Method in Theology*, 4, 14-25.

48. *Method in Theology*, 104, 265, 292.

49. *Method in Theology*, 20, 33, 101-108. For an excellent discussion on this point see Thomas J. McPartland. *Lonergan and Voegelin on Political Authority*. Paper presented at the American Political Science Association annual conference, Washington, DC. 2010.

50. *Method in Theology, 20-25.*

51. *Method in Theology*, 21.

52. *Method in Theology*, pp. 80 and 162.

53. Keith Owens, Classroom Critiques: Transforming Conformity into Creativity, *Industry and Higher Education*, v21 n5 pp. 345-351, Oct 2007.

54. Bernard, J.F. Lonergan, *Topics in Education, Collected Works of Bernard Lonergan. Vol. 10,* ed. Frederick E. Crowe and Robert Doran (Toronto: University of Toronto Press, 1993), 104.

55. *Insight,* 244-254.

56. *Insight*, 8, 21.

57. Mannheim, Karl. *Ideology and Utopia: An Introduction to the Sociology of Knowledge.* Translated by Louis Wirth and Edward Shils. (New York: Harcourt, Bracc & World) 1963.

58. Antonio Gramsci. *Selections from Prison Notebooks.* Q. Hoare and G. Newell Smith eds. (London: Lawrewnce and Wisehart) 1971.

59. Paolo Freire. *Pedagogy of the Oppressed.* Trans. Myra Bergman Ramos. (New York: Continuum) 1984.

60. Gerald Gutek. *New Perspectives on Philosophy and Education.* (Chicago: Pearson Education) 2009. 169-178.

61. *The Lonergan Reader*, 572.

62. *Insight*, 251-267.

63. *Insight*, 261-268.

SECTION II:

THE TEACHER'S SEARCH

FOR ORDER

Chapter 5

Eric Voegelin and the Art of the *Periagoge*[1]
John von Heyking, University of Lethbridge

Introduction and Biographical Information

Eric Voegelin (1901–1985) was an Austrian-American political philosopher and philosopher of history. He is best known for his *New Science of Politics* (1952), in which he characterized modern civilization in terms of the ancient Christian heresy, Gnosticism. In his magnum opus, *Order and History* (5 volumes, 1956–1987), he developed a theory of politics and history meant to understand equivalent experiences across Western and non-Western cultures.[2] He stated his thinking was an act of resistance against "stop-history" ideological systems such as those of Enlightenment intellectuals Georg Hegel and Karl Marx. He was inspired by an eclectic range of sources, including ancient Greek philosopher Plato, medieval mysticism, German political economist and sociologist Max Weber, ancient Egyptian meditations on death, and prehistoric cave paintings. The theory of humanity he developed over his career consisted of an attempt to understand the wide range of experiences conveyed by these sources. Voegelin believed that a political science that failed to understand such sources—or found ways of ignoring them—was not genuine science.

Voegelin spent his early career at the University of Vienna, where he received his doctorate under the supervision of legal scholar Hans Kelsen. He also came under the influence of Max Weber and members of the Stefan-George literary and academic circle. His time in Vienna was punctuated by the events of World War II (1939–1945). During this time he published books and newspaper articles critical of Nazi race ideology as well as his *Political Religions* (1938), which examined the religious nature of revolutionary ideology. These publications prompted the Gestapo to seek his arrest in 1938, and he fled from Austria.

He immigrated to the United States and taught at Louisiana State University between 1942 and 1958. During this time he published the first three volumes of *Order and History* (1956 and 1957), which covered the ancient Near East, Israel, and Greece. From 1958 to 1969, he directed the Institut für Politische Wissenschaft in Munich, Germany, and attempted to introduce the study of political science as part of the postwar reconstruction of German society. While at the University of Munich, he delivered his controversial lecture series, "Hitler and the Germans," which indicted a wide spectrum of German society for Nazism.

Voegelin returned to the United States in 1969 by joining the Hoover Institution at Stanford University. During that time he published the fourth volume of *Order and History*, titled *The Ecumenic Age* (1974), along with numerous articles detailing the theory of consciousness he regarded as the basis for a genuinely empirical political science. He died in Palo Alto, California, on January 19, 1985. Volume Five of *Order and History* was published in 1987, and the University of Missouri Press published the thirty-four volume *Collected Works of Eric Voegelin* between 1990 and 2007.

Despite the rigor and difficulty of his writing, Voegelin regarded political science as an activity in tune with common sense. Citing Aristotle, it is an exercise of *phronesis* insofar as it begins with an analysis of current political, moral, and spiritual disorder, and ascends to clarity, understanding, and above all, existence in truth. Teaching, therefore, was not simply a matter of replacing false or faulty opinions (*doxai*) with knowledge because the crisis of ideology in the twentieth-century meant that that view of teaching is inadequate. The crisis of ideology was a crisis in the use of reason because ideology represents a fundamental corruption of reason, and one's willingness to exercise reason. Like Leo Strauss, who once referred to the Enlightenment as the chamber below Plato's cave, Voegelin thought that the crisis of ideology was a matter of inducing students, to awaken students toward readiness to think, philosophize, and to live in truth. The challenge for teachers, who are dedicated to the life of reason in the current context, is how to induce a love of the life of reason among those who reject that reason has anything to say, for ideology forms a "secondary reality" whose premises the ideologue refuses to consider. He endeavored to bring to the light the preconditions for the use of reason in a culture where reason had been distorted beyond recognition.

For this reason, Voegelin's understanding of teaching draws directly from Plato's description of it as the "art of the periagoge." Plato describes the "turning around" of the soul that the teacher induces to bring the student out of the cave and into the light, the ascent from becoming to Being:

> Then there would be an art to this very thing, I said, this turning around (*tes periagoges*), having to do with the way the soul would be most easily and effectively redirected (*metastrophe*), not an art of implanting sight in it, but of

how to contrive that for someone who has sight, but doesn't have it turned the
right way or looking at what it needs to.[3]

The art of the periagoge is a matter of turning the entire person around from
becoming to being. It helps to cultivate the virtues Plato describes, but ultimately "the educator can do no more than turn this organ of vision, if it exists in
the soul of man, around from the realm of becoming to the realm of being and
the brightest region of being—'and that, we say, is the Agathon' (518c)." The
teacher can do no more because knowledge cannot be put into the soul, as the
sophists believe. Moreover, periagoge must be distinguished from religious conversion to a beatific vision. Instead, it leads to "literally a heightened sense of
Daimonia, which the Daimon in the psyche will reach when he engages in cultivation (*paideia*) through association through the eudaimonic Agathon."[4] We
shall elaborate how Voegelin understood and applied this insight to his teaching.
For now, it is sufficient to observe that the "turning around" from becoming to
Being has nothing to do with escapism or other-worldly mysticism. Rather, it is
a heightened awareness and openness to all of reality that issues in wisdom
(*sophia*) of the Good as well as makes possible practical wisdom (*phronesis*).

Voegelin's understanding of teaching has a strong "civic" dimension to it,
and it is incumbent on societies to ensure, though public education, the spiritual
formation of its citizens.[5] He sharply contrasts the Platonic "art of the
periagoge" from modern conceptions of education because the former cultivates
the spiritual order of the individual and society. It is a political or civic exercise.
He distinguishes this from the Humboldtian model of cultural formation
(*Bildung*) that dominated Germany in the second part of the nineteenth-century
and played a role in forming the elites of Germany in the nineteen-twenties and
thirties. The Bildung model is a trickle-down model of education because it
forms presupposes that cultural elites (or "scum," as Voegelin remarks) with an
education in the social sciences that, "in a mysterious way engenders order in
the interiority of the nation."[6] The Bildung ideal aspires to create an apolitical
citizenry under the assumption that a political or civic education hinders the
unfolding of one's personality. However, for Voegelin, the very opposite happens because it leaves out the political aspect of citizenry, which is spiritual. In
another essay, Voegelin generalizes this point as the feature of modern education, which he contrasts with the Platonic "art of the periagoge": "Education is
the art of adjusting people so solidly to the climate of opinion prevalent at the
time that they feel no "desire to know." Education is the art of preventing people
from acquiring the knowledge that would enable them to articulate the questions
of existence. Education is the art of pressuring young people into a state of
alienation that will result in either quiet despair or aggressive militancy."[7]
Voegelin's assessment of the Humboldtian paradigm, which governs the research universities of the West today, reminds one of the dangers inherent when
the ideals of scientism are the guiding principles of a political regime. For
Voegelin, the "art of the periagoge" is a spiritual turning-around or conversion
that encompasses the entire personality of the student, and this necessarily

means too that it involves a political education because one's political nature is included in one's spiritual formation.

The Problem of Teaching in a University:
How Social Science Deforms Periagoge

Eric Voegelin's lifelong work was an act of resistance against the dehumanizing ideologies of the twentieth-century, as well as the "softer" forms of intellectual confusion in liberal democracy that shared some of the philosophical lineage as the more aggressive ideologies.[8] His teaching efforts, described in greater detail later in this essay, were directed at inoculating students against those ideologies, and to instill *periagoge* to those students who would listen. Voegelin saw social science (*Wissenschaft*) as less destructive than some other political thinkers of the twentieth-century, including Michael Oakeshott and Leo Strauss, though he was no less critical of its practitioners, including Max Weber.[9] Weber's greatest achievement was in underlining the importance of being open to new developments in science, new discoveries in particular. The significance of Weber, which Voegelin attempted to continue, was in incorporating the discoveries of non-Western cultures into a general theory of humanity. Weber failed at developing a theory of humanity, but Voegelin credits him for seeing the importance of trying. Voegelin's full explanation is worth quoting:

> If Weber nevertheless did not derail into some sort of relativism or anarchism, that is because, even without the conduct of such analysis, he was a staunch ethical character and in fact (as the biography by his nephew, Eduard Baumgarten, has brought out) a mystic. So he knew what was right without knowing the reasons for it. But of course, so far as science is concerned, that is a very precarious position, because students after all want to know the reasons why they should conduct themselves in a certain manner; and when the reasons—that is, the rational order of existence—are excluded from consideration, emotions are liable to carry you away into all sorts of ideological and idealistic adventures in which the ends become more fascinating than the means. Here is the gap in Weber's work constituting the great problem with which I have dealt during the fifty years since I got acquainted with his ideas.[10]

In explaining the Weberian starting point of his life's work, Voegelin situates it in the student's need to have the activity of science explained. In other words, Voegelin recognizes how central the existential truth of science is to students, perhaps more central to them than for their elder professors. Weber recognized the dead-end of specialization, but could not adequately develop an account of political and historical reality that could unify the details of new knowledge whose study he pioneered. For Voegelin, the example of Weber demonstrates the possibility for philosophical openness in social science which is infrequently followed.

For Voegelin, "openness," a concept he derived from philosophers including Plato and Henri Bergson, meant viewing the empirical materials as they are.

Ideologies are a form of self-assertion, or *libido dominandi*, because they distort empirical materials into a ready-made self-image. Materials that do not fit get discarded or one pretends they do not exist, an intellectual move whose most extreme political expression is the concentration camp.[11] The "softer" form of this self-assertion can be found in the positivist methodologies that sustain American (and German) political science.

Voegelin's criticisms of social science date back to his early career in the late 1920s during his time at the University of Vienna, where academic and political life was strongly influenced by Hans Kelsen's legal positivism and neo-Kantian methodologies.[12] Neo-Kantian Normlogik made two moves that Voegelin came to reject. The first was the positivist position that anything that lies outside of the capacity of the physical sciences to examine, including theology, philosophy, history, etc., was not an appropriate object of science understood as empirical analysis. Yet, the neo-Kantian did not reject the existence of such topics. Rather, this led to the second move, which was to regard these topics as "values," as Max Weber did. But such a move assumes that the scholar who examines them "approximates the function of the transindividual evaluating subject (transcendental ego) of cognition, if and insofar as he himself incorporates the cultural value of being a cultivated person."[13] The effort of the German educational effort of *Bildung*, then, was to create this cultivated person who could stand above the empirical materials. Voegelin's extended criticisms of neo-Kantianism point out why this bifurcated view of reality—raw and disorganized empirical data on the one hand, and the transcendental ego who wills his own reasons for organizing those data—is untenable. Voegelin would carry these criticisms to the United States when he would criticize the less sophisticated versions of positivistic and historical political theory in the Anglo-American world.[14]

Let us return to Voegelin's assessment of Weber, whom Voegelin saw as closely connected to neo-Kantianism. Voegelin admired Weber's "openness" to new possibilities but thought he lacked a deeper sense of openness, or Platonic eros, that might have enabled Weber to formulate a deeper sense of humanity out of the fragments of materials he collected. Reflecting upon Weber's continued attempts to formulate the human spirit in the modern age (e.g., his admiration for Tolstoy), Voegelin concludes Weber's transcendence was unresolved.

Voegelin cites two key episodes of Weber's biography pertinent to our discussion of *periagoge*. The first is Weber's existential reflections inspired by his illness. He told his wife that "Some time I will find a hole, out of which I rush up again into the heights."[15] Voegelin considers the symbol of a rocket shooting out of a hole one of an ideological activist, who rushes out from oppression up to the heights. However, Weber was no ideological activist, as his resignation over the modern age was leavened with an inarticulate longing for transcendence: "Beside this, one thinks of the Platonic parable of the cave and of the man who is open to transcendence and feels himself compelled to turn himself around in order to carry out of the *periagoge* and ascend toward the light. Quite differently Max Weber: He rushes like a rocket out of the hole. The symbol for that age and for its unresolved tension could hardly be more characteristic."[16]

A few pages later Voegelin cites Weber's exchange with his wife, Marianne, over his question to her whether she could think of him as a mystic. His rejoinder to her negative response is poignant:

> "I suppose it could be that I am one. Since I have dreamed more in my life than one should really allow oneself to do, I am also nowhere at home with complete certainty. It is as if I could and would also completely withdraw myself from everything." That is a splendid formulation of the Pauline hos me, the as-if-not, of the Christian counsel, "Be in the world, but not of it. Live in the world as if you did not live in it and belong to it" (cf. 1 Cor. 7:29–31).[17]

For Voegelin, the stakes of unresolved transcendence, stunted *periagoge* if you will, are high because failure to bring out the highest erotic longings in human beings can be catastrophic. As Voegelin found with Weber, and with Plato, eros is a terrible force that can be good or evil. The purpose of education, then, is to evoke the experience of *periagoge* in the Platonic sense, but starting from the spiritual disturbances of the modern age, of which Weber was one of the greatest articulations. Voegelin's analysis of Weber shows the limits of an education in social science, but also points beyond those limits.[18]

Turning around (Periagoge) from Ideology to Philosophy Via Common Sense

Recall that Voegelin's lifelong philosophic and scientific work is rooted in the responsibility the teacher has to explain to students "why they should conduct themselves in a certain manner." His was an effort to explain the life of philosophy and science as an existential question of how one should live one's life, and for students with whom the teacher lives as an example and in community. The responsibility of the teacher, in conducting the "art of the periagoge," then is to inculcate wisdom (*sophia*) and practical wisdom (*phronesis*). This is no small task in an ideological age when much effort must be exerted in resisting ideology, and where the social sciences in universities are so oblivious to the challenges facing us. The difficulty is compounded by the teacher's responsibility to demonstrate to students that what he offers is not yet another ideology, but life in truth. Somehow, the teacher must teach the student how to interpret his own eros. A consideration of this problem in Voegelin's writings is a prelude to our glimpse of Voegelin in the classroom.

The immanentization of the eschaton, pneumopathology, Gnosticism, It-reality, balance of consciousness, apperception, *metaxy*, compact, ecumenicity, differentiation, dogmatomachy, historiogenesis, nonexistence, intentionality, *epekeina*, luminosity, second reality, and a host of untranslated Greek terms confront the unsuspecting student of Eric Voegelin's work. His scientific terminology has turned off a lot of readers due to its difficulty. But does his scientific terminology obscure or illuminate reality? Can it communicate anything meaningful to common sense?

One of Eric Voegelin's great achievements was to reestablish political science within the realm of practical wisdom: "Not without reason did Aristotle identify the *episteme politike* with the virtue of *phronesis.*"[19] Beginning perhaps with his first visit to the United States in the 1920s, Voegelin was impressed with common sense philosophy and the civilization that itself is based on common sense (though not necessarily and exclusively on common sense philosophy). Referring to Thomas Reid, who cites Cicero, common sense is a "compact type of rationality" and "habit of judgment and conduct of a man formed by ratio."[20] To speak, then, of common sense and its relationship to science is to point to two central axes of Voegelin's theoretical preoccupations: 1) the common world of society and 2) the theoretical tools that arise from that common world and that reflect upon it. Voegelin was intensely aware of the problématique of the second axis that, one might say, is in the common world but not of it. The problem of most political science is that it is oblivious to this problématique, which leads it no longer to be even part of the common world.

Voegelin sought to inculcate *sophia* and *phronesis*, via common sense, in a Socratic manner. Ellis Sandoz explains: "[He] encouraged students sympathetically to involve their own common sense, intellectual, and faith experiences in understanding demanding material in personal reflective consciousnesss, implicitly somewhat on the pattern of the Socratic 'Look and see if this is not the case'—i.e., by validating the analytical discourse through personal understanding and questioning."[21] This section consists of an exploration of Sandoz's observation.

Voegelin explains that common sense "presupposes noetic experience, without the man of this habit himself possessing a differentiated knowledge of noesis....[W]e characterized this habit as that of the *spoudaios* without the luminosity of consciousness...."[22] Common sense participates in ratio which means that the explication of ratio itself requires one to move outside the bounds of common sense. Common sense on its own is insufficient, especially when ratio itself is threatened: "Common sense can rest assured of its ability 'to judge of things self-evident' but it cannot oppose the ideologies on their level of differentiated argumentation, common sense has at its command no explicit noesis."[23] Voegelin's work consists primarily of an attempt to articulate an "explicit noesis," and this endeavor required new terminologies that required him to move beyond those he inherited from the collection of symbols and meanings that human history had hitherto developed. He needed to move beyond the *episteme* of Aristotle and the *intellectus* of Aquinas. This required him to develop new symbols, and some of these (e.g., Gnosticism) he used for a while before replacing them with more refined symbols for whom those unfamiliar with his thought could be quite bewildering (e.g., pneumopathology, secondary reality, It-reality).

Common sense fails to recognize the demonism of ideologies, and, because it lacks an "explicit noesis," it also fails to recognize the spiritual and erotic habits upon which the exercise of reason depends. Common sense lacks capacity to explain either the turning around of the soul as in the case of the philosopher, or the closure of the soul, as in the case of the pneumopathological ideologue. Common sense cannot account for the "art of the periagoge." In an ideological age, common sense runs the risk of becoming its own ideology on account of its being too "rest assured," which can be seen in various forms like pragmatism or, more generally, in Tocqueville's observation that Americans are Cartesian empiricists without ever having read a word of Descartes. In our own time, one observes how quickly rugged self-reliant libertarians and pragmatists are quick to believe in conspiracy theories about Barack Obama, 9/11, and so on.[24]

Voegelin's common sense appears least common sensical in his considerations of "explicit noesis," in his analyses of concrete consciousness as well as in the deformation of reason, in his analyses of open souls and in closed souls; or put another way, in philosophical eros and in demonic eros.

Most of Voegelin's students (especially in the United States) as well as most today are common sensical, but the common sense they manifest is limited. They are typically small-l liberals who prize maximum freedom for individuals and regard external limitations on their freedom as a form of coercion and therefore unjust. For this reason, they also have an instinctive distrust of religious authorities that makes them instinctively to think a free society is also a secular one. Their vision of society corresponds roughly with that sketched by John Stuart Mill in *On Liberty*.

Students have not considered the philosophical, spiritual, and indeed religious preconditions for a free society. Therefore, their common sense is "rest assured" which makes them vulnerable to ideological replacements for the genuine preconditions for a free society. They tend to view theirs as an "open society" in the sense of Karl Popper, not of that Henri Bergson; Voegelin describes Popper's version as a mechanism for preventing "public collisions between private opinions."[25] Thus, speaking of Mill's discussion of liberty, Voegelin claims "today it is the *readiness* to discuss that is the subject of investigation."[26] We can no longer be as optimistic as Mill that obstacles to discussion could be "warded off through the medium of rational discussion" because *ratio* itself is now in question. And with ratio itself in question, the possibility of *common sense* is threatened.

Students' instinctive love of freedom corresponds to their unreflective readiness to characterize their society "secular." They are not necessarily Comtean secularists because they generally wish freedom for religious people to worship the gods they choose. Moreover, they do not necessarily think being religious is a prima facie reason to have one's perspective removed from public debate. However, they do not think religion should have an authoritative voice in society. Thus, they respond with perplexity and perhaps some resentment when I point out to them that reason does not stand on its own, and presupposes something like faith to sustain it. They can be like Voegelin's students who are "flabbergasted, especially those who are agnostics, when I tell them that they all act, whether agnostics or not, as if they were immortal. Only under the assumption of immortality, of a fulfillment beyond life, is the seriousness of action intelligible that they actually into their work and that has a fulfillment nowhere in this life however long they may live. They all act as if their lives made sense immortally, even if they deny immortality, deny the existence of a psyche, deny the existence of a Divinity—in brief, if they are just the sort of fairly corrupt average agnostics that you find among college students today. One shouldn't take their agnosticism too seriously, because in fact they act as if they were not agnostics!"[27]

An instance of the manner by which "fairly corrupt average" agnosticism deforms the souls of students is seen in a letter Voegelin wrote to his friend Robert Heilman on an event that occurred on the Lousiana State University campus.[28] A New Orleans stripper came to campus to entertain the (male) students, who promptly rioted:

> It certainly was a psychologically interesting affair, and as a matter of course, not appreciated in its full juicyness. The mob outbreak of the attack on the stripping lady by the very persons who had come there for the purpose of watching her performing her antics, is something to ponder about. It seems to me the typical middle class attitude about which Karl Kraus has expressed himself at length and with poignancy....Since it was her misfortune to be born into our age and environment, she is reduced to taking her clothes off in public because that is about the only level of eroticism that is accessible to the senile lewdness of the middle-class youth of our time. The point is that the magnificent males whom I have just characterized congregate by the thousand to get their genital excitement, and then, somehow revolted by the mass exhibition of their baseness, take their revenge on the woman in whom this baseness is symbolic reality.

Voegelin observes, in a Platonic manner, that this eroticism is base on account of the lack of availability of higher forms of eroticism. Eros becomes deformed and ultimately violent when it has not been formed by the *agathon*. Without this erotic formation, the individual remains one of Plato's cave dwellers. The only form of transcendence these middle class students understand is bodily. This is a condemnation of their education, both in university and of their general cultural upbringing. As with the German ideal of *Bildung*, American pragmatic education fails to form the whole of a human being and the longings of his soul.

The common sense, then, of today's students is not entirely commonly sensical. But notice how Voegelin frames the art of periagoge in the last sentence of his characterization of "corrupt agnosticism": "because in fact they act as if they were not agnostics." Teaching "explicit noesis," while difficult in the sense that it requires the kind of scholarly work that encompassed Voegelin's entire scholarly life, is also straightforward because it entails explaining to students what they are already doing. Teaching involves understanding and explaining the paradox of what Voegelin termed the existential virtues, and how practice takes priority to theory.[29] The priority of the practical takes away some of the chal-

lenge of introducing scientific terminology and analysis because teaching becomes not a matter of replacing opinions with knowledge, but of refining opinions, of gaining illumination of one's present practices. The art of periagoge,
meant to move from common sense to "explicit noesis," entails an exploration
with students of their souls, which is conducted by examining the deformations
of consciousness as well as the symbols and testaments of souls that have
opened. Voegelin's scientific analysis of experience always comes back to the
soul's erotic yearnings, which is the locus of common sense.

Deformations

Before commenting on the deformation of consciousness in its extreme form,
consider how Voegelin treats the precondition for this extremism in a slightly
earlier essay, "Immortality: Experience and Symbol" (1967). This is important
because most students, in so far as they are common sensical, do not exhibit the
extreme forms of ideology (though they can do that too). However, they do frequently exhibit the symptoms of deculturation, the precondition of the more
extreme form of ideology. Voegelin explains deculturation and how opaque
symbols create the conditions where ideologies thrive. Experience of transcendence (or "phenomena of original account") degenerates into dogmatic exposition, which then gets rejected by skeptics, while those seeking the "ground" that
produced the original experiences go looking elsewhere for ersatz grounds. For
example, Plato's *Republic* becomes Platonism, which eventually produces the
host of modern ideologies; or, the Gospel splits into theology and philosophy, as
well as fundamentalism, which also fosters modern ideologies. The problem
students face is that they have received these doctrinal forms of philosophy but,
as such, these forms do not speak to their souls or how they should live their
lives. Thus, one needs to descend into the extreme forms, and then ascend towards truth in order to experience truth as truth, and not as doctrine.

Voegelin's discussion of pneumopathology and secondary reality in ideology pose the challenge of convincing students that, indeed, there is a common
world and that some people choose to opt out of it. This argument smacks them
of "elitism" or intellectual snobbery because it implies that some people are
more enlightened than others. Moreover, it stokes their skepticism that there is
no genuine distinction between knowledge and opinion, that philosophy is
merely the replacement of opinion with another opinion. Voegelin's praise of
Christianity in works like *New Science of Politics* and *Science, Politics, and
Gnosticism* also stokes their skepticism.

Even so, it helps that in *Science, Politics, and Gnosticism*, Voegelin frames
the distinction between ideology and philosophy in light of erotics immediately
at the beginning of the work: "In the experiences of love for the world-
transcendent origin of being, in *philia* toward the *sophon* (the wise), in *eros* toward the *agathon* (the good) and the *kalon* (the beautiful), man became philoso-

pher."[30] Voegelin grounds his scientific inquiry in the existential quest for truth that he regarded as the primary responsiblity of the teacher toward the student.

The demonism of ideology can be seen most vividly in his exposition in *Science, Politics, and Gnosticism*, of Karl Marx and of Friedrich Nietzsche. Ideologies are self-referential systems whose aim is not to illuminate our understanding but to change existence. The system is sustained by a considerable amount of world play that simultaneously confuses in order to defuse questioning, and explains phenomena in terms roughly similar to the classical tradition in order to provide a semblance of familiarity and intelligibility to the system:

> The purpose of this speculation is to shut off the process of being from transcendent being and have man create himself. This is accomplished by playing with equivocations in which "nature" is now all-inclusive being, now nature as opposed to man, and now the nature of man in the sense of *essentia*. This equivocal wordplay reaches its climax in a sentence that can easily be overlooked: "A being that does not have its nature outside of itself is not a natural being; it does not participate in the being of nature."[31]

Pointing out equivocation, which in this case almost amounts to Marx contradicting the law of non-contradiction, shows to the person of common sense how Marx breaks the ratio of common sense.

Common sense is also affronted by Voegelin's observation of Marx's removal of personal existence from his system and construction of history.[32] The expectation of the transformation of history is "supported by nothing but the empty formula of a 'being' which determines 'consciousness' and the equally empty assumption that a sinful humanity can be liberated from its libido dominandi through the revolutionary dictatorship of libidinous dreamers who pretend to be the vanguard of a sinless 'proletariat.' In brief, there is nothing in reality to support the expectation...." He concludes by contrasting wryly the ideological dreamworld with the place of the *spoudaios* in society according to Plato and Aristotle: "In the dreamworlds...the personal pièce de résistance of order and imperfection is eliminated by the dream of a Mature Man who, beyond freedom and human dignity, will no longer raise questions concerning the meaning of existence....Just as frequently as with Utopianism and Absurdity, we meet in their language with the symbols of a New Humanism and a New Humanity."[33]

By observing these and other examples, the student understands that the ideologue is not interested in sharing a common world of understanding. He understands the implications of Marx's claim in the *Theses on Feuerbach* that he is not interested in understanding the world, but in remaking it.

With Voegelin's subsequent discussion of Marx's prohibition of questioning, we get to the heart of his intellectual swindle and the demonic violence at its root. That this reminds some students of Orwell's view that a key method of control used by totalitarian regimes is to ensure people are incapable even of entertaining certain thoughts, suggests that common sense can, with guidance, enter the deepest malebolges of the closed soul.[34] This discussion also illuminates a limitation of common sense on its own terms because it shows how problematic common sense can be. Despite common sense being "rest assured," the individual of common sense is haunted by the possibility that not everything before his eyes is what it seems.[35] Unlike the ideologue, though, who simply treats the world of common sense as the world of deception (and his ideology as the key to unlock the door to higher consciousness), Voegelin raises common sense on its own terms; common sense is expanded, not displaced.

Even so, Voegelin's comment on Marx's prohibitioning, or rather, what he leaves out, has implications for our common sensical elucidation. For Marx, the question of human origins is nonsensical abstraction because it eventually leads to an infinite regress, "which in Ionian philosophy led to the problem of the *arche* (origin)."[36] In his late writings, Voegelin would reject the mode of such questioning of arche in Aristotle or in Aquinas' so-called proofs of God for being too rooted in cosmological experience, and not in the nature of ratio itself. If our common world is to be apprehended through our soul, the sensorium of transcendence, then that common world must come through our soul and not through the cosmos. As with Augustine, the arche is to be found within, and not in the cosmos.

Turning now to the "trick action" that the ideologue seeks to transfigure reality, we must recognize that Voegelin's analysis emphasizes the root of the "trick action" and not specific linguistic and sophistic tools to mislead; it looks at the deception itself. Because the ideologue wishes to transfigure reality—or, pretend to transfigure reality—he wishes to master history, which is to say to master the beyond of the horizon that surrounds human beings as questioners. The magic of the extreme "charms"[37] because it mimics the erotic attraction we have to the beyond of the horizon: "The mystery of the horizon that draws us to advance toward it but withdraws as we advance; it can give direction to the quest of truth but it cannot be reached; and the beyond of the horizon can fascinate as the 'extreme' of truth but it cannot be possessed as truth face to face within this life." The ideologue seeks mastery out of a wish to possess truth "face to face." He is in a rush; he wishes to confront truth and confront others, on his own terms and only wishes what he wishes to see. The ideologue wishes certainty over truth, which is something he shares with the person of common sense. The ideologue also wishes to gain mastery over the horizon of existence, but as Ellis Sandoz observes of Voegelin's teaching, he always reminded students that "you can't go 'back of revelation' and pretend it never happened."[38]

Even so, the ideologue's "magic trick" of controlling reality is only a trick because his desire to control reality is only made possible by reality: "the potential of deformation is inherent in a form that does not exist other than in the process of formation."[39] The ideologue wishes to master the "experiences of a human questioning (*aporein*) and seeking (*zetein*) in response to a mysterious drawing (*helkein*) and moving (*kinein*) from the divine side."[40]

Voegelin's discussion of Shakespeare's Sonnet 129 to describe the charm in the extreme is a masterful elucidation of the lust of domination:

Mad in pursuit and in possession so

Had, having, in quest, to have extreme
A bliss in proof and proved a very woe
Before a joy proposed behind a dream[41]

"The temptation of the 'extreme' will always endanger the balance, and the imbalance will ever be quite unconscious of its madness."

As a somewhat common sense way of illustrating the ideologue's "imbalance" of living in reality and in the dreamworld, I frequently use the example of erotic obsession. Whereas undergraduates may be unfamiliar with thinking about ideology in terms of erotic obsession, as young and somewhat unformed souls, they are likely to be familiar with the experience in their own lives and where it can lead. A recent example of a "celebrity stalker" makes my point: "The accused, who lives in High River [Alberta, Canada], said he first saw [the actress] when she was in a recent parade. 'She was apparently smiling and waving and he took this (to mean) there was something special between them,' he said. 'Since then he was repeatedly going to the Heartland set trying to get in, dropping off notes and stuff.'"[42] Erotic obsession leads one to imagine a narrative where individual events and gestures take on special meaning, and necessarily for the sake of the one erotically obsessed, around which the narrative revolves. This helps students relate better to Voegelin's claim that the ideologue who speculates a transfiguration of history also places himself at the center of the new vanguard, that the individual magician is necessarily the one who represents the new Humanity. Historical transfiguration, like erotic obsession, is always about the activist. Any undergraduate can also see the violence embedded in this erotic obsession, as they each know that no "stalker" can compel one to love. Love cannot be forced, and the one who thinks it can be is dangerous indeed. We turn now to love and Voegelin's restoration of political science.

Restoration

Voegelin's account of the "magic of the extreme" in ideology is significant for his understanding of education as the "art of the periagoge" because it demonstrates what one turns away from, the cave as it were. Additionally, it shows why education cannot be simply a matter of imparting information, but also of opening the student's existential awareness of the life of reason. Finally, facing the "magic of the extreme" demonstrates to the student the limits of their own common sense, and where their common sense may lead if left without "explicit noesis" and erotic formation. We turn now to the ascent from the cave.

Voegelin observes that when society has been decultured the ground of existence, the precondition to our existence and knowledge of our existence and love of our existence, has become obscured. It is not that the ideologue ignores the ground but that he displaces it elsewhere in motives such as power, profit, productivity, race, and so forth.[43] As suggested above, Voegelin's concern for deculturation was one he shared with the ideologues, and the large part of his work consisted of restoring for civilization a sense of the divine ground that those ideologues distorted.

Voegelin's late writings display his response. His meditations in volume five of *Order and History* and "Quod Deus Dicutur" overturn traditional and compact subject-object dichotomies. Now, to put it very simplistically, one's participation in "nonexistent reality" is a matter of being conscious of God's participation in the meditative process: "divine is itself an event within the reality we are questioning."[44] Voegelin agrees somewhat with Marx's rejection of the Ionian quest for the arche because it is too firmly rooted in cosmological experience. Aquinas's five proofs of the existence of God are also too firmly rooted in the cosmos, despite Aquinas having had "attained a certain degree of clarity about [the] paradoxic structure" of the quest.[45]

Even so, Voegelin's characterization of participation in "nonexistent reality" where "divine is itself an event within the reality we are questioning" risks falling into the same obscuration as Marx's empty categories of universal humanity and end of history. Does "nonexistence" signify nothing? Does having the divine "itself an event" mean "God is on our side" as part of some religiously-oriented revolutionary vanguard? Of course not. As Ellis Sandoz has argued, Voegelin's choice of terms and understanding of these meditations is inspired not only by Plato, but by the medieval mystics including the author of the "Cloud of Unknowing." He, like they, understood the limits of language and also understood that words, insofar as they are things, cannot possibly capture reality that transcends thingness. Thus Voegelin knew he had to develop a philosophical language about the quest's "paradoxic structure" that surpassed even Aquinas's "certain degree of clarity."[46] Even so, just as Plato has Socrates frequently observe the difficulty of communicating the truth of philosophy to a city who knows only sophists, so too does Voegelin's philosophical questioning run the risk of appearing as ideology. We are back to the student's perplexity at figuring out whether the philosopher really is any different from the sophist and the teacher's responsibility to show the student that they are different.

Voegelin elaborates a greater degree of clarity in "Quod Deus Dicitur," the final work he dictated, and which crystallizes his thoughts on the meditative quest found in previous writings. There lists seven pairs of symbols "dominating reflective language on the fringe of compactness and differentiation" that include philosophy and religion, philosophy and theology, faith and reason, science and religion, and so forth.[47] Today one might also add secularism and religion, and secular society and religious society. Each of these pairs is familiar to common sense, as they convey a set of experiences in our deculturated landscape. In other words, "rest assured" common sense, as seen in the opinions of my students, takes it for granted that each term among these sets of pairs refers to something, and the other term refers to a something that is its opposite. As Voegelin observes, "each of these dichotomies furnishes the occasion for indefinite debate on the compact level, without ever penetrating to the fundamentally paradoxic structure of thought that is peculiar to the participatory relation between the process of thought and the reality in which it proceeds."

It is unnecessary to summarize Voegelin's subsequent meditation, but only to point out that Voegelin overturns these common sense and yet sterile dichotomies. He does so not by displacing common sense as the ideologue does, but by expanding common sense. Referring to Leibniz's *Principles de la nature et de la grace*, Voegelin cites Leibniz's two questions concerning sufficient reason: why is there something rather than nothing? and why are the things as they are? Voegelin comments are worth quoting at length:

> The experience of contingent reality implies a noncontingent reason for what is experienced as contingent....What comes to the fore now is the inherence of the answer in the event of the question. And that imaginative characteristic which goes beyond the simple assumption of a revelatory symbol is due to the Cartesian insight of the answer being contained in the act of doubting and desiring. The experienced transition from an apparently certain *cogito ergo sum* to an imaginatively doubting and desiring ego is the meditative source of the understanding that there is no ego without a comprehending reality to be symbolized as the perfection toward which the imaginative ego strives. An ego that doubts and desires to go beyond itself is not the creator of itself but requires a creator and maintainer of its doubting existence, and that cause is the "God" who appears in the analyses of the *Third Meditation* and the *Principles*. There is no doubting contingency without the tension toward the necessity which makes the doubt evident as such.[48]

This and Voegelin's subsequent meditation shows that expansion of common sense entails the enlargement of reason because instead of appealing to the arche, which remains bound to cosmological experience, Voegelin appeals to the conditions of reason itself. Human beings reason about existence with their reason, and Voegelin illuminates the precondition of that activity. Students are thereby suddenly struck by the fact of their participation in existence. They are struck by the their newly expanded common sense observation that to question is to have the answer embedded in the question, and to question means also to be questioned. Those inclined toward religiosity see the "religious" roots of their rationality, and those inclined to be secularists see the insufficiency of their secular reason and recognized an expanded reason that is no longer hostile to faith. The "rest assured" dichotomies of common sense have broken down and given way to an expanded noetic existence.

Just as Voegelin's meditations invite the common sense student to deepen her noetic existence, so too do they invite the student to get more comfortable with her erotic restlessness. Their "doubting and desiring" is caused by their previously unrecognized participation in reality, and one that is drawing them toward itself. Having been plagued by the modern's anxiety that their experience of immortality is an illusion,[49] they now see their immortalization is in fact real because they now have a coherent set of symbols with which to symbolize the activity of immortalization toward the ground. They now recognize within themselves the truth of Voegelin's observation that "you can't go 'back of revelation'" because they have partaken in the revelation, in the periagoge. They recognize that the fool who says there is no God is genuinely a fool because "God" for them is no longer a reified symbol but a constituent partner in their own search whose stakes now have never been higher. Most undergraduate students then recognize the continuity between their questioning and the prayers of Anaximander, Plato, Anselm, Goethe, and of course Aquinas that conclude the essay.

The Daunting Adventure: Voegelin and His Students

Voegelin's capacity as a teacher gets mixed reviews.[50] Tom Flanagan took classes at the University of Notre Dame with both Voegelin and his colleague, Gerhart Niemeyer. He regards Niemeyer the better teacher. Niemeyer's teaching method was Socratic. He was "constantly asking people questions and getting them to explore. And he orchestrated all this so that we would also come together. I can remember all the books I read in Niemeyer's class. In contrast, I can't remember anything specific that Voegelin said, although he was there for an entire term."[51] Flanagan reflects the sentiment of many undergraduate students of Voegelin in noting he was "mesmerized" by Voegelin. He was "a good speaker" and "tremendously erudite and interesting." Reading in the same volume the recollections of Voegelin's students at the University of Munich, one is not surprised by Flanagan's reaction. Thus, Flanagan concludes, Voegelin "wasn't really a teacher, he was a phenomenon."

Flanagan's testimonial reflects the paradox of Voegelin as teacher. On the one hand, as others like Ellis Sandoz and Tilo Schabert report, Voegelin was outstanding at communicating extremely complicated ideas in simple terms for students. On the other hand, listening to Voegelin was akin to joining a high-speed intellectual adventure in which the student always lagged behind. Thus, Voegelin could be simultaneously "mesmerizing" in his intellectual flight, and Socratic in his ability to appeal to common sense.

Sandoz observes that "the lectures were arresting because of the force and clarity with which complex material was communicated extemporaneously from brief notes and outlines, never read. Every class meeting seemed to have its own special moments, and often there was a sense of adventure attendant upon an intellectual voyage into uncharted waters."[52] Part of this might be due to the fact that Voegelin was still an immigrant during his time at LSU. He was learning to become an American, and may have been learning this from his colleagues, as well as his students even while he was teaching them. One of the constants in their recollections is that it was obvious Voegelin was being magnanimous toward them. He was obviously a great man, and they took his magnanimity as old world generosity and style.

It seems Voegelin left LSU for Munich with the hope of recreating the *Geistkreis* of scholars he enjoyed in Vienna in his youth.[53] Either that or a school of scientists who could rejuvenate the activity of science in Germany.[54] However, this was not meant to be, in part due to his own (self-imposed) isolation and lack of friends.

As a teacher of undergraduates, Voegelin had a reputation among many for strictness and being unfriendly, but it seems this was a strategy to weed out ideological or simply stupid and lazy students. Recall Cooper's observation of Voegelin's impatience towards American social science debates he had dealt with twenty years previously. That impatience was also directed towards the willful ignorance at the root of ideological consciousness: "I have always had to explain to students at the beginning of my seminars all my life: There is no such thing as a right to be stupid; there is no such right as a right to be illiterate; there is no such thing as a right to be incompetent."[55]

According to Claus-Ekkehard Barsch, Voegelin's strategy benefited those who stayed. It seems it helped them gain clarity on the fundamental issues. Moreover, he observes how appreciative Voegelin was for students to talk to him in walks between classes. Voegelin's former students at LSU and the University of Notre Dame confirm this side of him.[56] For example, Denis Moran reminisces about his conversations with Voegelin and his colleague Anton Chroust in the Notre Dame dining hall. Ellis Sandoz notes how Voegelin gave undergraduate and graduate students a sense they were participating with him in the activity of science: "To this degree Voegelin was doing *science* as he taught, whether in lecture or in seminar–and everybody knew this is what we were doing: the students and class were to greater lesser degree participants in a persuasive inquiry, in something appreciated as a search for truth, for truth that mattered! I think this palpable sense of participation in the activity of inquiry was perhaps the chief source of Voegelin's popularity as a teacher."[57]

Voegelin also—probably unintentionally—evoked an erotic attraction, especially from some of his female students. Using an eclectic method of studying student behavior in all his classes, Barsch notes of Voegelin's brighter female students "their eyes were open and their legs were open. And they looked like they were in a mixture of relaxing and the opposite of relaxing...Tense! Always. I think that Voegelin had an erotic attraction. That was my general impression."[58] Voegelin exerted a Socratic eroticism of the soul that characterizes great teachers, and that reminds us this form of eroticism calls forth the entire person.[59] Plato expresses it well in the *Phaedrus* when he speaks of the lover "shuddering" while beholding his beloved whom he sees as the icon of the good.[60] This is the higher form of eroticism that his LSU students, who rioted during the stripper's visit, lacked.

The gap between the "phenomenon" and student narrows in the recollections of his graduate students. According to Tilo Schabert, he regularly invited his staff and students for gatherings at his Munich apartment and sometimes for a barbeque at his cottage in Weilheim.[61] He certainly preferred the company of his students to his colleagues. However, some of his students express frustration at his aloofness and incapacity for conversation.

All the limitations of Voegelin's personality and his aloofness seemed to dissolve for those graduate students who ended up participating in his own scientific investigations. He was in constant conversation and dialogue with them concerning the latest books, theories, and current events.[62] Sandoz describes an occasion in a reading group on Plato's *Protagoras*, in which Voegelin and his students studied the text line-by-line, when Voegelin discovered he had erred on an interpretive point in *Order and History*, volume two, and said he would have to revise it for a later edition. Schabert explains that Voegelin's "workshop" consisted of his immediate research assistants, but also those with whom he corresponded by letter, and his students in his lectures:

> After initiating a conversation—and without considering whether what was to follow would interest all who were present or would even be acceptable to them—Eric Voegelin would present the latest ideas that had come to him in the course of his thought, of his work. Manifestly, these were ideas that he wanted first to "test." They were delivered in that manner he always maintained: one of presenting them as conceptual discoveries that were absolutely unfamiliar, shocking and unorthodox, yet of a far-reaching significance. Voegelin usually proceeded in precisely the same way in lectures and presentations, especially during the discussion round. On such occasions, he appeared as the figure of the experimental mind that rebelliously probed to the furthest, least expected limit. The effect upon his audience was palpable: it too now brimmed with creative excitement as well. Voegelin regarded his lectures as a manifestation of his workshop that had no parallel anywhere else. As a matter of particular note: it was at just such lectures that Voegelin won others over to his thought and gained them for the study of his work.[63]

Students, who could not possibly fully understand what Voegelin was talking about, could still sense the significance and thrill of scientific inquiry. Here was a scientist's existential motion in truth. Of course, Voegelin was not a regular scholar in the sense of being a specialist. An exuberant gnat biologist can thrill his students by teaching them about its digestive organs. Voegelin, as we have seen, was attempting to move beyond Weber's attempt to develop a theory of humanity.

Thomas Hollweck elaborates Voegelin's invitation to students to "think with" him:

> Voegelin as a teacher, that means to me first of all, Voegelin as a keen observer of the person with whom he was having a conversation and as someone who visibly thought your thoughts with you, which my by no means meant that his thought processes would arrive at the same end as your own. This is when things would become extremely interesting; for then you knew that something important was going on, something that embodied to me the essence of *Wissenschaft* and philosophy. Voegelin never had any need to interrupt, except to interject "what do you mean. I do not understand," when I had once again failed to express my thoughts clearly.[64]

Under the circumstances of "thinking with" a talented graduate student, Voegelin displayed a Socratic sense of teaching deeper perhaps even than of Socrates, who, it seems, never "thought with" another interlocutor in the sense of treating him as an equal, at least in terms of the topic at hand.[65] His Socratic teaching was the result of his capacity to remove himself from the topic of inquiry: "It is the sign of a sovereign thinker that he has no need to mention his own writings on a particular subject and that he does not chew the cud of old accomplishments. When Voegelin invited you to read something he had written it was, as Tilo Schabert points out, 'work in progress.' Voegelin invited you to think with him, not about him, not against him, but about the subject matter."[66]

Of course, an inequality existed between Voegelin and his top students by virtue of Voegelin's intellect, which the students recognized: "What I personally valued more than anything else in Voegelin's thinking was its analytical power. He was the only man ever from whom I would accept statements about what cannot be proven, because I knew that if anyone ever had, he had thought it through and had not relied on intuition."[67] Even so, for several of his German students, the authority of his intellect meant something more than giving them the faith to take his word for granted on this or that topic. His German students grew up in the post-World War II period, which meant their own parents—fathers in particular—were directly affected by the war. The fathers of some were killed (which meant they barely would have known them), while others had been National Socialists.[68] Voegelin was a father figure for many of them for the same reason Socrates was a father figure for the dispossessed youth of Athens. The old order was either dead or corrupt, and he represented the new way for many of his students (though he seems not to have noticed nor cultivated this kind of relationship).

Voegelin as Founder

Many sides of Voegelin the teacher treated here so far are gathered up in the series of lectures, "Hitler and the Germans," delivered in 1964, that perhaps constituted the climax of his teaching career.[69] It is the best example of Voegelin's activity as a teacher involved in the art of the periagoge that consists of a liberal and civic education for students. As we have seen, many of Voegelin's students regarded him a mesmerizing "phenomenon" but his significance was not altogether clear to them. His significance to this audience, composed mostly of students, was clear because the topic was about them, or rather, about the society they had inherited from their corrupted parents. Purcell compares the performance to Socrates pulling Athenian youths out of their cave: "For his audience, encountering Voegelin delivering the lectures was like meeting someone coming up from the underworld of Plato's cave, would be their Socratic guide. In that sense, Manfred Henningsen remarked that their greatest impact was in their actual performance, 'in expectation of a German metanoia.'"[70] Purcell argues that Voegelin, for whom, like Socrates or Kierkegaard, philosophy is a way of existence instead of simply holding concepts, the lectures were intended to recreate the capacity for civic friendship in truth in Germany, a rebuilding of souls in "a community of existential concern": "That's perhaps the fullest significance of those lectures—they expressed Voegelin's own *philia politike*, his attitude of political friendship towards his audience. They were intended to ground the common *homonoia*—likemindedness in participation in the same divine nous—a new generation of German *spoudaioi*, of an inner dignity and external civic virtue equivalent to Max Weber's."[71] Like Socrates who refounds the beautiful city in the souls of the young with whom he converses, Voegelin attempted to reconstitute the life of truthfulness in a destroyed German society.

Purcell analyzes the method of Voegelin's attempt to evoke *periagoge* in his students. He draws upon Kierkegaard's program of eliciting in his audience three steps in conversion: aesthetic, ethical, and religious, as well as a fourth step, towards the truth of existence. These steps of ascent are attempts to practice the "art of the periagoge."

The first step toward conversion is to enter into the aesthetic by means of irony and satire. Efforts by post-war German philosophers, historians, and social scientists to explain the Nazi phenomena were pathetic because they too participated in the destruction of reality (which helps explain why the title of Voegelin's lectures was "Hitler *and* the Germans" (my emphasis), to show that Hitler does not arise in a cultural vacuum). Voegelin borrows heavily from Karl Kraus's satires on the Nazis and culture in the inter-war period to demonstrate, with a considerable degree of bluntness, how anyone should have seen the destruction of order in society. Satire exposes the destruction, but the ironic presentation of details enables the audience to distance itself from "the commonly accepted doxa of academic contemporary historiography."[72] Voegelin bluntly demonstrates to his students that the paragons of intelligence and morality in their society are stupid idiots. No wonder he was professionally isolated in Germany! Even so, Purcell singles out the aesthetic as Voegelin's first step toward evoking periagoge in students. Satire and irony are not meant to belittle or intimidate, as many of his students thought, but was "aimed at healing through cauterization." Of course, satire and irony can appear as mere insult to some, and, without the shared background of being young in a corrupt society like Voegelin's German students were, it would be difficult to determine the target of Voegelin's barbs.

An example of Voegelinian pedagogic irony from early in his career sharpens our analysis. Bruno Schlesinger took Voegelin's constitutional law class at the University of Vienna before he was dismissed. He describes how Voegelin used irony to handle Nazi sympathizers in his dissection of the Nazi constitution: "He didn't in any way denounce the Nazis; there was no kind of lashing out at them. It was almost a kind of bantering about them instead. He would even smile as he said it: 'Have you heard this and this?'...With a smile, he would mildly insinuate this or that and indicate that it was absolutely stupid or unlawful. He didn't say that they were stupid directly, of course: he just said, 'Can you imagine it? They have done this and that.'...I have never seen anything quite like it; it was really dangerous. Because at least some of them understood. At least a few knew what he was driving at, but he kept going."[73] This early example of irony insinuated truth into the souls of the students in a manner to avoid persecution, whereas Voegelin took a different ironic approach in the 1964 "Hitler and the Germans" lectures because he did not have to worry about persecution. Even so, both examples share the same mode of insinuating truth into ideological consciousness.

From the aesthetic, Voegelin in his "Hitler and the Germans" lectures moves to the ethical. It should be noted, though, that Purcell's Kierkegaardian categories (to which Voegelin does not refer) are existential, not temporal, ones. This means that each is present at each and every point of the lectures. One does not find the first lecture in the aesthetic, the second lecture in the ethical, and so on.

Having demonstrated the absurdity of the Nazis and their subsequent "scientific" interpreters, and having achieved an ironic distancing from the authoritative claims of the latter, Voegelin elicits ethical conversion expressed first as moral indignation and second as affirmation of moral order as a key constituent of scientific understanding of political reality. The absurdity of participating in the secondary reality of ideology deserves moral indignation, which is an affirmation of participation in a common reality. Voegelin uses the example of a journalist who criticizes a former Auschwitz prisoner for losing control on the witness stand and calling a former guard a murderer, even though the guard "merely" beat him into a cripple. Voegelin's indignation at the journalist is apparent: "For what it is saying is that one should peacefully allow oneself to be killed and shouldn't in any way shout 'murderer!'…As long as I have not been killed, I must not say that the other person is a murder. If I see that this other one is committing murder, I still may not say 'murderer!' before he has been convicted in a proper court."[74] One can see in the journalist a legalist mindset that would prohibit the former prisoner from speaking truth when doing so breaks the letter of the law.

Having affirmed the moral order in the conversion to the ethical, Voegelin then elicits religious conversion, or perhaps more accurately, "conversion to the transcendent."[75] From affirming the moral order in the ethical conversion, Voegelin moves into the transcendent under which the individual stands to be judged by that standard. Voegelin identifies the loss of reality, rooted in man's desire to be the creator of his own existence and values, as the source of German disorder, and cites one sentence of Novalis to summarize this sentiment: "'The world shall be as I wish it!' There you already have in a nutshell the whole problem of Hitler, the central problem of the dedivinizing and dehumanizing.'"[76] In contrast, Voegelin succinctly clarifies the transcendent, and empirically true, standard under which man exists: "The experience of reason and spirit agree on the point that man experiences himself as a being who does not exist from himself. He exists in an already given world. This world itself exists by reason of a mystery, and the name for the mystery, for the cause of this being of the world, of which man is a component, is referred to as 'God.' So, dependence of existence on the divine causation of existence has remained the basic question of philosophy up to today."[77] Of course, Voegelin was not a spokesman for Christianity or any other religion. But Christianity, as well as Socratic political philosophy, calls upon the individual to live his life in truth and to be judged by that truth. The "experiences of reason and spirit" tell us life is to be lived in existential truth, and that philosophy is not simply the holding of right or even true opinions and concepts. This enables Voegelin to devote considerable attention to criticizing the Christian churches during the Nazi era, for they failed to bear witness to transcendent truth. Willingness to live under judgment expresses the "openness" toward the divine ground discussed above. Only such souls are capable of political and philosophical friendship. That Voegelin was capable of eliciting such friendship in his university lectures testifies to his greatness as a teacher.

The "Hitler and the Germans" lectures appear to have been foundational events for those who heard them. Many in the audience went on to form important parts of the German regime. Our analysis of his teaching began with some reservations of his talents, which his former students explained to be the result of his greatness as a scholar, which tended to make it difficult for students to keep up with him. Those who were able to develop a working relationship with him identify his capacity to "think with" the student as the bond between them. Even so, Voegelin "pushed ahead" with his science and thinking, which risked leaving behind students. However, as we saw with Purcell's account of the "Hitler and the German" lectures, Voegelin was very capable of teaching to a wide array of intellects, and of condescending (in the good sense of the term) to the longings of the students.

Conclusion

Socrates in the *Symposium* explains how Diotima describes the multidimensional eros as: "courageous, stout, and keen, a skilled hunter, always weaving devices, desirous of practical wisdom and inventive, philosophizing through all his life, a skilled magician, druggist, sophist."[78] This list of attributes should unsettle anyone who fails to appreciate the complexity of teaching. Voegelin displayed all of these qualities because he understood teaching as an existential quest with students that ascends from ideological disorder to wisdom (*sophia*) and practical judgment (*phronesis*).

Teachers and learners form an existential community because together they turn, and have their souls turned, from becoming to being. For Voegelin, the "art of the periagoge" consists of inculcating the habits necessary for these existential virtues, and the methods used to inculcate them are various because they require the teacher to dig more deeply than reason into the souls of the students. As Voegelin indicates, his lifelong work is the result of the need to show students why the life of reason is indeed the pursuit of truth. His scholarship and teaching has as its core the moral aspiration for existential life in truth.

At the same time, though, Voegelin, like Plato, was aware that education is a matter of eliciting knowledge and not of inserting knowledge. As we have seen, Voegelin's self-understanding as a scholar is intimately connected to his self-understanding as a teacher. We saw how Weber could not explain his activity of being a scientist in terms of his science, which, as Voegelin notes, is a question at the forefront of the minds of students who wish to know on what basis their teacher is telling them to act the way he suggests. For Voegelin, the life of science is bound up with the activity of science and this means that so-called "research" and teaching are, in the end, two activities with the same end, the cultivation of society living in existential truth.

Notes

1. I thank Southern Utah University Press for their permission to republish parts of my essay, "Periagoge: Liberal Education in the Modern University," in *The Democratic Discourse of Liberal Education*, ed., Lee Trepanier. Another part of this essay was presented to the Eric Voegelin Society in 2011. I thank Tilo Schabert, Brendan Purcell, Barry Cooper, and Steven McGuire for their comments on previous instantiations of this essay.

2. These volumes have been published in the 34 volumes of the *Collected Works of Eric Voegelin*, (Columbia, MO: University of Missouri Press, 1990–2007). Voegelin's writings will be cited by title and the volume in which they appear (CW). *New Science of Politics* is in CW 5 and *Order and History* is found in CW 14–18.

3. Plato, *Republic*, trans., Joe Sachs, (Focus Publishing), 518d.

4. *Plato and Aristotle, Order and History*, vol. 3, (Baton Rouge, LA: Louisiana State University Press, 1956), 116.

5. For an early statement of Voegelin, first published in 1936, see "Popular Education, Science, and Politics," CW 9, 79–90.

6. "Democracy and Industrial Society," CW 11, 219.

7. "On Classical Studies," CW 12, 260.

8. For a description of "resistance," see Thomas W. Heilke, "Science, Philosophy, and Resistance: On Eric Voegelin's Practice of Opposition," *The Review of Politics*, 56 (Fall, 1994): 727–752.

9. Voegelin wrote several focused studies of Weber: "On Max Weber," *Published Essays, 1922–1928*, CW 7, 100–17; "Max Weber," *Published Essays, 1929–1933*, CW 8, 130–48; "Introduction" to "New Science of Politics," CW 5, 88–108; "The Greatness of Max Weber," (Eleventh Lecture), *Hitler and the Germans*, CW 31, 257–74. See also *Autobiographical Reflections*, CW 34, 39–41.

10. *Autobiographical Reflections*, CW 34, 40.

11. *Science, Politics, and Gnosticism*, CW 5, 264–65, 274–5.

12. For details, see Thomas Heilke and John von Heyking, "Editors' Introduction," *Published Essays, 1922–1928*, CW 7; Jürgen Gebhardt and Barry Cooper, "Editors' Introduction," *On the Form of the American Mind*, CW1, ix–xxxv.

13. Gebhardt and Cooper, "Editors' Introduction," CW 1, xv.

14. Voegelin, "Political Theory," in CW 33; "The Oxford Political Philosophers," CW 11, 24–46. Barry Cooper observes that Voegelin was impatient with American debates in the 1950s and 1960s over social science, methodology, and behavioralism be-

cause "he had already dealt with these issues at a philosophically more sophisticated level some thirty years earlier" (*Beginning the Quest: Law and Politics in the Early Work of Eric Voegelin*, (Columbia, MO: University of Missouri Press, 2009), 18).

15. Voegelin, "The Greatness of Max Weber," in *Hitler and the Germans*, CW 31, 270. Voegelin cites Eduard Baumgarten, *Max Weber: Werk und Person: Dokumente ausgewahlte und kommentiert von Eduard Baumgarten*, (Tubingen: J. C. B. Mohr, 1964), 638.

16. Compare with an earlier (1925) assessment of Weber, "On Max Weber," CW 7, 111–16, where Voegelin finds Weber's transcendental ego in the lonely company of his daimon. Yet, Weber's daimon functions differently from that of Socrates: "the ultimate meaning of life is not to find its meaning, but constantly to create it. For our consciousness there is a point before the world, where we are alone, so alone that no one can follow us there." Cooper describes Weber's daimon as "a somewhat Nietzschean way of referring to the neo-Kantian transcendental ego. However named, the task of the historical scientist was to marshal his will and ability to impress a concrete shape or form upon history" (Cooper, *Beginning the Quest*, 33). Writing in the 1920s, Voegelin would find the mightiest symbol of the age, and the clearest expression of the existential state of social science, was Weber's lonely conversation with his daimon (see also Heilke and Heyking, "Editors' Introduction," CW 7, 7).

17. "Greatness of Max Weber," *Hitler and the Germans*, CW 31, 273.

18. I have elaborated on the limits of social science education in "Obstacles to Liberal Education in the Modern University," *The Democratic Discourse of Liberal Education*, ed. Lee Trepanier, (Cedar City, UT: Southern Utah University Press and the Grace A. Tanner Center, 2010), 134–159.

19. Eric Voegelin, *Anamnesis*, CW 6, 411.

20. CW6, 411.

21. Ellis Sandoz, "Editor's Introduction," CW 34, 4.

22. CW6, 411.

23. CW6, 412.

24. See Jonathan Kay, *Among the Truthers*, (New York: HarperCollins, 2011).

25. "Immortality: Experience and Symbol," CW12, 72.

26. CW6, 297.

27. "In Search of the Ground," CW11, 228.

28. Letter to Robert Heilman, March 19, 1948, CW 29, 562.

29. "Since every man participates in love of the transcendent Being and is aware of such a ground—Ground, Reason, or Nous—out of which he exists, every man can, by virtue of this noetic self, have love for other men. In theory, this is the secondary phenomenon—in theory, not in practice. In practice, we love others right away without having a theory for it. But in theory that is secondary because there is no particular reason—reason, I say now—to love other men unless they also participate in that same divine Nous and have such a noetic self" ("In Search of the Ground," CW11, 230-1). This statement corresponds to the more compact statement of responsibility toward others that the common sense philosopher, Thomas Reid, affirms and that Voegelin quotes: "There is a certain degree of it which is necessary to our being subjects of law and government, capable of managing our own affairs, and answerable for our conduct towards others: this is called common sense, because it is common to all men with whom we can transact business, or call to account for their conduct" (CW6, 410–11). David Walsh emphasizes Voegelin's unfinished project of articulating the practical over the theoretical ("Voegelin's Place in Modern Philosophy," *Modern Age*, Winter 2007: 12–23).

30. CW5, 259.

31. CW5, 262, quoting Marx, "Nationalökonomie und Philosophie," in Karl Marx, *Der Historiche Materismus: Die Fruhschriften*, ed., Landshut and Meyer, (Leipzig, 1932), 333. Voegelin focuses on Marx's earlier, more "metaphysical," writings. Raymond Aron focused on Marx's later economic writings and also found them "equivocal," especially his discussion of "social class," a fact that Marx himself admitted (Brian Anderson, *Raymond Aron: The Recovery of the Political*, (Lanham, MD: Rowman and Littlefield, 1997), 79, citing Marx's letter to J. Weydemeyer (March 5, 1852)).

32. "Wisdom and the Magic of the Extreme," CW12, 320-1.

33. "Wisdom and the Magic of the Extreme," CW12, 320-1.

34. CW5, 262-4.

35. Thus, as Tocqueville observes, the tendency of democratic souls who are otherwise practical and common sensical to be drawn toward grand abstract visions of humanity, history, and society. At a more vulgar level, this might help explain the persistence of conspiracy theories in our own day (see Kay, *Among the Truthers*).

36. CW5, 262-3.

37. The title of Voegelin's essay of course derives from Nietzsche: "The charm (Zauber) that works for us…is the magic of the extreme, the seductive force that radiates from all that is utmost" (Nietzsche, *Will to Power*, 749) (quoted, CW12, 324). At one point, Augustine claims sin is rooted in the love of a false good that charms (see Augustine, *Expositions on Psalms*, CXIX, *A Select Library of the Nicene and Post-Nicene Fathers of the Christian Church*, ed., Philip Schaff, vol. viii, (Grand Rapids, MI: Wm. B. Eerdmans Publishing Company, 1989), 574)).

38. Ellis Sandoz, "Editor's Introduction" CW 34, 5.

39. "Wisdom and the Magic of the Extreme," CW12, 326.

40. "Wisdom," CW12, 326.

41. "Wisdom," CW12, 329.

42. "High River Man Charged with Stalking Heartland Star," *Calgary Sun*, June 23, 2011. (http://www.calgarysun.com/2011/06/23/high-river-man-charged-with-stocking-heartland-star).

43. "In Search of the Ground," CW11, 235.

44. CW 12, 376–77.

45. CW12, 378–380.

46. This leaves aside the question of whether silence would have been a superior form of signifying nonexistent reality, as even words, no matter how carefully used, still reify. But silence, as a mode of communication, has its own problems, as debates over esotericism show (see James Rhodes, *Eros, Wisdom, and Silence: Plato's Erotic Dialogues*, (Columbia, MO: University of Missouri Press, 2003), chaps. 1–2.

47. CW 12, 378.

48. CW 12, 380.

49. See "Immortality: Experience and Symbol," CW 12, 67.

50. Invaluable in this regard are the recollections of a large number of his students in Barry Cooper and Jodi Bruhn (eds.), *Voegelin Recollected: Conversations on a Life*, (Columbia, MO: University of Missouri Press, 2008). See also Sandoz, "Editor's Introduction," CW 34, 1–7. See also the interviews with former students in the video, "Eric Voegelin: Philosopher of Consciousness," (www.ericvoegelin.org).

51. *Voegelin Recollected*, 132.

52. Sandoz, "Editor's Introduction," CW 34, 3.

53. See comments by Tilo Schabert in *Voegelin Recollected*, 105. For details of Voegelin's life in Vienna, see *Voegelin Recollected*, 220–253. Voegelin describes the Geistkreis, which was composed of scholars who would remain his lifelong friends: "It

was a group of younger people who met regularly every month, one of them giving a lecture on a subject of his choice and the others tearing him to pieces....An important characteristic of the group was that we were all held together by our intellectual interests in the pursuit of this or that science, but that at the same time a good number of the members were not simply attached to the university but were engaged in various business activities." (*Autobiographical Reflections*, 35–36). The lack of identification with the University of Vienna reminds us of Stephen Miller's observation that the "clubbable men" of the Enlightenment pursued their most important conversations outside the parameters of the universities (*Conversation*, 79–118).

54. *Voegelin Recollected*, 111.

55. Voegelin, CW 33, 419.

56. *Voegelin Recollected*, 81.

57. Ellis Sandoz, "Eric Voegelin As Master Teacher: Notes For A Talk," Roundtable Discussion, American Political Science Association & Eric Voegelin Society, Annual Meetings in Chicago, September 4, 2004. I thank Professor Sandoz for sharing his notes with me. See also Sandoz, "Editor's Introduction," 5.

58. *Voegelin Recollected*, 82–3.

59. See William Deresiewicz, "Love on Campus," *American Scholar*, Summer 2007: 36–46 (http://www.theamericanscholar.org/su07/love-deresiewicz.html).

60. Plato, *Phaedrus*, 251a.

61. *Voegelin Recollected*, 89.

62. Tilo Schabert, "Die Werkstatt Eric Voegelins," *Zeitschrift fur Politik*, Marz 2002, 49(1): 83–95.

63. Schabert, "Die Werkstatt Eric Voegelins," 91. Translation taken from unpublished English translation. I thank Professor Schabert for sharing his manuscript with me.

64. Thomas Hollweck, "Roundtable Discussion: Voegelin as Master Teacher," Comments presented at Eric Voegelin Society, 2004 Annual Meeting of the American Political Science Association (http://www.artsci.lsu.edu/voegelin/EVS/2004%20Papers/Hollweck22004.htm).

65. This is a contentious claim, as Socratic ignorance, if we take it seriously, implies a genuine equality among Socrates and all men. Søren Kierkegaard brings this equality out very well.

66. Hollweck, "Voegelin as Master Teacher."

67. Hollweck, "Voegelin as Master Teacher."

68. *Voegelin Recollected*, 113.

69. Voegelin, *Hitler and the Germans*, CW 31. The following analysis draws upon Purcell's analysis of these lectures, which focuses on Voegelin's performance of them, instead of the published version ("Can a Philosopher Be a Prophetic Witness to the Truth?").

70. Purcell, "Can a Philosopher Be a Prophetic Witness to the Truth?", 2, quoting Henningsen, "Eine Mischung aus Schlachthof und Klapsmühle, Einleitung zu Eric Voegelin," *Hitler und die Deutschen*, (Munich: Wilhelm Fink, 2006), 38.

71. Purcell, "Can a Philosopher Be a Prophetic Witness to the Truth?." 6. Henningsen documents a number of students in attendance who would go on to form a cross-section of German *spoudaioi*, representing media, government, bureaucracy, and the academy ("Einleitung zu Eric Voegelin," 19).

72. Purcell, "Can a Philosopher Be a Prophetic Witness to the Truth?," 3.

73. *Voegelin, Recollected*, 228–9.

74. Voegelin, *Hitler and the Germans*, CW 31, 64.

75. Purcell, "Can a Philosopher Be a Prophetic Witness to the Truth?," 4.

76. Voegelin, *Hitler and the Germans*, CW 31, 88.
77. Voegelin, *Hitler and the Germans*, CW 31, 86.
78. Plato, *Symposium*, 203d-e.

Chapter 6

Gerhart Niemeyer as Educator:
The Defense of Western Culture in an Ideological Age[*]
Michael Henry, St. John's University

Near the end of his life Plato referred to Socrates in his *Seventh Letter* as a man who had been an "elder friend" (*philon andra emoi presbuteron*) to him in his youth and also the most just man of the time. Although Socrates, some forty years Plato's senior, was certainly someone who had taught Plato a great deal he does not refer to him as his teacher but as his friend, meaning that it was friendship offered by a man of remarkable character, a man who loved truth and goodness above all, that had ignited the similar love in Plato's soul. Alcibiades' recounting in Plato's *Symposium* his amazement at discovering beneath Socrates' satyr-like exterior a soul "of god-like beauty" was probably not intended to refer to the experience of only Alcibiades. From the dialogues that Plato wrote in the half century after Socrates' death it is clear that what he learned from his friend was not only the critical importance of an open-souled, wondering questioning and pursuit of Truth but also the nature of true teaching as grounded in friendship and the care of souls.

Whether or not he consciously intended to emulate Socrates in this respect, Gerhart Niemeyer's relationships with his students, particularly his graduate

[*] Students of Niemeyer whose published and unpublished writings contributed to this chapter are James Rhodes, John Gueguen, Gregory Wolfe, Donald Roy, Richard Bishirjian, Bruce Fingerhut, and William Miller.

students and even more particularly those whose dissertations he directed, were also primarily friendships, friendships of the kind that Aristotle would have considered as between unequals, but for Niemeyer the inequality was merely temporary because he saw his students as future colleagues. Although, or more likely because, Niemeyer was a superb teacher he did not want disciples but instead he always fostered a communion of minds and souls that loved the truth. Like Socrates he exerted such a magnetic attraction on those of kindred spirit that many can still vividly recall the first encounter with him as the sudden, electrifying realization of being in the mind-expanding and life-changing presence of an extraordinary man. James Rhodes, for instance, reports that his life changed forever when as a chemistry major he "wandered into" Niemeyer's course in Political Theory in 1959 and found a professor "thinking, luminously, about the ultimate questions of human existence," something he had never encountered before. He abandoned chemistry because, as he put it, in words that would resonate with many other Niemeyer students, "I realized soon that I wanted to spend all my years doing what he did, in the way that he did it."[1] Bruce Fingerhut encountered Niemeyer at a conference in Washington in the late 1960s and immediately decided that he had to apply to Notre Dame, even though at the time he did not even know where it was.[2] I myself was in the Philosophy Department when I enrolled in Niemeyer's graduate course in "The Concept of History" in the spring of 1970, and after he had spoken perhaps two or three sentences I knew that he was the teacher I had been searching for. What enabled Niemeyer to have such an immediate and powerful impact on students and what made him so remarkable a teacher was not only the luminosity of his mind and the breadth and depth of his knowledge but an unmistakable authority and core of conviction that illumined almost every sentence that he spoke and wrote. This was a matter of his character that antedated his religious and philosophical turn, for even as early as 1940, before he had arrived at most of the knowledge and beliefs that provided the substance of his Notre Dame courses, Princeton's student publication reported of him, "What does make him stand out in one's memory...is the steady look in his eye and the seriousness and assurance with which he tells you what he believes to be true."[3] There are teachers from whom one learns a subject and there are teachers who, through grace and friendship, profoundly nurture one's soul and shape one's life. For many of those who entered his classroom Niemeyer was the latter. As Rhodes put it, "I believe now that it was a case of a great, saintly soul humbly allowing God's light to shine through it."[4] How he became such a teacher and thinker (and these are inseparable in him) can be partially understood from his biography and his writings, as well as the insights of those who knew him well. The rest is the mystery that is each unique human soul in its silent solitude with God.[5]

I shall begin by tracing Niemeyer's intellectual development and describing him as a teacher, and then I shall attempt to illuminate the core of his thinking about political theory in general and education in particular, thinking which served as both the animating spirit and the purpose of his teaching. His intellectual development has been recounted more than once, in most detail in the excellent biography of Niemeyer by his son Paul. I will focus on the persons and events that had the greatest impact on him.[6]

Gerhart Niemeyer was born in Essen, Germany on February 15, 1907, to a family that was rather distinguished on both his mother's and his father's sides. Perhaps because law was a common profession among his ancestors and his father Victor was a well-known lawyer and his uncle Theodor taught law at the University of Kiel, he eventually settled on the study of law. He very happily spent the 1925–26 year at Cambridge, where he studied law, took long boat trips on rivers, and replaced the superficial Protestant faith of his childhood with an atheistic mixture of Labor Party Socialism, Marxism, and Fabianism, concluding that, as he later recalled, "no really intelligent person could be a religious believer. At any rate, I felt it was below my intellectual dignity."[7] When he returned to Germany he became a Social Democrat and enrolled at the University of Munich. However, Munich had too many distractions, particularly the constant allurement of mountain climbing in the Alps, so for the sake of his law studies in the fall of 1927 he transferred to the University of Kiel where he finished his J.D. degree in 1932. It was in Theodor's home that he met Hermann Heller, a prominent German political, legal, and socialist thinker and a prolific writer, who at the time was teaching in Berlin. According to Niemeyer's own account, he was working on his dissertation when he met Heller, and he soon went to Berlin to visit him and attend his lectures. In 1932 he became Heller's assistant at the University of Frankfurt. When Hitler came to power Heller was in England, but before he could return to Germany Niemeyer met him in Basel to convey a warning that Heller, who was a Jew, should not return.[8] Instead he went to Spain, where Niemeyer and his wife joined him in September, 1933 only to be present in November when Heller collapsed and died from a heart attack at the age of forty-two. His final, unfinished book, *Staatslehre [Political Theory]*, which was edited and published by Niemeyer in 1934, greatly influenced the development of Niemeyer's argument in the book on international law that he began in 1936 and published in 1941, *Law Without Force*.

Heller played a crucial role in Niemeyer's intellectual and personal development. In an article on Heller that he wrote for *The International Encyclopedia of the Social Sciences* in 1964 Niemeyer noted that "much of Heller's work concerned the political crisis of the West. He conceived it as a collapse of political order stemming from the destruction of political theory. The anti-political notion of an automatically self-regulating natural order had produced modern legal positivism which construed the concept of order without the state and apart from any concrete content. By way of psychological reaction there arose the modern cult of sheer force, the strong man, and the intrinsic value of a command."[9] Heller advocated a non-Marxist socialism because he believed that the unity of a democratic state had to be grounded in social homogeneity and on specific concrete realities, or "underlying historical forms of culture," which meant in the case of Germany "the community of the German language, the community of cultural forms of German life, the community of German historical traditions, etc."[10] What Niemeyer learned from Heller was an emphasis on *Wirklich-*

keitswissenshaft, the science of reality, which does not lend itself to the abstract systems of philosophers. Reality meant what concretely existing individual human beings actually chose to do in their living together in specific times and places. Because Heller was convinced that political science had to be founded on the richness, complexity, and concreteness of experience—all of it—he concluded that it is somewhat artificial to isolate the state and politics from the rest of a complex life-reality. As Niemeyer ended his article on Heller, "Man consists of both body and soul, society includes physical acts as well as spiritual meaning, legal order presupposes both norm and will, political theory must use not only causal but also normative analysis, etc. It was his ability to hold such tensions in his mind without trying to resolve them in the interest of a unified system that secured his rank as one of the strong voices of sanity in an age of political disorder."[11] These principles of the wholeness of concrete experience and the importance of grounding political theory in concrete reality would continue to guide Niemeyer as he explored their implications beyond the dimension of Heller's inquiry in his own efforts to be a voice of sanity through the rest of the twentieth century.

Moreover, Heller's whole character had a profound impact on that of Niemeyer. At the end of his preface to *Law Without Force,* his first attempt to come to grips with the crisis of his time, he paid loving tribute to the memory of Heller, who had inspired him with the desire to spend all his years doing what his mentor had done. It is helpful here to quote this in full because at the age of thirty-three he essentially laid out his plan of growth for the rest of his life.

> Herman Heller's teaching inspired me with his ideas; his living inspired me with the example of an extraordinary man, outstanding in qualities both of soul and of mind, a man to whom the rational mastery of political reality meant a profound human responsibility and thus a personal task. His urge to penetrate the phenomena of political association with the clarity of the spirit sprang not from a mere intellectual interest in his work but from the depths of his soul, which suffered from arbitrariness and the lack of order in politics much as a man may suffer from the moral inadequacies of his own nature. Yet the strength of his character made him look straight into the face of realities, without flinching from their ugliness or covering their features with the veil of wishful thinking. Hermann Heller's life and death were a constant and forceful proclamation of the idea that to realize a genuinely rational order in the political side of human culture is not merely a pragmatic, but an ethical requirement.[12]

Niemeyer had no way of knowing when he wrote these words in 1940 that he was describing precisely the way in which many of his future students would think of him.

After Heller's death Niemeyer remained in Madrid until the summer of 1936 when, while he and his family were on vacation in Germany, the outbreak of the Spanish Civil War prevented their return. Because he found life in Nazi Germany asphyxiating, in 1937 he and his family emigrated to the United States, about which he knew relatively little other than that it was a free and English-speaking country. He began his teaching career at Princeton where he taught courses on international politics, international law, and administrative law, and, beginning in 1939, "Conditions of Modern Dictatorship." Also, in 1939 he directed the dissertation of his first doctoral student, John Hallowell.[13] The dictatorship course was the result of Niemeyer's struggling to understand what had happened in Europe during the first four decades of the twentieth century. His personal experience of Nazism with its attendant barbarity and vulgar racist ideology was certainly the second important influence on Niemeyer.[14] Like Voegelin and others who were appalled by the destruction of civilization he believed it was his responsibility to understand how it had happened. Combating ideologies such as Nazism and particularly Communism, which he later studied extensively, would become the core of his life's work.

The crucial moment in his intellectual and spiritual development was his conversion to Christianity (along with his wife Lucie) after a lengthy internal search and struggle. Also, according to his account, he read Kierkegaard and had to acknowledge that there was at least one extremely intelligent person who did believe, passionately and profoundly, in God and in Christianity.[15] From this point on his writings increase in philosophical and spiritual depth, particularly after he began to read Augustine, who became one of his intellectual mentors. It was most likely in 1947 that he met Eric Voegelin, like him a scholar and a refugee from Nazism, and also a thinker who had found very little in his education that enabled him to comprehend the catastrophic disorders that erupted in Europe and therefore had undertaken the prodigious scholarship involved in searching for an explanation. Finally concluding that the key lay in consciousness, Voegelin developed a philosophy that focused on the relation between the human *psyche* and divine transcendence. Indeed, he believed that human existence is best understood as, simply, "openness to transcendence." Never dogmatic, Voegelin made it clear the human *psyche* must be open to all of reality which certainly included the spiritual and that ideologies were serious disturbances or pathologies of the spirit that he classified as forms of Gnosticism, a classification that Niemeyer himself adopted. Voegelin's influence on Niemeyer's growing awareness of the importance of ontology was considerable, particularly after the publication of *The New Science of Politics* and the first three volumes of *Order and History* in the 1950s. Niemeyer's later writings incorporate much of Voegelin's thought into his own philosophical and spiritual analyses of issues. (Unlike Niemeyer, Voegelin was not a devout Christian, although he took Christianity quite seriously as a way of symbolizing man's mysterious relation with transcendence.)

After several years of teaching at Princeton Niemeyer moved to Oglethorpe University in Atlanta in 1944 because, as he put it, he was attracted "by the prospect of there building an experimental model of liberal education."[16] This did not work out quite as he had hoped so in 1950 he left academia for five years while he worked in Washington at the State Department's Office of United Nations Affairs and in New York as a research analyst with the Council on Foreign

Relations, in both of which positions he greatly increased his expertise in foreign policy, international organizations, and particularly Communist Ideology. His understanding of the real nature of Communist Ideology and therefore of the Cold War produced some friction with his liberal colleagues, both in government and in universities, and almost ended his career. As he recounted it in a letter he was present at an academic gathering in 1954 at the home of a Columbia University faculty member when someone accused Senator Joseph McCarthy of being a Fascist. Niemeyer disagreed on the reasonable grounds that, as a refugee from Nazi Germany and a student of Communism, he had first-hand, detailed knowledge and experience of Fascism that enabled him to say that McCarthy, despite his faults, did not fit the criteria. His demurral provoked something like a firestorm and he soon learned that he was "barred from any consideration for employment by Columbia, and later by other universities." He observed to his correspondent that there was "an anti-McCarthy terror" in academic circles, that his one open disagreement with liberal orthodoxy nearly cost him his career, and that this was not the only problem he had had because he did not toe the liberal line.[17]

Fortunately in January of 1955 Fr. Stanley Parry, the chairman of the Government Department at The University of Notre Dame, offered Niemeyer a permanent appointment to teach courses on Communist Ideology, which he accepted.[18] This began the philosophically rich and productive second half of his life, a span of almost forty years. Not only did he write numerous essays, book reviews, and two books during this time, but he also participated regularly in Intercollegiate Studies Institute conferences, as well as others, and also taught at Hillsdale College from 1976 to 1982. And his thirty years of deepening Christian faith led to his ordination as an Episcopal deacon in 1973 and a priest in 1980. In 1993 he converted to the Roman Catholic Church. The liberal trends in the Episcopal Church, particularly those involving the ordination of women, dismayed him, because, he said, the ordination of women "cast a shadow on Jesus Christ," but he said that what ultimately determined his conversion was the new Catechism of the Catholic Church.[19] Although he sought ordination as a Catholic priest he was denied. By then he had retired from teaching, and his last publication appeared in 1994. After that his prodigious mental powers began to decline as a result of age and the cancer that took his life on June 23, 1997.

For the reader who did not know him such biographical details can only adumbrate Niemeyer's charism as a teacher. I shall try to sharpen the focus in the portrait of him as a teacher and then provide an account of the ideas about conservatism, ontology, and liberal arts education that provided the substance and purposes of his teaching.

Niemeyer was a man who combined an external old world formality and courtesy with, for those fortunate in becoming his friends, great personal warmth and generosity of spirit. Until he was eighty-nine I never saw him without a jacket (and only once, I think, without a tie). In the classroom he always addressed his students by their last names preceded by Mr. or Miss. Except when he was among family and close friends he was reserved and did not easily

engage in the sort of casual conversation that constitutes much of human inter-
actions. (In one letter he mentions his lack of small talk.[20]) Yet those who were
fortunate to get to know him well found in him a loving, supportive, and loyal
mentor, friend, and father.[21]

He was a German scholar ("a scholar to his toes," as Richard Bishirjian
described him), which means that was awesomely well educated (much of it
autodidactically, I should point out), fluent in several languages and able to read
two or three others, and a prolific writer.[22] His undergraduate survey course in
political theory, a requirement for government majors, consisted of twice-
weekly brilliantly concise lectures on major thinkers in political philosophy
given to large classes. His graduate courses were seminars, most which met for
two and a half hours in the evening without a break, since he would have considered any such interruption a ridiculous waste of time (as, in fact, it was). A
one-hour presentation by a student on the philosopher to be discussed was followed by ninety minutes of discussion by other members of the class with appropriate commentary and direction by Niemeyer. He always knew exactly what
he wanted discussed and if no one brought up the essentials he would continue
the class past its scheduled ending in order to point out the critical issues and
important passages.

The subjects of his graduate courses at Notre Dame ranged from the almost
entirely philosophical Concept of Nature and Concept of History to the two-semester critical analysis of modern ideologies and the two-semester course specifically on Communism (the first on Marx and Engels and the second on Lenin,
Stalin, and Mao). Another course he taught frequently was called Reconstruction
in Political Theory because one of his constant themes was reconstruction, restoration, renewal, re-founding, or recovery—he used almost every possible syno-
nym at one time or another. What he meant was the overcoming of the devastation of the modern mind wrought by ideologies and the recovery of the truth of
reality in all its dimensions. Also in the early 1970s he began to teach a two-semester course in Asian philosophy—Hindu, Buddhist, Taoist, and Confucian, as
I recall—in which the political was embedded in the often difficult metaphysics.
By this time Niemeyer had come to understand the political as the tip of the ontological iceberg and it was the deeper levels of the understanding of reality that
primarily interested him. At Hillsdale College he was able to expand his liberal
arts teaching to a Russian writers course that covered Turgenev, Dostoevsky,
Solzhenitsyn, and possibly Zamyatin,[23] as well as a course in Western writers
and totalitarianism that included Arthur Koestler's *Darkness at Noon,* Lionel
Trilling's *The Middle of the Journey,* and Thomas Mann's *Doctor Faustus,*
among others. All of these courses were taught as seminars in which Niemeyer
sought to instill in the students the openness to truth, particularly transcendent
truth, that learning required, as well as the willingness to engage in the labor of
thinking.[24]

Those who chose to study with him already had the philosophical *eros* for
learning, but while Niemeyer made us acutely aware of how dauntingly much
there was to learn, the drive to emulate him and the desire for his praise and fear

of disappointing him were significant motivators to exceed what we thought we were capable of.[25] He asked tough, mind-expanding questions and he demanded serious and open-minded attention to what was actually in a text—he once told me to analyze a text the way a dog worries a bone and he criticized students for failing to think carefully enough about the worldview of the thinker under discussion. He gave one student a C- on an otherwise well-written paper because the student had filled it with quotations from Voegelin's analysis of Plato (because he hoped to impress Niemeyer who he knew admired Voegelin) rather than addressing and grappling with the text himself. When he taught his two-semester course in Communist Ideology, an area in which he was an expert, he told his students that he wanted them to learn to think like Communists, without, of course, actually becoming Communists. Sometimes he even organized the class into "Communist cells" so the students could better understand Communist thinking from the inside before they engaged in critical analysis.[26] He assumed that the more thorough the understanding the more probing and effective the analysis.

Clarity of mind was important because he understood that not only was the failure to grasp the way in which Communists thought at the root of many foreign policy errors in the Cold War but the lack of clear thinking contributed to other disorders in the world. He wanted clear, precise, unpretentious language. As John Gueguen observed, "What I found most remarkable about Dr. Niemeyer was his lucidity of expression, the naturalness and confidence with which he spoke." He wanted his students to practice and attain the same lucidity and confidence. When an earnest student uttered the word "methodology" he announced, with a mischievous grin, that he was a charter member of a small society—and here he brought thumb and index finger very close together to indicate how small—founded with the single purpose of stamping out the self-important use of "methodology" when the intended meaning was simply "method." Above all he wanted his students to see reality for what it is, including especially spiritual reality. As he wrote in a personal letter, "I have never put in the title of any of my courses the word 'Christian,' or 'Religion,' yet to every one of my students it has become clear, without any indoctrination, that I was talking of reality *in* God, the 'in God' taken for granted as the only possible way of experiencing reality."[27]

Although he did not want disciples he did want "sons,"[28] intellectual progeny who would pass on the heritage of the wisdom of tradition and the love of truth "in God." John Gueguen comments that "This kind of family relationship was characteristic of Dr. Niemeyer's habitual attitude toward his students (and of them toward him). He understood his profession of teacher as a continual search for intellectual 'sons,' young men whose destiny it was to 'be a teacher' after his own heart (as 'father'). It goes without saying that this was a species of friendship." It was the kind of friendship that primarily involved the fostering of learning. When Gueguen asked him what "service" he would perform to earn his assistantship, Niemeyer replied, "The best way you can help me is by spending those hours studying well, becoming the best learner you can be."[29] With those of his students who were most his kindred spirits he did indeed enter into a friendship that lasted until his death, friendships which he nurtured quite actively.[30]

Niemeyer was indeed an "elder friend" who was certainly a father and mentor, but primarily a friend who recognized and nurtured in other souls the love of truth that animated him. Gregory Wolfe described Niemeyer the "elder friend" as follows:

> First, he taught me that philosophy consists not in the mastery of propositions or the deconstruction of propositions, but in the Socratic quest for truth in openness to the transcendent ground of being. But, more importantly, he showed me that faith shares with reason this structure of openness-in-love toward being. That is why an encounter with Gerhart Niemeyer is not merely a mental experience, but one which affects the whole person. In conversation with him, I have found that he is profoundly moved by the drama, as it were, of the education of mind and spirit. Whether he is describing the impact of a single book on a student, or recounting the success one of his former students has had in teaching prisoners, Niemeyer exhibits not only curiosity but compassion and, yes, humility. Perhaps that is why his influence on me has been so deep: he would as gladly learn as teach.[31]

Friendship, or "fellowship" as he often referred to it, was extremely important to him, as it is to all those who love truth and goodness, which is why he devoted several pages in *Between Nothingness and Paradise* to Aristotle's analysis of the most fundamental kind of the existential virtue of friendship, the friendship of the mature man, the *spoudaios,* with himself. This means that for a good man the emotions and desires in the soul "are lovingly devoted to the 'intellectual element,' which 'is thought to be the man himself,'" i.e. the *nous* which participates in the divine ground and directs the soul in "doing and wishing what is good."[32] This nurtured the many friendships he maintained among his peers, one of which was William F. Buckley, Jr., whom he met in 1951. In his eulogy for Niemeyer in *National Review* Buckley quoted a letter in which Niemeyer said, "Whenever I read something of yours like this [he wrote of an obituary in *National Review*...] I feel as if there were no distance, or time of absence, at all between us. There is an immediacy of presence which, again, is possible only through the realm of spiritual mediation."[33] Also, another aspect of friendship for Niemeyer, as Buckley noted in his Preface to Niemeyer's collection of essays *Aftersight and Foresight,* was that he loved to laugh. "Gerhart's love of laughter has always been a distinctive characteristic of this native of Essen. While acutely sensing the tragedy of this most awful century, he could always laugh....And there are different kinds of laughter, Gerhart's being of the generous kind, the laughter of gratitude: to the person who makes him laugh, and to the protocols of the cosmos that permit laughter, a divine revel...one laughs most salvifically to express thanks." Niemeyer was, indeed, a man full of gratitude—one of his favorite quotes was "Joy is praise of the whole" from Thornton Wilder's *The Eighth Day*—and in his essay "Reason and Faith: The Fallacious

Antithesis" he wrote that "Reason vs. faith…is a conflict not between two varieties of belief, but rather between an intelligible universe that opens up only as an individual submits to it with praise and thanksgiving, and one whose access risks no more than the acceptance of its axioms."[34] Also "reality has dimensions into which one must enter with faith, praise, and worship if one is to understand at all."[35] Therefore he tried to live his life and to teach ontologically, if one may put it that way, with friendship, gratitude, and praise, but also with humility and loyalty, two of the most important virtues to him because they both testify to the reality of the enduring goodness, the being, of reality.

If Niemeyer had had to sum up his philosophy and his approach to teaching in one word it probably would have been "ontophilia," the love of being, which is the opposite of the "ontophobia" that he found characteristic of modern ideologies as well as of the ancient Gnostics. As a thinker Niemeyer's main goal was to expose ideologies for the travesties of reality, the hatred of being, that they are and as a teacher it was to open his students' minds to the truth. Both goals he considered essentially conservative, for to him conservatism was not just a position on social or fiscal issues but was first and foremost an openness to reality. That is, conservatism is ontological. In his 1994 eulogy for Russell Kirk he noted that "conservatives know each other by their intellectual openness toward reality: the immediate reality of social, economic, and political relations, and the divine reality above and beyond this world."[36] He had earlier noted that "it makes sense to call conservatives instinctual ontologists," even if conservatism itself lacks a profound conception of being. His later writings are permeated by ontology and the essential intellectual openness to reality that he liked to call "deference to being." One of his particular themes was that true philosophers are conservatives because they have no ideology, so that "conservative ideology" is an oxymoron. He reserved the term "ideology" for the idea systems that create a dream world as a replacement for what is perceived as an unsatisfying reality. Conservatives dwell among the "solid blocks and boulders of reality," recognizing its concreteness and complexity as well as its limitations. He also believed that conservatism in the modern age is inherently pedagogical through its mission to combat modern ideologies: "Conservatives…will prepare the soil of the mind in many places throughout the country, to be ready for the seeds of truth when sowing time comes."[37] Conservatives always seek the truth of order, the truth of being, in response to the "threatening nihilism," the loss of faith in order that is the crisis of modernity. It was Niemeyer's rejection of all ideological distortions of reality that motivated his advice to students to approach a text, even a text by Marx or Lenin, with an open mind and it is what makes his own analysis of ideologies, philosophical theories and concepts, social phenomena, foreign policy, international relations, etc., so lucid and grounded in common sense.

Perhaps the best way to understand the grounding of Niemeyer's political thought is with the first paragraph of Eric Voegelin's introduction to *Israel and Revelation,* originally published in 1956.

God and man, world and society, form a primordial community of being. The community with its quaternary tructure is, and is not, a datum of human experience. It is a datum of experience in so far as it is known to man by virtue of his participation in the mystery of its being. It is not a datum of experience in so far as it is not given in the manner of an object of the external world but is knowable only from the perspective of participation in it.[38]

Voegelin goes on to say that man is engaged in participation in being "with the whole of his existence, for participation is existence itself" and we have no way of being certain of the meaning of this participation, but we must play the role "as an adventure of decision on the edge of freedom and necessity."

Voegelin's insight, which is very much in harmony with the less explicitly metaphysical sense of the wholeness of reality that Niemeyer received from Heller, provided the ontological grounding for Niemeyer's analysis of the crisis of Western civilization. As someone who thought holistically Niemeyer could not discuss political problems in isolation from the loss of the sense of participation in being that gave life its order, peace, and fulfillment but also provided much less certainty than the human psyche craves. As he succinctly phrased it, "Being human is a risky business, beset on all sides with insecurities and pitfalls."[39]

As a political theorist Niemeyer was, of necessity, an ontologist who sought to regain or reawaken the consciousness of our participation in being and our essential orientation toward transcendence which has been eclipsed by ideologies. As he wrote in a letter to the editor of *Social Order* in 1961, "the central issue of the time" is one which John Hallowell, rightly "defined in these words: 'Is reality something to which ultimately all of us must conform, or is it something we make to conform to our desires?'"[40] Modernity is a crisis of consciousness in which human beings have lost the true, substantive concepts of man, God, and society through the rebellion against God and against Christianity in the eighteenth and nineteenth centuries and tried to replace them with substitute realities more pleasing to desires. Ontology was at the root of everything for Niemeyer—religion, politics, society, virtue, culture, friendship—and his later essays focus increasingly on the origins and consequences of what Albert Camus called "metaphysical rebellion." Again and again he returns to the same issues but analyzes them from a different perspective.

Niemeyer diagnosed the disorder of modernity through its primary symptom, ideologies—mainly Communism, but also Nazism, Fascism, and Liberalism. Because he lived in the midst of a Cold War that, with the invention of nuclear weapons, required charting a course between the Scylla of nuclear annihilation and the Charybdis of civilizational destruction through appeasement and surrender to Communism, Niemeyer thought and wrote extensively about the requirements of preserving as much as possible of Western civilization and freedom. Hence his reason for devoting two semesters to the study of Communist Ideology, for while Marx and Engels provided the theory neither had ever possessed the slightest political power. The second semester was given to the study of those men who did and who shaped the development of America's major Communist adversaries.

From his studies of Communism and other ideologies Niemeyer developed the concept of the "Total Critique," by which he meant that ideologies by their nature cannot accept society, religion, human beings, and reality itself as they are but must ceaselessly, and "peacelessly," wage war against all manifestations of being. Ideologies are the refusal to participate in the mysterious, already existing reality into which we are born and the insistence on replacing it with a dream world, a "Second Reality,"[41] of which the ideologist is the creator and controller and which he insists on imposing on the true reality. The Total Critique is a "total condemnation of [the] community, be it the university, the society, or the civilization as a whole," as he noted in his *National Review* article on the New Left in 1970.[42] The discontent with a society equated with evil is limitless as

> is evidenced by the multitude of sweeping descriptions of society's evil which seem to be interchangeable. Our society is simultaneously defined as a world of death, a "world of violence," of materialism, racism, constraint, a system of exploitative capitalism, oppressive materialism, a culture of repressive tolerance, oppressive consciousness, mindless power....Society amount to instituted evil.[43]

This was, of course, the view of capitalism and liberal Western societies held by Communists who wanted to replace it all with a society built upon the notion that man is becoming a purely immanent and collective being with no loftier aspirations than to labor ceaselessly in a purely material reality devoid of God, spirit, and mystery. This rejection of the ontological depths of human existence Niemeyer classified as "substantive irrationality," although he recognized that Communists could be quite pragmatically rational in developing the strategy and tactics to achieve their short-term goals.

Like Voegelin, Niemeyer understood rationality as something far more than the eighteenth-century reduction of reason to pragmatic scientific thought. He understood it to mean what Plato and Aristotle meant by *nous,* the human faculty for conscious participation in reality through openness to transcendence. Human beings exist in a relation to a transcendent God and to an immanent reality which, even with all its imperfections, manifests an order of goodness that is the necessary basis of human community and presupposition of rational discussion. Perfection cannot exist in this ineluctably imperfect world, but ideologies demand that it shall in the future, therefore flattening the psyche's tension toward a mysterious transcendence into the tension of waiting for a predicted and fully comprehensible ideal future to arrive. The denial of real possibilities in favor of "possible realities" cannot succeed in realizing the dream world but it can wreak havoc in the real world.

It was this havoc that Niemeyer resisted, regarding "conservatism" as one name for the rational man's resistance to encroaching disorder. And he was deeply concerned with the increasing disorders of American society. Many of his later essays seem on the surface to be social commentary but they are more than this, ontological analyses of the roots of disorder. For instance, the same essay on the New Left quoted above ends with a commentary on the loss of ontological substance in Western democracy, which for the past hundred years "has defined itself more and more in terms of mere procedure, progressively neglecting or even banning problems of moral and intellectual substance."[44] In fact, in the current atmosphere of rampant positivism the banning of such problems is considered to be precisely progress. The result is that those with the power to make policy decisions are often precisely the people "who have allowed the substance of order to atrophy within their souls," and "during the last thirty years [i.e., since 1940] we have allowed the basis of public rationality to erode. Unless we succeed in stopping and reversing that course, and in recovering some knowledge of 'the things that belong to our peace,' our intellectual and moral anarchy may well end in a scene strewn with corpses, waiting for a Fortinbras in full armor to enter and take over."[45] Political theory was not merely an academic discipline for Niemeyer. It was an urgent struggle to see and live according to the truth.

Liberalism was yet another ideology that represented a loss of order, truth, and genuine goodness and at its heart is the "modern idea of the Self.... It is not the only force of modernity, but culturally possibly the most widely effective one. Its effect has been to dismantle one variety of authority after another, until no kind of authority is left." It has also led to the questioning of all norms and rules "in the name of the freedom of the self, until everything seems to be permitted, or permissible, until the 'why not?' is taken as a complete and irrefutable argument."[46] Liberalism led to the "autonomous self," which was isolated from communion with God and other human beings. It also produced the modern welfare state, which he called the "mandarin state" because its swollen bureaucracy became a self-perpetuating mechanism for supplying people's wants but also for limiting their freedom. The emphasis on the autonomy of the self (not an emphasis on the soul) has led to much disorder in Western culture and society.

Probably his most succinct indictment of Liberalism can be found in his 1986 essay "Is There a Conservative Mission?" in which he lists twelve ways in which Liberals have inflicted serious harm on the culture, among which are the replacement of individualism with a mass consciousness that results in dependence on government handouts and regulations; the reduction of Christianity to the status of one "party" among others so it appears legitimate to limit it in order to protect atheism; the radical secularization of American education, "so that American children are being raised in total ignorance of the faith that informed their fathers"; moral relativism; and the substitution of the belief in progress for the human hope of salvation.[47] He considered Liberalism "essentially sentimental benevolence. Liberals are in love with their own feelings rather than the reality at which their benevolence is aiming," and therefore they are not sufficiently open to reality.[48] And he saw this closing of the mind taking over the academic world.

In a 1959 review of *Germany and Freedom: A Personal Appraisal* by James Bryant Conant he made the following observation:

> It seems that Mr. Conant has not come to grips with the problem of how a deterioration of values in the hearts and minds of people can pave the way for demonically destructive forces....A spiritually agnostic educational program aiming chiefly at factual knowledge can hardly be a "potent influence" in preventing totalitarian madness, the communist as little as the fascist variety....he does not consider the hollowness of the intellectual and moral foundations of Weimar Germany, a regime governed by men without true convictions.[49]

Clearly he believed that education needed to be grounded in spiritual truth to avoid ideological, demonic destruction and that Liberalism, which had taken over many universities, was producing a spiritual hollowness in America akin to that in Weimar Germany.

Niemeyer did not, of course, fall into the illusion that the writings of philosophers such as himself could reverse the ideological disorders of the West, but he did seem to think that the more people were made aware of what had been lost the more open they would be to restorative experiences, although he feared the necessary experiences might need to be as "soul-shaking" as those of Aleksandr Solzhenitsyn, for whom Niemeyer had boundless admiration. He frequently turned to Solzhenitsyn in essays, lectures, and reviews because in the pit of the Soviet Gulag hell he had encountered the goodness of being, grace, spirit, faith, and God. He was what the totalitarian rulers in the Soviet Union most feared, a fearless and eloquent truth-teller and witness to spiritual order, who thereby became a rival and greater authority. If someone such as Solzhenitsyn could emerge "from under the rubble" of ontological destruction in Soviet society Niemeyer hoped that such seeds of renewal as he and other like-minded persons could sow might bear fruit in the West.

Given all this it is not surprising that Niemeyer was a strong advocate of liberal arts education, but it had to be the liberal arts of the tradition and not the caricature of liberal arts education inflicted on students in much of the modern academy because of the distortions of liberal ideology. At the beginning of an unpublished paper on the Liberalism of the Academy he illuminated the hollowness of much higher education with an indictment of "the liberal masters of Academe [who] wield power with an intolerant and oppressive exclusiveness that narrows the scope of discussion, bans certain questions or subjects, prevents certain legitimate views of society and policies from being vented, closes academic positions and publications to representatives of these views, and withal enthrones Liberalism as a kind of established religion of intellectuals."[50]

He had already begun to develop his argument about what type of education should be considered liberal arts education in general but also about Christian education, as specifically open to ontology, in particular. In his 1982 essay "The Glory and Misery of Education," originally published in *The Intercollegiate Review,* he traced the decline of liberal education as the understanding of human reason declined from *nous* to the instrumental view of reason as "a practical and useful faculty, an instrument of human power" in the "quest for certainty."[51] The inner unity of liberal education gave way to a "wine-tasting approach" in which students acquire a broad but shallow fund of disconnected information, most of which is quickly forgotten. A student graduates as a "modern barbarian" who is so ignorant that his "well-nigh unlimited gullibility...puts him at the disposal of any charismatic anti-Christ. Hence the misery of education redounds to the advantage of the demagogue, the feasibility of terroristic enterprise, the power of mobs, and the disposition for dictatorship." Since such a "liberal arts education" is worse than useless because its alumni are quite oblivious to their ignorance, Niemeyer found it essential to re-win "what it was that made meaningful education possible."

Niemeyer goes back to Aristotle for the core of education in the desire to know grounded in "the experience of 'seeing' the cosmos as a whole." It is a non-utilitarian sense of wonder.[52] "Here is the concept of liberal education, the education of free men in the setting of a 'free science,' subject to nobody and to no passion." It is the participation in the *koinos,* the "reality experienced as essentially common." Without the inner substance of ontological order the shell of liberal education produces disorder, barbarism, and dissociation. Niemeyer observes that students starved of intellectual and metaphysical substance will realize this in later years when they discover that their education has not given them the tools to help them "discern the character of the time" in which they live.[53] So he designed his courses precisely to provide his students with those tools, with visions "regarding the meaning of the whole."[54] He was not advocating indoctrination but education in beliefs "carefully and systematically examined," and particularly those beliefs that recognize the mystery that we are part of a whole. This meant that it was essential that education involve the transmission, critically examined, of tradition, the "public memory" that "undergirds a common culture and political order."[55] This "piety" toward the wisdom as well as the imperfection of the past "manifests respect, love, and loyalty for everything that bears a human face, for all human questing for the ground, the end, and the way."[56]

There is also the necessity of education in Christianity, which has been "the source and center of our culture, the ultimate truth that has shaped our past and is still shaping our present, regardless of what attitude to it particular persons may have."[57] Reality is concrete and Christianity has, in historical fact, played a decisive role in shaping Western civilization which cannot, indeed, be understood without Christianity. Modern ideologies are all perversions of the Christian understanding of salvation, with the parousia located at some time in the future, rather than in eternity transcending history. Ideologies attempt to resolve the unresolvable experiential tensions "between time and eternity, nature and transcendence, the world and heaven, the sacred and the profane."[58] Positivism, progressivism, liberalism—all those theories that deny transcendent beliefs— cannot grasp the nature of totalitarian mass movements. "Likewise, the student shaped by a liberal education that knows nothing of Christianity, faith, mysteries, and 'words adequate to God' (St. Basil's definition of theology), will remain unable to grasp the nature of our time and its political pitfalls."[59] Niemeyer somewhat pessimistically concludes that "the muddle that today passes for education" will have to produce much more misery "before people begin to run after a real teacher, seize him by the hem of his overcoat, and beg him to take charge of their children."[60]

Because so many schools were dominated by liberal and even Marxist ideologues the one place where Niemeyer thought genuine higher education had a chance of surviving was in the Catholic university. In 1975 he published an essay entitled "The New Need for the Catholic University" in which he argued that this was the one kind of institution that was able to continue the "inquiry into being" that was from the medieval beginning understood as the *raison d'être* of the Western university, which embodies not only "the concept of being but,...also a philosophical realism which presupposes that there is an external world independent of the mind, and that it is intelligible."[61] Furthermore, Niemeyer analyses three necessary aspects of knowledge: analysis of concrete objects in the world, which he calls *mens;* "the wider framework of understanding, comprehending essence, grasping the whole in which objects are parts, arriving at judgments,"[62] which he calls *intellectus;* and the primary existential tending to the objects of inquiry, the desire to know, which he calls *fides* because "one cannot desire knowledge unless that which is yet unknown can be desired before it is known." The Western university traditionally combined all three.

Necessarily then the search for knowledge brings up "the problem of God," the ground of being. Using a Voegelinian analysis Niemeyer points out that "raising questions about finite things propels the mind toward raising questions about transcendence which intrudes on all knowledge as the dimension of 'the beginning,' and on all human experience as the realm of 'the beyond.'" However, since Christianity has come to be identified with a set of concepts and propositions which post-Enlightenment rationality has made difficult to believe, "enlightenment" in the West (as Niemeyer knew from personal experience) tends to mean "a personal choice to be without God and transcendence."[63] The deracinated intellect falls into subjectivity, dream worlds, and human self-salvation that were symbolized by Prometheus in the nineteenth century. In modernity the increasing human pride in the scientific and technological mastery of nature has been accompanied by "an ever-deepening erosion" in the areas of spirit, morality, and political order.

Since universities are the centers of intellectual inquiry and since they have suffered "progressive devastation" in the "substance of culture and order"[64] they have lost the ability to transmit knowledge grounded in transcendence, a loss that has infected the rest of society. However, as Nietzsche pointed out, human beings cannot go on with business as usual after the death of God because this death leaves a cosmic void that must be filled. Human beings cannot change reality, so those who deny God are impelled to produce a substitute God. So in our modern enlightened world transcendence has often been replaced by "an idolatrous worship of the historical future," by "pseudoreligions and pseudomyths,"[65] "pseudo" because they are precisely efforts to conceal rather than gain insight into the truth, and as such they "bear witness to the inescapability of transcendence." The modern ideologies have taken root in the universities' positivist environment that first arose in the natural sciences, and "this is why the university as a whole, not merely the liberal arts departments, is at the root of the hurricane which is sweeping our culture."[66]

Niemeyer believed that this ontological devastation in secular universities has created the new need for the truly Catholic university "in which the pursuit of truth and the transmission of knowledge are systematically kept open to the presupposition of a divine creation and the reliance on divine salvation."[67] Niemeyer notes that the restoration of true reason has already begun with the work of "imaginative scholars" in classical, oriental, and biblical studies, comparative religion, and political science. He quotes Niels Bohr and Werner Heisenberg as indications that even physicists have retained a glimmering of awareness of transcendence.

Niemeyer's conclusion is that because cultural renewal is not likely to take root in the decultured secular universities where anti-metaphysical prejudices are too deeply entrenched, "today's Catholic university has the potential to be a trailblazer, ahead in its encouragement of the boldest and most penetrating scholarship of our times."[68] When he wrote this Niemeyer had been a non-Catholic faculty member at Notre Dame for twenty years, and he certainly had Notre Dame in mind here. To him it was not essential for a Catholic university to have a faculty consisting entirely of practicing Catholics. What *was* essential was a faculty and an institutional atmosphere open to transcendence in the natural and social sciences as well as the liberal arts.

Four years earlier, in March of 1971, the Provost of Notre Dame, the Rev, James T. Burtchaell, C.S.C., sent a letter to eleven members of the University community informing them that the Board of Trustees had "undertaken to initiate a thorough discussion of Catholicism at Notre Dame" and asking them to share their thoughts. Niemeyer sent a three-page reply that outlined what he later published. He notes that it is becoming impossible to deny the bankruptcy of all the ideologies that substitute something—anything—for God and therefore because of its "deeply-founded respect for the essential freedom of inquiry that arises when men commit themselves to a new basic insight and the countless new vistas it offers" and its "strong tradition of the autonomy of reason under faith," and its "basic attunement to the divine ground of being and...the Incarnation as the insight into that ground...the Catholic university is the one valid prototype of the Western university." He says that he came to this conclusion because of the student revolts of the 1960s and early '70s that erupted "at the most illustrious of the positivist, scientist, reductionist universities, which served mainly to demonstrate the extent to which Godless science "amounts to the end of order, meaning, and rationality." That left the Catholic university as "our civilization's last and best hope to regain the 'things that belong to our peace.'"[69]

It will have become evident to the reader that in Niemeyer it is impossible to separate the political philosopher from the ontologist and the man of faith, but also that these cannot be divided from the teacher who Socratically cared for the souls of his students, not only for their sake but for the sake of preserving and transmitting truth to future generations. As Walter Nicgorski put it, "His example endorses Whitehead's common-sense formulation, with a nod to Plato, that 'we live as we think.'"[70] He embodied the teacher as Josef Pieper understood Aquinas the teacher as someone who has entered into a "relationship with truth, the power of silent listening to reality." The importance of silent listening became of increasing importance to Niemeyer as evidenced by his references in his late essays to the Estonian composer Arvo Pärt who abandoned his original twelve-tone serialist composition style for years of silence until a radically different kind of music began to emerge, note by note, into his consciousness.[71] Like Aquinas, Niemeyer well understood and always sought to convey to his students that real learning must be "more than a mere acquisition of material," rather a "growing into a spiritual reality which the learner cannot yet grasp as all knowledge of any depth, not only philosophizing, begins with amazement." Then "everything depends upon leading the learner to recognize the amazing qualities, the *mirandum*" of what the teacher discusses so that the learner can embark upon "the road to genuine questioning. And it is genuine questioning that inspires all true learning." Moreover, Pieper continues, the teacher does not claim to provide "comprehensive answers, but throw[s] the gates open to an infinitude of further seeking" into "a boundless unknown." The teacher educates the students in the openness to reality that is the attitude of the loving questioner, the love presupposing, of course, that the reality in which we participate is ineffably good. Aquinas was able to do this because, amidst the fierce polemics of his time, "he concentrated upon the totality of reality;…wrapped in the silence that filled the innermost cell of his soul he simply did not hear the din of polemics in the foreground;…he listened to something beyond it, something entirely different, which was the vital thing for him."[72]

Niemeyer's students characteristically found their encounter with him to be an experience of amazement, superficially at him, but really at the previously unsuspected depth of reality, beyond all the din of political argumentation and conflict, to which he introduced them. James Rhodes characterized the vocation in which Niemeyer had formed him as "wondering questioning." For Niemeyer, who strove to be the Aristotelian mature man, it was precisely the awakening of this response that was the essence of his own vocation as a teacher of political philosophy. This was also his defense of freedom and Western civilization because, "Totalitarian's ultimate enemies are those who remain aware that reality is not man-made but rooted in deep grounds, to explore which is man's wisdom, and to revere, man's nobility."[73]

Notes

NDA refers to the Archives of The University of Notre Dame. It is followed by the collection code and box/folder number. The title of the folder is also given.

1. James Rhodes, "Gerhart Niemeyer: Seeker for the Way," in *Logos: A Journal of Catholic Thought and Culture,* Vol. 10, No. 2 (Spring, 2007), 113.
2. Bruce Fingerhut, "Look for the Lift: A Biographical Essay of Gerhart Niemeyer," in "A Symposium on Gerhart Niemeyer," ed. by Michael Henry, in *The Political Science Reviewer,* Vol. XXXI, 2002, 34.
3. Quoted in Paul V. Niemeyer, *A Path Remembered: The Lives of Gerhart and Lucie Niemeyer* (Wilmington: ISI Books, 2006), 176.
4. Rhodes, 113.
5. This is certainly how Niemeyer came to think of this mystery of spirituality. For instance there is this passage in his eulogy for Russell Kirk: "[F]or eyes without ideological blinkers, a conservative is recognizable when we meet him. We intuitively prefer his company to that of liberals with their secular dogmatism. We enjoy the many facets of such a personality, the generosity of his soul, the gentility of his manners, and, seeking to look through all this to the core of his secret, we faintly taste the peace of God." "Russell Kirk and Ideology" in *The University Bookman,* Fall 1994, 38.
6. There is no substitute for reading Niemeyer, but for those who would like an introduction to his thought there is the Symposium on Gerhart Niemeyer in *The Political Science Reviewer,* Vol. XXXI (2002), 70-116. The essays were written by Bruce Fingerhut, Walter Nicgorski, Michael Henry, V. Bradley Lewis, and Gregory Wolfe. For a beginning in Niemeyer's own writings I recommend *Aftersight and Foresight: Selected Essays* (Lanham, MD, The Intercollegiate Studies Institute and The University Press of America, 1988). The biography by his son Paul is cited in note 3.
7. *A Path Remembered,* 124.
8. Niemeyer reports this in a letter dated August 2, 1978, to Herr Professor Dr. Josef Kühne at the Institut für Rechtswissenschaften in Vienna: "Er [Heller] war in England, als Hitler zur Macht kam, und ich bin im März nach Basel gefahren um ihm dort eine Warnung seines Freundes Beyerle zu überbringen, dass er nicht nach Deutschland zurückkehren sollte, da ein Haftbefehl gegen ihn vorläge." NDA, CGNM 1/22, Correspondence 1978, Letter of 8/2/78.
9. Gerhart Niemeyer, article on Hermann Heller for the *International Encyclopedia of the Social Sciences.* The quotation is taken from the typescript of the article that is in the NDA, CGNM 2/17, Heller 1963-1991, "Letter to Miss Elinor G. Barber," 2-3 of the typescript, which is attached to the letter.
10. Niemeyer, letter to Miss Elinor G. Barber of the *International Encyclopedia of the Social Sciences* regarding his article on Heller, May 22, 1964. See note 8.
11. Article on Heller, page 4 of the typescript. See note 8.
12. Gerhart Niemeyer, *Law Without Force: The Function of Politics in International Law* (New Brunswick: Transaction Publishers, 2001), xxvi. The book is dedicated "To the Memory of Hermann Heller, The Man, The Teacher, The Friend." He began writing this book in Germany in 1936. Paul Niemeyer supplies the list of his Princeton courses and the name of his first doctoral student in *A Path Remembered,* 175-176.

13. Niemeyer recorded his reminiscences of the conditions and events that precipitated his resolve to leave Germany and of his experiences as a new arrival in the United States in an unpublished essay entitled "From Europe, With Love," dated July 4, 1976, the bicentennial of American independence. (NDA, CGNM 8/04. Ancient [offprints 1940-1988]). This essay will be published in the forthcoming volume of his writings *The Loss and Recovery of Truth: Selected Essays of Gerhart Niemeyer,* ed. by Michael Henry, from St. Augustine's Press.

14. Compared with his extensive work on Communism Niemeyer wrote relatively little on Nazism. One can, however, discern something of the impact that Nazism had on him from his essay "From Europe, With Love." See note 12.

15. In a letter to William F. Buckley, Jr., dated October 16, 1993, he wrote that the acknowledgement about Kierkegaard "was no more than a light touch on my shoulder, on God's part, after which I was fully ready (and what is much more of a miracle, found Lucie fully ready) to accept God's reality." "Letter to Bill" in NDA, CGNM 1/07, Correspondence 1993. At the time they met in 1929 Lucie was an agnostic.

16. Gerhart Niemeyer, unpublished Curriculum Vitae from around 1989. Paul Niemeyer devotes chapter X (223-243) to Niemeyer's Oglethorpe years.

17. "Letter to Susan B. Little" in NDA, CGNM 2/10, Correspondence 1967. In addition to this incident he also mentioned his work in the State Department, "at a time when Eisenhower was elected president. I had supported him and voted for him. When the change of regime hit the State Department, though, it was I and not my Democratic fellow employees who was dismissed. What I am telling you is no isolated incident. I could match it with a number of similar incidents in the case of other professors who failed to join the anti-McCarthy bandwagon."

18. But his actual appointment required letters of recommendation from several respected liberals to overcome the Rev. Theodore Hesburgh's reluctance to hire him.

19. Niemeyer specifically liked the French edition of the Catechism and in his letter of October 16, 1993, advised William F. Buckley to get it.

20. "Letter to Bill," May 12, 1988. NDA, CGNM 1/07, Correspondence 1993. [This is not William F. Buckley, Jr.]

21. To one of his former students who found himself in some difficulties Niemeyer said that he would "put [his] hand in the fire" for him and no doubt many of his students could testify to his unflagging loyalty, interest, and support. I can testify that he was willing to go more than the extra mile.

22. Lest the reader derive the mistaken impression that he did little more than read and write I should point out that he was a lifelong sportsman who loved the outdoors and was an ethusiastic Notre Dame football fan, a musician who played the bass viola da gamba at chamber music evenings at his home, a frequent traveler, a man who maintained lifelong friendships and a voluminous correspondence, a priest and hospice volunteer in the latter part of his life, and, not least, a devoted husband and father of five children.

23. Yevgeny Zamyatin is the author of *We,* a scathingly and often hilarious satirical novel of collectivist society.

24. For the account of his Hillsdale College teaching I am indebted to Gregory Wolfe. For Wolfe's account of Niemeyer's interest in literature and the arts as possible sources of cultural and spiritual renewal see his essay "Discerning the Spirits: Gerhart Niemeyer as Culture Critic" in *The Political Science Reviewer* Symposium on Niemeyer, 162-182.

25. Bruce Fingerhut recalls that after his first class with Niemeyer at Notre Dame "It took another six months for me to get to know the heart of this man, to meet and love his

wife Lucie, to witness his tender care of his students (how well I remember the pained look on his face when a student, usually me, said something so untenable that only a graduate student could utter it, the face of one who had just been told mid-mouthful what lutefisk really consisted of)." Congratulatory note in *The Good Man in Society—Active Contemplation: Essays in Honor of Gerhart Niemeyer,* ed. By John A. Gueguen, Michael henry, and James Rhodes (Lanham: The Intercollegiate Studies Institute, Inc., 1989), 302. When asked how Niemeyer got students to learn Richard Bishirjian replied tersely, "fear." We all feared the pained look because we hated to disappoint him.

26. This was reported to me by Donald Roy who took the Communist Ideology course after I did. He also reported that he was the only student to sign up for the second semester of the course, so Niemeyer invited him to his home where he subjected him to a solitary and "withering cross-examination" on the material before giving him a beer to recover. It seems that for almost the first decade of his career at Notre Dame Niemeyer did not invite students to his home, but beginning with Richard Bishirjian, who arrived in late 1964 or early 1965, he began to do so. By the time I became his student it was quite common for students to visit him at home to discuss work. He occasionally held an evening class at home, although with Donald Roy it was the entire course. Students were also sometimes invited for dinner. His wife Lucie was indeed an excellent cook and hostess.

27. "Letter to Bill," May 12, 1988.

28. Niemeyer was also quite happy to have "daughters" but, at least at Notre Dame, there were very few women who took his courses. Until the early 1970s only women in religious orders were admitted to the graduate school, few of whom studied political theory.

29. Private communication from John Gueguen.

30. Speaking from my own experience, which I am sure is representative, he regularly sent letters with encouragement, praise, gratitude, warmth, support, and humor, book recommendations and newspaper clippings, and whenever he was in my vicinity he would arrange a meeting. Sometimes he sent offprints of his essays. He also recommended me for teaching positions whenever he could. When, after four years of searching for a teaching position I finally found a part-time job his congratulatory reply addressed me as "my dear colleague."

31. Congratulatory note in *The Good Man in Society: Active Contemplation: Essays in Honor of Gerhart Niemeyer,* 303-304.

32. Gerhart Niemeyer, *Between Nothingness and Paradise* (Baton Rouge: Louisiana State University Press, 1971), 194-195.

33. William F. Buckley, Jr., "Gerhart Niemeyer, R.I.P., *National Review,* 7/28/97, 16-17.

34. Gerhart Niemeyer, "Reason and Faith: The Fallacious Antithesis," in *Aftersight and Foresight: Selected Essays* (Lanham, MD, The Intercollegiate Studies Institute and The University Press of America, 1988), 237.

35. Niemeyer, "Reason and Faith," 239.

36. Gerhart Niemeyer, "Russell Kirk and Ideology," 36.

37. Gerhart Niemeyer, "Conservatism and the Modern Age," in *The Review of Politics,* Vol. 29, No. 1 (Jan. 1967), 120.

38. Eric Voegelin, *Order and History, Vol. I of Israel and Revelation* (Louisiana State University Press, 1956), 1.

39. Gerhart Niemeyer, "Reason and Faith: The Fallacious Antithesis," in *Aftersight and Foresight,* 249.

40. Gerhart Niemeyer, "Political Science Today," in *Social Order,* May 1961, 237.

41. Like Voegelin Niemeyer borrowed Robert Musil's "Second Reality" to characterize the dream worlds of ideologies.

42. Gerhart Niemeyer, "The Homesickness of the New Left," in *Aftersight and Foresight,* 51.

43. Niemeyer, "The Homesickness," 51.

44. Niemeyer, "The Homesickness," 54-55.

45. Niemeyer, "The Homesickness," 56.

46. Quoted from a lecture called "The Things Worth Fighting For" that also says "ISI East, 1981." Evidently an Intercollegiate Studies Institute lecture. NDA, CGNM 7/12, ISI 1981, "The Things Worth Fighting For, [Number] I."

47. Gerhart Niemeyer, "Is There a Conservative Mission?" in *The Intercollegiate Review,* Spring 1986, 10.

48. "Russell Kirk and Ideology," 35-36.

49. Gerhart Niemeyer, review of *Germany and Freedom: A Personal Appraisal* by James Bryant Conant, in *The Journal of Politics,* Vol. 21, No. 1 (Feb., 1959), 148.

50. Gerhart Niemeyer, "Confrontation of Opinions or Dialectical Discussion?" in NDA, CGNM 2/06, Correspondence 1971.

51. Gerhart Niemeyer, "The Glory and Misery of Education," in *Aftersight and Foresight,* 337.

52. Niemeyer, "The Glory and Misery," 340.

53. Niemeyer, "The Glory and Misery," 341.

54. Niemeyer, "The Glory and Misery."

55. Niemeyer, "The Glory and Misery," 344.

56. Niemeyer, "The Glory and Misery," 345.

57. Niemeyer, "The Glory and Misery."

58. Niemeyer, "The Glory and Misery," 347.

59. Niemeyer, "The Glory and Misery."

60. Niemeyer, "The Glory and Misery," 348.

61. Gerhart Niemeyer, "The New Need for the Catholic University," in *Within and Above Ourselves: Essays in Political Analysis* (Wilmington: The Intercollegiate Studies Institute, 1996), 244. Originally published in *The Review of Politics* 37 (October 1975), 479-89.

62. Niemeyer, "The New Need," 245.

63. Niemeyer, "The New Need," 246.

64. Niemeyer, "The New Need," 249.

65. Niemeyer, "The New Need."

66. Niemeyer, "The New Need."

67. Niemeyer, "The New Need," 250.

68. Niemeyer, "The New Need," 253.

69. "Letter to James T. Burthchaell" in NDA, CGNM 2/06, Correspondence 1971. In 1967, when Notre Dame was transferred from clerical to lay control, Niemeyer sent to the Rev. Theodore Hesburgh a letter with his views on the significance of a Catholic university. He noted the "anti-Christian pressures increasing throughout our culture" that lead to courses that promote a secular worldview. "By contrast with the demonic irrationality" of the assumptions of such secular courses, "the Christian university represents the fullest rationality of scientific inquiry in that it begins with a commitment to a Creation in which it makes sense to look for order, purpose, and goodness." Niemeyer was concerned about the "defensive appearance" of the move to lay control. "It is likely to impress people like a concession that the Christian faith in the academy is out of place, or that it has no more significance than as an inspiration to charitable conduct. It seems to grant to the

other side the all-important ontological premise." He ended by suggesting that the defensive impression be offset by "a clear initiative re-asserting the rationality of scientific inquest stemming from Christian faith." "Letter to Rev. T. Hesburgh" in NDA, CGNM 2/10, Correspondence 1967.

70. Walter Nicgorski, "Politics, Political Philosophy, and Christian Faith: Gerhart Niemeyer's Journey" in "A Symposium on Gerhart Niemeyer," 44. (Nicgorski was a colleague, not a student, of Niemeyer.)

71. I believe that Niemeyer's understanding of the importance of silence grew out of his prayer life. In a taped interview in 1995 he said, "Prayer is essentially an emptiness of ourselves with the view of having the emptiness filled by God....The basic prayer is one in which the praying person has to dismiss all the problems of his life, all the engagements in this world, all that he seeks or tries to do, all that has been done against him....There is a point then at which there is a great silence in oneself and the silence is an emptiness, and at that point sometimes you feel precisely that God is filling the emptiness, which does not occur every time, but it occurs often enough that you feel God is a living reality. And the emptiness is the only contribution that we can make to a living relation with God."

72. Josef Pieper, *Guide to Thomas Aquinas,* chapter VIII. I am indebted to James Rhodes for making me aware of Pieper's discussion of Aquinas the teacher. Rhodes gives page numbers for the quotations that he uses, but since, more technologically advanced, I am using a Kindle, I can give only the chapter number.

73. Gerhart Niemeyer, "The Reality of Totalitarian Despotism," in *National Review,* 1/4/74, 36.

Chapter 7

Ellis Sandoz as Master Teacher:
Consistent in Belief, Steadfast in Purpose
Charles R. Embry, Texas A & M University at Commerce

Introduction

Professor Ellis Sandoz, the Hermann Moyse, Jr., Distinguished Professor of Political Science at Louisiana State University and Director of the Eric Voegelin Institute for American Renaissance Studies, was born in 1931, a descendent of Swiss immigrants who came to Louisiana in 1829. He attended and received a Bachelor of Arts degree in 1951 and a Master of Arts degree in 1953 from Louisiana State University. In 1965 he received his doctorate—*Dr. oec. publ.*—under the direction of Eric Voegelin from the University of Munich. Professor Sandoz has taught political philosophy at three colleges: Louisiana Polytechnic Institute (1959–1968); East Texas State University—now Texas A & M University-Commerce (1968–1978); and Louisiana State University (1978–present).[1]

In the pasts of many teachers and political philosophers there stands an existential encounter with another philosopher and teacher, in many cases a master teacher, whose character, insight, erudition, intellect, and presence inspired the student to become who he is already. In other words, the future teacher in the present student is evoked from the encounter with the master teacher. In a sense this existential encounter gives form to the pre-existing, inchoate, unformed teacher, identifying the vocation that student and future teacher is destined to follow. This existential encounter is sometimes so "drastic" that it effects a change in the student, a change that challenges and/or inspires that student to fulfill his potential both as a teacher and as a human being. There are, of course, famous precedents for this model of the teacher-student encounter. One readily calls to mind Plato's encounter with Socrates and its result: that Plato gave up his intent to become a playwright and politician in order to live the life of a philosopher.

Near the beginning of Plato's *Gorgias,* Socrates instructs Chaerephon to ask Gorgias Who he is, thereby establishing the crucial question—the existential question—whose answer will reveal the character of the sophist Gorgias and his student, Callicles. Ultimately, the truth of character—Who a man *is*—reduces itself to the revelation of what he loves. And what he loves is revealed in those activities in which he engages, for "by his fruits ye shall know him." Socrates, in opposing the sophist and his student Callicles, now a politician and lover of power, maintains that the philosopher, in contrast, is simply "a lover of wisdom," for "Only the god is wise."

The Encounter

In 1949, Ellis Sandoz, an eighteen year old undergraduate student at Louisiana State University encountered an inspiring teacher and philosopher of remarkable character and courage, Eric Voegelin. This encounter determined the path that Sandoz would follow throughout his life and that he continues to follow today. It would sustain him through his undergraduate years and early graduate work with Voegelin, through his brief stint in the US Marines, and would lead him back to Voegelin in Munich to complete his *Dr. oec. publ.* It has continued in a massive program of publication, education in a public sphere both here in the United States and abroad, and in a legacy of fostering generations of teacher scholars.

Embedded in this encounter were two fundamental principles that would influence the young Sandoz and move him to philosophical and pedagogical avenues of exploration and discovery. The first of these was Voegelin's recognition that the primary problem of philosophy is the central human experience of transcendence: the divine-human encounter. In 2002, Sandoz recalled:

> From the time I first heard him lecture as a young undergraduate in 1949 I never doubted that Voegelin was profoundly Christian whatever the ambiguities of his formal church affiliation. It never dawned on me at the time to think otherwise, since the whole of his discourse was luminous with devotion to the truth of divine reality that plainly formed the horizon of his analytical expositions in class and of his scholarly writings as well, as I later found out. That youthful judgment was valid then and, with appropriate qualification, remains so long years later.[2]

The second, perhaps more crucial at least insofar as teaching is concerned, was the principle that the science of philosophy and its central problem of transcendence is controlled by experience. In 2004, again commenting on his encounter with Voegelin as a young undergraduate, Sandoz wrote:

> Voegelin's teaching method managed to communicate the meditative grounding of his thought. GOD was not a dirty word, and he often stressed to his secular-minded audiences that *science* is controlled by *experience*—and you can't go back of revelation and pretend that pneumatic experiences never happened. This basis of *faith* was more firmly in place in America, esp. in Louisiana where he taught for 16 years. He was always telling the "saving tale of immortality," in a variety of ways—out of a conviction that the experience of transcendence is essential to man's existence as human. This was not argued "religiously" or blandly assumed but buttressed scientifically through the facts of experience.[3]

Voegelin's openness to the horizon of human experience that includes the divine-human encounter,

> often induced students sympathetically to involve their own common sense, intellectual, and faith experiences in understanding demanding material in personal reflective consciousness, somewhat on the pattern of the Socratic imperative: "Look and see if this is not the case."[4]

The rooting of science in experience, interpreted by Sandoz as the Socratic "Look and see if this is not the case," would become the technique through which he would later invite his own students to participate in the philosophical search.

At any rate, it was this encounter that set the student, Ellis Sandoz, on the road to becoming a master teacher himself. It must be made clear, however, that this "setting on the road" is not something that is done to a student in the sense that the student is passive and the teacher is actively intending a particular path for the student. The relationship is much subtler. While the teacher's intent is certainly to persuade the student of the truth of existence in openness to all realms of reality accessible to him by virtue of his own composite nature, the persuasion itself is rooted in the ability of the teacher to evoke from the student what is already present. Concomitantly, the evocation depends upon the openness and willingness of the students to "involve their own common sense, and intellectual and faith experiences in understanding demanding material in personal reflective consciousness."[5]

The Political Philosopher

From the two fundamental principles—that experiences of transcendence are the central focus of philosophizing and that these experiences are subject to validation by every human being—flow other premises central to Sandoz's political philosophy.

In his study of Dostoevsky's Grand Inquisitor, Sandoz reminds his readers that philosophical anthropology is an essential component of political philosophy. He writes:

> it will be appropriate to recall the pertinence of anthropology and ethics to political theory. The basic connection is of the utmost simplicity. Because political science is a search (*zetema*) for the truth of things political, it is of necessity concerned with man as human and as citizen (*polites*) and with the axiological factors which give order and cohesion to the lives of individuals and communities. The science of man is anthropology, and the science of the goods which order human existence is ethics."[6]

Sandoz's anthropology is rooted in Classical Greek philosophy as confirmed, complemented, and completed by Christianity. Voegelin's discovery that in Greek philosophy there exists an element of divine revelation and that in the divine revelations of Judaism and Christianity there is an element of reason, led him to the insight that transcendence is the central problem that philosophers must explore, and that the consciousness of an embodied individual human being is the locus of the divine human encounter. It is the human being's responsibility to fulfill his nature by seeking the Good (Aristotle) or God. As Sandoz writes:

> Through spirit man actualizes his potential to partake of the divine. He rises thereby to the *imago Dei* which it is his destiny to be. The integrity of the individual human person thus conceived, with its reflective consciousness, is the spring of resistance to evil and responsive source of the love of truth.[7]

But there is, however—especially in the Christian tradition that manifests itself in the thinkers of the American Founding—a seamier side to human nature. Man may be a little lower than the angels, and above the beasts of the field, but he is also a fallen creature, and the potentialities of his higher nature—to rise "to the *imago Dei* which it is his destiny to be"—are often sacrificed to his baser nature. As Sandoz says "human beings in addition to possessing reason and gifts of consciousness are material, corporeal, passionate, self-serving, devious, obstreperous, ornery, unreliable, imperfect, fallible, and prone to sin if not outright depraved."[8]

A second and crucial element for Sandoz's political philosophy is what Voegelin called "the Platonic Anthropological Principle" or in Plato's formulation: The State is Man Writ Large. Voegelin interpreted this principle to mean that the substance of society is spiritual. This means essentially three things: that various dimensions of human nature could be more readily understood if one examined the various parts of the larger entity of the state; that the character of a particular human being could be identified by observing the part of his soul that dominated his actions and thus revealed his character; and finally that the political scientist could judge the nature and type of a particular polis by discovering what type of character was dominant in that state. From Plato's famous construction in *The Republic*—of the best form of government as the rule of the philosopher-king who embodies Reason (and represents the best human character) and the various degenerating forms of government (and thus less admirable types of humans)—we come to understand that ethics and politics are intertwined. The order of the soul is reflected in the order of the polis and the type of order/disorder that is present in a state determines the type of state. It must also be pointed out that even if the best polis of the philosopher king could be established on earth in historical time, it would always degenerate into its less ordered forms because of refractory human nature.

Plato's student Aristotle recognized that politics and ethics are intertwined and, while interested in the necessity of the philosophical search for the Highest Good—since all men act to achieve some end and that end is the *Summum bonum*, catalogued empirically the virtues of the mature man—the *spoudaios*—of Athens. In his great works on ethics and politics—the *Nicomachean Ethics* and *Politics*—he defined politics as a prudential science and thereby focused attention on the possibilities of establishing the best form of government possible given the circumstances of a particular society. Recognizing Aristotle's maxim that politics is a prudential science, Sandoz tempers his defense of the politics of truth by asserting that

> truth's blazing luminosity cannot sustain itself perfectly given the facts of refractory historical existence, not least of all the vividly attested mystery of evil. The politics of truth thereby implies some degree of prudential tempering, if it is not to succumb to perversion. It is there that the idealist becomes impatient, indignant, or even disgusted with the statesman. Compromise appears to be necessary, and this always seems an unwholesome business.[9]

Addressing the faculty at the University of Palacky, Czech Republic, Sandoz argues that "if we can acknowledge that politics is art as well as science, and that even as science it can never be more precise than its subject matter permits [Aristotle], we set foot on the road to sound government."[10]

A third element of Sandoz's political philosophy is his focus on human liberty and its corollaries: liberty under law, individual freedom, and personal responsibility. As one of his students Jeremy Mhire puts it:

> One knows two things about Ellis: Voegelin and America. How and why he reconciles the two the way he does is a question for his immense contributions to scholarship. One has the sense that Voegelin taught Ellis to see that the best of American political thought and practice opened up to, indeed was a contrib-

uting part of, the openness and true freedom that is preserved in and through western civilization.[11]

Mhire's "sense" that Voegelin enabled Sandoz to see the importance of America's historical contribution to western civilization is accurate, I think, for Voegelin saw that his establishment of the Political Science Institute at the University of Munich, provided him the opportunity to build "curriculum that had at its center the courses and seminars in classical politics and Anglo-American politics with the stresses on Locke and the *Federalist Papers*."[12]

Sandoz found in his own tradition a ready field for exploration and development. In his essay, "Reflections on Spiritual Aspects of the American Founding," he wrote that "the founding was the re-articulation of Western civilization in its Anglo-American mode."[13] In his study of this period he came to appreciate the important contributions that the itinerant preachers—in addition to the revolutionaries and constitution-makers—made to the development of a civic consciousness. He writes in "Foundations of American Liberty and the Rule of Law" that

Undergirding all of the "events" [of the Founding period] lay a concerted education of the general populace of America in the political theory and jurisprudence of liberty and rule of law that created the *civic consciousness* of citizenship essential to the formation of civil community or society and to the foundation of the nation. It seems likely to me that the origins of a national American community with a special destiny in world history lay in the work of George Whitefield and other itinerant preachers who crisscrossed the country for decades, bring the Great Awakening to America from 1739 onwards, sporadically right into the Revolutionary and constitutional periods.[14]

Forming the bedrock upon which this education of the general public was built is a Christian anthropology that articulates the experiences of having been created—Sandoz often reminds his students that "We live in a house we didn't build"[15]—and of being free beings. Introducing his anthology of political sermons of eighteenth-century America, he writes that the itinerant preachers saw

Man, blessed with liberty, reason, and a moral sense, created in the image of God, a little lower than the angels, and given dominion over the earth (Psalm 8; Hebrews 2:6-12), [as] the chief and most perfect of God's works.
    Liberty is, thus, an essential principle of man's constitution, a natural trait which yet reflects the supernatural Creator. Liberty is God-given. The growth of virtue and perfection of being depends upon free choice, in response to divine invitation and help, in a cooperative relationship. The correlate of responsibility, liberty is most truly exercised by living in accordance with *truth*.[16]

Since human beings are "flawed" creatures in addition to being free, they require governance that will assure their liberty because "among the chief hindrances to this life of true liberty is the oppression of men."[17] "The trick of poli-

tics and the demand of statesmanship," Sandoz says, in obedience to the principles of Aristotelian prudential science,

> are to embody the idea—truth and justice—in recalcitrant human reality within
> tolerable limits.... Experience—the culture of habit and the institutions avail-
> able to the society and its political leadership—is generally a limiting factor,
> but the particulars always are decisive. In fact, the plausibility of the argument
> in favor of the rule of law rather than of men always has been that law is the
> distillation of reason and justice. But men possess an element of the beast, so
> that anger and passion pervert the minds of rulers, even when they are the best
> of men. Aristotle first said this, and James Madison and the American founders
> believed him and partly based their constitutional design on separated powers
> with checks and balances on the validity of this anthropology.[18]

If we consult Professor Sandoz's students about his political philosophy we find
that they clearly understand both the content and intent of his teaching. Scott
Segrest asserts that

> Despite, or perhaps in a sense because of, the mystical overtones of Sandoz's
> treatment of spiritual foundations, he is, as Adams was, a hard-headed realist
> about human affairs, emphasizing human limitations and the human proclivity
> to vice, corruption, and, all too often, outrage. When Sandoz is hopeful, he is
> always cautiously hopeful. When he celebrates Western and American
> achievements, as he often does, his praise is almost always qualified and he
> never lets us forget the tenuousness and fragility of the hard-won benefits.
> Sandoz has no trace of Jeffersonian enthusiasm for revolutionary projects. If he
> strives to keep us in mind of transcendence, he knows, with Madison, that men
> are no angels.
>   The result of all this is a political philosophy that is at once inspirational
> and bracingly sober. I can think of no contemporary scholar who has so
> consistently struck the right balance of hope and solid common sense.[19]

Nicoletta Stradaioli, a researcher at the Eric Voegelin Institute and an advisee of
Professor Sandoz, describes his work as an "alliance of philosophy and faith, of
mind and spirit":

> By means of thorough study of the American Founding, focusing on the themes
> of liberty, liberty under law, religion and the role of classical ideas in American
> Republicanism, Professor Sandoz reveals the perennial questions of human na-
> ture. Sandoz's interpretation of the Founding Fathers' vision of political reality
> examines the Classical and Christian roots of their thinking emphasizing how
> the American Founders strengthen the notion of the individual human person as
> possessed of certain inalienable rights that are God-given in an indelibly defin-
> ing creaturely-Creator relationship. Thus, the general understanding of human
> existence hints at a human being living in truth under God. A human being's
> vertical tension toward transcendent divine reality has a horizontal form of ac-
> tion in history that is best exemplified by the American Founding political
> thought.[20]

Sandoz's encounter with Voegelin not only evoked from him his vocation, supplied the principle of experiential validation and led him to develop his own political philosophy, but also led him to overt personal commitments beyond (although consistent with) his substantive political philosophy: to embrace the Truth and to resist the Lie.

There are, however—even within Sandoz's and Voegelin's commitment to Truth—many truths within the Truth of Existence. We recall here Voegelin's principle that ordering experiences of divine-human encounters in various traditions are equivalent even if the symbolizations of these are linguistically and metaphorically different.[21] We may also note, as does Sandoz, that Voegelin often referred to Jean Bodin's caution against religious intolerance. Sandoz writes that "the insistent exclusivity of putative Christian (doctrinal) truth, Voegelin tempered with the mystic's tolerance as expressed by Jean Bodin who wrote: "Do not allow conflicting opinions about religion to carry you away; only bear in mind this fact: genuine religion is nothing other than the sincere direction of a cleansed mind toward God."[22] Finally, we must heed Sandoz's qualification and warning about Truth.

No truth is immune if dogmatically insisted upon .... Truth as grasped in human cognition is, thus, neither monolithic and doctrinaire nor comprehensive. The truths of the human realms of time and space, historical truth, must be distinguished from eternal or everlasting verity. Even under the best of circumstances, human knowledge achieves no more than representative truth grounded in the perspective of participation, and it is never the comprehensive Truth of omniscience.[23]

Sandoz's own resistance to untruth has taken two forms. First, his resistance has taken the form of research and publications that have included not only his explication of Voegelin's philosophical work, but also his own extensive work on the Anglo-American historical tradition of resisting tyranny in the name of liberty under law; the political philosophers and lawyers who buttressed and aided this struggle for freedom; the thought of the American Founders themselves; and, finally the contributions of the religious leaders of the American Founding to a civic consciousness that supported the establishment of a political system based upon the principles of liberty under law, individual freedom, personal responsibility, and constitutional limitations upon the exercise of power. Although various publications of Professor Sandoz report his findings, his collections of essays *A Government of Laws: Political Theory, Religion, and the American Founding*; *The Politics of Truth and Other Untimely Essays*; and, *Republicanism, Religion, and the Soul of America*, give ready access to the range of his research.[24]

The Teacher

Upon this extensive research he has built a second tier of resistance to untruth that is more "politically" active although educational in form. In both his classroom and in the educational conferences that he has organized, directed, and participated in he has relied upon a combination of Classical Greek, Christian, Voegelinian, and Anglo-American writings. And in both of these educational venues, the primary aim is to persuade his interlocutors of the Truth of Existence—not as he himself formulates it, but as they experience it with his help and support. The teacher-philosopher must

> ineluctably live the open quest of truth, however, as a *participant* in the In-Between or metaxic common divine-human reality: there is no Archimedean point outside of reality from which to objectively study it, nor is the leap in being or experience of the transcendent Beyond a leap out of the abiding reality of the human condition.... Thus, within the limits of possibility and persuasion, the philosopher is called actively *to resist* untruth through searching noctic critique, grounded as in Aristotle in robust common sense which is the foundation of prudential rationality and of political science itself....[25]

The teacher becomes the model of resistance to untruth, but persuasion is not a rude imposition upon the students or interlocutors to accept every word out of his mouth as absolute. Instead, the student must be invited to "Look and see if this is not the case" and thereby be included in the philosopher's search and resistance. The student must freely respond to the invitation and enter into the search for truth in a free and open exchange of ideas. As Sandoz says in his Teaching Philosophy, "true education is always self-education." The teacher cannot persuade the student to the truth, only the student can discover the truth when he truly looks into and explores his own consciousness. This mode of teaching is risky because it depends absolutely on the spiritual authority of the teacher. And the spiritual authority of the teacher must be firmly grounded in the love of the Good and the genuine respect for the individual person of each student that comes of this love. If the former is not present the latter will be absent also. Randy LeBlanc confirms that Sandoz demonstrated in his seminars his respect for students: "he allowed, in fact insisted, that students follow their own trains of thought before bringing them back to the matter at hand. He appreciated the work of philosophy, and he did not have to agree with a student's perspective in order to respect the student and his or her work."[26]

Professor Sandoz's philosophical vocation as demonstrated to him by Voegelin—"to love the Good, to serve the truth of Being in its highest dimensions, [to] live in attunement with it, and to resist untruth"[27]—inspired him to engage in a number of activities that honor the legacy of his mentor in numerous ways. While some of these activities occur outside the traditional classroom, they are rooted in the conviction that in a free society it is essential that scholars address the philosophical underpinnings of politics and that it is their obligation to encourage the development of a civic consciousness that grounds liberal democratic political systems in "self-evident truths." These activities include his organizing and leading the Eric Voegelin Society as a related group of the American Political Science Association, his conceiving and persuading Louisiana State University to establish the Eric Voegelin Institute for American Renaissance Studies, and his participation in Liberty Fund conferences.

Eric Voegelin Society

In 1985, Sandoz led the movement to found the Eric Voegelin Society. Sandoz assumed the leadership of the EVS and in his role as Secretary of the EVS, he began organizing programs that first met in 1986 in conjunction with the annual APSA convention. That initial program presented two panels. Over the intervening years since the founding of the EVS, he has organized 26 annual programs—presenting 180 panels. From 1986 through 2011 these programs have included over 400 individual scholars. Even though many of the panels and papers over the years have focused on interpreting the work of Eric Voegelin, its relation to various philosophers and religious thinkers, as well as its implications for contemporary politics, Professor Sandoz has invited all scholars who wish to discuss the philosophical dimensions of politics to submit panel and paper proposals.

Eric Voegelin Institute for American Renaissance Studies

In 1987, the Board of Supervisors of Louisiana State University, with a initial $50,000 grant from the Exxon Foundation secured by Sandoz, established the Eric Voegelin Institute for American Renaissance Studies and appointed Professor Sandoz as its Director. After the initial establishment of the Institute, Sandoz continued to raise funds—reaching an apex of $10,000 per month for a time—to support the various activities and publishing ventures sponsored by the Institute. In order to support the work of the Institute, Sandoz has continued to secure funds from benefactors—individual, corporate, and foundational. In 2009, for example, he secured for the Institute major grants from Earhart Foundation and the Hamel family totaling $40,000.[28] The bulk of the funds Sandoz has generated for the past twenty-five years has supported the varied works of the Institute, to include various publication projects as well as the sponsorship of several conferences held in Eastern European nations after the dissolution of the Soviet Union.

Eric Voegelin Institute Publishing Programs

The primary publication endeavor supported by the Eric Voegelin Institute was *The Collected Works of Eric Voegelin*. Thirty-four volumes prepared and published over more than a twenty year period, for which Sandoz served as the general editor. In addition, he also edited and wrote introductions for six volumes from 1990 to 2006.[29] Each volume of the *Collected Works* received a $5000 subvention from the EVI to support its publication for a total subvention of $170,000. Beverly Jarrett, former Director of the University of Missouri Press wrote:

> Sandoz led the editorial board and me as we laid out plans for publication of the thirty-four volume *Collected Works of Eric Voegelin*, [and] it is...appropriate to record the fact that Ellis Sandoz was the one human who worked hardest to assure that *The Collected Works* was not allowed to falter. Whether it was volume editors, translators, a dedicated publisher, or money that needed to be secured, it was Ellis Sandoz who worked tirelessly to locate those necessities.[30]

Under the leadership of Sandoz, the Institute also established two monograph series entitled *Eric Voegelin Institute Studies in Political Philosophy* (26 monographs published to date) and *Studies in Religion and Politics* (7 monographs published to date) in conjunction with the University of Missouri Press. Each of these volumes received a $2500 subvention from the Institute to support its publication for a total of $82,500 for subventions alone. The Institute also supplied monetary support for copy-editors and indexers for many of these monographs.

Eric Voegelin Institute Conference Organization, Direction, Participation, and Support

After the Soviet Union disintegrated and the Eastern European nations were liberated from Soviet dominance, Ellis Sandoz, as Director of the Eric Voegelin Institute, seized the opportunity to organize and direct conferences focusing on liberty, law, and constitutionalism in Czechoslovakia and Poland. The first of these, Anglo-American Liberty, Constitutionalism and Free Government: A Workshop on *The Federalist Papers,* was sponsored by the Institute under contract to the United States Information Agency and held in Moravia, Czech & Slovak Federal Republic in 1991. The second, Anglo-American Liberty, Constitutionalism and Free Government: John Locke and the Foundations of Modern Democracy, was sponsored by the Institute in cooperation with the Jan Hus Foundation, and held at at Palacky University, Olomouc, Czech Republic in July 1992. The third, Anglo-American Liberty, Constitutionalism and Free Government: A Workshop on *The Federalist Papers,* was sponsored by the Institute in cooperation with the Jagiellonian and Kosziusko Foundations at Jagiellonian University, Krakow, Republic of Poland in July 1992.

Eric Voegelin Institute Scholarship Program

Numerous political theory students have received Institute scholarships that supported their graduate studies. For example, from Fall, 2008 through Spring 2011, the Institute awarded $20,000 to students from the Eric Voegelin Scholar Fund and the Sidney Richards Moore Fellowship in Political Philosophy.[31] In addition, Professor Sandoz has generously supplied travel stipends for students to attend various domestic and international conferences from Institute funds.

Liberty Fund Conference Organization and Participation

Since 1985, Professor Sandoz organized for the Liberty Fund[32] twenty-seven conferences focusing on readings as disparate as classical Islamic texts, the Magna Carta, St. Augustine, St. Bonaventure, Milton, Leo Strauss, and Eric Voegelin. In addition, he organized and participated as a discussant in three Liberty Fund conferences that were held in the Czech Republic, to wit "Crisis, Liberty, and Order" in 1994, "Rule of Law, Liberty, and Civic Consciousness" in 1995, and "Montesquieu and Burke on Constitutionalism, Liberty and Human Nature" in 1996.

While these varied activities grow naturally from Professor Sandoz's encounter with Eric Voegelin and the subsequent development of his political philosophy, the most important outcome (and the reason for this essay) is what Professor Sandoz does in the classroom. Below I describe the instrumental elements—principles that he identifies as part of his teaching philosophy, readings that he requires in his courses, and the general demands that he makes upon his students—of his teaching, followed by a description of his teaching techniques and classroom presence as reported by his students.

In his Teaching Philosophy Sandoz identifies three principles as central to his teaching: "the student is the most important person in the classroom," "all education worthy of the name is self-education," and "a professor bears the name because he or she professes something, and that something is the scholarly ascertained scientific truth of the course subject-matter under discussion as the objective content of instruction." Developing the third principle he asserts that the professor must know his business and be prepared to "use all appropriate means to provoke interest, to respectfully engage the critical faculties of each and every student in class and to push them beyond their own suspected limits."[33]

Sandoz indeed makes rigorous demands upon his students: "reading sources beyond the textbook and lecture coverage, and writing analytical essays at test and exam times were (and are) required, and making an 'A' is a distinct challenge. Since I respect the material I teach, the writings we study together, I expect students to respect it also and to do their best to understand and master it."[34] The most challenging aspect of Sandoz's courses are the extensive and difficult readings. For example, the reading list of his undergraduate ancient and medieval political theory includes five dialogues by Plato; Aristotle's *Nicomachean Ethics* and *Politics*; Thomas Aquinas, *Political Ideas of*; St. Bonaventure, *Journey of the Mind to God*; Edward S. Corwin, *Higher Law Background of American Constitutional Law*; and Sir John Fortescue, *On the Laws and Governance of England*. Student grades in the course are then based upon two essay exams covering the readings and lectures and the final essay examination that is cumulative. The difficult of the reading lists and assignments however is complemented by the approaches that Sandoz takes in classes.

Fundamental to his basic approach in all his classes is his unwillingness to impose his own ideas on students. Rather, he encourages them to think through political and philosophical problems with his help and support. Angela Miceli appreciates this openness in Sandoz's teaching. She writes that "I always sensed that Dr. Sandoz put the care of students first. He has been a model of what a teacher is called to do: to serve. Ellis was never the type of self-aggrandizing professor who shoved his own opinion or ideology into his student's brains, nor did he ever demand their allegiance to his beliefs or interests."[35] Not only does Sandoz refuse to impose his own opinion on his students, he also urges them to think for themselves. Scott Robinson confirms the openness that Miceli appreciates in Professor Sandoz. He maintains that

> as far as the teacher-student classroom relationship was concerned, I did not know what Professor Sandoz's political philosophy was, precisely because Professor Sandoz was encouraging me to develop my own political philosophy: to think through political issues on my own and not become an ideological drone. Of course, his appreciation for classical philosophy, the truth, reasonableness, etc, could not be missed. It is, however, his *open-minded* appreciation for these ideals that is most note-worthy.[36]

And even though Sandoz often uses Voegelin's work in courses he does not impose his own interpretations of Voegelin or Voegelinian interpretations of other texts on his students. As one of his students, Glenn Moots, notes: Sandoz "would not only abide non-Voegelinian readings of texts, he assigned texts that Voegelin himself considered unoriginal or even dangerous and taught students to appreciate the virtues of those texts…. He wasn't interested in transmitting a Voegelinian orthodoxy."[37]

Although Sandoz is certainly committed to teaching the core texts of western civilization, the students recognize that he also respects other traditions that contribute to the development and sustenance of civilizational and social order. Former student Alan Baily recounts his experience of Sandoz's response to the events of September 11, 2001.

> In the spirit of Voegelin's dictum that "science" is whatever sheds light on the phenomena in question, Professor Sandoz could always be counted on to pursue fruitful, and often unexpected parallels and comparisons, across history and cultures, motivated by the quest to understand history, and the present, under the aspect of the human condition, *sub specie* aeternitatis. This philosophical generosity is all too rare in our time, when the prevailing fashion among intellectuals dictates that sympathy for other traditions necessitates the rejection of one's own, or worse, as among some "conservatives," such sympathy is taken for a sign of weakness or irresolution. A defining example of Professor Sandoz's philosophical sympathy was his decision to offer a seminar on Islamic political thought just after the terrorist attacks of September 11th, 2001….Rather than pore over radical propaganda, students became acquainted

with much of "the best that has been thought and said" in Islamic thought, from Averroes and Avicenna, to Ibn Khaldun.[38]

Sandoz uses various techniques and approaches in his teaching in order to persuade his students to participate in the philosophical conversation that has gone on through the ages and continues today. In one setting he may resort to a hortatory style of lecture that mirrors that of a Baptist preacher (as one student notes) while in another setting his approach will be to encourage a student who has genuine doubts about a particular philosophical position to pursue her own thinking. In another instance he may encourage a student to study with a colleague at a different university. John Baltes reports his formative experience in class in response to the first technique.

> At the end of a lecture on Plato/Voegelin…Sandoz projected an aura of earnestness and gravity even the ordinarily earnest and grave sage did not usually possess. He gripped the lectern fiercely and pronounced—I can't forget this—that "the price of 'progress' is the loss of one's soul." Each word was punctuated by his hand pounding the podium. My eyes were opened; I don't say this lightly.
>   This was the moment when I was "released and suddenly compelled to stand up, to turn [my] neck around, to walk and look up toward the light." I am neither a Voegelinian nor a Platonist…thus I wouldn't use the language of "truth" to describe what was going on (though it seemed to me at the time to be a question of truth), but the metaphor of chain-breaking and liberation perfectly captures my experience of it. *I was free.* I understood Plato, then, as a liberator from superstition, sloppy thinking, custom, habit, power—Sandoz had peeled back the curtain on a "higher, transcendent" world that shimmered with beauty and verity and possibility. Philosophy didn't demand faith; it demanded questions. I was positively enamored of philosophy from that point forward, though my understanding of it has changed considerably. Nevertheless, this was as close to a moment of conversion as I can imagine.[39]

What can evoke such a powerful existential response from a student? Baltes continues with his own assessment of Sandoz as a teacher and as a philosopher, which to a large extent answers the question of what makes Professor Sandoz a master teacher. He asserts

> [it] was less a question of *style* or *teaching philosophy* and more an issue of substance and a Socratic harmony between his words and deeds. I had the sense I still have the sense—that Sandoz *is* what he *says*, that his life is governed by the ideals he holds and teaches, that there is no space between the virtuous, noble, and beautiful ideas he holds and how he lives. In him, they are "inwardly digested, evident in the fine wool they produce." The power and authority conferred by this harmony is stunning; it was akin to studying with Aristotle or Socrates or Epictetus. Here was a man who was the incarnation of his philosophy, a man whose deeds were living proof of his virtue; I could sense this immediately.[40]

In a different vein, Randy LeBlanc writes of his own experience of Sandoz's teaching and its impact on his personal development. He says:

> After getting my philosophical legs under me, I realized that there were deep difficulties in Voegelin's perspective for me. Professor Sandoz allowed me to challenge myself by challenging the Voegelinian perspective. Knowing I was serious, that I was not rejecting anything, but merely challenging what I perceived as weaknesses, Professor Sandoz took on my challenges. He took them seriously, often quite gently, and allowed me to develop intellectually in a way others might not have. As a result, Professor Sandoz demonstrated how a teacher handles difference or dispute to the best effect. This pedagogical lesson has been critical in my development as a teacher, a mentor, and a scholar.[41]

On Sandoz's advice Scott Robinson after earning his MA under Sandoz pursued his PhD with Don Lutz, a close friend of Sandoz at the University of Houston. He remembers:

> Although Lutz is decidedly more liberal than Sandoz, he approached the philosophy of politics with the same common sense attitude that I had grown fond of in Sandoz. A really interesting aspect of their friendship is that they probably do not agree on a tremendous amount when it comes to policy; they share a common sense methodology regarding political philosophy, and it is this, not the politics of either man, that make them both admirable professors of political philosophy and good, decent men. (The reason for Eric Voegelin's disdain for ideology is clear after studying under both of them: intelligent individuals can indeed disagree about policy specifics without either of them being foolish or pig-headed; this is too easily overlooked in American society these days.)[42]

And finally, there is the report from Angela Miceli that demonstrates Sandoz's willingness to tolerate dissent with a genuine respect for students. Angela recalls that "after a student animatedly and rudely told him he was wrong, [Sandoz replied:] 'Well, I could be wrong, you know, but I don't think so.'"[43]

Sandoz consciously uses the rigor of his courses to challenge students to work up to their full potential. As Scott Segrest remarks "the first thing that leaps to mind about Sandoz's teaching philosophy is his evident view that if he made high demands of his students, they would rise to meet the challenge."[44] Many students have risen to the challenge and report that if you performed well, "he could make you feel like a million bucks."[45] He seems to have the capacity as a teacher to make almost impossible demands of his students and then joyfully to acknowledge excellent work turned in by students who exceed their own expectations. Scott Robinson recalls both how Sandoz encouraged him to produce better work and then on a later occasion recognized that work.

> He was by no means an easy professor. On the occasions when I turned in less than acceptable work, it was made abundantly clear to me, both through the grade, written comments, and facial expressions that Sandoz knew I could do better and that he expected better of me. These occasions were perhaps too fre-

quent, but in contrast I remember one occasion in particular, when I wrote an especially good final exam; he called me into his office just to tell me that he was proud of the paper, and his facial expressions said a lot on that occasion too. I do not think he was proud of any particular insight. He was, instead, proud of the hard work and extra library hours I spent on that particular paper. He taught me a tremendous amount about the value of hard work.[46]

Many former and current students, while acknowledging Sandoz's rigor, also experience him as a tolerant and compassionate teacher who is genuinely concerned for each individual student. One doctoral student, Todd Myers, remembers that Sandoz "lit into him" about how bad the rough draft of his dissertation was. Todd admits that "I was a bit emotionally shaken but had to agree. The dissertation was a spiritual journey for me and I guess I had hit the point of the dark night of the soul. He then shifted gears to find the merits of the work and gave me some direction on how to make it a better piece of work. I later came to discover he was tough with all of his graduate students. Ellis was tough but compassionate."[47]

Over the fifty-two years of his teaching career, students have responded to Sandoz's demands by committing themselves to demonstrate to him that they can excel on his assignments. One former pre-law student, Steve Cowan, recalls that in his first class with Sandoz, he earned a B+. Since this grade did not fulfill his own desire to make As in order to bolster his chances of being admitted to law school, he signed up for Russian Political Theory in order to prove to himself and Sandoz that he could make his A. After doggedly studying all the texts, class lectures, and suggested readings, after reciting the whole course back to Sandoz, he had written 20 pages in pencil (because he could write faster) and only finished the first of two required essays. He was sure that he had blown his chances for an A. Forty years later he remembers:

When Dr. Sandoz came in with the graded papers, he told the class that he didn't give A plusses, but if he did, he would have given one this time. I received my test back with an A in red pencil at the top with one word written on the paper, "Able." Just A-B-L-E. That one word comment from a teacher I admired has stuck in my brain for 40 years. I have used it to encourage my sons and even used it to describe a retiring judge after a long and distinguished career.

I suppose he knew I could have answered question two if I had managed my time better. In the margin, he wrote "next time don't use a pencil."[48]

Although Sandoz does not overtly acknowledge that he is in the business to help students "complete the building of their souls,"[49] the students recognize that his teaching addresses the spiritual dimensions of their individual humanity and that he is genuinely concerned that they live good lives. Nicoletta Stradaioli writes that "Professor Sandoz highlights a responsible personal way of living and the moral and political principles (human dignity, morality of liberty and justice...) that an individual has to accomplish for an ordered societal existence."[50] Todd Myers emphasizes that the material he brought to class was existentially significant. It was meant to engage the learner in the process of soul building. If I understand his role as teacher correctly, his understanding of a liberal education was to equip people for the spiritual journey of a human life while meeting the material needs of that life. Completely balanced ...That is the mark of a great teacher.[51]

Alan Baily points out that Sandoz's conception of liberal education

> has its roots in the classical understanding according to which education is a work of character development—a *paideia*—that intends both material and spiritual dimensions of reality and addresses itself to human existence: a complex whole in which the experience of intersecting realities of God, man, world and society give rise to variegated symbols pregnant with human significance.... For Sandoz, Liberal education is humanistic education; and the common thread of humanity, far from being the mere drive for self-preservation and material comfort, is the "knowing questioning and questioning knowing" of conscious beings sensitive to human experience between the poles of immanence and transcendence.[52]

David Whitney observes that Sandoz's teaching method, following Aristotle, begins "with common opinions about the topics covered and tries to move the student beyond those opinions to get at the truth of the matter [and] he is adamant about the importance of 'checking' reason with experience. The two must go together. Citing Socrates, he always implores the students to "'look and see if it's the case.' In other words, check your own experience."[53]
Paideia, of course, is dependent upon persuading the students to become active members in their own education by inviting them, as well as often reminding them, to check the ideas found in their texts or discussed in class against their own experience. When students are invited to "Look and see if this is not the case" they know at an experiential level that they too can become participants in "the great dialogue that goes through the centuries among men about their nature and destiny."[54] Jeremy Mhire observes that Sandoz's "teaching philosophy involves getting students to see for themselves what is, and what is not, worth preserving. That includes acquiring a vast acquaintance with canonical texts, as well as an ever-deepening understanding and appreciation of history."[55] This is a very powerful and liberating experience for students know that they are engaged for a lifetime in the work that Sandoz has invited them into. As Scott Robinson recalls

> I had and still have the impression that Sandoz cares more about the well being of his students than he cares about any idea in particular; this is a healthy and hopefully infectious state of mind. If Sandoz's students teach their students the way that Sandoz taught us...well, if one follows this train of thought through, one cannot help but to see the tremendous potential good to be wrought from Professor Sandoz's character and efforts.[56]

Angela Miceli experiences Sandoz's teaching as joyful guidance through complex and difficult readings. She writes that he "has a way of making the truth very relatable to common human experience, and yet he is guided by the highest mystic thinkers and writers. He encourages students not to fear engaging these thinkers and joyfully guides them through texts to discover the truth about what it means to be a human person living in the world."[57]

Not only does Sandoz guide his students through difficult texts, but he also demonstrates the significance of the formative effects of the classical works of western civilization in his own life. One student from the 1970s, in an unsolicited message sent to Sandoz in 2008 wrote:

> When I was in college I did not attend church regularly, but one Sunday I attended First Baptist Church in Commerce and you were there. I don't know anything about your religious beliefs then or now, but your presence at church said a great deal to me. It said that if a man with a mind and an education like Dr. Sandoz can have a place for God in his life, then I, too, can have a healthy life of both the mind and the spirit.[58]

Finally, it is the existential commitment of Professor Sandoz that impresses upon his students the *essential* importance of philosophy, understood as the love of wisdom, of the Good, of God, for both personal and social order. Indeed, it is from the integration in his person of Classical Greek Philosophy and Christianity, a union taken to heart from the example of his own teacher in 1949, that students learn they too can "have a healthy life of both the mind and spirit."

Select Bibliography of Published Works by Ellis Sandoz

A Government of Laws: Political Theory, Religion and the American Founding. Baton Rouge: Louisiana State University Press, 1990. 2d revised ed. Columbia: University of Missouri Press, 2001.

Conceived in Liberty: American Individual Rights Today. North Scituate, Massachusetts: Duxbury Press, 1978.

Political Apocalypse: A Study of Dostoevsky's Grand Inquisitor. Baton Rouge: Louisiana State University Press, 1971. 2d revised edition. Wilmington, Delaware: ISI Publications, 2000.

Political Sermons of the American Founding Era, 1730-1805. Editor with introduction and annotations. Indianapolis: Liberty Press, 1991.

Republicanism, Religion and the Soul of America. Columbia: University of Missouri Press, 2006.

The Roots of Liberty: Magna Carta, Ancient Constitution, and the Anglo-American Tradition of Rule of Law. Editor and Introduction. Columbia: University of Missouri Press, 1993.

The Voegelinian Revolution: A Biographical Introduction. Baton Rouge: Louisiana State University Press, 1981.

Volumes of The Collected Works of Eric Voegelin *edited by Ellis Sandoz.*

Voegelin, Eric. *Autobiographical Reflections.* Revised, with a Voegelin Glossary and Cumulative Index. Edited by Ellis Sandoz. Vol. 34 of *The Collected Works of Eric Voegelin.* Columbia: University of Missouri Press, 2006. [Note: *Autobiographical Reflections* results from a series of interviews Sandoz conducted with Eric Voegelin about his work in 1973.]

———. *Hellenism, Rome, and Early Christianity.* Edited with introduction by Athanasios Moulakis. Vol. I of *History of Political Ideas.* General Introduction to the Series by Thomas Hollweck and Ellis Sandoz. Vol. 19 of *The Collected Works of Eric Voegelin.* Columbia: University of Missouri Press, 1997.

———. *In Search of Order.* Edited with introduction by Ellis Sandoz. Vol. V of *Order and History.* Vol. 18 of *The Collected Works of Eric Voegelin.* Columbia: University of Missouri Press, 2000.

———. *Published Essays, 1940-1952.* Edited with introduction by Ellis Sandoz. Vol. 10 of *The Collected Works of Eric Voegelin.* Columbia: University of Missouri Press, 2000.

———. Published Essays, 1953-1965. Edited with introduction by Ellis Sandoz. Vol. 11 of *The Collected Works of Eric Voegelin.* Columbia: University of Missouri Press, 2000.

————. *Published Essays, 1966-1985.* Edited with introduction by Ellis Sandoz
and epilogue by Jürgen Gebhardt. Vol. 12 of *The Collected Works of Eric
Voegelin.* Baton Rouge: Louisiana State University, 1990.

Notes

1. *Acknowledgments and a Note on Sources.* Professor Sandoz was kind enough
to send me a wealth of information to include: a list of all the graduate students whose
theses and/or dissertations he directed, students' narrative responses from various course
evaluations, course syllabi, a copy of his Teaching Philosophy, a copy of the 2010 Report
of the Eric Voegelin Institute to the administration of Louisiana State University, copies
of e-mails or letters sent to him by former students, and a copy of his Curriculum Vitae
that includes his various teaching-related activities in addition to a bibliography of his
publications. Much of this information was already known by me (especially his publications, his work with the Eric Voegelin Institute at LSU, and his work with the Eric
Voegelin Society), but to have it in a consolidated form and in one place was quite helpful. Steve Ealy, Senior Fellow, Liberty Fund, Inc., graciously answered my questions
about Liberty Fund conferences and supplied me with a list of the Liberty Fund Conferences that Professor Sandoz conceived and organized. Information describing Sandoz's
teaching—its nature and impact with illustrations —was solicited from former students in
the form of "interviews." These "interviews" consisted of sending six open-ended ques-
tion-prompts to his students asking them to respond in writing and e-mail these responses
back to me. In addition to those responses solicited by me from his students, Professor
Sandoz sent me several unsolicited "testimonials" sent to him by former students. I would
like here to acknowledge and thank all of the students of Sandoz who responded to my
questionnaire for their thoughtful, insightful, and extensive narratives. Even though I
have not been able to use all of the material they generously supplied to me, all of the
responses contributed to what, I hope they will agree is an accurate portrait of their
teacher. Finally, I thank my wife, Polly Detels, for her invaluable help in revising and
editing this essay for publication. Of course, all the mistakes and missteps that squeak
through remain my responsibility.
2. Ellis Sandoz, "Carrying Coals to Newcastle: Voegelin and Christianity," 1.
Voegelin and Christianity: A Roundtable. American Political Science Association and
Eric Voegelin Society, Annual Meeting, Boston, August 30, 2002. Accessible at
http://www.lsu.edu/artsci/groups/voegelin/society/. A slightly revised version of this
paper appears in Ellis Sandoz, *Republicanism, Religion, and the Soul of America.* (Columbia: University of Missouri Press, 2006), 114-120.
3. Ellis Sandoz, "Eric Voegelin as Master Teacher: Notes for a Talk," 2-3. Roundtable Discussion, American Political Science Association and Eric Voegelin Society,
Annual Meeting, Chicago, September 4, 2004. Emphasis in original. Accessible at
http://www.lsu.edu/artsci/groups/voegelin/society/.
4. Ellis Sandoz, "Eric Voegelin as Master Teacher: Notes for a Talk," 2-3.
5. Ellis Sandoz, "Eric Voegelin as Master Teacher: Notes for a Talk," 2-3.
6. Ellis Sandoz, *Political Apocalypse: A Study of Dostoevsky's Grand Inquisitor.*
(Wilmington, DE: ISI Books, 2000), xvii-xviii.
7. Sandoz, "Carrying Coals," 2.

8.   Ellis Sandoz, "The Politics of Truth," in Ellis Sandoz, *Politics of Truth and Other Untimely Essays: The Crisis of Civic Consciousness* (Columbia: University of Missouri Press, 1999), 39.

9.   Sandoz, *The Politics of Truth*, 38.

10. Sandoz, *The Politics of Truth*, 40.

11. Jeremy Mhire (student 2000-2006), personal e-mail communication to me, July 25, 2011.

12. Quoted by Sandoz, "Eric Voegelin as Master Teacher," 2.

13. Ellis Sandoz, "Reflections on Spiritual Aspects of the American Founding," in *A Government of Laws: Political Theory, Religion, and the American Founding*, (Columbia: Unversity of Missouri Press, 2001), 151.

14. Ellis Sandoz, "Foundations of American Liberty and Rule of Law," in *Republicanism, Religion, and the Soul of America* (Columbia: University of Missouri Press, 2006), 57.

15. Joshua Deroche (present student), personal e-mail communication to me, November 28, 2011.

16. Ellis Sandoz, ed. Foreword. *Political Sermons of the American Founding Era, 1730-1805.* Volume 1. (Indianapolis: Liberty Fund, Second edition, 1998. Foreword, 1991), xvii-xviii.

17. Ibid., xvii.

18. Ellis Sandoz, "The Politics of Truth," 39.

19. Scott Segrest (student 1998-2005), personal e-mail communication to me, July 26, 2011.

20. Nicoletta Stradaioli (researcher and advisee at Eric Voegelin Institute 2001; 2005-2008), personal e-mail communication to me, July 23, 2011.

21. Eric Voegelin, "Equivalences of Experience and Symbolization in History," in volume 12, *Published Works, 1966-1985*, ed. with introduction Ellis Sandoz, *Collected Works of Eric Voegelin*, (Baton Rouge: Louisiana State University Press, 1990), 115-133.

22. Sandoz, "Carrying Coals to Newcastle," 8.

23. Sandoz, "Politics of Truth," 40.

24. See attached Selected Bibliography of Published Works by Ellis Sandoz.

25. Sandoz, "The Philosopher's Vocation: The Voegelinian Paradigm," *Review of Politics* 71 (2009), 57. Emphasis in original.

26. Randy LeBlanc (student 1993-1997), personal e-mail communication to me, July 22, 2011.

27. Ellis Sandoz, "Mysticism and Politics in Voegelin's Philosophy," American Political Science Association and Eric Voegelin Society, Annual Meeting, Toronto, Ontario, Canada, September 4, 2009. Accessible at http://www.lsu.edu/artsci/groups/voegelin/society/.

28. Summary Report of Activities, Eric Voegelin Institute 2009 as Updated for 2009-2010, 2.

29. See attached Selected Bibliography of Published Works by Ellis Sandoz for specific volumes.

30. Beverly Jarrett, "Publisher's Note," in Charles R. Embry and Barry Cooper, eds., *Philosophy, Literature, and Politics: Essays Honoring Ellis Sandoz*, (Columbia: University of Missouri Press, 2005), vii.

31. Summary Report of Activities, Eric Voegelin Institute 2009 as Updated for 2009-2010, 4.

32. The Liberty Fund Foundation, founded by Pierre F. Goodrich in 1960, sponsors small scholarly conferences that include participants from various occupations and aca-

demic disciplines to include economics, history, law, political thought, literature, philosophy, religion and the natural sciences. Mr. Goodrich who read widely in the Great Books tradition believed "that education in a free society requires a dialogue centered in the great ideas of civilization. He saw learning as an ongoing process of discovery, not limited to traditional institutional settings or specific ages." These conferences are organized to promote Goodrich's conviction "that the best way to promote the ideal of a society of free and responsible individuals is through [a] full and open [Socratic] discussion among people of varying ages, backgrounds, and occupations." This information was accessed at the Liberty Fund, Inc. site (http://www.libertyfund.org here) on various days, the last being December 7, 2011.

33. Ellis Sandoz, "Teaching Philosophy," October 2007.

34. Ellis Sandoz, "Teaching Philosophy," October 2007.

35. Angela Miceli (student 2005-2011), personal e-mail communication to me, July 25, 2011.

36. Scott Robinson (student2002-2006), personal e-mail communication to me, June 17, 2011. Emphasis in original.

37. Glenn Moots (student 1991-1993; 2000-2001), personal e-mail communication to me, June 17, 2011.

38. Alan Baily (student 1999-2003), personal e-mail communication to me, July 20, 2011.

39. John Baltes (student 1994; 1998-2002), personal e-mail communication to me, July 17, 2011. Emphasis in original.

40. Ibid. Emphasis in original.

41. Randy LeBlanc (student 1993-1997), personal e-mail communication to me, July 22, 2011.

42. Scott Robinson (student 2002-2006), personal e-mail communication to me, June 17, 2011.

43. Angela Miceli (current student), supplied as a supplement to her personal e-mail communication to me, July 25, 2011.

44. Scott Segrest (student 1998-2005), personal e-mail communication to me, July 26, 2011.

45. Sam Whitley (student 1970-1972), personal e-mail communication to me, June 17, 2011.

46. Scott Robinson (student2002-2006), personal e-mail communication to me, June 17, 2011.

47. Todd Myers (student 1992-1997), personal e-mail communication to me, July 17, 2011.

48. Steve Cowan (student, 1971-1972), personal e-mail communication to me, November 28, 2011.

49. Werner Dannhauser, "On Teaching Politics Today," *Commentary*, March 1975, 74.

50. Nicoletta Stradaioli, Universitiy of Perugia (researcher and advisee at Eric Voegelin Institute 2001; 2005-2008), personal e-mail communication to me, July 23, 2011.

51. Todd Myers (student 1992-1997), personal e-mail communication to me, July 17, 2011.

52. Alan Baily (student 1999-2003), personal e-mail communication to me, July 20, 2011.

53. David Whitney (student 2004-2010), personal e-mail communication to me, July 17, 2011.

54. Eric Voegelin in a letter to Robert B. Heilman, August 22, 1956a, in Charles R. Embry, ed. *Robert B. Heilman and Eric Voegelin: A Friendship in Letters, 1944-1984* (Columbia: University of Missouri Press, 2004), 157.

55. Jeremy Mhire (student 2000-2006), personal e-mail communication to me, July 25, 2011.

56. Scott Robinson (student 2002-2006), personal e-mail communication to me, June 17, 2011.

57. Angela Miceli (student 2005-2011), personal e-mail communication to me, July 25, 2011.

58. A copy of this e-mail message was supplied to me by Ellis Sandoz. I have withheld the name of this person because my attempts to contact him have been unsuccessful.

Chapter 8

John H. Hallowell: Principled Pragmatist
Timothy Hoye, Texas Women's University

John H. Hallowell (1913–1991) was born thirteen years into the twentieth century and died nine years short of its end.[1] In the course of his life, he witnessed, as a diligent, scholarly observer of politics, history, and philosophy, the rise and demise of unprecedented totalitarian forms of government in the heart of Europe, a New Deal approach to government and a long delayed civil rights movement, to which he was committed, in the United States, two world wars, the beginnings of a nuclear age, a cold war between competing ideologies, numerous shifts and turns in domestic and global politics, economics, and civilizational dynamics, and profound changes both in his discipline and in higher education in general, changes which deeply threatened what Hallowell called, in a letter to Dean Ernestine Friedl on September 10, 1981, his "rather old-fashioned view" of his professional duties (Hallowell Papers, Box 6). Hallowell taught political philosophy at Duke University for almost forty years. He also taught, at various times, at UCLA, Stanford, Munich, the University of Illinois, Stetson University, and, as a Fulbright exchange scholar, at the University of South Wales in Australia. Despite an early reputation for outstanding scholarship, he always considered teaching his primary professional responsibility and consistently held his students in the highest regard. This is perhaps best illustrated by his dedication of *Main Currents in Modern Political Thought* to "My Students Past and Present." Toward the end of his long tenure at Duke he wrote to Dean Friedl again, on September 15, 1981, as follows: "I entered this profession because I wanted to teach. In my opinion a university consists of teachers and students primarily. I have always considered teaching my first and most important responsibility" (Hallowell Papers, Box 6). This, however, was written in frustration. He could not understand how his department chair and colleague seemed to dismiss the importance of teaching. As he had expressed it in his earlier letter to the Dean, of September 10: "It does come to me as something of a surprise to learn that teaching is not considered by my department chairman to be all that important. I would have thought it was the most important activity in which a professor could be engaged" (Hallowell Papers, Box 6). For Hallowell, political philosophy was centered in the teaching and guiding of students. This always came first.

Early in his career, in 1951, as further illustration that his primary concern was with teaching, are his comments on "Goals for Political Science," a report of the American Political Science Association's Committee for the Advancement of Teaching. There, Hallowell expressed substantial concern with much of what the committee had reported on the subject of education, particularly education to citizenship. It was "parochial in the extreme." Among his largest concerns was an emphasis in the report on education as participation in the political process. Hallowell raised the question as to whether "the only effective way to understand politics is to participate in it." This view, for Hallowell, is "fallacious." Rather, one "learns to think by thinking, as he learns to evaluate by evaluating and no amount of 'practical' observation or participation will teach him automatically how to do either." The textbooks of "our greatest statesman," he continued, "were the classics and moral philosophy figured prominently in their education." The educational process, for Hallowell, is "a mutual search for truth." In this mutual search, students, with respect to their professors, should "be encouraged to take issue with him when they feel so inclined and be free always to reject his judgments, as well as to accept them if they find them sound." The goal of the political scientist, of the political philosopher, of the scholar, of the student, inside and outside of the classroom, is "practical knowledge of the best means of promoting justice among men" (Fesler 1951, 1005–1010).

Hallowell was sharply critical of the mainstream in his discipline, a position but symptomatic of a far larger concern with what he called the "crisis of our times" (Hallowell 1950, viii). Among Hallowell's greatest contributions to the discipline of political science and, indeed, higher education in the United States, is his role in making the works of émigré scholars, escaping fascism in Europe, better known within his profession, among his students, and across academia in general. Few scholars have had a greater impact on their discipline than this group of émigrés from pre-World War II Europe who came to America and challenged political scientists here in their most basic assumptions. These émigré scholars, as they have come to be called, brought a more philosophical approach to the study and teaching of political science compared to a mainstream approach rooted in a positivist tradition within what Bernard Crick has called the "American science of politics" (Crick 1959). Among these scholars are Leo

Strauss, Hans Morganthau, Carl Friedrich, Eric Voegelin, Hannah Arendt, Theodor Adorno, Herbert Marcuse, Arnold Brecht, and Max Horkheimer, among many others, scholars whose students today teach, or have taught, and whose students in turn teach at America's leading universities. According to one scholar, it was Hallowell "whose work would become one of the principal conduits through which the ideas of the émigrés entered political theory and whose voice would come to represent the new mood in the field" (Gunnell 1988, 75).

In his tribute to Hallowell, published in the *Political Science Reviewer*, former student Walter B. Mead wrote that Hallowell "devoted his attention for some four decades to formulating a critique of modernity, informed by a fundamental commitment to classical concepts and principles, Greco-Roman as well as Judeo-Christian" (Mead 1994, 5). More than four decades earlier, in his response to the publication of Hallowell's first book, *The Decline of Liberalism as an Ideology,* theologian Reinhold Niebuhr wrote, in a letter to Hallowell dated March 2, 1944: "I think you have made a real contribution, particularly in your distinction between the early liberalism and its later corruption" (Hallowell Papers, Box 1).[2] Hallowell knew, from his earliest days as an undergraduate at Harvard, that at the heart of "modernity" was the rise of ideological politics and that any critique of the modern age, or the modern study of politics, would have to focus on the rise and decay of political movements rooted in ideological styles of thought. His Master's Thesis at Duke was a lengthy study of *The German National Chamber of Culture* established in September, 1933, only eight months after Hitler came to power in Germany, and directed by Joseph Goebbels. In his dissertation at Princeton, two years later, Hallowell argued that National Socialism in Germany was the product of a decadent liberalism, a point of view upon which he expanded in his first book. His dissertation adviser, émigré scholar Gerhart Niemeyer, wrote the following in a letter to Hallowell on July 5, 1943, upon publication of the book: "...the complicity of decadent liberalism to the growth of fascist ideas has often been asserted, but never been proved in any book accessible to English readers" (Hallowell Papers, Box 1).

To counter "decadent liberalism," Hallowell labored throughout his long, distinguished career to articulate the principles of political philosophy in the classical and Judeo-Christian traditions, with particular dedication to the works of Plato, Aristotle, St. Augustine, and Thomas Aquinas. He deplored labels. But on at least three occasions he chose to position himself, once early in his career in response to an inquiry from Arnold Brecht, in 1946, once late in his career in response to a request from a student in class, and in his lectures on the moral foundation of democracy at the University of Chicago. In the first instance, in a letter to Brecht of November 23, 1946, he wrote that his position was "essentially that of the Christian humanist and it is that position I shall seek to defend" (Hallowell Papers, Box 4). In the second instance, after a considerable pause, he replied to the student: "principled pragmatist." Yet, drawing on the work of John Wild in his Walgreen Lectures in the spring of 1952, Hallowell positioned himself as a "classical realist:" "My argument will rest upon what might be called the principles of classical realism, principles that commend themselves to common sense." He proceeded to summarize these principles as including the view that there is a "meaningful reality" a "cosmos, not a chaos," the existence of which not depending on our knowledge of it; that human beings are "endowed" with the capacity to discover meaning in this cosmos, however dimly; and that "being and goodness belong together," that those qualities essential to the development of a good person are "identical" to those that make "life in society possible" (Hallowell 1954a, 22, 23). Hallowell never expounded in a lengthy work a fuller view of his epistemological first principles. He did, however, maintain a consistency within the broad outlines of classical realism above sketched. It is important to stress that classical realism, for Hallowell, included the wisdom found in Christian classics, such as by "St. Augustine, St. Clement of Alexandria, St. Thomas Aquinas, Luther, Calvin, Richard Hooker, and others" (Hallowell 1956, 22) and more contemporary Christian humanists, among whom being C. S. Lewis, Reinhold Niebuhr, Etienne Gilson, Emil Brunner, Jacques Maritain, William Temple, and Hoxie Neale Fairchild.

The following study will be organized according to five particularly important focal areas that defined and sustained the trajectory of Hallowell's scholarly development, bearing in mind that throughout his professional development he never lost sight that his was a "mutual search" with his students, within a classical realist tradition: his understanding and critique of liberalism; his sketch of the "main currents" in modern political thought; his insistence upon the "moral foundation" of modern democracy; his civic and professional activism; and his practice, throughout his career, of a *maieutic* art. Eric Voegelin was among those who admired Hallowell's gifts as a teacher, and he wrote of this in a letter to Hallowell on November 11, 1975: "Your students, John, show the effect of your training. They are really good; they are interested and ask the right questions" (Hallowell Papers, Box 6). Voegelin here glimpses what Hallowell's students knew, and know intimately: in the classroom, in his office, in his home, at professional conferences, even in otherwise casual conversation, each of the above focal areas remained for Hallowell the central issues in that "mutual search" of student with *sensei.*[3]

Integral and Decadent Liberalism

Upon completion of his undergraduate studies, and at the urging of his friend and lifetime associate Taylor Cole,[4] Hallowell went to Germany to study at Heidelberg University. Among his professors there was philosopher Karl Jaspers. Hallowell from time to time recounted to his students stories of his experiences there which illustrated life in a totalitarian society governed by a rigid ideology: speaking in whispers huddled over a coffee table, for example, mindful that the children in the house were rewarded at school for sharing what their parents discussed at home; watching indigenous, German students stop coming to lectures by Jaspers, among others, because of SS agents in the hall outside of class periodically looking in and writing down names. Regrettably, Hallowell opted not to include letters, papers, notes or other materials from this period in his young life in his papers at the Duke University Archives. According to John G. Gunnell, however, Hallowell witnessed faculty members who "greeted each other with the Nazi salute." He also observed that "half the faculty appeared in uniform at the first convocation" (Gunnell 1993, 202). His experiences in Germany were clearly of great importance in his formulation of research problems, both for his Master's degree at Duke and his doctorate at Princeton. Regarding the latter, Hallowell explored, in his dissertation, the relationship between the demise of what he called an early modern, integral liberalism that grew out of the European Renaissance and its relation to the rise of National Socialism in Germany. Published in book form in 1943, Hallowell begins as follows: "With the rise to power of the National Socialists in Germany liberal political institutions collapsed like a house of cards tumbled over by a gust of wind" (Hallowell 1943, ix).

But what was this "integral liberalism" that had "tumbled over?" Integral liberalism is characterized by three particular developments in the seventeenth-century. First, faith in a rule of law, of impersonal rules rather than faith in personal authority such as characterized feudal relations, as the foundation of social order. Second, belief in a natural order that includes both society and the individual. And third, belief in natural rights which the state not only cannot deny but must protect. In *Main Currents*, Hallowell concedes that "liberalism" is a complex concept and "defies succinct definition." The term itself is unknown prior to the early nineteenth-century. Still, there is a "classic expression" of liberalism as a "political philosophy" and it finds that classic expression in the works of Hugo Grotius and John Locke. In an attempt to give a measure of precision to "integral" liberalism Hallowell identifies ten specific "beliefs:" a belief in the spiritual equality of all individuals; in "the autonomy of individual will;" in the "rationality and goodness" of man; in the inalienable rights of "life, liberty, and property;" a belief that the state exists by consent to protect these rights; that the state also exists by contract with individuals retaining a right of revolution; a belief that order is best secured by law; that the government which governs least governs best; a belief in individual freedom "in all spheres of life;" and "in the existence of a transcendental order of truth which is accessible to man's natural reason and capable of evoking a moral response" (Hallowell 1950, 110, 111). Particularly important in the integral liberal scheme is the concept of law, which has two dimensions: Two logically independent notions of law, then, are embodied in integral liberalism. First of all, there is the notion that law is the product of individual wills and the expression of subjective, personal interests. In this view it is the irrational compulsion behind the law which makes the individual submit to it. On the other hand, there is the notion that the law is the embodiment of truths and values transcending individual will and interest—that law is found, not made. In this view it is the rational recognition of the inherent justice of the law that imposes obligation. The source of law is thought of, in the first instance, as individual wills; in the second, as reason, nature, or the "order of things." What holds these competing concepts of law together is "reason guided by individual conscience," in "an uneasy compromise." What proved to be a problem was that the appeal to "conscience" was founded on a Christian ethic which proved to be "without weight." This "conscience" could not survive "the separation of reason from faith and the repudiation of the authority of the Church (Hallowell 1950, 91, 92). When the formal conception of law as the product of individual wills alone came to predominate, a development hastened by the widespread acceptance of positivism and historicism in the nineteenth-century, the integral character of liberalism eroded, over time, and took on a decadent form. Though this was particularly evident in Germany, where it led to the rise of National Socialism and the Third Reich, "decadent" liberalism is equally characteristic of the Western liberal democracies of the post war era.

In his review for the *Journal of Politics* Eric Voegelin commended Hallowell for aptly stating the problem and he recommended the study "particularly for its insight that the totalitarian ideas are not an event superseding liberalism, but the logical outcome of the initial inconsistencies of the liberal position." Yet, Voegelin did not think Hallowell went far enough: "In his presentation, the integral liberalism of the seventeenth-century looks a bit more integral than it actually was; and, correspondingly, the disintegration of the nineteenth-century looks more nefarious than it would in a better proportioned view" (Voegelin 1944, 108, 109).

Peter Drucker, as expressed in a letter of December 7, 1943, was less impressed: "I wonder whether you intentionally side-stepped the question— whether 'integral liberalism' was ever integral, that is whether it ever was a whole" (Hallowell Papers, Box One)?

Ideological and Philosophical Main Currents

Mindful that "decadent liberalism" was only one dimension of the modern era, Hallowell turned his attention next to other "main currents" in modern political thought. Though the focus of the study is on political thought since the sixteenth century and includes much detail on peripheral, but related currents, Hallowell identified the three most powerful currents as liberalism, socialism, and nihilism and organized his study accordingly. Inasmuch as all three had roots in the Renaissance and Reformation, however, either directly or indirectly, both the Renaissance and Reformation being rebirths of ancient thought, Hallowell began his study with brief considerations of classical and medieval thought as background and to understand transitions. And he began with a consideration of the meaning of political philosophy. Such a discipline of the mind is defined in part by what it is not. For Hallowell, among the principal tasks of political philosophy is "to bring men's political beliefs to self-consciousness and to subject them to the scrutiny of reason." Political philosophy is less concerned with institutions than with "the ideas and aspirations that are embodied in institutions" (Hallowell 1950, 9).[5] For example, one might consider the following. If we look to the basic institutions of American national government, Congress, the presidency, and the

federal courts, there is certainly much to behold. At the center of the design are
the separation of powers and checks and balances, principles sketched out at the
opening of virtually any text on the market designed for courses on American
government and politics. There is the variety in methods of selection, two and
six year cycles for Congress, House and Senate respectively, a four year term for
the President, chosen by a select group of electors acting on behalf of majorities
in the states, and presidential nomination with Senate confirmation for federal
judges, who serve during "good behavior." This is all standard, introductory
information. Yet, and few texts include this, there is also the faded residue, at
least, of "ideas" and "aspirations" associated with a classical tradition with roots
in Greek philosophy, Roman law, and Christian theology. This residue is more
likely to be found in common sense than in texts. Among the classical ideas is
that Congress, the legislative body, should "aspire" to moderation, the first of
the cardinal virtues of the ancient Greek polis. The current Tea Party Movement
in American politics is surely a common sense response to a perceived lack of
moderation in Congress today, both with respect to taxing—"taxed enough already"—and spending (the debt crisis). Similarly, with respect to the wider culture, the Occupy Wall Street movement is surely a common sense protest of a
lack of moderation in the private sphere. Hallowell, today, might wonder if there
isn't an Occupy Harvard Yard, or something kindred, just over the horizon in
reaction to immoderation in the academy—rising tuition rates, rising student and
parent debt, larger classes, online education, online degrees, online "academies,"
technology in the classroom, high tech cave walls via powerpoint lectures, ru-
brics with quantitative measures to the hundredth decimal point for evauating
student performance, SLO directives (Student Learning Outcomes), corporate
modeling, and burgeoning bureaucracies, among other excesses. What, a political philosopher in dialogue with his/her students might wonder, is being midwifed by these developments and what, more importantly, do these trends contribute to the life of the mind, or the life of the modern, democratic nation-state?

Among classical ideas is also, to return to institutions of the modern American state, that the one, be it Pericles, Caesar, Marcus Aurelius, or George Washington, embody, or at least aspire to, courage. Surely when the average American voter measures his/her presidential selection this quality weighs heavily in
the balance. Courage is clearly demanded of the commander-in-chief, but it is
also demanded of a chief legislator willing to take on the most challenging domestic issues of the day. U.S. Senator John F. Kennedy of Massachusetts, in the
1950s, was surely aware of this common sense dynamic when, with dreams of
the White House, he wrote his Pulitzer Prize winning account of *Profiles in
Courage*. And that judges aspire to justice, in the original scheme at least, is
nothing less than a self-evident truth. It is why they are called justices. All of
this is a faded residue also of the mixed constitutional ideal of the one, the few,
and the many of ancient Greek philosophy, Roman jurisprudence, and early
modern political theory in Europe. Shakespeare's *Julius Caesar* is the classic
study in literature, though one could make the case that Melville's *Moby Dick*
and *Billy Budd* are similarly structured and focused. But considerations such as

the foregoing have, at best, gone underground. Modern political thought has developed in mostly ideological "main currents," which have eroded such common sense connections. In addition to liberalism, Hallowell examined in *Main Currents* utilitarianism, idealism, positivism, conservatism, socialism, nihilism, existentialism, nationalism, fascism, and national socialism, to name the most predominant.

Reviews of Hallowell's study of modern political thought were mixed. Among positive reviews was that of Eric Voegelin. Hallowell had asked Voegelin, in a letter dated October 7, 1949, to review the manuscript for Henry Holt and Company prior to publication: "I am anxious to avoid any really serious errors of fact and of interpretation, and I know of no one better qualified than you to suggest such changes" (Hallowell Papers, Box 4). Three weeks later, after submitting fifteen pages of commentary to the publisher, Voegelin wrote to Hallowell, on October 27, 1949, that the manuscript "has given me great pleasure." He offered his "congratulations for your fine piece of work." Voegelin was not without concerns: "I have the impression that you are perhaps relying too much on the neo-orthodoxy of the type of Niebuhr and Barth as the answer to our problems" (Hallowell Papers, Box 4). In his letter of October 26, 1949, Voegelin wrote to C. A. Madison, editor at Henry Holt, that he found Hallowell's manuscript to be "enormously superior to any other book in the field." He expressed his intention of using it himself upon publication. "I for one shall certainly use it as compulsory reading in my course on modern political theory." He especially liked Hallowell's treatment of "liberalism" and "democracy." For Voegelin, the manuscript was "among the best that has been written on the subject" (Voegelin Papers). The review in the *Journal of Politics*, written by Fred V. Cahill of Yale University, was more critical. Though Hallowell was complimented for a "clear" style, Cahill "with some regret," found that Hallowell's "results" do not "achieve the same level as the intention." He finds that Hallowell is "cryptic," that readers will sometimes have a feeling that "something is being done with mirrors, but just what is being done is not certain." He further notes that certain terms are "employed rather more freely than precisely." He specifies here Hallowell's particular references to "liberal," "Christian tradition," and "positivism" (Cahill 1951, 104-107).[6] Robert C. Hartnett, Editor of the national Catholic weekly *America,* offered this advice in a letter dated December 12, 1950: "If I may say so, I think you have done enough work in non-Christian writers and have devoted enough time to pointing out their shortcomings. What we profoundly need is spokesmen for a positive Christian solution" (Hallowell Papers, Box 4). Yet, Hallowell explicitly states in the Preface to *Main Currents* that the "presuppositions" from which his book is written are those of "the classical Christian tradition, as I understand it" (Hallowell 1950, viii). His concluding chapter is on Christianity and the Social Order. There he examines liberal Protestantism, Protestant neo-orthodoxy, Protestant unity, Roman Catholicism, and Anglicanism. In his conclusion, Hallowell states that though Christianity "is not a political philosophy" it nonetheless can help save us from the "illusion" that we can "establish a system which is perfect or make a reform that is final." Christianity can also help us realize that "the task of achieving a just social order is an ever-continuing one and that justice is a goal to be striven after rather than finally attained." Finally, it places our "political, social, and economic aspirations in proper perspective, subordinating them to an aspiration which should include but transcend them" (Hallowell 1950, 692, 693). This Christian dimension of Hallowell's study was among its strengths for Voegelin. As he further wrote to editor Madison in his letter of October 26, 1949, the "greatest merit" of Hallowell's text was that it presented a "consistent interpretation of modern politics from a Christian position." *Main Currents*, wrote Voegelin, is the "first book in this field that adopts this position." It is "just the thing people are looking for—even those who do not know yet that it was that what they wanted" (Voegelin Papers). Bernard Crick, writing on "The Science of Politics in the United States," and considering Hallowell's work as a whole, referred to Hallowell as "gently grinding a Thomist axe" (Crick 1954, 316).

Morality and Modern Democracy

Hallowell's success with *Main Currents* led to an invitation to present a series of lectures at the University of Chicago, in the spring of 1952, as part of the Charles R. Walgreen Foundation study of American institutions. Jerome G. Kerwin, Chairman of the Foundation, in a letter of December 7, 1950, suggested a wide range of possible topics: "the decline of natural law concepts in American thought, justice as the foundation of politics, liberalism in America, and the crisis of our times." Hallowell asked the advice of Professor Niemeyer, who responded on January 26, 1951: "In my mind there is nothing which is as urgent in our day as the working out of the theoretical position vis a vis the communist assault. How about the 'Moral Basis of Freedom?' I don't know whether that is in your line but I certainly would like to see someone deal intelligently with the topic" (Hallowell Papers, Box 4). After much deliberation Hallowell chose as his theme the moral foundation of democracy. He presented six lectures between April 7 and April 18, 1952, in Room 122 of the Social Sciences Research Building at the University of Chicago, each about fifty minutes with no questions. These lectures became the basis of Hallowell's book published, in 1954, under the same title, by the University of Chicago Press. Chairman Kerwin was especially pleased with Hallowell's performance as he expressed in a letter of April 29, 1952: "Once again I would like to assure you that you fulfilled all my fondest expectations in your lectures, and I am especially pleased with the excellent reactions that increasingly come to me. I feel that the point of view that you gave in your lectures is profoundly important for the development of political science in this country and it is time that our colleagues in the field were apprised of this approach (Hallowell Papers, Box 4).

Hallowell began his analysis with a lecture on "Democracy—Fact or Fiction?" He put forth for consideration the increasingly popular theories of Italian sociologist Vilfredo Pareto, for whom all governments, no matter what name is attached to them, are "always rule by the few in their own interest." For Pareto this represents the findings of modern science. Hallowell points out, however, that it is also the argument both of Thrasymachus in Plato's *Republic* of the fourth century BC and of Machiavelli's writing in the sixteenth century. What Pareto has done, according to Hallowell, is simply "restate the ancient Sophistic arguments under the guise of scientific research." Hallowell proceeds to compare Pareto's concept of "derivatives" to Marx's concept of "ideologies," Sorel's concept of "myths," and Freud's concept of "rationalizations," all of which, despite differences of nuance and degree, are in accord that human beings are "motivated more by irrational considerations than by rational ones." From such a perspective, concepts such as "justice, natural law, and natural rights," indeed the concepts of "reason" and "democracy" are but "words" which "refer to no objective reality" and can be "used in any fashion anyone wants to use them, and there is no way in which we can challenge his right to do so."

This idea that democracy is a fiction is especially widespread, according to Hallowell. As further illustration he draws on the work of American scholar Thurman Arnold, author *of The Symbols of Government* and *The Folklore of Capitalism*. For Arnold, the concept of the "thinking man," cherished by traditional democratic theorists and politicians is an "illusion." To believe in an objective reality of "law, justice, and rights" is, for Arnold, "infantile." The only real wants of human beings are "prestige" and "income." There is much in Arnold's work about the need for "good men" and "respectable people" to guard against the cruelty in the leadership such as all have witnessed in Germany, Italy, and Russia under National Socialist, Fascist, and Communist dictators. But as Hallowell points out: "He cannot maintain at one and the same time that all ethical judgments are nonsense and resort to an ethical judgment as the bulwark of his theory" (Hallowell 1954a, 3-13). Hallowell chose to focus on Pareto and Arnold because each is especially representative of a widely shared attitude among scholars that modern democracy is a fiction with no relation to objective reality, that concepts such as justice, morality, conscience, indeed reason, are but words signifying if not nothing, little. But if such views be accepted what is the future of democracy or principles of good government in general? For Hallowell we are fortunate in that the conflict between philosophical realism and various forms of sophistry is nothing new. And in his subsequent Walgreen Lectures, he makes the case for philosophical realism and a democratic future based upon a moral foundation.

He first critiques T. V. Smith's argument that democracy is essentially the "art of compromise." For Hallowell, rather, this in effect means that legislators in a democratically elected assembly cannot reject the claims of any group on the grounds that the claims are unreasonable or unjust. All proposals by all represented interests are assumed to equally legitimate. The "substance" of any compromise would then depend upon "the relative strength of the opposing groups." Such a view, for Hallowell, reduces politics to "domestic warfare."

Smith also assumes that representatives of the competing interests are "equally honest." But this is assuming "more than is credible or justified by experience." For Hallowell, compromises, if they are to "approximate a solution," must "embody what is best in all proposals, what will best promote the common good." This is only possible "by appealing to those purposes and values that are shared" (Hallowell 1954a, 29-31). As democracy is more than the art of compromise, so also is it more than its institutional framework. This is the subject of the third lecture. Certain "institutions," however, are essential. First among these is the "whole range of civil liberties" (Hallowell 1954a, 44). Essential also is a popularly elected legislative assembly. But, drawing on Montesquieu, Hallowell cautions that the idea that all are qualified to choose does not mean that all are qualified to be chosen. Political parties have also become essential institutions in modern democracies. But contrary to the findings of Arthur Bentley and others, Hallowell cites Madison in the tenth Federalist to the effect that governments should control the effects of factionalism not simply reflect what factions are able to get which is implied in the work of scholars such as Bentley for whom politics is simply "pressure politics," what Harold Lasswell called "who gets what, when, and how." In a letter to J. Roland Pennock at Swarthmore College, dated February 8, 1952, just two months prior to Hallowell's lectures at Chicago, he expressed surprise at Pennock's "take" on Lasswell's work: "I must confess I was somewhat startled by the admiration I detected for the recent work of Harold Lasswell. Personally I am inclined to think that it is a lot of pretentious jargon, but maybe I am to hard on him" (Hallowell Papers, Box 4). To say that parties are essential institutions is, for Hallowell, to agree with Edmund Burke that they unite persons who wish to promote "the national interest, upon some particular principle in which they are all agreed" (Hallowell 1954a, 47). But most important is the recognition that modern democracy is government by persuasion and deliberation. And the process "implies a reciprocal relationship between those in positions of public responsibility and the electorate" (Hallowell 1954a, 54). Finally, democratic government is "constitutional" government. Drawing on the work of his former professor at Princeton, C. H. McIlwain, Hallowell contends that constitutional government is a "practical manifestation and reflection of the idea of natural law," the idea that government is "restrained by the dictates of a law more fundamental than that enacted by the legislature...." (Hallowell 1954a, 57). But there is no democratic institution that is not subjected to possible corruption or subversion. Quoting Nikolai Berdyaev, Hallowell concludes his third lecture by emphasizing the importance to the continuation of democracy of a concept of liberty allied with a concept of truth: "Liberty will be saved by its union with Truth—it cannot be saved by indifference to Truth" (Hallowell 1954a, 60). The fourth lecture is on the close relationship, historically, between democracy and liberalism. Here Hallowell presents, in condensed form, the arguments he had made both in *The Decline of Liberalism* and *Main Currents*. In a word, the liberal goal of freedom must be tempered with "concern for the community welfare" and it must think of the latter "in more organic terms." Freedom is not an end in itself, but, "as the classical liberal was inclined to believe," an "essential means to the development of moral and spiritual perfection" (Hallowell 1954a, 78).

The final two lectures are on, respectively, "Human Nature and Politics" and "The Moral Foundation of Democracy." In the first, Hallowell reviews the optimistic views of eighteenth-century theorists regarding the very perfectability of human nature. Through education, social engineering, or psychoanalysis theorists such as Helvetius, Condorcet, Robert Owen, and Harold Lasswell see future society as all but devoid of conflict. Latent in many of these modern approaches and made explicit by William James is the idea that truth is not something to be discovered but something to be made. In his famous, often quoted formulation, truth "happens" to an idea. Through the work of James' disciple John Dewey, among others, the idea of "social salvation by science" becomes prevalent. At the heart of these developments, for Hallowell, is an overarching question of political philosophy: "Is there something inherent in human nature which demands the state and defines and limits its function, or is the state simply a conventional and arbitrary instrument of human will?" That human nature is "nothing more than the reflection of social conditions" seems for Hallowell to be a "self-evident presupposition of most modern thought." But all of this is counter to the Hebraic-Greek-Christian tradition which teaches the necessity of human beings to conform to a reality that is not made but given. The meaning of history from this perspective is not Marx's "man pursuing his own aims" but the restoration of human personality "through redemption from evil." Specifically, human beings need redemption from the evil "which is manifested in pride, avarice, envy, anger, greed, lust, and sloth" (Hallowell 1954a, 85-90). In his concluding lecture Hallowell relies on the arguments of Plato, Cicero, St. Augustine, and Yves Simon to make the case of Socrates against Callicles on the meaning of freedom. For Callicles, as for many in the modern world, freedom is "the power to do what one wants." For Socrates it is "a means to promote justice and the common good." For Hallowell, that Socrates be victorious over Callicles is not an academic question. It is "a question of the life or death of modern civilization" (Hallowell 1954a, 117-120).

In his review of *The Moral Foundation of Democracy* for the *Journal of Politics*, Walter E. Sandelius found "substance presented clearly and with sustained convincingness" (Sandelius 1955, 688). The same could be said of all of Hallowell's published work. Regarding a clarity of style, Eric Voegelin, in a letter of February 4, 1953, in a postscript, relayed a compliment: "Incidentally, the reviewer mentioned above in parenthesis referred to your style as a model that I should seek to imitate." (Hallowell Papers, Box 4). Regarding "substance," there is that dimension of freedom represented by Socrates that calls one to "service" to "one's fellow-men" (Hallowell 1954a, 119).

Civic and Professional Activist

Despite his criticisms of Clinton Rossiter, and others, in his comments on the APSA's Committee for the Advancement of Teaching in 1951 regarding partici- pation in the political process, Hallowell was very active in the civic commu- nity, within his discipline's community of scholars, and within the Episcopal Church. With respect to community service he chaired a Citizens Committee to help address tensions in Greensboro, North Carolina, amidst the sit-ins and ef- forts to desegregate lunch counters in 1960. Four years later, he chaired the North Carolina chapter of Professors for Johnson/Humphrey, for which he re- ceived a letter of gratitude, on December 15, 1964, from Vice President Elect Hubert Humphrey: "President Johnson appreciates the important work of the Professor's committee, just as I do" (Hallowell Papers, Box 5). Some years later Hallowell wrote, in a letter to President Jimmy Carter dated September 18, 1977, that he worked enthusiastically for Carter's election in 1976 and that he was "a lifelong Democrat" (Hallowell Papers, Box 6). Yet, four years later, in a letter to Duke President Terry Sanford, dated August 27, 1981, he wrote that he was "a conservative politically who voted for President Reagan" and that he "generally support(s) the policies of the Reagan Administration." The letter to Sanford was with regards to the issue of whether to support the building of the Nixon Library on the Duke campus. Sanford was active in promoting the idea, while Hallowell was an outspoken member of CANDL, Committee Against the Nixon-Duke Library. Regarding President Nixon, Hallowell wrote in the letter of August 27, 1981, to Sanford: "With shamelessness he is now engaged in try- ing to rehabilitate his image and seeks to enlist Duke University in that effort." He continued: "Let us not be seduced by the lure of 'a great collection of papers' into providing a memorial for a man who will live in infamy" (Hallowell Papers, Box One). Years earlier, during Watergate, Hallowell frequently wrote to prin- cipals urging impeachment and conviction of the President. To his Congress- man, Ike Andrews, he wrote, on October 20, 1973, that not "since the Civil War has our system of government been in as dire peril as it is today" (Hallowell Papers, Box 6). On the same day he wrote to U.S. Senator Sam J. Ervin (D/NC), Chair of the Senate Watergate Committee: "I hope that you will use the prestige of your office and your current popularity based upon your courageous activity of recent months to see that justice is genuinely done and that the law applies equally to those in high political office and to the ordinary citizen. I know that you are a staunch defender of the rule of law, and if this goes, our entire system of constitutional democracy goes with it" (Hallowell Papers, Box 6). He wrote him again the very next day: "Never have we had a President who has behaved with greater arrogance nor an administration more permeated with corruption and hints of corruption. Please support impeachment..." (Hallowell Papers, Box 6). The following year, after President Ford's pardon of President Nixon, Hallowell wrote numerous letters expressing his serious disappointment. To Representative John J. Rhodes (R/AZ), Minority Leader during the Watergate crisis, Hallowell expressed himself candidly in a letter of September 11, 1974: "You are quite wrong in believing that the American public does not want to see Nixon in prison. If he is in fact guilty of any crime, that is precisely where he belongs" (Hallowell Papers, Box 6). He also wrote letters criticizing the pardon to Walter Mondale (D/MN), Vice President Nelson A. Rockefeller, Speaker of the House Carl Albert, Special Prosecutor Leon Jaworski, and President Ford.

Professionally, and in addition to his regular contributions to the American and Southern Political Science Associations, noted above, Hallowell was especially active in bringing distinguished speakers to the Duke campus through his chairmanship of the Lilly Endowment Research Program in Christianity and Politics. Among the scholars who visited campus and lectured under this program were Arnold Toynbee, in May, 1958, John Wild, in November, 1958, Kenneth W. Thompson, in March, 1959, Paul Ramsey, in May, 1960, Eric Voegelin, in December, 1960, Edgar Brookes, February, 1963, and Carl J. Friedrich, March, 1963. In November, 1964, as President of the Southern Political Science Association, Hallowell hosted the Rev. Martin Luther King. In his introduction, Hallowell said that not only was Dr. King "one of the outstanding leaders in the movement for the recognition of Negro rights (one might better say 'human rights')" but also "one who is seeking to liberate the white man from the bondage of fear and prejudice" (Hallowell Papers, Box 5). Secretary of State Dean Rusk, two years later, in a letter dated May 13, 1966, invited Hallowell to a National Foreign Policy Conference for Educators to be held June16, 17, 1966, in Washington, D.C. (Hallowell Papers, Box 5). From 1961 to 1964, Hallowell served on the Council of the American Political Science Association, served as the Editor of the *Journal of Politics* for three years (1957–1960), and, at various times, served on the editorial boards of *The Journal of Church and State*, the *Political Science Reviewer,* and the journal *Interpretation.*

Maieutic Artist

Throughout his life, Hallowell was honored as an outstanding scholar. In 1975 he was awarded a James B. Duke Professorship at Duke. In January 20, 1981, on the inauguration of President Ronald Reagan, the *Wall Street Journal* published an article on "The Conservative Ideas in Reagan's Victory." Noting that "many names" could be mentioned as influential in the formation of the Reagan vision, five stand out as having had a "pervasive influence." The five are "Ludwig Von Mises, Richard Weaver, Leo Strauss, Gordon Keith Chalmers, and John Hallowell" ("Conservative" 1981).[7] His first book on the *Decline of Liberalism* was translated into Spanish in 1949, and Japanese in 1953. *The Moral Foundation of Democracy* was translated into Arabic in 1956, Korean the same year, and French in 1970. His work was analyzed, with that of Irving Kristol, in a doctoral dissertation at Fordham University in 1977. He was also the subject of a Master's thesis by William R. Stevenson, Jr., at East Carolina University, in 1978, entitled *The Political 'Physician:' John H. Hallowell: Diagnosing the Crisis of Our Times.* Hallowell's primary concern as a research scholar, a concern that grew rather than subsided with age and experience, was with what might be called democracy's demise. His research as a young scholar brilliantly traced the symbiotic relationship between what he conceptualized as integral liberalism and the rise of modern democracy, and the subsequent threat to the latter with the decay of the former into a decadent, one dimensional liberalism. His analysis of the main currents in modern political thought examined this decay more fully, calling into question what any of the modern, supposedly "scientific" ideologies could contribute to the good life or advance in any way beyond the insights of the towering figures in a classical realist tradition with roots in the ancient Greek polis, the Roman republic, and ancient Hebrew and Christian communities. What could modern ideologies, modern "isms," with claims to truth regarding the "logos" of history, add to the perennial wisdom to be found in the works of Plato, Aristotle, Cicero, St. Augustine, St. Thomas Aquinas and scholars over two millennia who have found wisdom and inspiration in their works? But as rich as his insights, as persuasive as his community service understood civically, professionally, and religiously were to all who studied his works, studied with him, or worked with him, John H. Hallowell's most lasting legacy is as a *maieutic* artist both inside and outside of the classroom. It was in his role as teacher, *sensei,* that Hallowell had the greatest impact and for which he is best remembered.

Hallowell's teaching was not confined to the traditional classroom. He gave numerous visiting lectures and directed two National Endowment for the Humanities summer seminars for college teachers on "Politics and Morality," one in 1975 and one in 1976. When it came to teaching style, Hallowell gave much credit to Taylor Cole. He expressed this in a letter to his lifelong friend on March 5, 1975: "I vividly remember your technique of questioning that forced us to discover our own presuppositions, your insistence that we consider the alternatives, that we define our terms with some precision. It is a technique I have tried to incorporate into my own teaching" (Hallowell Papers, Box 6). When Mary Evelyn Blagg Huey became the first woman president of Texas Woman's University, the largest university in the United States primarily for women, she wrote to her former professor, who directed her dissertation, in the spring of 1977 (n.d.): "The high standards and noble ideas which we talked about so frequently twenty-five years ago are with me every day. I hope that I will be true always to those principles that we hold so dear" (Hallowell Papers, Box 6). Hallowell gave the keynote address at her inauguration on April 15, 1977. Upon returning to Durham, he received a letter on April 19 from Randall C. Jackson, a former regent of Texas Woman's University, who was in the audience: "Your inaugural address was one of the best I have ever heard" (Hallowell Papers, Box 6).

All of the scholars featured in this tribute to political philosophers as teachers practiced, or are practicing, in the long, classical tradition of Socrates, a *maieutic* art according to which the first priority of the teacher is to midwife the latent curiosity and creativity in the life of the mind of students, and less to communicate "information." John H. Hallowell was fond of reminding his students that truth is "self-authenticating." This somewhat faded approach to teaching raises serious questions about current trends in modern pedagogical practices such as the encouragement of large classes, shorter time lines, standardized testing, PowerPoint presentations and lectures, laptops, iPads, and iPhones in the classroom, group assignments, rubric designs, all things associated with "student learning outcomes," and, perhaps most of all, online courses and degrees. Were Hallowell with us today, he would surely be on the front lines challenging the wisdom of embracing these developments. Francis Canavan, in the Preface to *The Ethical Dimension of Political Life: Essays in Honor of John H. Hallowell*, quotes from the citation that accompanied the honorary Litt. D that Hallowell received from the College of the Holy Cross in 1963. Hallowell was a "teacher's teacher" (Canavan 1983, viii). In the final analysis, as a teacher, sometimes explicitly, always by example, John H Hallowell posed but a single question to his students. It is the question that Diotima, the stranger of Mantineia, posed to Socrates as related in Plato's *Symposium*:

> What may we suppose to be the felicity of the man who sees absolute beauty in its essence, pure and unalloyed, who, instead of a beauty tainted by human flesh and colour and a mass of perishable rubbish, is able to apprehend divine beauty where it exists apart and alone? Do you think that it will be a poor life that a man leads who has his gaze fixed in that direction, who contemplates absolute beauty with the appropriate faculty and is in constant union with it? Do you not see that in that region alone where he sees beauty with the faculty capable of seeing it, will he be able to bring forth not mere reflected images of goodness but true goodness, because he will be in contact not with a reflection but with the truth? (Plato, 212c).

And, as with Socrates, Hallowell's students, being persuaded of the "truth" in Diotima's question, have gone out to "persuade others."

Notes

1. I want to thank here Hallowell's former students Bruce Douglass, Charles R. Embry, and Timothy Lomperis for sharing their personal recollections of Professor Hallowell.

2. Niebuhr was especially instrumental in Hallowell's turn to Christianity, as he explains in his contribution to *Modern Canterbury Pilgrims:* "While I was writing the dissertation I 'happened' one Sunday to attend a church service in the Princeton University Chapel. The speaker was Reinhold Niebuhr. I had not been to a church service for years and I had come out of curiosity to hear the man who some of my friends said was an unusual preacher. He was, indeed. He discussed with great profundity and intellectual clarity problems that I had encountered in writing about the decline of liberalism. Indeed, he seemed to have a greater grasp of the reasons for the decline of liberalism than I had.

If these insights were the product of Christianity, then Christianity was certainly relevant to what I was attempting to do. I cannot say that I immediately appropriated them as my own, but I did begin to think about Christianity in a serious way" (Hallowell 1956, 21).

3. It seems particularly appropriate to refer to Hallowell as *sensei*, given that the term has a richer connotation in Japanese than the common translation as "teacher." The two *kanji*, or Chinese characters, mean, on the left, the *sen* character, "before," and, on the right, the *sei* character, "to live." The suggestion is that a *sensei* has so mastered the essential principles of his/her cultural milieu that it is as if he/she has "lived before." Hallowell so mastered the classics of the Western civilizational milieu and encouraged his students to do the same.

4. In a letter of March 5, 1975, Hallowell expressed his deepest debt to Taylor Cole as follows: "...it is your qualities as a man that I cherish most and would like most to emulate. Institutions, political systems, civilizations come and go—it is the example of good men which endures and inspires others to try again" (Hallowell Papers, Box 6).

5. In his critique of Karl Lowenstein's *Political Reconstruction*, Hallowell stressed this point: "The author is so intent upon the preservation of democratic institutions that he gives little or no attention to the philosophy of man and society that must exist if those institutions are to have a fertile soil in which to grow" (Hallowell 1946).

6. Cahill was especially critical of Hallowell's analysis of positivism: "No historian of political theory can be unaware of the frequency with which a term will be applied to widely diverging concepts. He ought therefore to be more than ever alert to avoid identifying the legal positivists with the sociological positivists—two groups which have, or so it seems to me, little, if anything, in common. And in connection with the legal positivists, it can be suggested that Dean Pound's later and somewhat ill-tempered strictures concerning his jurisprudential brethren should not be accepted at face value without at least carefully assaying some of his earlier writings for traces of the same positivism. In any event, it seems a bit odd for a man of Professor Hallowell's views to accept aid with such alacrity from the father of 'sociological jurisprudence'" (Cahill 1951, 106, 107).

7. It is commonplace to come across Hallowell's name in connection with postwar "conservatism." But Hallowell, as noted earlier in the text, deplored labels. And he was certainly not immune to criticizing other, better known, conservatives. The following is from his review of Russell Kirk's *The Conservative Tradition from Burke to Santayana:* "This reviewer, at any rate, finds the uncritical nature of his partisanship more disturbing than the partisan attitude itself. One wishes that he had indulged in fewer eulogies of conservative thought and sought rather to separate the good from the bad in conservative thought. We are more likely to appropriate the wisdom in conservative thought if we are not made to feel that we must accept the errors as well" (Hallowell 1954b, 152).

Works Cited

Cahill, Fred V., Jr. 1951. "Review of *Main Currents in Modern Political Thought*, by John H. Hallowell. *The Journal of Politics* 13 (1): 104-107.

Canavan, Francis, ed. 1983. *The Ethical Dimension of Political Life: Essays in Honor of John H. Hallowell.* Durham: Duke University Press.

"The Conservative Ideas in Reagan's Victory." 1981. *The Wall Street Journal*, January 20.

180   Timothy Hoye

Crick, Bernard. 1954. "The Science of Politics in the United States." *The Canadian Journal of Economics and Political Science/Revue canadienne d'Economique et de Science politique* 20 (3): 308-320.

———. 1959. *The American Science of Politics: Origins and Conditions.* Los Angeles, California: University of California Press.

Fesler, James W., et al. 1951. "Goals for Political Science: A Discussion." *American Political Science Review* 45 (4): 996-1024.

Gunnell, John G. 1988. "American Political Science, Liberalism, and the Invention of Political Theory." *American Political Science Review* 82 (1): 71-87.

———. 1993. *The Descent of Political Theory: The Genealogy of an American Vocation.* Chicago: University of Chicago Press.

Hallowell, John H. 1943. *The Decline of Liberalism as an Ideology, with Particular Reference to German Politico-Legal Thought.* Berkeley: University of California Press.

———. 1946. "Review of *Political Reconstruction,* by Karl Lowenstein. *The Journal of Politics* 8 (3): 414-417.

———. 1950. *Main Currents in Modern Political Thought.* New York: Henry Holt and Company.

———. 1954a. *The Moral Foundation of Democracy.* Chicago: University of Chicago Press.

———. 1954b. "Review of *The Conservative Tradition from Burke to Santayana,* by Russell Kirk." *The Journal of Politics* 16 (1): 150-152.

———. 1956. "John H. Hallowell." In *Modern Canterbury Pilgrims, And Why They Chose the Episcopal Church,* edited by James A. Pike, 15-30. New York: Morehouse-Gorham.

———. 1964. "Plato and His Critics." *The Journal of Politics* 27 (2): 273-289.

———. 1972. "Existence in Tension: Man in Search of His Humanity." *Political Science Reviewer* 2 (1): 162-184.

———. Papers. Duke University Library Archives, Durham, North Carolina.

Mead, Walter B. 1994. "John H. Hallowell: A Political Philosopher's Critique of His Profession's Paradigm." *Political Science Reviewer* 23 (1): 5-49.

Plato. 1971. *Symposium.* Translated by Walter Hamilton. Baltimore: Penguin Books Ltd.

Sandelius, Walter E. 1955. "Review of *The Moral Foundation of Democracy,* by John H. Hallowell.*" The Journal of Politics* 17 (4): 688-689.

Voegelin, Eric. 1944. "Review of *The Decline of Liberalism as an Ideology, with Particular Reference to German Politico-Legal Thought." The Journal of Politics* 6 (1): 107-109.

———. Papers. Louisiana State University Archives, Baton Rouge, Louisiana.

SECTION III:

THE TEACHING OF NATURAL RIGHTS TODAY

Chapter 9

Leo Strauss's Two Agendas for Education
Michael Zuckert, Notre Dame University

Like several other of the authors discussed in this volume, Leo Strauss (1899–1973) was an émigré from Germany, driven into exile by the disastrous events of the 1930s in his homeland. Born a Jew in an out of the way part of Germany, Strauss was of course vulnerable to the anti-Jewish Nazi regime. He left Germany just as Hitler was coming to power, travelling first to France, then to England, and, finally, to the United States, where he eventually became a citizen and established himself as one of the major political philosophers of the twentieth century.

Strauss described his family home as one deeply immersed in Jewish observance but lacking in Jewish learning. In his early years he was much engaged in the political Zionist movement, but at the same time procured a standard German secular philosophic education. Two events were probably most decisive for setting him on the path that led to his mature philosophic orientation: The first was his education. He was primarily educated in the neo-Kantian tradition, the leading light of which in Strauss's younger years was the German-Jewish thinker Hermann Cohen. Cohen died before Strauss reached the university, but Strauss ended up writing his dissertation at University of Hamburg under Cohen's successor as leader of the neo-Kantian movement, Ernst Cassirer.

Although Strauss worked under Cassirer, Cassirer does not appear to have had a major impact on him. Even as he was studying neo-Kantianism Strauss was attracted by more modern, more philosophically radical movements. He started reading Nietzsche while in gymnasium and remained in thrall to him until age thirty or so (Smith, 20).[1] He was also exploring more formally some of the newer philosophic movements. Thus he went to Freiburg for a post-doctoral year in 1922 to study with Edmund Husserl, the founder of phenomenology. At that time he became aware of Husserl's young assistant, Martin Heidegger, who was ten years Strauss's senior. Strauss always admired Husserl, but the young Heidegger swept him away (See Smith, 15). He heard the latter lecture on Aristotle and was awed by the seriousness and penetration of Heidegger as a reader of old texts and thinker of new thoughts. Strauss was apparently not present at the famous debate at Davos in 1929 between Cassirer and Heidegger, a battle of titans representing the old and the new thinking respectively, but he was greatly impressed by reports of Heidegger's performance.

These three thinkers of his formative years—Nietzsche, Husserl, Heidegger—always remained important for him and elements of what he learned from them remained in his mature thought. But he did not end up a follower of any of them any more than of neo-Kantianism. The three turned out to be a springboard for an attempt by Strauss to recover earlier Greek thought. The effort was midwifed by his life-long friend Jacob Klein, who had studied with Husserl and was influenced by Heidegger, but who saw in them a possibility they had not seen in themselves—the possibility of recapturing ancient Greek thought, in this case ancient mathematical thinking—not merely in a more adequate historical way, but as a truer grasp of the nature of mathematical reality than modern mathematics contained. In the 1930s Strauss set off on a similar path—a return to ancient political philosophy. This meant breaking with the historicism of two of his early philosophical guides—Nietzsche and Heidegger—a historicism that in effect decreed such a return to be impossible and unworthy. In setting off in the direction in which Klein had gone, Strauss committed himself to two themes that came to define and indeed dominate his mature thinking—the battle against historicism and the attempt to return, even if in a tentative or hypothetical manner, to the ancients. (*CM,* 11)

Strauss's philosophic reorientation overlapped to a considerable extent with the political disaster unfolding around him. The late 1920s made clear to all who could see, as Strauss might say, that the Weimar regime, the liberal democracy established in Germany following the German defeat in WWI, was collapsing. It lurched from crisis to crisis and the moderate liberal center seemed powerless when caught in the pincers of the communist left and the ultra nationalist right, the most determined representative of which was Hitler's National Socialist Party (LAM, 225).

There was an uncanny and important coincidence between these two major formative forces in Strauss's life, for the philosophers to whom he was attracted, especially Nietzsche and Heidegger, were at the forefront of challenging the kind of liberal/enlightenment thought that inspired Weimar in its noblest aspirations. From the failure of Weimar at the hands of the political extremes and the failure of enlightenment philosophy as shown by the pens of Nietzsche and Heidegger, Strauss inferred that the liberal Enlightenment project was not viable. At first he seems to have concluded that the vacuum caused by the failure of liberalism could be filled only by a movement of the right, like Mussolini's early Fascist movement: only a movement of the right, not the old and now discredited appeal to "the rights of man," could fend off the "shabby" Nazis or the communists. Strauss believed, on the basis of the Weimar experience unfolding before his eyes and the testimony of the philosophers he most admired, that the liberal democratic experiment had proven a failure. His experience in England and America, and their experience in World War II led him to greatly revise his opinion, especially when, as his understanding of classical philosophy deepened, he came to see that liberal democracy, viewed in the perspective of the classics rather than the moderns, had much greater potential than he had at first believed. He became, as he said in one of his essays on education, "a friend and an ally of democracy." Of course, being a "friend and an ally" is not the same as being himself in a straightforward way a liberal democrat. (LER, 28)[2] His perspective was never the same as that of the ordinary champion of liberal democracy, but on the basis of classical political science he came to affirm liberal democracy as the best regime possible for the modern world.

After leaving Germany and finally settling in America, the externals of Strauss's life were much less eventful. He first taught at the New School for Social Research in New York, as one of the army of émigrés employed by that haven for émigrés. He left the New School for University of Chicago in 1947, personally recruited by its President, Robert Maynard Hutchens. Strauss spent the bulk of his remaining career at Chicago, publishing his best known books while there, including *Natural Right and History, Thoughts on Machiavelli*, and *The City and Man*. He retired at the then mandatory time in 1967, moving first to Claremont Men's College as a colleague of his former student Harry Jaffa and then to St. John's College where he was reunited with his old friend and one-time mentor, Jacob Klein. His post-Chicago years were productive but were mostly years of ill health, to which he finally succumbed in 1973.

Strauss's Two-Fold Intention

"I own that education is in a sense the subject matter of my teaching and my research" (LER 1). Thus Leo Strauss in an essay on liberal education. Yet he wrote relatively little directly on the subject and in one place went to some lengths to speak of his "apprehension," of his "bewilderment," and to indicate with much hemming and hawing his reluctance to write explicitly on the subject when asked to do so for a conference sponsored by the Fund for Adult Education. Overcoming his apparent reluctance he wrote the requested essay for the conference as a follow-up to his one other essay on the general subject of liberal education written the year before.

The two essays on liberal education, published in 1961 and 1962, were written for particular occasions and particular audiences. The first was delivered as a commencement address at the Basic Program of Liberal Education for Adults at University of Chicago. That address prompted the second essay, for the organizer of the conference on adult education requested Strauss to expand on some sentences of his first essay for a conference the following year (Nicgorski, 233).

The essays were addressed, respectively, to an audience of adult graduates, and to an audience of "professional educators" (LER, 3). Strauss's way of addressing or relating to these two audiences differs markedly, as is visible even in his use of first person pronouns. In the essay addressed to the graduates, Strauss employs first person plural pronouns (we, us, our) eighty-six times as opposed the mere six times he uses first person singular pronouns (I, me, my). That is, he uses the first person plural more than fourteen times as often as the first person singular. This stands in marked contrast to the essay addressed to the professionals, where he uses the singular and plural forms an almost equal number of times (forty-one and forty-five respectively). He distinguishes himself from his audience of professionals (as "I") *much* more often than he does from his audience of liberal arts program graduates. As he emphasizes in the latter address, "the teachers [in liberal arts education] themselves are pupils and must be pupils" (WILE, 1). As such a teacher and thus as a fellow pupil Strauss shares much more with "the less experienced pupils" he is addressing than he does with the professionals, and thus he can more readily speak to and of them as "we." Almost as striking as the relative distribution of singular and plural pronouns is the aggregate usage of all pronouns in the two addresses. The address to the professionals is roughly three times longer than the other (twenty-nine paragraphs to ten) but uses first person pronouns fewer total times (eighty-six) than the much shorter address to the graduates (ninety-two times). In place of the personal pronouns of the shorter essay we find the rise of the impersonal pronoun "one" in the longer essay (three and twenty-one times, respectively).

Strauss signals with his use of pronoun how he stands toward his two audiences. Though a professional educator himself (LER, 1), he identifies much less with those who claim to be the professionals than he does with his pupils. The difference between him as a teacher and the profession of teachers is indeed one of the subtle but pervasive themes of the essay. He is very different from them. He announces himself, for example, to be "almost solely concerned with the goal or end of education...and very little with its conditions and its how," the latter two, he implies, being the chief concerns of his audience (LER 1). Although Strauss might consider it presumptuous to compare himself to Socrates, yet the situation he faces, as he presents it, is rather like that Socrates faced in Plato's *Protagoras*—a lone man of integrity in a room full of sophists, which may be why Strauss makes the following curious point in his opening paragraph: "I thought that it was my job, my responsibility, to do my best...with students wholly regardless of whether they are registered or not," i.e., regardless of whether they pay for instruction. Strauss is no sophist, for one of the distinguishing marks of sophists is that they teach for money. Thus Strauss illustrates a certain point in this address by adducing the example and teaching of Protagoras from Plato's dialogue of that name as one who "came to the democratic city of

Athens in order to educate human beings, or *to teach for pay*...the political art"
(LER, 8; emphasis added). Moreover, since he is attempting to sell his wares in
democratic Athens, Protagoras must flatter the Athenians and accept or even
cater to the premise of the democracy "that everyone is supposed to possess the
political art somehow" (ibid). Strauss is careful to distinguish himself and his
practice from that of the sophist: "We are not permitted to be flatterers of democracy" (LER, 28).

Strauss shares less with the professionals and therefore shares with them
less of himself, as ironically evidenced by the much greater presence of "I" in
his address to them. That impression is confirmed by his insistence at the outset
of the address that he has not chosen his topic, indeed that it was assigned or
imposed on him, and that he does not even wholly understand the topic as given
to him (LER, 1–2). His address is in some important sense not voluntary; it is, if
not exactly coerced, nonetheless not a presentation he chose for himself. The
address to the graduates has nothing of that coerced or forced character, nothing
of that alienation from his own topic that marks the address to the professionals.
Indeed, he speaks to the graduates on the topic "What is Liberal Education," one
of only two pieces in his entire corpus explicitly raising in its title *the* Socratic
question, the "what is" question (Also see WIPP, 1). Strauss's two speeches on
liberal education thus relate to each other as the two kinds of Platonic dialogues
that Strauss identified—the voluntary and the involuntary.

"What is Liberal Education?" addresses a topic Strauss apparently wishes
on his own to address: it concerns a matter near and dear to him. "Liberal Education and Responsibility" addresses a topic Strauss is less spontaneously eager
to discuss, but which he is somehow compelled to address. In Strauss's interpretation of the Platonic corpus perhaps the involuntary or coerced dialogue par
excellence is the *Republic*. Would it be too much to say that this address is
Strauss's *Republic* even more than or while simultaneously being his *Protagoras*?

As the example of the *Republic* shows, the involuntary dialogue is not in itself of lesser importance. Indeed it is not entirely the case that the topic of "Liberal Education and Responsibility" is alien to Strauss. As he tells it, he was
asked to expand upon some sentences of his earlier address, i.e., to explain
something he had already said in his spontaneous speech (LER, 3). Moreover, it
is difficult to say the two addresses differ fundamentally when both culminate in
the same recommendation for the practice of liberal education in our day—the
study of the great books (WILE 1, 6; LER, 27).

Yet it would be a mistake to jettison the numerous indications that the addresses differ, despite their common advocacy of great books education. In order
to understand Strauss's two-fold intention let us begin with the statement he
signals to be more fundamental—the shorter Socratic inquiry, "What is Liberal
Education?" Midway through that address Strauss identifies liberal education as
"education to perfect gentlemanship, to human excellence"; "liberal education,"
he says, "consists in reminding ourselves of human greatness," which means
attending to "Plato's suggestion that education in the highest sense is philoso-

phy" (WILE 5, 6). The highest theme, the theme of "What is Liberal Education," is education to or in light of philosophy as the peak of "human excellence," "human greatness." Accordingly, Strauss in this speech makes one of the most extensive comments in his corpus on the nature and goodness of philosophy (WILE 6–10).

"Liberal Education and Responsibility" also touches on the relations between liberal education and philosophy. "In the light of philosophy, liberal education takes on a new meaning," i.e., new to the line of argument Strauss had been pursuing to that point, the classical understanding of liberal education as education for "gentlemen." In "the light of philosophy...liberal education, especially education in the liberal arts, comes to sight as a preparation for philosophy. This means that philosophy transcends gentlemanship," especially with regard to the virtues developed by and in the respective types of education (LER 10–11). At this point the second address looks as though it is making the same turn as the first address—to liberal education as philosophic education. But Strauss abruptly turns away from that theme "by assuming that the philosophers are not as such a constituent part of the city," and from that point forward taking his bearings by the relation between liberal education and the city, thereby allowing him to fulfill his imposed obligation to speak of "liberal education and responsibility." Taking one's bearings by philosophy would not allow him to discharge that responsibility so well, for, as he emphasizes, the philosopher has only very limited responsibility to the city (LER 13).

On both occasions Strauss addresses the topic of liberal education; on both occasions he promotes the cause of great books education as the proper form of liberal education in our day. But in the one address he looks at liberal education in light of philosophy; in the other in light of the city or politics. The two speeches thus epitomize the themes of Strauss's life work—philosophy and politics. That the address to the graduates corresponds to the "voluntary" Socratic conversation and the one to the educators to the involuntary or compelled Socratic dialogue now makes perfect sense. The two addresses together also reveal that liberal education lacks a single goal and a single method. The two together address the problematic of liberal education today—the difference, amounting, it seems, to a tension between liberal education as understood and practiced in the light of philosophy and liberal education as understood and practiced in the light of the political. Strauss's reflections on liberal education take the form of asking what that kind of education can contribute to the health or well-being of a human individual versus what it can contribute to the health or well-being of a political community. But since, he insists, philosophy transcends, and is even in tension with the city, it cannot be the case that the two-fold end of liberal education can readily be combined into one educational practice. I would tentatively conclude, therefore, that the question posed by Strauss's writings on liberal education, as well as by his practice of liberal education, is how the tension or disproportion between the two goals of education can be negotiated or held together in one practice of education, and why that one practice is great books education.

Philosophic Education and the Great Books

Why should education to philosophy or in light of philosophy be great books education? Given the tendency within the contemporary study of philosophy to ignore or depreciate the history of philosophy, it is clear that those in charge of philosophic education in the modern university would not agree with Strauss. But these are authorities he would reject out of hand. Consider his comments on contemporary teachers of philosophy: they should no more be confused with philosophers than art historians should be confused with artists (WILE, 6). Nonetheless an authority for whom he has much greater respect, Plato, also does not present the education to philosophy as education in great books (cf. *Rep.*, Bk. 7).

Strauss presents three distinct arguments in favor of liberal education as great books education. The three relate to each other dialectically. The first argument occurs in the very first paragraph of "WILE" as an implication of his first proffered definition of liberal education as "education in culture or toward culture," where culture is understood on the model of agriculture, in this case as "the cultivation of the mind, the taking care and improving of the native faculties of the mind in accordance with the nature of the mind" (WILE 1). The cultivation of the mind is performed by teachers, the equivalent in this sphere to farmers in agriculture. But the teachers in turn are pupils, or have teachers until one reaches the very greatest minds, "who are not in turn pupils," but are the originators or greatest practitioners of the art of mind-cultivation. Such great minds are rare and are met "only through the great books." Therefore, liberal education is defined as "studying with proper care the great books which the greatest minds have left behind" (WILE 1).

This definition of liberal education and accompanying defense of great books education proves to be unsatisfactory and Strauss announces very soon that he must "make a fresh start" (WILE 2). He provides a number of reasons for the need to begin anew, among which is that "the greatest minds do not all tell us the same things regarding the most important themes." That disagreement among the greatest minds is matched by the fact that there would appear to be not one but many types of "culture," a "variety of cultures." Strauss suggests that the difficulty may perhaps lie in our too flexible notion of culture, according to which "any pattern of conduct common to any human group" is called a culture; to the extent that is so, the notion of education to "culture" can supply us no definite guidance for education.

A moment's reflection reveals that the difficulty with Strauss's first definition of liberal education goes deeper. It depends on the analogy between agriculture and education and implies that there is a natural end of human development as there is a natural end to the products of agriculture. It implies that in education we can unambiguously take our bearings by nature. But the facts of disagreements among "the greatest minds" and of the "variety of cultures" indicate that nature cannot so readily guide education as it can guide farming. Better and worse agriculture will produce better and worse crops of wheat, but no kind of agriculture will produce a crop of corn from seeds of wheat. But that is more or less the situation with mind-culture: one model of a "greatest mind" will be a Plato, another a Heidegger. One sort of mind culture will produce a "culture of suburbia" and another "a culture of juvenile gangs" (WILE, 2). One will produce an Athens, another a Maori tribe.

Strauss's initial definition of liberal education fails for at least the reason that it abstracts from convention and proceeds as if nature is all, or as if the nature of a human being is no more complex or problematic than the nature of an ear of corn. In response to the one-sidedness of his first definition Strauss tries another tack: liberal education somehow relates to modern democracy. This movement in the argument is meant to give an answer to the question "what can liberal education mean here and now" (WILE, 2). To ask about the "here and now" is to implicitly recognize what his first approach to the question ignored by taking for granted that liberal education takes its bearings by something timeless and universal, "the nature of the mind" (WILE 1). "Here and now…liberal education is the counterpoison to mass culture" or "the necessary endeavor to found an aristocracy within democratic mass society" (WILE, 4). Although modern democracy began in the hope of producing a "universal aristocracy," it seems rather to have produced "mass culture," a kind of culture marked by the dominance of mediocrity or less (WILE, 4), belying those hopes that democracy would lead to the elevation of mankind. "Liberal education" serves as "counterpoison" to this kind of modern culture in so far as it "reminds those members of a mass democracy who have ears to hear, of human greatness" (WILE, 4). Once again Strauss connects the idea of human greatness to the great books, for these are, as he said, products of the greatest minds. Proper study of the great books would indeed counter the mediocrity of mass society and contribute to the elevation of that society by reminding of how much more can be aspired to than the normal run of intellectual achievement and human depth achieved within mass culture.

Strauss's first definition of liberal education and his accompanying first defense of great books education proceed on the basis of a very common notion of education as the development or perfection of natural human faculties. It looks at education as a means to individual self-development. The second set of definitions takes its bearings by another very common notion of the point of education—to serve social or political ends, to fit individuals to serve the common good. Strauss has folded into that basic idea several of his most characteristic themes: society as such is an abstraction and one must rather think in terms of regime, or the ordering of authority within a society. The regime gives to the society its character. Concerned with the "here and now" Strauss limits his attention to the regime dominant today, modern democracy.

The dominance of mediocrity within modern democracy means that it needs something more than mass culture provides. Democracy, even as the home of mass culture, "requires in the long run qualities of an entirely different kind [from those typically produced within mass culture]: qualities of dedication, of concentration, of breadth, and of depth" (WILE, 4). Liberal education, in this account, is required for the sake of the public good of modern democracy, i.e., as a requirement of regime maintenance. Liberal education as "counterpoison to mass culture," as an instrument for producing higher or more strenuous qualities, as a "reminder of human greatness" supplies the transition to the third and last discussion of liberal education. Given that it is a transition to liberal education as preparation for philosophy, the transition is curiously made via appeal to the authority of Xenophon and Plato, and not on the basis of philosophy itself: The transition to philosophy must occur in the pre-philosophic and therefore must occur non-philosophically.

The emergence of human greatness understood as philosophy seems to return to the initial definition of liberal education on the model of agriculture. That impression is correct in so far as the third treatment of liberal education returns to an individual perspective. The impression of return to the first definition is also mistaken, as can be seen if we notice what is missing from this third discussion. There is no mention of "culture" either in the sense of cultivation or in the sense of "any pattern of behavior" and belief. Where the first definition spoke very generally and vaguely of the end of education as "improving…the native faculties of the mind in accordance with the nature of the mind," the third speaks far more concretely of philosophy as that end.

The concreteness of Strauss's evocation of the end of education is not matched by the clarity of his discussion of that end. He is obscure and even apparently contradictory in what he says of this highest human activity. The difficulty of his discussion turns on two deep equivocations in the discussion. "Philosophy," he tells us, "is quest for wisdom or quest for knowledge regarding the most important, the highest, or the most comprehensive things." But the wisdom or knowledge sought in philosophy "is inaccessible to man." The conclusion he draws is "we cannot be philosophers…but we can love philosophy; we can try to philosophize" (WILE, 6). The two equivocations occur right here. He seems to be using "philosophy" in two different senses—first, as the quest for wisdom, etc., and second as the achievement of wisdom, etc. In the second sense we cannot be philosophers but in the first sense we can try to philosophize. In the second sense there are no philosophers, but at the same he tells us that the "philosophizing" that we can try to engage in "consists…in listening to the conversation between the great philosophers." These "great philosophers" existed and would then seem to be philosophers in the first sense, seekers after and lovers of wisdom, etc. A parallel equivocation occurs in Strauss's use of the pronoun "we" in this part of his address. After asserting the unavailability of wisdom per se he concludes "we cannot be philosophers," referring, apparently, to all human beings. In the immediate sequel, however, he seems to use "we" to refer to him and his audience, or to human beings of our time and place, for he emphasizes that the form of education in which we can engage is to listen "to the conversations between the great philosophers."

Surely as careful a writer as Strauss is aware of the equivocations in his text. Let us try to sort out the various points raised in this puzzling discussion.

First, he is bringing out the gap between the philosophic aspiration and the philosophic achievement, a theme he returns to many times in his corpus (e.g., *WIPP*, 11, 38-40). That theme in turn leads to a most pressing problem—why philosophy, if philosophy is such a "Sisyphean" enterprise? (*WIPP*, 40). He will return to this question at the end of WILE.

Second, he is bringing out the particularly problematic character of philosophy in the "here and now," i.e., in modernity. This too is a common theme in his work. His general point could be stated as follows. Philosophy is always a difficult enterprise and a rare achievement. Although human beings are in a sense naturally ordered to philosophy, much in them stands in the way. Few have the time or leisure for it since most human lives are and must be devoted to the lower but far more urgent tasks of survival. Moreover, as social beings, humans live in communities held together by authoritative norms and myths. Much pressure exists in these societies to maintain these norms, while philosophy requires intellectual questioning or challenging of all authoritative norms. The moral pressure of society is thus arrayed against philosophy. Finally, that Sisyphean character of philosophy disappoints and hence discourages many from the pursuit. These are universal factors standing between human beings and philosophy.

There are other forces too that particularly afflict us moderns. Thus for us it seems much harder to philosophize than it was, say, for individuals of Socrates' time. Thus Strauss says "we cannot be philosophers" at the same time that he recommends to us the study of the philosophers of the past. What is not possible for us was possible for them. Strange to say, Strauss sees the very existence of a philosophic tradition as itself a barrier to philosophy. The tradition leads to a misunderstanding of the nature of philosophy: it makes us think that philosophy is doctrinal, systematic, and dogmatic, whereas it is not doctrines but a way of living, and it is not systematic or dogmatic but zetetic. Moreover, as he argues in *NRH*, the tradition pre-shapes our beginning points for thinking philosophically and thereby estranges us from the proper beginning points in pre-theorized opinions or "common sense." One reason it is much more difficult to philosophize today derives from the fact that unlike Socrates or Aristotle, we must struggle to find the starting points, for common opinion has been completely infected by residues of the philosophic tradition.

For us, study of the great books is the necessary propaedeutic to the recovery of philosophy. Particularly important is the conflict among the great thinkers, which invites or spurs us to attempt to judge between them, a task that pushes us toward philosophizing. Strauss notes more than once in WILE the irony or even absurdity of the task liberal education poses: we who are probably lesser must judge those who are probably greater in intellect and depth.

The absurdity implicit in the task of liberal education in the here and now is obscured for us, Strauss suggests, by "a number of facile delusions" two of which he explicitly identifies. The first is the "delusion" of progress, the view that our modern point of view is superior to that of thinkers of the past and according to which judging between them is not very difficult, for the philosophic teaching closest to dominant opinion in our day is taken to be the most correct.

Study of the great books under the reign of that view will never lead to philosophy or to serious engagement with the thought of the past.

Closely related is the more relativist or historicist view that all thinkers are related to their times and situations in such a way that "none can be simply true" (WILE, 8). This too cannot lead to philosophy or serious engagement. Both "delusions" are variants of the problem that most besets us moderns—the problem of history. The deepest problem we moderns face derives from our views of history or human historicity, views that are themselves the latest and most challenging products of the philosophic tradition itself. We moderns dwell, Strauss sometimes said, in a "cave beneath the cave" that Plato had spoken of in his *Republic*. Not merely do we need to struggle to free ourselves from the illusions and restraints within the cave, but we must struggle to find our way back to the cave so that we can struggle to free ourselves from the cave.

Strauss's view of liberal education as education to philosophy thus finds us painted into a corner with no clear prospect that the paint will ever dry. We must have recourse to the tradition to find our way, but the tradition has closed off the means by which we could make good use of the tradition.

Strauss, however, is more optimistic than he has to this point of his argument led us to expect him to be. In his closing paragraphs he addresses the two large problems of liberal education as path to philosophy, the problem deriving from our modern situation and the problem deriving from the universal situation of philosophy as necessarily incomplete and frustrated in its aims. Our situation renders us particularly unable to fulfill our task of judging among the great books—and yet Strauss remarkably reverses his diagnosis. We must face our responsibility to judge in the face of our incompetence to do so, and of our delusional view that judging is either unnecessary or impossible.

As it seems to me, the cause of this situation is that we have lost all simply authoritative traditions in which we could trust, the *nomos* which gave us authoritative guidance, because our immediate teachers and teachers' teachers believed in the possibility of a simply rational society. Each of us here is compelled to find his bearings by his own powers, however, defective they may be (WILE, 8).

Strauss's thought near the end of his address is difficult to follow because he is effecting an astounding reversal. Philosophy is actually in some ways more evidently necessary for us now than it has been in the past precisely as a result of the work of the philosophic tradition, which heretofore appeared as a source of the occlusion of philosophy. The Enlightenment philosophers—the projectors of a "simply rational society" and the formulators of the delusion of progress—have quite unintentionally helped provide the basis for a return to philosophy in the destruction they wrought of *nomoi* that provided "authoritative guidance" for all previous societies and that constituted the chains that held us captive in the cave. Ironically, the cave beneath the cave provides the preconditions for freedom from the initial or "natural" cave. We have no authoritative guidance and thus are aware of our need to "find [our] bearings by [our] own powers, however defective these may be." The destruction of all dogmas must therefore include the destruction of the historicist dogma as well. Such at least was the point Strauss made in one of the most common practices in his teaching: nearly every course began with a demonstration of the self-contradictory character of the historicist position, as prerequisite to opening the minds of his students to the possibility of that bold and even presumptuous act of judging that constitutes the step into philosophy.

Perhaps it should go without saying, but in affirming the possibility of philosophizing via the great books Strauss is not implying that a nation of philosophers is possible. He has no illusion that the rational society sought by our predecessors is possible. The education into philosophy is for a few and has little likelihood of being transformative for society (cf. LER, 28). As he emphasizes in "Liberal Education and Responsibility," "the city as city is more closed to philosophy than open to it" (LER, 13). "Philosophy can then only live side by side with the city" (LER 13). That living side by side is particularly possible in modern democracy, for there is "the obvious fact that by giving freedom to all, democracy also gives freedom to those who care for human excellence. No one prevents us from cultivating our garden" (LER 27). To cultivate one's own garden—that seems to be the philosophic vocation.

Our present paradoxical situation does not, contrary to first impression, rule out liberal education as a path to philosophy. But what of the more universal problem of philosophy—its Sisyphean character? Here too Strauss is more hopeful than we might expect.

We cannot exert our understanding without from time to time understanding something of importance; and this act of understanding may be accompanied by the awareness of our understanding, by the understanding of understanding, by *noesis noesos*, and this is so high, so pure, so noble an experience that Aristotle could ascribe it to his God.

Philosophy may not be able to achieve its goal of wisdom but Strauss in an uncharacteristically poetic passage indicates its goodness despite its limits. The conscious experience of understanding, of progress in knowing, is enough, enough to make us aware "of the dignity of the mind...the true ground of the dignity of man and therewith the goodness of the world, whether one understands it as created or as uncreated, which is the home of man because it is the home of the human mind" (WILE, 9). Philosophy may not be capable of settling the question of created vs. eternal world, but it can settle a yet more fundamental question—what is the place of man and man's mind within the whole. These pleasures and the insight into the correspondence of man and world make philosophy a life worth living, and the basic experience of understanding is open to many if not all, for the experience of understanding is not limited to the "greatest minds."

Strauss emphasizes that it is the act of understanding more than the particular content understood that matters. "This experience [of understanding] is entirely independent of whether what one understands primarily is pleasing or displeasing, fair or ugly" (WILE, 9). It is in the spirit of that claim that we must understand Strauss's parting words: "Liberal education supplies us with experience in things beautiful" (WILE, 10).

Liberal Education and Modern Democracy

The organizers of the conference at which Strauss delivered the talk "Liberal Education and Responsibility" charged him to expand his comments on liberal education as means "to found an aristocracy within democratic mass society" (LER, 3). The organizers perhaps noticed what we have briefly adverted to. One of the three perspectives from which Strauss views liberal education in his first address is the political. In that perspective liberal education was identified as the "counterpoison" to the mass culture of modern democracy, a function it serves by reminding of human greatness in a context in which such reminders are necessary in order to maintain democracy. However, perhaps for reasons of time constraints, Strauss no sooner introduced the idea of human greatness than he slid away from the political function of liberal education to its role as road to philosophy. Since his topic was the Socratic question "what is liberal education," it is understandable that he was eager to ascend to the highest aim or purpose of liberal education, philosophy. But in rushing so quickly to philosophy he almost completely slighted the political theme he had raised.

Partly because of the prodding of the organizers Strauss was compelled to address the relation between liberal education and responsibility, a concern, he makes clear at the opening of his essay, that is strictly moral and political, for "responsibility," he concluded, was a substitute for more directly moral phenomena, such as "duty," "conscience," or "virtue" (LER, 2). But whatever that substitution means (Strauss seems to claim not to know) "responsibility" remains a political-moral phenomenon. His assigned task thus pushed him to put liberal education in a completely different light than what he did in his first address.

Strauss's second address is much longer than the first and covers a much wider array of topics. It covers more but does not go as deep: although it raises the issue of philosophy and liberal education, it is not nearly so revealing about the nature of the philosophic life. The scope of the second essay is so great that in it Strauss moves from liberal education in its "original political meaning" to "the prospects for liberal education within mass democracy" (LER 4, 28; WILE 3).

Originally, liberal education was the education suited to "a man who behaved in a manner becoming a free man," that is to say, education for those not subject to the necessities imposed by slavery or by earning a living. It was education for men who could live a life good for its own sake and not subject to external necessities (LER, 4–5). The original liberal education is not primarily bookish education, although it contains some bookish elements. "It consists above all in the formation of character and taste. The fountains of that education are poets," not philosophers. But it largely consists in "experiential learning" based on "familiar intercourse with older or more experienced gentlemen." Original liberal education "requires leisure" and is therefore "the preserve of a certain kind of wealthy people" (LER, 5). It is emphatically not based on commitment to the proposition that "all men are created equal" (LER, 15). The original liberal education is geared to men who are to rule their societies (LER, 6–8). Thus, it definitely relates to "responsibility," the assigned topic of Strauss's paper: This education "not only fosters civic responsibility: it is even required for the exercise of civic responsibility" (LER, 9).

These gentlemen—aristocrats as it were—have two main pursuits or activities—politics, to which Strauss has devoted much of his attention, and philosophy, to which he turns in the tenth paragraph. But the philosophy with which the gentlemen concern themselves is not philosophy "understood strictly"; it is rather "what is now called intellectual interests" (LER, 10). But philosophy in the strict sense is relevant to understanding the situation and nature of the gentlemen, and therewith the liberal education they receive. There is both an important discontinuity and on important continuity between them and the philosophers. Philosophy is higher than gentlemanship. "The gentleman's virtue is not entirely the same as the philosopher's virtue," for they have different ends and goods, captured well enough in the characteristically political life of the gentleman and the apolitical life of the philosopher (LER, 11). "According to classical philosophy, the end of the philosophers is radically different from the end or ends...[of] the nonphilosophers" (LER, 22). Since they have different ends the education they receive perforce is different or at least has different aims. So far as liberal education is education toward gentlemanship, it is governed by the fact that "the gentleman accepts on trust certain most weighty things"—the fundamental moral, political, and theological beliefs of the gentlemanly class—"which for the philosopher are the themes of investigation and of questioning" (LER 11). Although he does not dwell on it, this difference is immense and necessarily affects the character of liberal education "all the way down." Education that "accepts on trust" or even inculcates those "weighty things" and education that encourages the questioning or even challenging of these very "weighty things" are two very different practices indeed. But since the young do not come pre-labeled as gentleman or philosopher, the serious question immediately arises: how does one combine in one educational practice these two different— opposite—educational regimes? In his essays on liberal education Strauss does not explicitly address that decisive question, but his well known answer concerns that kind of speaking and writing that says different things to different people.

Despite the very great difference between the virtue of the gentleman and the philosopher Strauss makes the perhaps surprising claim that "the gentleman's virtue is a reflection of the philosopher's virtue; one may say it is its political reflection" (LER, 11). The basis of this extraordinarily important claim lies in the feature of the gentleman's moral orientation that Strauss emphasizes on several occasions: "The gentlemen regard virtue as choice worthy for its own sake, whereas the others praise virtue as a means for acquiring wealth and honor. The gentlemen and the others disagree, then, as regards the end of man or the highest good; they disagree regarding first principles" (LER, 21, 22). But the philosopher agrees with the gentlemen relative to the non-gentlemen: there is a human activity choice worth for its own sake and not "as a means for acquiring wealth and honor." The philosophers, as Strauss sees it, are entirely correct in their judgment, while the gentlemen have but a "reflected," i.e., distorted, view, but they nonetheless embody the crucial claim that allows the gentlemen to elevate their entire society when they are sufficiently prominent in it, the claim of a good beyond the lower goods of survival, pleasure, wealth, and honor, the claim that there is a good or ground of moral judgment, the noble, beyond the merely instrumental (cf. LER, 21).

The relation of liberal education to politics changed considerably in modern times, setting the particular political task of liberal education in the here and now. These changes resulted from changes in both political life and in education (LER, 14, 21). Strauss speaks of three moments in the evolving relation between politics and liberal education in the modern era. Modern politics in all three moments differs from earlier politics in that it affirms "the natural equality of all men, and it leads therefore to the assertion that sovereignty belongs to the people" (LER, 14). There can be no question then of the gentlemen or the philosophers ruling in their own right. But originally at least, modern politics was marked by the distinction "between the sovereign and the government," which meant that though the people were sovereign they did not need to rule (LER 14). Indeed, the early moderns generally accepted an arrangement according to which elites, who were responsible to the people, ruled (LER, 15). The people, who held an ultimate power under this arrangement, were to be formed by a religious education "based on the Bible...to regard himself as responsible for his actions and for his thoughts to a God who would judge him" (LER, 15). There was no thought of a universal enlightenment. The elites in turn would be prepared for their task via liberal education, which in the case of classic early moderns like Locke still had many echoes of classical liberal education. It was to be "education in 'good breeding,'" based in large part on classical literature and modern political philosophy (LER, 15).

But as modernity progressed, this solution did not hold. "The enlightenment was destined to become universal enlightenment" (LER, 21). The relatively clear distinction between popular sovereignty and government was blurred as the norm of ever more democratic governance spread (LER, 15). The ideal of enlightenment spread but the need for special liberal education receded—"the only thing which can be held to be unqualifiedly good is...a good intention, and of good intentions everyone is as capable as everyone else, wholly independently of education." Indeed, education may be a disadvantage: "the voice of nature or of the moral law speaks in [the uneducated] perhaps more clearly and more decidedly than in the sophisticated who may have sophisticated away their conscience" (LER 24).

We now live in a third phase marked by "tension between the ethos of democracy and the ethos of technocracy," a tension that apparently replaces the earlier tension between the city and philosophy. Our situation is the ultimate result of the various innovations introduced by modern philosophy. In one of his most pregnant formulations Strauss identifies the genesis of modern philosophy in the identification of "the end of philosophy...with the end which is capable of being actually pursued by all men," or "more precisely," in the subordination of philosophy to the end "capable of being actually pursued by all men." Most men—the non-philosophers and the non-gentlemen—pursue preservation, wealth, and honor. The new aim of philosophy can be captured in the Baconian formula, "the relief of man's estate" (LER, 21).

With the collapse of the distinction of ends between the philosopher and non-philosopher comes the collapse of the distinction between the gentlemen and the non-gentlemen. All human beings and all human aims are now assimilated to the latter class. Philosophy became a means to power and thus becomes technologized. Morality becomes instrumentalized, i.e., merely the rules best suited to achieving the non-moral goods (LER, 22).

The advanced stages of these various processes leaves us with a mass democracy—ever larger political societies governed by or responsible to the masses—and the authority of science, which leads to a new conception of education and our present situation. Science has had two particularly potent effects in addition to the large increase in power put in the hands of modern humanity. On the one hand, science has come to pronounce itself unable to produce "rational knowledge of 'values,' that is, the science or reason is incompetent to distinguish between good and evil ends" (LER, 25). This is the development Strauss often speaks of as positivism and as one of the elements of the "crisis of our times." The other development sponsored by the triumph of modern science is the growth of specialization; which produces individuals, according to the now familiar adage, who know more and more about less and less. Our predicament, in a word, is that we have ever increasing power and ever weaker resources for controlling it and putting it to good use, in part because no one has broad enough vision to see the whole landscape and in part because we are increasingly unable to say what the good ends are.

Liberal education is of importance in this context; it is needed to overcome the narrowness of specialization and the aimlessness promoted by current thinking about "values." Strauss is not particularly optimistic that liberal education can fill the needs of the day. The universities are dominated by the very intellectual trends that need to be countered. Under conditions of mass democracy "the insufficiently educated are bound to have an unreasonably strong influence on education" (LER, 26). It is thus difficult to find the lever by which education can be moved to counter the present situation.

So far as there is hope it lies in liberal education understood as great books education (LER, 27). We must, of course, recall his warnings from "What is Liberal Education?" about the modern delusions that will prevent us from deriving any benefit from the great books. To the warnings about historicism of the first essay must be joined the warnings about positivism of this essay. So long as either science or history leads to the dismissal of value questions great books will neither lead to political good nor prepare the way for philosophy. Thus in Strauss's own educational practice the critique of positivism and historicism almost inevitably prefaced every inquiry into political philosophy. Strauss sometimes seemed obsessive about these twin demons, but as he saw it, they are the threshold barriers the overcoming of which is required for liberal education to be of any value.

The great books of the past are particularly adept at providing the broadening and deepening required in our age of technocracy and democratism because they were produced by men of particular intellect and humanity. They were produced by thinkers not themselves under the sway of technocratic specialization and democratic willfulness. Strauss does not expect liberal education, even when pursued well, to have an indoctrinating effect of any sort. "We cannot expect that liberal education will lead all who benefit from it to understand their civic responsibility in the same way or to agree politically" (LER, 28). He cites the examples of Marx and Nietzsche, two extraordinarily liberally educated individuals, who disagreed with each other as much as possible politically. The political aim of liberal education today is not the inculcation of one or another political ideology but rather the fostering of political moderation, a moderation that stays away from the one extreme of "visionary expectations from politics" as well as the opposite extreme of "unmanly contempt for politics" (LER, 28). In its political or moral bearing liberal education is not to promote the tending of one's own garden and is to encourage moderation rather than mania.

The theme so prominent in Strauss's first essay—the conflict and disagreements among the great thinkers—must be in part the basis for his lopes that liberal education will promote moderation. That disagreement, which we are so incompetent to adjudicate, discourages hasty and one-sided conclusions. It fosters the kind of moderation that sees a point in various alternatives, and thus hesitates to put all its eggs in any one basket or alternative. Strauss, writing not too long after the horrors of World War II and in the midst of the Cold War, also counts on our experience of "the grandiose failures" of the political regimes that less moderate projectors like Marx and Nietzsche had fathered or grandfathered (LER, 28). The chief political lesson Strauss hopes liberal education can impart is that "wisdom requires unhesitating loyalty to a decent constitution and even to the cause of constitutionalism" (Ibid). He attempts to reproduce within modernity the effect of liberal education in pre-modernity: "thus it may again become true that all liberally educated men will be politically moderate men" (Ibid). Nonetheless, he cautions, the most we can expect are "palliatives," not "cures" (LER, 29).

Strauss's Educational Practice

As is now clear, liberal education understood in light of philosophy and liberal education understood in light of politics and morality point in two different if not simply conflicting directions. Strauss leaves us with the conundrum of how to combine those two ways into one educational practice. As it happens we probably know more about Strauss as a teacher than we do about many other historical political philosophers. From some time in the late 1950s until the end of his career Strauss's classes were audio taped and the transcripts from these tapes are now or soon to be available on the website of the Leo Strauss Center (leostrausscenter.uchicago.edu). Moreover, several of Strauss's students have left reminiscences of him as a teacher, many of which are also available on the Strauss Center website.

I too was student of Strauss's in his very last years at Chicago, years marked by physical frailty, and can add some observations of my own to those of others who had a fuller and richer experience of him in the classroom. By the time I was in Strauss's classes he was a major figure in the world. Many of us had come to Chicago expressly to study with him and we did not have the experience many of his older students had of coming upon him unknown and being astonished by the power of his mind and the stimulation of his classroom persona. We, on the contrary, were primed for him. We were prepared to be impressed and for the most part we were. Sometimes too much so, as his method of teaching allowed a certain passivity in his students. Almost all his courses in my time were graduate seminars—although they were not the small group experiences one thinks of when one thinks of seminars. He had perhaps fifty students in the average seminar and thus had to meet in a regular classroom, not a seminar room. I believe that not all fifty persons in the room were ordinary registered students, for many were older students writing dissertations, or even beyond the dissertation stage; many were walk-ins from outside the university. As Strauss said in "WILE," he never turned away non-paying students.

His seminars were all conducted in the same way. They ordinarily covered only one text. In my time he taught Grotius; individual dialogues of Plato (*Gorgias, Protagoras, Meno, Apology and Crito*); Aristotle's *Politics*, Kant *On History*, Hegel's *Philosophy of History*, Nietzsche's *Beyond Good and Evil* and *Genealogy of Morals* (an exceptional two books), and Montesquieu's *Spirit of the Laws* and *Persian Letters* spread over two quarters. He taught a full range of texts from across the history of political philosophy, focusing a bit on areas of current interest to him, but also making it a practice to teach on a regular basis basic texts that he thought the graduate students needed to know. In my years he was deepening his knowledge of the turn to history in political philosophy, and thus the courses on Montesquieu, Kant, Hegel and Nietzsche. At the same time he was extending his knowledge of Plato. But he also taught the *Politics* twice, a text he believed all political science students should know.

He ran his seminars in a hybrid Germanic-American manner. He divided the text to be considered into as many segments as there were class sessions and assigned out the segments to the registered students. Each class period began with the presentation of a student paper—a strict twenty-minute limit on the papers—followed by an on the spot commentary on the paper by Strauss. He then turned to a more or less systematic treatment of the text for the day. He was very careful to get through the entire assignment, which meant that for some of the longer texts he skipped across the material, while for some, like the shorter Platonic dialogues, he was able to proceed almost line by line. Occasionally he paused to deliver something more akin to a mini-lecture, providing more of an overview than the passage by passage treatment allowed. In my day he had a reader who read aloud the passages Strauss wished to comment on. Strauss combined this German mode of comment with a more American discussion centered format, although more in his earlier years than in my day. Some of the transcripts are remarkable for how much lively discussion Strauss provoked and how open he was to learning from the students. He always had great authority in the classroom but he also encouraged students to contribute by calling attention to passages that puzzled him or which raised issues in need of airing. He was courteous in an old-world sort of way and always treated students with respect and encouragement. He could be critical of student presentations but never presented his criticisms harshly. He was not the sort of teacher who reduced his students to tears.

But of course no description of the externals of his procedures or of the atmosphere of his classroom can explain how his practice of teaching related to his understanding of the task of liberal education in our day. Perhaps most obviously, Strauss called for great books education and that is what he provided—he taught the works of "the greatest minds." He taught them in such a way as to bring the great texts to the fore. A Strauss class was not about him, not about his particular philosophic or political views. He faded into the background and tried so far as he could to let or help the thinkers speak to his listeners. In his writings and in his classroom teaching Strauss entered into the thought of the thinker and presented the thinker in the thinker's voice so far as he could, whether he, Strauss, agreed with that thinker or not. Occasionally, but only occasionally, he commented on the thought from his own point of view, but he found it more important to help modern readers understand the authors as they understood themselves than to judge them in the facile ways modern readers are prone to do. His classroom style thus does not strictly conform to the task he laid out in that we must judge among the great thinkers. It is not that he ever put the question of the truth of the thought aside, but he modeled for students the idea that one had to understand a thinker properly before one could judge him. The foregrounding of understanding the thinkers adequately by learning how to read them "with the proper care" is one of the ways in which Strauss combined in one pedagogy the two different ends of liberal education.

Another way in which he acted on his notions of liberal education is the aforementioned and nearly universal practice in both the classroom and in his writings of critiquing positivism and historicism. Nearly every course began with some version of this critique, a part both of liberal education toward philosophy and toward moderate and decent politics. Moreover, a large part of the substantive emphasis of his teaching was directed against historicism. That doctrine held that thinkers necessarily reflected their times; Strauss attempted to show that that was far from true and that the appearance that it was true was largely an artifact of the "art of writing" philosophers of the past employed. For various reasons they presented themselves as much more in harmony with reigning opinion of their times than they actually were. Strauss's attempt to respond to historicist claims at this empirical level led to some of the very controversial readings of the philosophers that he produced.

Strauss's activity as a teacher was not, of course, exhausted in the classroom. His many books were also acts of teaching, and he was always conscious of the difference between what was appropriate to the classroom and the book. When teaching Hegel, for example, he pointed to the much greater accessibility of Hegel's lectures compared to his books. The same certainly holds for Strauss as well. The books clearly go deeper and are far more challenging than his classroom proceedings. But there is a great continuity between his classroom teaching and his scholarly works as well. The best way to characterize that continuity, I believe, is in terms of what I have elsewhere called pedagogical reserve. Pedagogical reserve is perhaps the chief means by which Strauss holds together the two dimensions of liberal education in his own pedagogical practice. I am referring to that aspect of Strauss's writing and speaking that often leads readers and critics to attribute to Strauss the kind of esoteric writing he attributes to some of the thinkers in the tradition. It is certain that Strauss withholds much in his communication. He sometimes withholds conclusions—what he thinks follows from arguments he is presenting. He sometimes withholds parts of the argument but gives us his conclusions. He sometimes scatters his points though his writing, requiring of the reader an effort to remember what was said somewhere else that is deeply relevant to what is immediately at hand. The omissions, the scatterings, his subtle qualifications of points, the often difficult to penetrate structures of his writings are best understand, I think, as invitations to those more philosophically inclined to go deeper with him. Both in the classroom and in his books Strauss was a teacher who proceeded by offering such invitations. He certainly offered something to those who did not often take up these invitations—they came away with some good and certainly very interesting intellectual history. They came away with the firm message Strauss emphasized in his second essay on liberal education, the desirability of political and moral moderation, and the misguided character of the modern thinking that took its bearings from positivism or historicism. Those who took up his invitations came away with more—but not really different. Pedagogical reserve is not another name for "noble lying" as some of Strauss's recent critics have charged. He really believed in the value of political moderation; he really believed that positivism and historicism were misguided guides to understanding human thought. Strauss was, in sum, a man who practiced liberal arts education as he preached it.

Notes

1. I have left all references in the text. The works cited are the following: (Smith): Steven Smith, "Leo Strauss the Outlines of a Life' in Steven Smith ed. *The Cambridge Companion to Leo Strauss* (New York: Cambridge University Press, 2009); (CM): The City and Man (Chicago, Rand McNally, 1964; (LAM): Leo Strauss, *Liberalism Ancient and Modern* (New York: Basic Books, 1968); (LER): "Liberal Education and Responsibility," in LAM, 1–8; 1968); (Nicgorski): Walter Nicgorski, "Leo Strauss and Liberal Education" *Interpretation*; (WILE): Leo Strauss, "What is Liberal Education" in LAM 9–25; (WIPP): *What is Political Philosophy?and Other Essays*, (Glencoe, The Free Press, 1959).

2. References to LER and WILE are to paragraph number.

Chapter 10

Stanley Rosen: The Nemesis of Nihilism
Nalin Ranasinghe, Assumption College

Although his writing style has changed more than once, Rosen has always sought to defend the lifeline between cosmos and logos; he has always insisted that the bond between philosophy and ordinary language is sacred and indissoluble. From this vantage his amazing ability to yoke together and drive the unruly black horse of ordinary language and the ideal steed of metaphysics seems godlike. Accordingly, bearing in mind his teacher's famous assertion that the depth of things resides precisely in their surfaces, it is appropriate that my tribute by should begin by describing Stanley Rosen in the place where his unsurpassed mastery of both philosophy and ordinary language are most evident: the classroom.

I first took a class with Stanley Rosen almost twenty years ago, at Penn State, in the fall of 1985. What transpired in Rosen's seminar that afternoon was something that I have never experienced, either before or since, with any other teacher. My other instructors that semester were Joseph Kocklemans and the late David Lachterman, professors of rare erudition perfectly capable of making difficult texts clear and accessible. However, only Rosen, could seamlessly integrate philosophy into ordinary experience while enormously enriching his students' awareness of both. He was an amazing combination of Platonist, stand-up comedian, Dutch uncle and social commentator. Like Socrates, he could bring philosophy down from the heavens and do the most difficult topics justice in the language of the agora—or gridiron. His students saw that Rosen came before them neither to praise ordinary language—at the expense of philosophy, nor to bury it—in abstract jargon. Rosen made me aware of how flat and stale it was to make a living by opposing philosophy to everyday life; Platonism, as he embodied it, was distinguished by a robust sense of reality. A philosopher who cannot use the direct evidence of the everyday exercise of reason to justify the good life is worse than useless; he is dangerous.

This is why Rosen, America's most distinguished Platonist, has made it his mission to ceaselessly warn against the nihilistic foundations of what his teacher memorably called "the joyless quest for joy." By thoughtlessly denouncing the so-called elitist experience of excellence, our egalitarian ethos is powerless to defend the very virtues that must sustain a democracy. For one thing, any talk of high and low, noble and base or good and evil is expressed purely in terms of selfishness, sentimentality or superstition. Alternately, and even more dangerously, any "value language" that cannot be quantified is deemed either meaningless or, horror of horrors, judgmental. Consequently we find ourselves "thrown" in a world in which ordinary speech is hopelessly incompatible with the technical jargon and quantitative measurements that rule and constitute the increasingly artificial and illusory everyday reality we dwell in. Yet Rosen does not zestfully denounce Modernity in the stern constipated tones of Cato the Elder; self-consciously anachronistic speech only serves to widen the gap between eternal verities and present-day exigencies. He is of the view that human beings can only maintain the essential connection between reason and the good by living the good life in the present. Ancient self-knowledge and Modern liberality cannot be understood as virtues that mutually exclude each other.

Rosen's metaphysics of the ordinary becomes startling relevant when we realize that the hundreds of billions spent on weapons that could blow our planet up many times over are as inconceivable in terms of human experience as the immeasurably tiny particles of matter and energy used by computer technology to hold our world together. Reality today is such that even the President of the United States cannot hope to master all the data at his disposal and gain an accurate world-view without a large number of advisors and advisors of advisors, all operating from their own limited and limiting perspectives. Furthermore, by a perverse reversal of Heisenberg's Uncertainty Principle at the macro level, it seems inevitable that the very efforts made to measure and report this chaotic mass of raw matter itself result in distorted pictures of the whole that only further disorient the various entities constituting it. Consequently order, no matter how arbitrary or violent, is affirmed for its own sake. Renouncing higher notions of justice and personal integrity, both the technocratic West and the fundamentalist East shamelessly kneel before the altar of necessity. Human society becomes generic and machine-friendly, and the loudly proclaimed advances in cloning only promise to superficially embody what educational institutions have been doing to the minds of impressionable students for many decades. Under these conditions, when nobility and even uncorrupted speech seem to be all but impossible, a man who can practice ordinary language to remind us of virtue and excellence can only be compared to Tiresias in the Underworld: "alone retaining his wits while the others flitted around like shadows." Yet such is the dis-ease of this state that even many students fear those rare teachers who can deliver them from Hades.

For fifty years, Stanley Rosen has unceremoniously dragged thousands of students out of the ghetto of jargon and compelled them to speak and think in ordinary language. This is why many righteously tolerant academics have been appalled by his use of "judgmental" language and unprofessional examples to gratuitously indicate the nihilistic foundations of their schizophrenic existence. Now, as then, many highly intelligent students of philosophy prove to be utterly incapable of living their lives in accordance with the principles they pay lip service to in academese. Nihilism, an unbalanced disposition towards reality, which often results from a death-obsessed "care" or ego-maniacal authenticity, is preferred over the "logocentric" procedures of judgment and rank ordering that provide meaning and virtue in a world conspicuously deficient in both qualities. Unfortunately, the question of whether "being judgmental" is worse than being a hypocrite is one that few care to address in our simultaneously over-tolerant and over-righteous times.

Many students (and professors) still view philosophy as a disease (or way of being articulately neurotic) that they just happen to be good at. Of course, this sophisticated *diaresis* finds has no way of distinguishing between Wittgenstein and Woody Allen—and perhaps it shouldn't. In other words, philosophy becomes just a means of paying one's bills; the unquestioned end is normalcy— understood in the most banal and mimetic terms. Any setback will cause philosophers of this variety to not unhappily pursue some other, often more lucrative, career path that would better advance either "family values" or Epicurean lifestyles. Furthermore, following the example of Wittgenstein and the Logical Positivists it has become acceptable, and indeed downright philanthropic, for philosophers to set about the liquidation of philosophy itself—with a view to delivering normal people from its annoying questions and perplexities. Unfortunately, this Socratic "speed-bump" is the last obstacle to the flattening out of everyday reality and its rapid bifurcation into the mutually inclusive extremes of McWorld and Jihad.

By inconsiderately philosophizing in everyday language Rosen makes it far harder for his audience to maintain a "double-truth" relationship between philosophy and everyday existence. He has never treated philosophy as a language game that is played strictly within the pages of scholarly journals and becomes irrelevant or dangerous the moment we re-enter the real world of Xanthippe and Crito. The Good must have precedence over Being, even in our thoroughly historicized surroundings. Indeed, one could argue that Rosen has always followed Zarathustra's imperative to "be faithful to the earth" and never been seduced by ontic or even ontological exigency. Whilst those least worthy of philosophy only pursue it instrumentally, better but more timorous scholars have sought to make the world safe for philosophy and only succeeded in debasing both philosophy and the world. Vigorously eschewing both of these false oppositions, Rosen believes that true philosophers can and must justify existence through their "robust sense of reality." It follows that "rank-ordering" is an essential aspect of the distinctive manner in which a philosopher views the world and judges that it is still possible to practice virtue. Even though seeing things as they are is certainly not easy, and the task frequently seems to be as impossible as it was for Socrates or Rousseau to penetrate the encrusted outer shell of Glaucus, Rosen points us towards an abiding structure that, in his own words "isn't the eternal order but yet is the natural foundation for willing the eternal order to be."[1] It is noteworthy that despite the cryptic language, this formulation is far more positive than its equivalent in Strauss's thought: eternally recurrent problems that let philosophers stand beyond good and evil to rescue us from the chaotic mire of historicism. By his emphasis on this structure that allows noble deeds and thoughtful words to remain timelessly meaningful, Rosen defends the reality of both ordinary language and human virtue.

Furthermore, despite his passionate interest in moral and political questions, Rosen has consistently been critical of irrationalism and skepticism; both poses conveniently conclude that "everything but judgmental language is permitted" once we are either desperate or "cool" enough to assume the absurdity of existence or the final inaccessibility of ultimate reality. As a result, the world is delivered up to extremists on both ends of the political spectrum. Contrariwise, throughout his extraordinarily successful and productive career Rosen has demonstrated that ordinary language *is* sufficient to guide human life when it is governed by rational judgment—rather than mindless imitation. Conversely, ideas and facts cannot be separated from each other without consequences even more dangerous than those following the splitting of the atom. Neither does Rosen's model of human existence place man somewhere between an illusory physical world and a wholly transcendent heaven; he prefers to derive the ideas used to measure qualitative excellence from human cognitive activity itself— thus deriving depth from surface. In this important regard he once again separates himself from those who pride themselves on their ability to create values *ex-nihilo* by imposing order on the chaotic *hyle* of reality. Rosen's scathing criticisms of historicism and pseudo-aristocratic nihilism are founded in his recognition that it is possible for human beings to take their stand in the real world and resist both fundamentalism and sophistry.

Stanley Rosen, a self-described New Deal Democrat, has remained constant in his political views while instructing three generations of students. Temperamentally unsuited to occupy the Vicarage of Bray, he has never failed to warn against the worst tendencies of the ideology most in vogue among his students— even at the risk of being associated with political views that he is least sympathetic towards. His characteristic defense of prudence in eloquent but seemingly immoderate language has very little resemblance to our contemporary tendency to use insidious methods to promote extremism. Far from being the kind of man who would prescribe Nazism to ward against the corruption of Weimar, his criticisms of nihilism and Post-Modernism have always been undertaken in the name of moderate enlightenment. It is far nobler to be a Platonist accused of sounding like a Nietzschean than to be a Nietzschean impersonating a Platonist.

Rosen's well-known unwillingness to suffer fools gladly derives precisely from his awareness that many fools are yet capable of excellence; he does not allow a false sense of charity to alienate him (or them) from the experience of quality in the world. His high expectations of others have always been accompanied by genuine authenticity in personal relations with individuals. Having been educated in the company of many truly brilliant eccentrics at the University of Chicago in its glory days, and being himself the possessor of an artistic temperament, Rosen has always understood the thin line that separates genius from madness. He has never mistaken an artful plodder with a high IQ for a genuine philosopher. In a situation where students typically expect professors to be either their equal or an unapproachable superior, Rosen has refused to play either role for the sake of gaining drinking-buddies or disciples. Differently put, he has never been known to be afraid of being himself or of speaking his mind. Consequent to this refusal to conform to stereotype, humorless students (and colleagues) at both extremes have decided that he is either unprofessional or an elitist. Their pathetic inability to appreciate Rosen's unsurpassed sense of humor has always served as a kind of *pons asinorum* separating the children who approach him from the goats, sheep, camels and lions making up the intellectual order of rank. By refusing to take himself too seriously, and by never seeking to make disciples, Stanley Rosen always pointed beyond himself. The exaggerations and self-caricatures that made members of the afore-mentioned menagerie regard him as an egomaniac were in fact the productions of an artist always keenly aware of the enigmatic relationship between image and original. It followed sadly but necessarily that those incapable of understanding this basic Platonic distinction proved that they were unworthy of studying with our greatest living Platonist. Some of the most egregious misinterpretations of Plato have been committed by persons firmly convinced that a philosopher will never write or speak humorously.

Of course, any talk concerning Stanley Rosen and student teacher relationships is necessary incomplete without a discussion of his attitude towards his own teacher, Leo Strauss. Since much of Rosen's own work could be regarded as an ongoing response to certain fundamental themes in Strauss's work, and because Rosen himself has had much to say about his former teacher, we could gain valuable insights into the thought of both thinkers by directly addressing this topic. Accordingly, this will be the theme of the second half of this introduction. Just as Strauss's amazing success as a teacher is attested to by the large number of disciples garnered by this unprepossessing man, the strange fact that the charismatic and ebullient Stanley Rosen has actively refused to make disciples says a great deal about his deepest philosophical beliefs.

Rosen first met Strauss in 1949 shortly after the latter had moved to the University of Chicago after over a decade at the New School for Social Research in New York City. Rosen at the time regarded himself as a poet. He was also busily engaged in completing the requirements for a Bachelor's degree from Chicago in one year a feat that was also performed by his distinguished contemporary Seth Benardete. Rosen's hilarious account of his encounter with

Strauss awaits publication, but it suffices to state that on the occasion of their first meeting, after having introduced himself as a poet, he responded to Strauss's inquiry whether he knew what Plato said about poets by saying that he didn't care because as a poet he knew more about his art than Plato possibly could. This was the unpromising beginning of a very long and animated conversation that ended with an invitation to study with Strauss.

It is highly significant that Rosen was one of a very small number from the Philosophy Department at Chicago to attend Strauss's lectures; Richard Rorty was another. Most of the participants were either from Strauss's own department of political science or the Committee on Social Thought. Among these were intellectual luminaries such as Seth Benardete, Victor Gourevitch, Muhsin Mahdi, and Allan Bloom. Rosen was also the only one of Strauss's students to come to him from poetry. This fact is of course not unrelated to Rosen's interest in language and its, often tenuous, relationship to everyday reality. By his own account, he was also initially virtually uninterested in politics,[2] an attribute that, needless to say, also separated him from the vast majority of those who attached themselves to Strauss. Put differently, one could say that he preferred to study causes rather than effects; it has been noted on many occasions that Rosen's interests in metaphysics and epistemology also make him almost unique among Strauss's students. Because of his departmental affiliation, every official course offered by Strauss had to do with political science; however there were several private groups reading philosophical and theological works that he presided over as well.

By his own admission, Rosen attended virtually every meeting of Strauss's seminars over the five years he spent as a graduate student at the University of Chicago. It was soon readily apparent to him that Strauss "transcended the faculty members of the philosophy department in virtually every significant way." Accordingly, after taking his master's degree, Rosen transferred to the Committee on Social Thought where he was able to write a dissertation on Spinoza under the supervision of Leo Strauss. Shortly after completing his degree, marrying, and spending a year in Greece, Rosen secured employment at the Pennsylvania State University and left Chicago. This did not however end his association with Strauss. They corresponded often by letter and in 1958 Strauss visited Rosen and his wife at State College, Pennsylvania. Strauss, who had often defended Rosen against criticisms concerning his student's colorful temperament by giving assurances that he was "getting better," was very pleased at his student's success. He is said to have boasted to colleagues in Chicago that Rosen had "made it" and was now the proud owner of a house and automobile. Rosen continued to visit Strauss on many occasions, the last such visit taking place shortly before the latter's death in 1973. On that occasion, upon hearing that Rosen was preparing a book on Hegel, the ailing teacher pointed him towards what turned out to be a vitally important passage in the *Greater Logic*. This incident confirmed Rosen's adamantly held conviction that Strauss's true genius was to be found neither in his pronouncements as a statesman or prophet, nor in his metaphysical or poetic powers, but in his remarkable ability to read a text.

Rosen has stated elsewhere that Strauss rescued him as a teenager from a "transcendentally grounded nihilism." While he came to share a number of his teacher's central views and retained many of them throughout his life, Rosen says was never at any time a "Straussian."[3] Strauss never required him to become a Straussian "as a price for the extraordinary benefits he bestowed on his students."[4] Despite fully acknowledging how much he benefited from Strauss's immense learning and "sober madness" Rosen believed that there were certain important differences, largely concerning the issue of esotericism, which caused him to separate himself from the Straussian mainstream. As readers of his numerous books and articles are well aware, Rosen is in considerable sympathy with the courage and generosity animating the "Moderns" in their revolution against tradition and nature. Yet Strauss, who according to Rosen regarded courage as the lowest of virtues,[5] was often critical of what he perceived as Rosen's excessive boldness. It is worth repeating the expression *'epater le bourgeois'* (shocking the bourgeoisie) that summed up Strauss's disapproving opinion of his student's more exoteric writing style.[6] As Rosen's student, I am temperamentally incapable of not drawing attention to the obvious inference that this criticism had more to do with style than substance.

Even though Rosen's celebrated book *Nihilism* was written to work out the general features of Strauss's analysis of the nihilistic roots of modern philosophy, its "spiritual father," while commending the work highly, also commented that he himself lacked the courage to write such a book.[7] This goes to the heart of the fundamental difference between Strauss, a refugee from Nazi Germany, and Rosen, a native of Cleveland Ohio. Strauss had served in the German Army in occupied Belgium during the unprecedented carnage of the Great War; he had also lost all of the members of his family who remained in Germany to the Holocaust. It is easy to see why the author of such works as *Persecution and the Art of Writing*, a man who rediscovered the long forgotten art of esotericism by reading heretical political theologians, preferred not to express his truest opinions freely on most matters of importance. The question as to whether this had to do more with temperament, personal safety (lack of courage) or fear of corrupting his readers (*epater le bourgeois*) cannot be answered conclusively or in mutually exclusive terms. It is also not unrelated to their different views on whether it is more desirable and or practical to gain fame or disciples. There are reasons for and against the belief that Strauss, the prudent Ancient, obeyed the Greek warning against seeking fame in one's own lifespan. It is likewise unclear whether Rosen, the courageous and generous Modern, embraced Machiavelli's advice to trust in his own arms–even if they held *Fortuna* within them.

While Rosen has always defended the phenomenon of esoteric writing, it is his contention that our plight today is such that 'shocking the bourgeoisie' is far less dangerous than allowing them to persist in complacently nihilistic modes and orders already producing a cultural and economic meltdown. Put bluntly, esoteric writing is useless in a decadent time where success is measured by power, rather than wisdom, and even the best students are barely literate, certainly not pious, and often incapable of ever being more than good students.

Consequently, the true meaning of Strauss's teachings failed to reach the best minds and most able politicians of the present day. Importing esotericism to America is ultimately almost as quixotic as transplanting democracy in Iraq; in both cases one can best deflect the accusation of esoteric knavery by drawing attention to exoteric folly.

An emphasis on rigorous interpretive procedures aiming at the utmost clarity, ultimately expressed in ordinary language, rather than reliance upon oracular pronouncements and/or dogmatic assumptions concerning perfectly constructed texts that could only be decoded by infallible interpreters, starkly distinguishes Rosen's approach from methods common to both Heideggereans and Straussians. These procedures only separate student from interpreter while promoting the latter to an intellectual pantheon that confirms their qualitative kinship with the Ancients: "Where I go, you cannot follow." Additionally, dogmatic doctrines concerning perfect texts tend to create subterranean virtual realities presided over by sophistical shadow-shapers. The idea that there is only one perfect unchanging esoteric doctrine beyond good and evil denies the reality of the productive disagreements between equally great thinkers that have contributed so much to Western Civilization. It also deprives writers from past times of what while they would most desire in ours: intelligent readers capable of ascending from the signifier and sign-painter to the signified. The idea that Shakespeare could only have learned about the soul by reading Xenophon and Thucydides by candlelight denies the possibility that an intelligent man could gain much wisdom by observing human affairs. It is far more plausible that Shakespeare and other great minds gained access to that "natural foundation for willing the eternal order to be" that Rosen alludes to.

It is quite obvious that many great writers write in such a way that the deeper implications of their works would only be apparent to more astute readers. However, the view that great works are flawless masterpieces of logographic necessity takes away the only quality that makes interpersonal communication of goodness truth and beauty between very different times and places possible: shared finite humanity. Consequently, a certain kind of historicism, based upon dark oracles concerning the withdrawal of Being or caves below caves, necessitates revelatory exegesis by a superhuman mediator when unnecessarily befuddled students cry out "Only a god can enlighten us!" Conversely, by refusing to resort to obscurantism, and providing constant verbal and nonverbal reminders of his robust humanity, Stanley Rosen has never 'hermenutered' his students and left them incapable of reading for themselves. He recalls Strauss smiling broadly and quoting Nietszche's assertion that the best thing a student can do for his teacher is to kill him. Teacher-student relationships modeled after the doctrine of original sin, which opens up an infinite moral and qualitative abyss between creator and creation, are not appropriate in rational—as opposed to revelatory—contexts. In other words, teachers who produce disciplined disciples often cast a long shadow that makes emulation of the master's virtue by the disciples, or even recognition of it by later generations, all but impossible. Shakespeare put it best in *Julius Caesar*: "The evil that men do lives after them; the good is oft interred with their bones."

Rosen has stated that Leo Strauss "regarded Heidegger as the enemy of the heritage of Platonism in the late Modern world." Accordingly, he sought to "inoculate his students against Heidegger by training them in the Platonic tradition."[8] It was in the service of this cause that Rosen published two works that took direct aim at Heidegger: *Nihilism* and *A Question of Being*. Yet Rosen's singular experience was that Strauss very rarely mentioned Heidegger by name, even in private conversations and reading groups, and never referred to Heideggerean texts.[9] It was only shortly after leaving Chicago that Rosen became aware of Strauss's lecture *An Introduction to Heideggerian Existentialism* a revised version of which was published by Thomas Pangle in 1989. This document concludes with a description of Heideggerean Being or *Esse* as a synthesis of the Platonic Ideas and the Biblical God. *Esse* is said to be as impersonal as the former and as elusive as the latter.[10] It is exceedingly curious that Strauss himself, in his famous 1953 lecture *Progress or Return?* claimed that the secret of the vitality of the West depended on the continuance of the unresolved conflict between Reason and Revelation, Jerusalem and Athens.[11] Bearing in mind Heidegger's famous pronouncement in his *Introduction to Metaphysics* (also published in 1953) that the idea of a Christian Philosophy was about as meaningful as a round square,[12] we must entertain seriously Rosen's thought that, despite their respective foci on ontology and politics, the man his teacher called "the only great thinker in our time,"[13] exerted a great deal of influence on Leo Strauss.[14] Did Strauss believe in either the round or the square? Does he subscribe to the Nietzschean view that a culture is created *ex nihilo* out of the dialectical interaction between two fictions? Or did he follow Heidegger's example and effectively function as a revelatory interpreter?

Perhaps we could say that Strauss, who claimed to be only a scholar,[15] rejected the poisoned chalice of Reason and preferred to find upright shelter in the enduring stormy tension between the impersonal and the elusive. In less poetic words, he preferred political philosophy to metaphysics. Viewed in this light, it is likely that his setting up of the famous quarrel between the Ancients and Moderns was undertaken with the intention of reconfiguring the debris remaining from Heidegger's *destruktion* of the Western Tradition in a way that protected the West from the consequences of nihilistic enlightenment. This solution amounted to forcing both Faith and Reason to co-operatively assume defensive postures against their common enemy, the juggernaut of technology, instead of exposing each other's offensive deficiencies. Unfortunately, the exigencies of the Cold War forced the West to embrace this very enemy in self-defense. Heidegger warned against this danger, but of course his own doctrines had contributed greatly towards the Western Tradition's weakened condition. Rosen himself believes that Strauss was imprudently prudent "too pessimistic concerning human creativity, too enamored of nature and so too forgetful of the fact that nature is both good and bad"[16] to employ a more positive attitude towards Caliban-like modernity. While we deplore the liberal tendency to celebrate raw potentiality as actuality, this is no reason to embrace the conservative fallacy of justifying, anointing and acclaiming what *is* as what *ought* to be. This is but another form of historicist fatalism. While they might flatter the rich and pander to the powerful, language games of this kind can only breed hubris and stupidity in the real world.

Strauss's preoccupation with such theorists of strife as Thucydides, Hobbes and Machiavelli, as well as his preference for those two noted anti-Socratics Aristophanes and Nietzsche, justify the inference that he esteemed the Ancients for their noble pessimism than out of any belief in the classical good life. This view is also supported by the fact that his celebrated re-discovery of Platonic political philosophy occurred through the esoteric, atheistic, and decidedly pessimistic medium of Islamic political thought. While Strauss's call for the revival of spiritedness was altogether justified in dark days of the Cold War, Cassandra-like, he drowned out his own warnings that the less immediate but gravest threats were posed by intellectual and religious decadence. In our present hegemonic predicament the unformed ambition of Alcibiades is more dangerous than the prudent timidity of Nicias. When our foes are unified by their hatred of us, we can no longer depend on our enemies to remind us of our virtues.

Leo Strauss's prudent interpretations of old, esoteric, texts have little to say to our unlettered, thoughtless and thoroughly exoteric times. His praise of martial virtue seems redundant besides our sanguine bellicosity, and his guarded revelations of well-concealed wickedness fail to shock our shameless and insatiable appetites. The sad truth is that all attempts to reproduce the singular *virtues* of this great exegete have been markedly unsuccessful. Mindless imitation of ideal hierarchical relationships between infinitely wise oracular teachers, noble young aristocrats, and invincibly ignorant *Hoi Polloi* do little good and generate a great deal of mischief in our cynical, illiterate, and thoroughly materialistic society. Today, the grand alliance promoted by Strauss between Reason and Revelation yields a distressingly large harvest of knowledgeable knaves, lustful libertarians and fanatical fools. By contrast Rosen's accounts of the essential connection between Reason and the Good provides a richly comprehensive erotic Platonism that is agreeable to the generous heart and fevered temperament of modernity. He believes that poetry can mediate successfully between sad reason and crass politics[17] and he has shown that a new robust metaphysic can be derived from the enduring phenomena of ordinary experience. While fully aware that nihilism is a permanent human possibility, Rosen's speech and deeds are animated by his confidence that humans are not inherently incapable of the self-knowledge needed to educate their desires and lead a good life. In one of the most beautiful passages of *Nihilism* he stirringly reminds us of the contagious example of a virtuous human being:

> The good man…is not "useful for…" in the same sense that tools, food, acts even just and beautiful things exhibit utility…there is a certain fulfillment, completeness, or perfection which shines forth from such a man, and which we too admire, even perhaps without envy or desire because of its splendor. This is

what we mean by "genuine goodness" or "purity of character." The shining of a good man's splendor may illuminate and help us to complete our own lives, whether by virtue of its nobility, or because we are able to see better what to do ourselves when that noble light permeates the otherwise dark contours of our lives.[18]

These winged words best express what Stanley Rosen has meant to many of his students.

Notes

1. Stanley Rosen, *Hermeneutics as Politics* (Oxford: Oxford University Press, 1987), 127.
2. See Stanley Rosen, Preface to the Portuguese Translation of *Nihilism*, (South Bend: St. Augustine's Press, 2000), xxii.
3. Rosen, Preface to the Portuguese Translation of *Nihilism*, xxiii.
4. Rosen, Preface to the Portuguese Translation of *Nihilism*.
5. Rosen, Preface to the Portuguese Translation of *Nihilism*.
6. Rosen, Preface to the Portuguese Translation of *Nihilism*.
7. Rosen, Preface to the Portuguese Translation of *Nihilism*, xxii–xxiii.
8. Rosen, Preface to the Portuguese Translation of *Nihilism*, xxiv.
9. Rosen, Preface to the Portuguese Translation of *Nihilism*.
10. Leo Strauss, "An Introduction to Heideggerean Existentialism" *The Rebirth of Classical Political Rationalism,* ed. Thomas Pangle (Chicago: University of Chicago Press, 1989) 45.
11. Leo Strauss, "Progress or Return?" in *Jewish Philosophy and the Crisis of Modernity*, ed. Kenneth Hart Green (Albany: State University of New York Press, 1997) 116.
12. Martin Heidegger, *Introduction to Metaphysics* (New Haven: Yale University Press, 1958), 7.
13. Strauss, "An Introduction to Heideggeran Existentialism," 29.
14. Stanley Rosen, Preface to Chinese Translation of *The Quarrel Between Philosophy and Politics*, 1.
15. Strauss, "An Introduction to Heideggeran Existentialism," 29.
16. Rosen, Preface to Chinese Translation, 2.
17. Rosen, Preface to Chinese Translation.
18. Stanley Rosen, *Nihilism* (New Haven: Yale University Press, 1969).

Chapter 11

Harvey Mansfield:
Teaching Not Differently, But Further Than the Parties
Travis D. Smith, Concordia University

The Man

Harvey C. Mansfield is the William R. Kenan, Jr. Professor of Government at Harvard University. He has published several books on modern political thought examined from the vantage point of one who prizes the wisdom of the ancients, scores of articles and reviews in scholarly journals and edited volumes, as well as extensive commentary on American politics and higher education in magazines and newspapers, not to mention original translations of works by Machiavelli and Tocqueville.[1] He is the worthy recipient of many prestigious distinctions, including most recently a 2011 Bradley Prize, the honor of delivering the 2007 Jefferson Lecture in the Humanities, and the National Humanities Medal in 2004. He joined the Harvard faculty in 1962 and calls himself "deep-dyed Crimson,"[2] essentially having been a permanent fixture on campus since enrolling as a first-year in 1949.

Mansfield is usually seen in public decked out in bespoke suit and fedora.[3] Man is made of both body and soul (cf. *SL* 8; *TP* 274; *Lev* xiv.2; *Rep* 572e) and Mansfield cares for the former as well, remaining ever trim and fit. He is fond of observing formalities and always heeds etiquette and protocol.[4] His tranquil temperament and charming demeanor disarm many who hitherto knew him by reputation alone. At countless conferences, *"That's* Harvey Mansfield?" has echoed in the audiences among the previously unacquainted, among whom some came prepared to loathe him. He speaks in a trademark semi-conspiratorial half-whisper modulated via cresting emphases and punctuated by forceful declarations and bursts of mirth. (I remember how nothing completed his "Ha!" quite like a scolding sigh from the late Delba Winthrop. "Oh, Harvey.") He manages to mix curmudgeonly lamentation, genial disputation, and quick-witted mischief. He has a talent for choosing exactly the right words in any situation and on the spot, so rich with meaning that further consideration on them usually yields supplementary though not necessarily complimentary connotations. Always courteous when speaking with journalists and others who are not entirely his peers (cf. *TP* 15; *DA* 177; *NE* 1124b20),[5] Mansfield is adaptable but not in an unlimited fashion. You might say that he "lack[s] the common touch" (*DA* xxii).[6]

Mansfield has earned a reputation as America's archconservative academic intellectual. His is a sophisticated patriotism, admiring most the America of the Founding Fathers as articulated by the foremost champions of the Constitution. If I had to put a label on his political-philosophical position, I might at first stab christen it semi-Machiavellian anti-Machiavellianism.[7] Well versed in that mastermind's modes he appropriates and redeploys them to recoup the orders the Florentine attempted to belay, though not exactly, since Aristotelianism itself recognizes the need for adaptation to changed circumstances (*MV* 21–22; *NE* 1134b30). Mansfield would not endorse the restoration of ecclesiastical authority, for example, but he does not disparage the religious culture intrinsic to America (cf. *MV* 26; *D* I 12.1).[8] He offers a non-theological way of questioning the modern project and combating the materialism that undergirds and propagates Marxism and postmodernism. To attach any "-ism" to his thought, however, does it a disservice. He has penned no treatise blueprinting the just society. The book of his of which he is most proud is presented in the form of a commentary on a commentary on a portion of a work of ancient history. No doctrine derived from conjured conjectures or abstract axioms bears his name (cf. *DA* xliii), although those who know his work can identify Mansfieldian themes, phrases, and flourishes. He endeavors to be scientific, as Aristotle was scientific, in contrast with present-day empirical political science and contemporary political theory, both of which are demonstrably biased despite their vaunted commitments to neutrality and inclusivity. His politics are ultimately friendly to liberalism (*SL* vi, cf. x), democracy (*DA* 400), republicanism, and religion, without being faithfully liberal, democratic, republican, or religious. And like a true friend, he practices tough love.

To the non-academic public, Mansfield is a model of the old-fashioned gentleman, one who is "gentle out of policy, not weakness" (*Man* 14, cf. 146), somewhat out of place nowadays but never out of style. Those who appreciate the contemplative life will recognize how that label falls short, however. Now, I know myself well enough not to presume to call him wise. He calls himself a professor at times (e.g., *SGPP* 1), which states a fact, but he also speaks abusively of professors as a category (e.g., *Man* 158). He permits others to say that he is a philosopher, but he prefers to reserve that appellation for "thinkers of the highest rank" (*Man* 252n18). He self-identifies as a Straussian, and in the context of American politics since the 1960s, a conservative. He will, however, always assert that, for him, philosophy is prior to politics,[9] going so far as to say that if Harvard (or America, by extrapolation) somehow became too right-wing, "I'd be happy to change…I'd probably turn liberal."[10] He has somewhere analyzed and criticized every major modern author, and elevated some thinkers commonly ranked in the second tier (cf. *Man* 24). His modern political-philosophical preferences and influences are predominantly English and American (e.g., Locke, Burke, Publius), alongside the uncommon friends of England and America found among the French (e.g., Montesquieu and Tocqueville). He attends to "the Germans, not so much,"[11] but Hegel lurks in the background, being the culmination of Machiavellianism (*Man* 230; *SGPP* 51), and Nietzsche gets treated at length in *Manliness*, although not in a manner that would gratify Nietzschephiliacs. Nietzsche, he says, "was too brilliant to read Plato carefully" (*Man* 118), and Mansfield gives Nietzsche the same back on Plato's behalf while taking aim at the legacies left by the vulgar Nietzscheanism. All in all, aware that there can be no objective substantiation that the contemplative life is best except in its particular incarnations (*NE* 1179a15–30), Mansfield takes it upon himself to offer a living example, as if one could seek an image of aristocracy in the man himself (cf. *DA* 13). One might venture that he likes America because he is like America, an experiment in self-government. Besides, America is fair; every type of soul may reside there (*Rep* 557c–e).

In what follows, I shall try to describe Professor Mansfield at work, teaching students at Harvard, then attempt to relate his teaching style to the tenor of his political thought.[12] I should like my portrait of Mansfield as a teacher to convey the impression of a man who puts on display the gamut of Aristotelian virtues, from courage, moderation, and generosity, to modest ambition (*NE* 1124b30), mildness, civility, truthfulness, and wit. In grand fashion, Socratic irony, Lockean elusiveness, Montesquieuean complexity, Hamiltonian boldness, and Tocquevillian perspicacity all coalesce and find refinement in him.

The Professor

An education in philosophy is not eminently practical, but it is the route to independent thought and it is indispensable in unearthing and untangling the roots of the opinions encountered in everyday life. While the true purpose of a liberal education rightly understood "is to make a beautiful soul,"[13] Mansfield will stage a utilitarian defense of an education in the history of philosophy as something vital to good citizenship in a free society. The content of newspapers, magazines, television, movies, and even talk radio are but the proverbial shadows on the wall, imitations of imitations of ideas best expressed and therefore best studied in the great books composed by the greatest authors. Thought and action are interrelated. We can ascend to the philosophical from the everyday (*SGPP* 2–3), and the everyday is derivative of the philosophical. Action "trickle[s] down from the top," and behind even the more thoughtless actions of ordinary people are the ideas of great thinkers.[14] Thus, philosophical inquiry is needed to understand and reform our education.[15] As the ancients understood, education must be conceived of broadly, as involving everything that shapes the thoughts and habits of people, lending direction to their actions, conditioning their souls, and affecting their capacity for flourishing. The manner and content of the education of the youth is predictive of the kind of regime they will be suited for in adulthood. Mansfield finds that the education young people presently receive is indulgent, lacking in rigor and standards, and obsessed with issues of personal identity and authenticity. It flatters and flattens students rather than enriching and elevating them. When protected from everything that would make them feel uncomfortable, students become overly sensitive and self-absorbed. But, "Learning is not self-expression," stresses Mansfield.[16] Upon enrolling at university, even bright and promising students are ill-prepared. Harvard College matriculants are no exception. They will encounter a steep learning curve on entering Professor Mansfield's classroom. They must be shown not only how to learn but to want to learn, which offends their democratic sensibilities since it means acknowledging their inferiority. They have been trained to call into question the legitimacy of all authority and resent taking instruction from someone who knows what they need better than they do. Learning to think independently entails taking seriously the ideas of minds much different from and far superior to one's own. Mansfield justifies the prioritization of Western texts as the most critical resources to take on this expedition on account of Western civilization's unparalleled capacity for self-criticism.[17] He also recommends digging deeply into some particular culture (one properly so-called, featuring some cultivation of what is best in man and offering itself a model of the good society), by studying its language, history, and literature,[18] in contrast with the wishy-washy multiculturalism that reigns today, feigning immense respect for everyone and everything while never vacating the comfort zone of a vain and vacuous relativism resting on "lazy dogmatism" (*SGPP* 5).

Harvard is blessed with the best existing student body, Mansfield affirms, although individual students are not equally extraordinary. He is unsure that their time at Harvard improves them, as the curriculum, faculty, and campus environment tend to instill bad habits and inculcate bad ideas. "At least at the time they were chosen they were meant to be the best," he remarks.[19] Today's students are pampered, easygoing, and irresponsible, and yet at the same time anxious, which betrays inklings that something is lacking in them and their education despite their sense of privilege and self-importance. There is a tension between the students' ambitiousness and their aversion to risk that leads them to become clever and opportunistic. Harvard students in particular are sordidly career-oriented and so busy with extracurricular activities that their formal schooling ranks about third on their priority list. Among them Rory Gilmores and Paris Gellers abound, founders and presidents of multiple associations to cure AIDS in Africa, support schools for orphans abroad, and raise consciousness about this or that—and, as it happens, grow their résumés.[20] Mansfield wistfully recalls the heady days of the 1960s when students were excited about politics and ideas, even if their youthful exuberance was misguided. Such fervor could conceivably make a comeback. To be fair, a number of his students are dedicated above all to being excellent students, but they are not the majority. Mansfield caters to them while troubling a bit the others who choose to sign up, winning the occasional convert—not necessarily to his views, but to his approach to education. He cannot help being a fisher casting pearls.

One of Machiavelli's maxims reads, "a prudent man should always enter upon the paths beaten by great men" (P VI 22). Mansfield imposes this rule on his undergraduate students by conducting courses in which only primary source texts are assigned, whether in ancient political philosophy, modern political philosophy, or American political thought. He is not unaware that there is no great inclination among Americans to think theoretically or savor intellectual pleasures, although this is not new (DA 50–51, 288, 403–4, 430, 434, 451). The great books "give you the main alternatives behind our way of life" and "open you to the permanent problems of mankind and of human nature, the questions that return again and again."[21] "The best thing to do is to try to study these great minds," Mansfield argues, "because that's the most direct confrontation with human wisdom, or with the possibilities of human wisdom."[22] He concentrates on the original sources of teachings that turn into ideologies, mining the founders rather than minding their followers. He teaches Marx and Nietzsche rather than Frankfurters and sundry continentalists, let alone the current literature by third-rate commentators. "Why not go for the gold? Why be content with the dross?" (SGPP 1).[23] The great books also supply an encounter with eloquence in an age of mass and social media ever more bereft of it. Mansfield's lectures on them are exhibitions in what it means to read such books with care, inspecting their arguments, searching their meaning, considering their significance, ascertaining their purposes, and assessing their truth. (It's curious how pronouncements of truth can be controversial at an institution with veritas as its motto.) Students are shown the merit of withholding fatuous expressions of agreement or disagreement on the basis of personal convictions or with respect to prevailing public opinion (cf. DA 409–10). Expressions of disapproval are especially appealing to smart young people, who are paradoxically inclined these days to believe that everybody is equal and yet determined to prove that they are smarter than these supposedly obsolete authors. At the beginning of a course, Mansfield provides students with rules for reading the assigned texts: 1. Come only to learn; 2. Empty yourself of prejudices toward the author; 3. Apply no external method to the text; 4. Don't read passively, but rather, think along and argue with the author as you go, as if you were engaging in a dialogue with him.[24] Try to understand each author on his own terms and be open to the possibility that the experience may change your mind about some things. Critical analyses of any thinker are, anyhow, made more impressive when addressed to a sympathetic and generous reading of him. Certainly do not begin any investigation determined to draw a preordained conclusion. Can you imagine, for example, the tedium of always knowing in advance that Y is to blame and that X is the solution?

Day in, day out, in the lecture hall, Mansfield breathes new life into old books and gives students a glimpse of what might be taken away from them should one put so much into them, inviting them to take a chance and give it a go. Mark Blitz relates the experience of attending a lecture by Professor Mansfield in this way:

> Mansfield developed a style of his own that features exquisitely polished set pieces delivered with characteristic flair and rapid pace. One struggled desperately to get down every word including—especially including—the jokes. To miss a step was to fall hopelessly behind. The effect was like having a hundred Koufax curveballs aimed mercilessly at one's head.[25]

And as Mary Ann McGrail reports,

> so far from talking down to or on the level of his students, he pitched his lectures well over the heads of almost everyone in his classes, engendering puzzlement, confusion, frustration, even, and often indignation and laughter as his approach to the great thinkers he taught exposed the superficiality of contemporary cant. His teaching was designed to draw students closer to the great thinkers of political science rather than making them accessible...He made them, at least initially, more inaccessible, awakening in his students an appreciation for the vast divide between their own intellectual powers and learning and those of the great thinkers in the Western tradition.[26]

The unspoken premise behind the level of difficulty his lectures sustain is, "This is Harvard! If you aren't up for a challenge, then why are you here?" I once inquired as to whether he would consider publishing a volume or two of his lectures on the history of moral and political philosophy, and he demurred. Everything in them worthy of publication has already been published, he replied.[27] As challenging as his lectures are, he does the students one favor. Whereas other professors are prone to using jargon to obfuscate and impress, Mansfield keeps to ordinary speech.[28] When lecturing on one author, often over the course of several days or weeks, he offers what seems like a running commentary with occasional digressions, allusions, and offhand remarks. He takes each author's side as best he can and works out their ideas in a friendly fashion, highlighting their best insights while drawing attention to tensions, mysteries, and incongruities, always assuming that the author is no dummy.[29] He makes inferences about their assumptions and draws out the implications of their arguments, furthermore connecting their ideas to those of other authors or recent events, often with discretion but sometimes with blunt force. He leads his students through these books in a spirit of wonder, wondering at the very strange doctrines they contain. He causes students to wonder about themselves, the things they hold dear, and the words they have been rewarded for repeating. Half of the time he makes you wonder if *he* is being serious. He leaves the lines between exposition and interpretation, or observation and criticism, intentionally blurry (cf. *SGPP* 31f),[30] and there is some honesty in that. There is rhetorical power in making it difficult to distinguish his own positions from those of the authors he presents, as well as in his way of holding some things back. These strategies force students to draw their own conclusions, internalizing and taking possession of them. Simply being told what others said and what to think about it only makes it easier to reject and forget the given information. Only after he has worked through some puzzles, assembling the pieces from the author's standpoint, does Mansfield shift to offering criticisms in his own voice. He draws attention to problems in a suggestive fashion rather than presenting definitive conclusions.[31] He raises more questions than he resolves. Sometimes his points seem peculiar or a little too pat, as do his answers to many students' questions, as if he is daring students not to take his word for it, but rather, go back to the text and figure things out for themselves (cf. *MNMO* 13; *MV* xvi).[32] At least to some, "An invitation to struggle is an incitement to excel" (*TP* 278).

Teaching the history of political philosophy, for Mansfield, is not simply to recount a he said/she said (he'd tease, "he said/he said") of what various authors happened to say way back when. Neither is it a dreary hunt for logical fallacies so as to establish our rational superiority. Nor is it an exercise in historicism, explaining away works of political thought as mundane politicking masquerading as something more, all products of their own time relevant only to an understanding of the localized struggles of the past. Mansfield does not pontificate upon a theory of his own invention for obsequious students to ape.[33] He neither requires nor desires flattery (cf. *D* III 21.3), so students cannot get around offering thoughtful arguments of their own by simply taking what they presume to be his side. On the flipside, every term half of the students who turn up during shopping period seeking the spectacle of an extremist professor using his classroom as a soapbox for outmoded and outrageous ideas, practically begging to be offended, leave disappointed. He'll unease you, but not just to displease you. His lectures are not overtly conservative, although in giving all sides a fair hearing he is guilty by inclusion not omission.[34] His task is to make every student feel "equally uncomfortable" so that they may begin to reconsider their prejudices and presuppositions.[35] Intransigence and indifference are the enemy, astonishment the means of combating them. It is not his job to transform you, but to appeal to you to reform yourself.

The assignments in Mansfield's classes traditionally instruct students that references to the scholarly literature or other materials apart from the assigned texts are neither required nor recommended.[36] Until one has grappled with the original texts, one cannot begin to judge the quality of the commentary on them. In the hands of most undergraduates, the secondary literature is a crutch the use of which confers the illusion of sophistication while concealing an unwillingness or inability to assume responsibility for reading a difficult book attentively and meditating on it. Picking authorities to appeal to is like journalists choosing which experts to consult, a way of advancing one's own opinions without owning up to it. Plus, a student's reasoning skills cannot be assessed or improved if they only report what others have said. Mansfield is much less concerned with the particular conclusions students draw than with the way they reach them, and he has no expectation that students will agree with him.

His nickname is infamous enough that Mansfield once stood on the 50 yard line during the halftime show while the HUB encircled him in a "C-" formation. But grades that low are scarce even in his classes anymore. As a scare tactic he announces that he is not averse to Machiavellian instruments in the evaluation of students' work, citing the salutary effects upon an "A student" of receiving the occasional undeserved B or C, to deflate and motivate. Students who grieve about their grades should not see them raised; a lesson in injustice benefits them more than seeing their complaining rewarded. Professor Mansfield is well known for the use of what he dubbed the "ironic grade." Students receive two grades on their assignments: an ironic one, used in calculating the grades that appear on transcripts, and another, kept confidential, representing an honest appraisal.[37] Some students are distressed at having their pretensions punctured, but he reports that they are generally grateful for the candor (so long as it does not hamper their chances for internships at Goldman Sachs or admission to the choicest law schools)—another sign that they know something is amiss within the system. They are aware that they are insufficiently challenged and left unaware of their deficiencies and therefore unsure as to how to improve themselves.

The Supervisor

I have fewer things that I want to say about how Professor Mansfield teaches graduate students. He has an uncanny capacity for quickly sizing up anyone and speaking to him or her in a fashion that is fitting (*NE* 1128a1). What he teaches and does not teach each of his advisees undoubtedly varies from one to another since he has to take each of them as they are (*TP* 46–47; *NE* 1180b5). What little control he may exercise over the admissions process, he trusts that it calls forth certain types (cf. *TP* 60). Mansfield's approach to graduate student supervision is largely hands-off. He does not wish to rule, and his students do not feel as if they are ruled (*D* xlii; *TP* 114, 140). It is not that he would "avoid the appearance and evade the responsibility of ruling" (*TP* 33; cf. *Man* 226), but rather, his approach is closer to saying *watch and learn*—without actually saying it, of course. His supervisory authority is left ambiguous in its particulars but everpresent in the backdrop, leaving it to the imagination of any student to guess at where they stand, supposing that he worries about them at all (*P* IX 40).[38] Training graduate students to rely on themselves, he trusts that they will figure out what they need to do, and if they cannot or will not, that's on them.[39] Encouraging and discouraging words alike are from him infrequently heard. His door is always open to discuss matters of importance, but his time is not to be wasted with idle chit-chat. Practicing political theory requires courage, self-assertion, self-examination, resilience, and risk-taking (*Man* 56–57, 69–70, 218–24, 232). Constant reassurances only nurture timidity and vanity, a reliance on approval that does not propel one forward into the unknown. Mansfield lets students make their own mistakes and waits for them to recognize and rectify them.

There is almost something futile in trying to exert direct force over graduate students in political philosophy. As a breed they are inherently obstinate and poor judges of their interests (cf. *TP* 48–49). As an advisor Mansfield teaches much more indirectly than directly, through the example he provides as a scholar, teacher, host, gentleman, and citizen. "The natural way to improve mores and manners is," he knows, "through mores and manners themselves" (*TP* 244). Witnessing his intellect in action inspires admiration and emulation.[40] He does not demand conformity to his methodology or interpretations, although his ideas have a way of inceiving themselves (*MV* xvi; *TP* 147). For someone whose political positions are so well established, it is impressive how diverse his students are. Some of them are liberals! Some of them are women. This fact accords with his avowal that, for him, partisan politics is subordinate to political science. Mansfield does not begrudge his students the right to take a different side, but whatever side they take he will show them not to be ideologically one-sided. As Sharon Krause says of him,

> Harvey's like this as a teacher too, non-partisan. He has a side for sure, but it's the side of always pushing you to think harder and deeper, more fearlessly. He does this by making questionable the things you always assumed were true, by inviting and answering your arguments, and by showing you by example what it looks like to seek the truth with real courage and persistence…without ever telling you what to think.[41]

Always beginning with a brief but instructive treatment of the readings, Mansfield's graduate seminars are mainly an opportunity for students to work through their thoughts on them aloud, if groping around. What students get out of his seminars is proportional to what they put into them, although they will always leave with a greater sense of what they still do not understand than what they have a handle on. "It can sometimes be a disadvantage to be too quick in your intellect. You come to have too much confidence in your first impression, and you don't fully think things through," Mansfield explains, and this is "one of the things that a professor can teach a brilliant person."[42]

Mansfield is notoriously sparing in his feedback on students' work. His students painstakingly examine each minuscule remark from every angle, keeping in mind the exacting care with which he selects his words.[43] He does not mind dispensing nuggets of interpretive assistance or professional advice when it is solicited, but it is often quizzical, leaving students free to make their own choices (*Man* 204, 229).[44] He does not want them to think that impressing him is paramount. He prepares them for a way of life in which they must ultimately take responsibility for themselves, not only with respect to their career paths, but more importantly, for the quality of their minds and souls. Philosophy is an activity that defines you. It is not principally a job.[45] Some would call it a calling.

Mansfield may be called a master, but in the sense of a teacher of something mastered, a master of apprentices who may someday become masters themselves and not remain forever servile (cf. *MV* xiii; *NE* 1160b1–10; *P* XX 83).[46] How well his students reflect on him is related in part to how they refract or rarify his teaching. Mansfield does dedicate a significant amount of time to training graduate students in their role as teachers, overseeing and advising them on the evaluation of students' work. He also provides many opportunities for learning outside of the classroom. He assists in making connections with networks of scholars and encourages involvement in conferences, seminars, and symposia. His Program on Constitutional Government funds education in languages, Greek and Latin especially (cf. *DA* 452). He sponsors many outstanding guest speakers in the Department and at the Faculty Club.[47] To me, the most memorable events were the biannual post-election autopsies led by William Galston and William Kristol, presented in part as a remedy for the tendency of political scientists to care too little about actual politics and public affairs.[48]

On Campus

Despite its flaws, of which he may be the chief accuser, Harvey Mansfield loves Harvard.[49] He loves it because it is his own and because it is good.[50] He may even love Harvard more than America; it is older and may last longer. Perhaps it is the idea of Harvard that he truly loves—the idea of the very best school in the world (cf. *ACS* 205), or rather the Idea of a School. He loves it as a critical friend, exhorting Harvard as he finds it toward his vision of what it should be. The Harvard community in turn, he says, retains him as a tokenistic "mascot for their tolerance."[51] The criticisms of a conservative sometimes sound like hopeless nostalgia, but for any Aristotelian, the past is not the standard; the best is. Harvard University is too good not to have someone like Harvey C. Mansfield holding it to a perceived higher standard, against what he sees as a decline, waging a noble battle against what may be a lost cause.[52]

Savoring the role of the gleeful gadfly on campus, when the press calls him for an inflammatory remark Mansfield is usually more than happy to oblige.[53] Part of his role as archconservative is to play it a little arch. One columnist in the *Crimson* likened Mansfield's predilection for sparking outrage to "a semi-annual dance."[54] I will not here recite the particulars of each issue on which he causes a sensational stir. They range from political correctness and affirmative action to grade inflation and deflated standards, and from inadequacies in the curriculum, including too much identity politics, to the ideological imbalance that slants the faculty, with its consequences for the broader culture.[55] It is mostly a matter of public record, and not hard to dig up.[56]

Aristotelian ethics, Tocquevillian analysis, plus a pinch of Machiavellian nerve, account for Mansfield's unpopular positions. His objections to political

correctness and affirmative action, for example, are tied to the view that atti-
tudes, sentiments, and intentions, let alone involuntary qualities or circumstances, are no basis upon which to dispense praise or allocate benefits (*NE*
1111b5–12b10). Democracy tends toward a self-congratulatory and stifling uni-
formity of opinion, which is still a form of majority tyranny even if its mouth-
pieces are well-meaning. Beset by those who would suppress freedom of
thought and speech, the responsible thing to do is to keep controversy alive (cf.
DA lvi–vii). It is especially irresponsible to submit to censorship at the premiere
institution where intellectual freedom should reign. "Sensitivity," Mansfield
explains, "is letting other people's reactions to you decide your behavior. So
instead of choosing to do what you think is right and then defending it," you
adapt to what you anticipate others will demand.[57] It is no coincidence that those
who make it their business to ensure that students feel welcome, comfortable,
and unthreatened are also busiest with policing thoughts, applying shame, and
silencing dissent. Those who lead campaigns against bullying—the cause du
jour—need to remember that, hey, bullies are people too.

All of Mansfield's criticisms are based on his assessment of what prevents
Harvard and its students from being superlatively excellent. He objects to complacency with, cooptation by, and subjection to prevailing public sentiments and
dogmas generated by democracy but detrimental to democracies. An egalitarian
ethos misguidedly defers to students and short-changes them instead of cultivating the pursuit of excellence, fostering independent thought, and building strong
character. Harvard is embarrassed about being an elite institution, Mansfield
says, and its students feel guilty about being so privileged.[58] Since "the faculty's
surrender to the students" in the 1960s,[59] the university has been derelict in its
responsibilities to its students and the public at large by not teaching responsibility. Should students counter this claim by insisting that they are motivated above
all by a sense of responsibility to care for people, they do so in accordance with
ideologies that undermine in principle and diminish in practice the sense of and
capacity for responsibility among the very people they aim to aid. It is as if we
were training elites to preside over subjects poor in goods and in spirit rather
than educating leaders of a free and able people (cf. *Pol* 1310a10–30). William
Kristol describes Mansfield's "unpopular and principled" criticisms of Harvard
as part of his effort "to help his fellow Americans to succeed in our honorable
effort to vindicate the capacity of mankind for self-government."[60] While some
of Mansfield's criticisms pertain to Harvard specifically, much of it applies
across academe.

The Teacher

It is not possible for me to offer a critical analysis of Mansfield's political
thought here, but I can try to show the connections between his political teaching and his teaching methods, especially as they pertain to the theme of responsibility. Within Aristotelian ethics, if I may set aside the case for the contemplative life (*Man* 203; *NE* 1177a10–79a30), the pursuit of happiness is portrayed as

being dependent on being responsible for our character and our conduct, for
acting rightly, voluntarily, upon prudent deliberation, informed by right habitua-
tion and relevant experience.[61] "It is up to you to improve your life by behaving
as if it were important,"[62] but when this truth is suppressed men need someone
to remind them of it. Mansfield states the importance of teaching responsibility
most powerfully in the conclusion to *Taming the Prince*, where he writes,

> So the political scientist must become a philosopher and a teacher of responsi-
> bility. Teaching responsibility to others is very different from taking it on one-
> self. To teach it, one must leave room for others to claim their due and exercise
> their choice. The teacher must not try to do everything himself, leaving nothing
> for his pupils to attempt. (*TP* 292)

In connection with the designs of the American founders, he elaborates,
"they wished to encourage responsibility. That is the only responsible thing to
do. Since one cannot oneself rule everything...it is irresponsible to leave no responsibility to others" (*TP* 292). Aristotelian kingship may be the best regime in
theory, but it is hardly practicable (*Man* 206; *SGPP* 5, 14; *TP* 43f, 45; *Pol*
1284b25–30, 1288a15, 1288b1, 1325b10). Machiavelli, his executors, and their
executives aim at indirect governance, which is "to evade the responsibility of
improving politics" (*TP* 292). While remaining decidedly modern, especially in
incautiously embracing a technological approach to the world,[63] the American
constitutional regime partially represents something of a strategic "return to Aristotelian responsibility," Mansfield argues (*TP* 293, cf. 188, 252, 256, 261–62,
276; *ACS* 200). The American regime mixes democratic and oligarchical elements (*DA* l–li, lxxx–xi; cf. *SGPP* 16; *TP* 36, 50, 52, 185, 254; *Pol* 1293b30–
94b40)[64] in a fashion that remains fundamentally republican, while summoning
forth something that approaches natural aristocracy (as Thomas Jefferson so
graciously put it) (*SL* 8, 15, 38).[65] It sets ambitious men against each other in a
competition to serve the interests of others rather than allowing them to unite
against the rest (*ACS* 123; *SL* 10). It profitably deflects the majority of ambitious
men in the direction of money-making within a relatively depoliticized market-
place that primarily allows people to succeed by satisfying the desires of others
(*MNMO* 157; *SL* 23; *TP* 270; cf. *ACS* 43). It also corrects for the deficiencies of
pure republican theory (*ACS* 143; *TP* 252ff), partly through the establishment of
the Presidency, a virtually kingly office restrained from becoming tyrannical so
long as constitutional forms and formalities are respected (*MNMO* 154; *TP*
xxvii, 1, 38f, 69–71, 189, 192f, 289–91; *TVSI* 27; *D* I 58.4, III 17.1).[66]

Given its democratic "point of departure" and "social state" (*DA* 30, 46),
America tends to become increasingly democratic over time. It centralizes authority (*TVSI* 23–24, 93–94; *DA* 84ff, 646ff),[67] and propelled by class conflict
and cultural divides alike (*Pol* 1302a25–30, 1303b15) it becomes susceptible to
demagoguery, which Mansfield regards as "the main danger" (*TP* 289, cf. 82,
266, 273, 280–81; *DA* 188–89; *Fed* No.1 35; *Pol* 1296a1, 1308a20, 1310b15,
1311a15; *Rep* 565c–d). Despotism, though mild, looms forebodingly (*DA*

662ff), its culmination forestalled through the resistance of two types of people: responsible citizens, too proud to forfeit the freedom to make their own choices and hold their own beliefs in exchange for the passable satisfaction of their material interests and the promise of the provision of their security (*ACS* 82, 139, 214, 218; *Man* 49, 60, 233; *MNMO* 264; *TP* 208; *TVSI* 81f);[68] and the responsible leaders who represent them, steadfastly upholding the idea that it is impossible to live well without liberty of thought and action, ready to win honor by confronting the hazards and repairing the damage wrought by other people's irresponsible choices (*ACS* 129–30; *Man* 217f; *SL* 67, 79; *TP* 66–67, 270; *TVSI* 81; *Fed* No.57 353). Despite its projected trajectory, foreseeable with reference to Plato and Tocqueville, it is noteworthy that Mansfield remains optimistic about America's future.[69] Nature, which includes human nature, "is fundamentally on our side,"[70] and it will not permit the permanent triumph of a partial view of man and society. Men will resist even beneficent, rational control (*SL* 7; *TP* 23, 29, 32, 40, 48–49, 57–58).[71] Fortunately, Americans have their founding to point to and guide them as a moderate, internal standard for reform (*D* III 1.2; cf. *MNMO* 300; *MV* 60, 230),[72] to be contrasted with the immoderate drive for egalitarian revolution that nowadays goes by the euphemism "systemic change" under the banner of progress.

To combat the prevailing ideologies of modernity, part of Mansfield's teaching is to tenaciously affirm the truth of various "facts" that problematize the wishful thinking characteristic of his opponents (*NE* 1111b15–20, 1112a30). It is irresponsible to not take the facts into account and try to engineer the impossible, or succumb to utter defeatism or destructive nihilism because perfection is unattainable (*Man* 226; *SL* 86; *TP* 47, 221).[73] A genuinely philosophical or scientific theory of politics takes into account the whole of human nature, including an acknowledgment of its limitations. A responsible political regime likewise respects the limits that nature imposes, bounding the realm of the possible (*ACS* 218; *TP* 50, 56, 286f),[74] cognizant that "the law cannot control nature" (*TP* 18; cf. *Man* xii; *MV* 56). Talking like this is anathema to all modernists, especially Marxists and postmodernists. Modernity is founded on the idea that the purpose of human thought and action is to conquer and transform nature, because nature, both our own and out there, is our enemy (*ACS* 106; *Man* 231; *MNMO* 229; *MV* 70; *SL* 59–60; *TP* 133f, 287, cf. 117). On this theory, man has no reason for gratitude toward God or Nature.[75] Even the idea of nature itself is to be reckoned an artifact.[76] Nothing that is possible should be called unnatural, and nothing should be called impossible (*TP* 129; cf. *MNMO* 163). Mansfield is hardly oblivious to the multifarious reactions that his plain talk about nature prompts. Mankind's conversion or capitulation to the idea that it is us versus the cosmos was the true Machiavellian moment. Even if Machiavelli himself did not blatantly advocate changing human nature,[77] that initiative soon finds its instauration in the version of his vision proposed by his first great pupil, Francis Bacon, who understood that transformative change involves destruction (cf. *MV* 75). Zealous defenders of this project believe that we shall finally achieve peace in our hearts and on earth through it and only through it. At the center of Mansfield's thought is a rejection of these premises and promises. No wonder he makes people angry.[78] He's an infidel. We cannot know and do everything. Security eludes us. Perfect rational control escapes us (cf. *MNMO* 421; *TP* 56f). Its pursuit is therefore irrational. Because risk is part of our permanent condition, moderate risk-taking is rational (*Man* 101,[79] cf. ix, 53, 203, 227–28; *MNMO* 59). Machiavelli's vow to forgo consideration of imaginary republics (*P* XV 61) in the pursuit of a politics of power and security results, in effect, in the proliferation of romantic utopias (*MV* 114),[80] the attempted manufacture of which brings about great insecurity in our hearts and around the world.[81] There is no final political solution that will satisfy and fulfill us (*SL* 87; *TP* 45, 66).[82] The effort to abolish risk proves reckless (*Man* 106). It is irresponsible to take responsibility for everything (cf. *Man* 171–72). It is furthermore ruinous to the very people who attempt it. In order to be capable of anything, they have to be willing and able to do and become anything (*TP* 280f; cf. *NE* 1144a20–35).[83] Such people do not take seriously taking good care of themselves. Seeking wisdom or honor or good character or God's will would constitute inconveniences and create conflict (*TP* 128). It belonged to Machiavelli's third great pupil, Thomas Hobbes, to convince everybody that it is scientific to think of ourselves as bodies without souls, calculating appetite-satisfiers with no higher purpose (*ACS* 108; *MV* 122; *TP* 175).[84] According to his scheme, the smart thing to do is agree to submit to an incomparable power that assumes full responsibility for securing our comfort and simultaneously divests itself of any responsibility, operating as an authorized representative of the people.[85] Even the ways people fill their bellies and tickle their fancies shall come under its purview. Hobbes's democratic anthropology is designed to universalize democratic psychology, transforming men into wimps and naïfs desperate for a combination wet-nurse/governess to aid in sating their cravings, assuaging their fears, and imprinting their brains. Tocqueville's insight that individualism yields collectivism was anticipated and intended by Hobbes. Democratic theories to this day echo Hobbes, probably none more so than that of John Rawls, the most successful professor of political theory over the last century when reckoned by counting minions and citations.[86]

In contrast with many contemporary theorists, whose every other sentence mentions morality or justice or both,[87] it is noticeable how infrequently the word "justice" appears in Mansfield's writings.[88] He prefers to broach the subject of justice indirectly through its relationships to the other virtues (*NE* 1129b25–30). "Moderation," he argues—not justice—"is *the* political virtue," because "wisdom knows its own ignorance, and recognizes that perfect justice is not humanly possible," making its pursuit inherently immoderate (*SL* 52f, cf. 70; *Man* 218; *MV* 257). It is not that Mansfield is unconcerned about justice, but rather he keeps Aristotelian justice in mind, a standard that deems the supremacy of unadulterated egalitarian justice unjust (*Man* 36, 211; *Pol* 1280a10; *Rep* 558c). Primary among the aforementioned facts that Mansfield highlights is the fact of inequality (*Man* 205; *SGPP* 20; *DA* 431),[89] asking, "what else is variety but unequal qualities in different individuals?" (*SL* 97). Natural and conventional inequalities alike are inescapable facts, and what is more, that is fine.[90] Plenty and equality cannot be achieved simultaneously (*DA* lxvii; *NE* 1121a30–b5; *Pol* 1320a30). The rich we will always have with us, but it is not just that. Intellectual inequality is particularly ineradicable (*DA* 51, 432, 513). Democrats are always partial to more equality, mistaking equality the whole of justice (*TVSI* 49; *DA* 52, 426–28, 479–82; *Pol* 1317a40–18b5). They will never get enough of it (*DA* 189, 513). The very pursuit of perfect equality confounds itself, establishing inequalities among those who prove superior or inferior in effecting or worshipping it (*MNMO* 150; *SL* 3, 67; *TP* xvii, 167, 173–74; *TVSI* 63).[91]

Constitutions and laws affect the formation of citizens, but institutional meddling cannot wholly substitute for good character (*ACS* 45; *SL* 71). The condition of men's souls is what truly matters (*DA* lxiii, 8; *SL* 39; *TVSI* 36), not broad historical movements or the system of relations between people. Since we are stuck with character as our primary concern, Mansfield decrees, "when all else fails—and it will—be virtuous" (*TP* 294; cf. *FH* xiv; *MV* 122). To be virtuous, men must be free and responsible. Thus, responsibility for others must not extend so far as to relieve them of learning to practice responsibility for themselves, lest in serving them one renders them servile (*SL* 11, 49). Beware of one who boasts of being brothers' and sisters' keeper (*DA* 430). Going too far to safeguard the dignity is indignifying.

Every actual regime is partial, including democracy (*Man* 206, 212; *MV* 112–13; *SGPP* 2; *TP* 108). From his Aristotelian perspective, Mansfield endeavors, like Tocqueville, "to see, not differently, but further than the parties" (*DA* 15).[92] While the political philosopher may transcend the parties in theory, he recognizes the permanence of the parties in fact (*Fed* No.10). The political philosopher sees the errors and dangers on all sides, and in practice labors to compensate for the former to obviate the latter (*SGPP* 2–3; *SL* 4ff). When the political philosopher reflects on politics and offers counsel, he should respect the opinions of ordinary people, allowing for and duly appreciating the claims made by all parties.[93] He knows that he will appear partisan too, even though he aims at improving not only the side he takes but the regime as a whole and its citizenry thereby (*SGPP* 4–5; *SL* 17; *SPG* 246; *TP* 249, 286–87). In ordinary practice, there is no getting "beyond partisanship" (*ACS* 15), and most people are capable of it only momentarily in thought (*ACS* 128; cf. *MNMO* 383). The purported postpartisan candidate is sure to govern in an ultrapartisan fashion when elected. Universal inclusivity is a mirage and a ruse. Politics as usual, so often decried, is something Americans should be thankful for given the realistic alternatives that history and other nations provide. In this world one has to take sides. One who says otherwise is taking sides against those who recognize the necessity of it (*Man* 268n58). I can only speculate that Mansfield takes the side he does based on the judgment that America today is exceedingly democratic,[94] and in a democratic age (*DA* 6–7, 13), the responsible thing to do is support the side that bucks the trend while cooling its excesses, too.[95] Espousing liberty, applauding excellence, and emboldening men must still be done in a fashion amenable to democracy, and in part on behalf of democracy (*TP* 248, 296). One should document "the abuses of enlightenment without renouncing enlightenment" (*TP* 218).

I was wrapping up at Harvard as preposterous accusations were circulating that a Straussian-neocon conspiracy controlled the White House. It was fascinating. I remember Mansfield in interviews at the time joking that he did not worry about those of his advisees who do not land academic jobs. He can always just send them to Washington to rule the world. But seriously, is it conceivable that there is any truth to the accusation that Mansfield is party to some sort of conspiracy?[96] I suppose so, in as much as whenever two or three people speak in agreement about the way things are heading and how they could and should be otherwise they are, technically speaking, conspiring, given that the Latin root of the word means simply to breathe together. One of the great things about America is that people can rally for change in broad daylight. Is it totally crazy to accuse Mansfield of being some sort of revolutionary? Mansfield explains that not every revolution is of the inadvisable overnight variety. Some occur gradually, perhaps over generations, in which time a regime and its citizens are significantly altered despite outward and official continuity (*ACS* 204; *MV* 113). Something like this has been going on in America since, at least, the Roosevelts (*MNMO* 318; *MV* 255; *TP* 74; cf. *D* I 10.6). "To conserve," however, "it is necessary to reform,"[97] for change in this world always moves forward in time. Technically speaking, therefore, it is revolutionary to argue even for just a gradual restoration of some of the principles, institutions, and virtues of the founding (*MNMO* 87; *Pol* 1289a1).[98] Surely it is unwise to wait until the republic has become the very thing it swore to destroy before raising an alarm (*SL* 80). Hopefully it is a long time before America becomes something for which the heroes of its great wars would not have fought. Mansfield is nowhere near dishonest enough to pretend that the United States is something eternal. Not even America is too big to fail.[99] In the meantime, it is imperative to take a shot at keeping America and Americans free and good (cf. *SGPP* 17).

Where then does Harvey C. Mansfield stand as a teacher of America? He looks to rise above ordinary politics, like a philosopher, but he does not proclaim himself a peer of Aristotle or Machiavelli. He seems content to play the part of John the Baptist vis-à-vis a second Marsilius (*TP* 118, cf. 100; *MNMO* 12, 227; *MV* 296). Even so, he has opted to drop the "Jr." from his name. Perhaps in time men will add "of Cambridge."

Notes

1. Harvey C. Mansfield's books to date, prefaced by the abbreviations by which they are cited if they are referred to in this essay, are as follows:
SPG   *Statesmanship and Party Government: A Study of Burke and Bolingbroke* (Chicago: University of Chicago Press, 1965)
SL   *The Spirit of Liberalism* (Cambridge: Harvard University Press, 1978)

MNMO *Machiavelli's New Modes and Orders: A Study of the Discourses on Livy* (Ithaca: Cornell University Press, 1979; Chicago: University of Chicago Press, 2001)

Thomas Jefferson: Selected Writings, Crofts Classics, ed., with introduction (Arlington Heights, IL.: AHM, 1979; rpt. Wheeling, IL: Harlan Davidson, 1987)

Selected Letters of Edmund Burke, ed., with introduction (Chicago: University of Chicago Press,1984)

P   Niccolò Machiavelli, *The Prince*, trans., with introduction (Chicago: University of Chicago Press, 1985; 2nd ed. 1998)

FH   Niccolò Machiavelli, *Florentine Histories*, with Laura F. Banfield, trans., with introduction (Princeton: Princeton University Press, 1988)

TP   *Taming the Prince: The Ambivalence of Modern Executive Power* (New York: Free Press, 1989; rpt. Baltimore: Johns Hopkins University Press, 1993)

ACS   *America's Constitutional Soul* (Baltimore: Johns Hopkins University Press, 1991)

MV   *Machiavelli's Virtue* (Chicago: University of Chicago Press, 1996)

D   Niccolò Machiavelli, *Discourses on Livy*, with Nathan Tarcov, trans., with introduction (Chicago: University of Chicago Press, 1996)

DA   Alexis de Tocqueville, *Democracy in America*, with Delba Winthrop, trans., with introduction (Chicago: University of Chicago Press, 2000)

SGPP *A Student's Guide to Political Philosophy* (Wilmington, DE: ISI Books, 2001)

Man   *Manliness* (New Haven: Yale University Press, 2006)

TVSI *Tocqueville: A Very Short Introduction* (Oxford: Oxford University Press, 2010)

Thorough bibliographies of Mansfield's publications are found in the two festschrifts dedicated to him. See Mark Blitz and William Kristol, eds., *Educating the Prince* (Lanham, MD: Rowman & Littlefield, 2000), 307–16, and Sharon R. Krause and Mary Ann McGrail, eds., *The Arts of Rule* (Lanham, MD: Lexington Books, 2009), 403–15.

All quotations and citations in this essay are attributed to works published or statements made by Harvey Mansfield unless otherwise noted. Works of political philosophy not by Mansfield but referred to in this essay's citations are:

2T   John Locke, *Second Treatise of Government*, ed. C. B. Macpherson (Indianapolis: Hackett, 1980)

Fed   *The Federalist Papers*, ed. Clinton Rossiter (New York: Penguin, 1961)

Lev   Thomas Hobbes, *Leviathan*, ed. Edwin Curley (Indianapolis: Hackett, 1994)

NE   Aristotle, *Nicomachean Ethics*, trans. Terence Irwin (Indianapolis: Hackett, 1985)

Pol   Aristotle, *The Politics*, trans. Carnes Lord (Chicago: University of Chicago Press, 1984)

Rep   Plato, *The Republic*, trans. Allan Bloom (New York: Basic Books, 1968; 2nd ed. 1991)

2. C-SPAN, In Depth with Harvey Mansfield, September 4, 2005, http://www.c-spanvideo.org/program/188451-1, hereafter "In Depth." There are many lectures, panels, and interviews featuring Professor Mansfield online. They are all relatively recent and many are more informal, yet they remain instructive as instances of Mansfield's efforts to educate the broader public. I refer to only a small sampling in this essay, preferring to rely on his published works, mainly his books. Quotations are drawn from the following and cited as follows: C-SPAN, Booknotes: Alexis de Tocqueville's Democracy in Amer-

ica, December 17, 2000, http://www.booknotes.org/Watch/159774-1/Harvey+Mans-
field.aspx, hereafter "Booknotes"; Big Think, Experts: Harvey Mansfield, undated (c.
2006), http://bigthink.com/harveymansfield, hereafter "Experts"; Hoover Institution,
Uncommon Knowledge: Harvey Mansfield—the Left on Campus,
http://www.hoover.org/multimedia/uncommon-knowledge/48261, hereafter "Left on
Campus," September 14, 2010.

3. One can imagine him donning special robes when he retires to his private study
to commune with his lords. See Machiavelli's letter to Francesco Vettori, December 10,
1513 (*P* 109–10).

4. His posture is proper at all times and his table manners are impeccable (cf. *ACS*
195). He will finish a meal without you seeing him take a bite, as if he didn't require
bodily sustenance since he started imbibing the alchemical elixir that keeps him so spry.

5. Confrontational interviews with spokespersons for the zeitgeist are less his forte.
In such environs Mansfield is exceeded by his most versatile student, William Kristol,
although he does alright. See, for instance, C-SPAN, After Words with Harvey Mansfield, March 15, 2006, http://www.c-spanvideo.org/program/191618-1. In an April 2,
2006 interview on *CBC News: Sunday*, a broadcast journalist embarrassed herself by
behaving sassily and condescendingly toward him. My wife discerned, however, that
Mansfield was not really speaking with this intrepid reporter; he was instead speaking
directly to the audience at home, to people like her. Mansfield admires ambitious women
who succeed in competitive fields like the mass media but understands them better than
they do themselves insofar as he recognizes that they are no more representative of or
role-models for all women generally than secretaries or housewives. Naturally, he would
indicate that they are less so.

6. He can hold his own on *The Colbert Report* (April 5, 2006) but he looks out of
place at a place like Charlie's Kitchen. Harvey's hamburgers are ordered rare, by the
way, providing an illustration of the opposition between manliness and health regulation.

7. Cf. *TP* 184. "The peculiar character of Machiavelli's political science emerges
only by contrast to Aristotle's," Mansfield points out (*MV* xiv; cf. *TP* 25). Of his own
relationship to Machiavelli, he explains, "one cannot help liking him, because he's so
impressive in his skill, in his intelligence, and in his humor," clarifying later on, "I am an
admirer of Machiavelli, but I didn't say that I agree with him." Machiavelli "seems much
less philosophical than he is," he adds, "and I rather like that." "In Depth"; cf. *Man* x;
MNMO 10f. In his book addressed to novices, Mansfield writes, "We may be intrigued
and impressed by Machiavelli, but I am obliged to say it would be wrong to approve of
him" (*SGPP* 35). Cf. René Descartes' September 1646 letter to Princess Elizabeth of
Bohemia, in *The Philosophical Writings of Descartes,* vol. III, trans. John Cottingham,
Robert Stoothoff, Dugald Murdoch, and Anthony Kenny (Cambridge: Cambridge University Press, 1991), 292. In another interview, he remarks, "I don't think I do [agree with
him], but, nonetheless, I somehow love him and love his writing because he punctures
our moral complacency." "Booknotes." When reading Machiavelli, Mansfield confesses,
"I have to make my way on my knees" (*MV* xii).

8. Mansfield maintains that among Machiavelli's principal errors was the assumption that religion is freedom's worst enemy, as explicitly atheistic regimes conduce to
totalitarianism (*Man* 237; *TP* 279ff). Mansfield counts among his friends and students
adherents of various religious traditions, counting on them to alert him when the end
times arrive so that he may align his allegiances as need be. According to classical philosophy, good luck and god's favor are indistinguishable. I would wager that Mansfield
estimates that there are better odds in favor of Jesus saving than Marxism emancipating.

9. "My gods live higher in the sky than conservatism," reveals Mansfield, who positions himself "closer to Plato and Aristotle." "In Depth"; cf. "Experts"; *SL* x. "The ancients promoted a virtue without sanctions that would be practiced for its own sake," he explains (*TP* 206, cf. 226). I remember being surprised when, as a very young undergraduate, my teacher, Janet Ajzenstat, indicated that the world still knows individuals for whom the *Ethics* serves as a surrogate for Scripture.

10. Quoted in Janet Tassel, "The 30 Years' War," *Harvard Magazine*, September–October 1999, 58. Contrast Heidegger (*SGPP* 49; cf. *Man* 136, 228).

11. "Booknotes."

12. In executing the task assigned by the editors of this volume I have decided to rely on myself alone rather than consult my cousins, preferring to be personally accountable for any blunders this text may contain, confident that it won't be altogether bad. My recollections are drawn from my experience as a student in Professor Mansfield's classes and as head teaching fellow for two of his courses. Cf. *AXM* vol. 3 no. 14 (June 2006), 11–14. My account of Professor Mansfield here is unavoidably partial due to my indebtedness and my defects. I was an improbable student of his—too green, irreverent, apprehensive, churchgoing, democratic in my breeding, and flighty, and worst of all, I didn't have the good sense to be born in the USA. Cf. *Man* 77; *MNMO* 325; *SL* 36; *NE* 1095a1. Much of my inaptness remains unreconstructed, as "people are not so easily got out of their old forms" (*2T* §223; cf. *NE* 1103b20–25, 1104b10, *Rep* 561a–b), but I shall drag myself against my inclinations and aim high (*NE* 1109b5; *P* VI 22). In preparing this essay I have endeavored to avoid lyrical panegyric and Harrington's error (*TP* 183). I have tried removing my postgraduation goggles but remain wary of misspeaking. Consider the Correspondence in *Claremont Review of Books* 7.3 (Summer 2007). I would ask Professor Mansfield's forgiveness for any misrepresentations discovered herein if he hadn't once sternly instructed me to stop apologizing like a Canadian. As "you cannot blame the teacher for the pupil's failures" (*Man* 226), I voluntarily bear all my faults upon myself. I certainly intend him no dishonor (*NE* 1124b10–15, 1163b1–15).

13. NEH, "Translating Politics: A Conversation with Harvey Mansfield," May 2007, http://www.neh.gov/news/humanities/2007–05/Political_Origins.htm.

14. "Experts." Words matter because ideas rule (cf. *TP* 296). This is a modern reality. Admittedly, political philosophy does not predate all human society, but political activity anywhere and anywhen always implies the possibility of it (*SGPP* 3–4).

15. Mansfield is skeptical of newfangled (i.e., increasingly democratic) approaches to education. As Tocqueville observes, "It is impossible, whatever one does, to raise the enlightenment of the people above a certain level. It will do no good to facilitate approaches to human knowledge, to improve the methods of teaching and to make science cheap; one will never make it so that men are instructed and develop their intelligence without devoting time to it" (*DA* 188).

16. "Our Coddled Students: How Harvard Compromised Its Virtue," *The Chronicle of Higher Education*, February 21, 2003, B8.

17. "Political Correctness and the Suicide of the Intellect," *The Heritage Lectures*, no. 337, June 26, 1991, 5; cf. "Left on Campus."

18. "In Depth."

19. "In Depth."

20. For Mansfield's depiction of Harvard students, see "Coddled" and "A More Demanding Curriculum," *Claremont Review of Books* 5.1 (Winter 2004). One can almost imagine a Harvard student fast-tracking to the Presidency because it would look good on his C.V. Thankfully, the founders built a regime that does not always require outstanding leadership, although it usually calls it forth in times of emergency (*Fed* No.10 80; cf. *TP*

256, 274; *DA* 190f). More disturbing is the prospect of a President who hopes to be America's Gorbachev (cf. *TP* 66–67). On the danger of audacious men, refer to Abraham Lincoln's 1838 Lyceum Address, one of Mansfield's favorites.

21. "Left on Campus."

22. "In Depth."

23. Maybe the odd women's studies devotee will discover for herself when she actually reads their works that not only do authors like Hobbes and Locke defy the postmodernists' caricatures of them, but these old fogeys are much more subversive than the common critique-monger. One downside to the primary sources only approach is that advanced students may set their standards so high that they realize that their own reflections are not worth reading, hence not worth writing. Nancy Rosenblum has been known to say that in stark contrast to their advisor's prolificacy and to their own detriment, Mansfield's advisees tend not to publish enough.

24. These instructions come from my notes on the first day of class in Moral Reasoning 17 "Democracy and Inequality" (Spring 1999). That course began with Plato's *Republic*, summed up as "an argument for inequality as a whole." That book is so comprehensive that it should be called simply *The Book*, declared Mansfield, except that there is another one out there that has already appropriated the name.

25. Mark Blitz, "Harvey C. Mansfield: An Appreciation," in *The Arts of Rule*, 398. "Trying to understand Machiavelli is like wrestling with a teacher who demonstrates the holds as he throws you," says Mansfield (*MNMO* 12), who puts on a comparable clinic in the classroom himself.

26. Hudson Institute, "The Arts of Rule: Essays in Honor of Harvey C. Mansfield" (transcript, February 19, 2009). Mansfield approaches translation similarly. "It is not the translator's business to make everything familiar" (*P* xxv).

27. This hardly implies that his writings express all that he has learned and understood (*MNMO* 13).

28. On the "jargonized wishful thinking" suffusing the social sciences, see "Sociology and Other 'Meathead' Majors" *The Wall Street Journal*, May 31, 2011; cf. *SGPP* 4.

29. Regarding Aristotle's *Politics*, for instance, Mansfield recommends that despite its appearance as "a hodge-podge of obscurities, repetitions, and inconsistencies" the reader must "suspend this belief and consider the text afresh with the hopeful hypothesis (which one must never fail to test) that the obstacles placed in his way are puzzles arranged for his instruction" (*TP* 28).

30. Consider his summary of Hamilton's positions at *TP* 276–78. Is he reporting or endorsing?

31. Read, for instance, chapters 8 and 9 of *TP* on Locke and Montesquieu to see how Mansfield weaves together charitable exposition, careful examination, and critical evaluation-although he states his own positions more straightforwardly in his published work than he does in the classroom.

32. Mansfield has a tell when he's bluffing. A slight and sudden waist-high punching motion indicates when an argument or answer is not entirely satisfactory, that something has been oversimplified or left unsaid, but he's moving on, leaving it up to you to take note of the lapse or lacuna. In the classroom he is deliberately "provocative or outlandish," he admits, "I also try to go perhaps too fast or too far so that you have something that you're not quite understanding as you walk out of the classroom....I want to give them something that they don't or aren't expected really fully to understand the first time they hear it...to keep them alive in between classes." "In Depth."

33. In addition to his regular lectures, however, he has delivered several sermons at the campus chapel. The one on charity from February 12, 2008, is relevant to the discus-

sion of treating those with whom one disagrees with respect so as to fortify one's own position. "The Common Form of All the Virtues," *Claremont Review of Books* 8.2 (Spring 2008).

34. "Conservatives," Mansfield argues, "are more tolerant [than liberals] because conservatives don't expect that liberalism is going to disappear, whereas liberals expect that conservatism will disappear." "Left on Campus"; cf. *SGPP* 5; *Man* 95, 204; *MV* 56. "Progress goes against diversity," is another way of putting it, "because progress makes certain ideas obsolete." "In Depth." Whereas progressivism's advances are held irrevocable and oblige compliance (*ACS* 141), Mansfield knows that you cannot wish away the dreamers.

35. "In Depth." He adds, "I do get a lot of conservative students because if you're a conservative at Harvard, or at a place like Harvard, you have no friends among professors in the classroom—and so they look for someone who will try to reassure them that what they think isn't totally crazy...[but] my job is not to reassure them but to make them uncomfortable too." Mansfield is not against equal treatment in all things always. Whatever their leanings, all students must be reckoned equally ignorant, inexperienced, and swayed by passions. Mansfield also asks equally devastating questions of every theorist the Department invites to speak. I personally miss the spectacle of the ol' one-two that he and Richard Tuck would deliver in tandem, leaving most guests, especially job candidates, reeling.

36. In the same spirit I guarantee to my own students that in the sum of what lies between the covers of any one of the great books and what is found between their ears there is sufficient raw material for an untold number of compelling essays.

37. Teaching fellows in courses issuing ironic grades must realize that the practice suggests something about the value of the grades they receive on their graduate level work, too.

38. Mansfield's persona is extraordinarily mild, for "No one is more ridiculous than an angry professor" (*SL* 52). He will show flashes of anger when he is most displeased, such as when a teaching fellow—one of his arms—gives away too many As, or when a one of his friends in the academy makes a disappointing choice. He also knows how to play the ferocious guard dog. See "Reply to Pocock," *Political Theory* 3.4 (November 1975): 402–5; cf. *NE* 1124b25. As an aside in that context, if one really could "identify Machiavellians merely by counting references to the name Machiavelli" (*TP* 184), it would turn out that some of the most Machiavellian scholars are the very ones who maintain that Machiavelli was not such a bad guy. (Should that be surprising?)

39. Incidentally, Mansfield is the most preeminent Straussian not formally schooled by Strauss.

40. That said, impersonating Mansfield's distinctive mannerisms outright should be avoided. It always comes off as parody. When it isn't intended as parody, the result is inadvertent self-parody.

41. Hudson, "Arts of Rule." For more on his "anti-dogmatism as a teacher and mentor," see Sharon R. Krause and Mary Ann McGrail, Introduction, *The Arts of Rule*, viii, cf. xi.

42. "In Depth."

43. One small example: in returning the first essay I submitted for one of his seminars, he grinned and assured me that it was "monumental." It was twice as long as assigned.

44. Then again, do not bother to ask him whether it is a good idea to write a dissertation on Nietzsche, or depend much on numerology in one's research (*MV* xvi).

45. To be sure, Mansfield recognizes the value of a decent job and certainly does what he can to help (*NE* 1153b15). Teaching in Quebec, where the inhabitants supply ample evidence that the love of one's own is a part of human nature, I have the fortune of observing the descent into *le despotisme doux* from the front row balcony. Montreal specifically is renowned for fine dining and summertime festivals (a/k/a bread and circuses), boasts more gentlemen's clubs than gentlemen, and caters to individuals with few responsibilities (cf. *SL* 49). As a native of Brantford I am delighted to have recently resettled in the province of Ontario.

46. For some cryptic remarks by Mansfield on the relationship between a teacher and his pupils, see Hudson, "Arts of Rule."

47. I recall that on the day that Baghdad fell Mansfield had the Faculty Club serve champagne in celebration. It would have been a shame if nobody did, he said, and to be sure, nobody else would have. See "Our Courage in Danger," Hoover Institution, *Endangered Virtues* essay series, 2011.

48. "A political scientist is supposed to study politics," but the professionals and their students "try to distance [themselves] from current politics and abstract from it using mathematical formulae" and by "chang[ing] the words," which "distracts [them] from dealing with actual political questions." NEH, "Translating Politics."

49. "I love Harvard wisely and not too well," he remarks, "just a little more than it deserves." Quoted in Tassel, "30 Years'," 58.

50. *Pol* 1262b20. Mansfield fastidiously avoids calling "that place in New Haven" by name. His dutiful rooting for the Red Sox exemplifies the due respect owed to the human propensity to love one's own even when it is not the best. However, since 2004, his team no longer represents the traditional idea of the Red Sox. Their aptly-named rivals have always provided evidence in support of the proposition that that power is proof of virtue (*Pol* 1255a10–15). To become champions again at long, long last, the Red Sox had to ever more emulate that evil empire their loyal fans hate most (cf. *ACS* 167), such that now, from far enough away, say Wrigley Field, these two franchises are relatively indistinguishable. Tangentially, Mansfield once mentioned that Leo Strauss founded "an informal school, like Red Sox Nation." "In Depth." That fandom became official and started granting members "citizenship" in 2004.

51. "In Depth."

52. "Manliness loves, and loves too much, the position of being embattled and alone against the world" (*Man* xiii).

53. During one televised Q&A, Mansfield acts piqued when a caller complains that his remarks are "a bit inflammatory." He means to be "a lot inflammatory." "In Depth."

54. Marc. J Ambinder, "The Aggressive-Passive Mr. Mansfield," *The Harvard Crimson*, February 26, 2001. As I write this essay I espy a screed by two feisty and fiery young women in the December 12, 2011 *Crimson* entitled, "Mansfield's Myth of Manliness." Here we go for another round.

55. "The liberalism of the media," imparted to public opinion, "comes from the liberalism of academia." "In Depth"; cf. *SL* 40; *TVSI* 49; *Lev*, xxx.14. As things stand, if he could practice the virtue of magnificence, Mansfield foresees funding "high culture" rather than the universities. "Experts."

56. Need I supply a disclaimer to the effect that Mansfield's views regarding Harvard do not necessarily represent my own? (I remain in the dark as to which plus factors gained me admission.) For a sampling of his criticisms, see: "More Demanding"; "Political Correctness"; NEH, "Translating Politics"; "Grade Inflation: It's Time to Face the Facts," *Chronicle of Higher Education*, April 6, 2001; "The Cost of Affirmative Action,"

The Harvard Crimson, June 4, 2008; and "Pride and Justice in Affirmative Action," in *ACS*.

57. "Left on Campus." It should not be impermissible to proclaim from rooftops and tell it on the mountain that Joseph Smith is a false prophet. Every non-Mormon insinuates it without uttering it, as every Mormon knows. Among civilized people it is out of civility that one does not make such a scene, not out of fear of reprisal—whether from the offended party or those who presume to preserve the potentially offended from insult on grounds not shared but gladly exploited by them. Now, if amidst the multitude of mild-mannered Mormons worldwide there were some brutal savages lying in wait, not content to remain exotic and remote, a civilized people would be absolutely right to declare that much publicly, and maybe go so far as to fight them. In any event, besmirching their prophet remains improvident.

58. See "Principles That Don't Change," *City Journal*, May 17, 2011, particularly on what "dropping the H-bomb" means.

59. "Left on Campus."

60. William Kristol, Introduction, *Educating the Prince*, xii.

61. Mansfield elaborates, "virtues are not suggested to us but are demanded of us, and Aristotle does not want to give excuses for not being virtuous based on human weakness." "Is Courage A Masculine Virtue? Yes, sort of..." *In Character*, January 1, 2009. Aristotle's treatment of voluntary action in Book III of *NE* raises the question of just how free human beings really are. Assuming that we are not all entirely unfree by nature, it is evident that some men become freer than others due to various combinations of nature, fortune (including nurture), reason, experience, and action (*Pol* 1332a40; cf. *Rep* 564e). It remains a political question how free we should say that people are. If we generally attribute to them less responsibility than they might obtain, then individuals are apt to become less responsible than they would have otherwise been. As Mansfield says, "if [men] do *not* choose, they will lose the power of choice" (*MNMO* 232). If we hold men to a higher level of culpability, they will generally take greater responsibility for themselves. Liberals of the tax-and-spend (-and-spend) variety lean the one way, traditional or "classical" liberals tend the other. Locke is the principal theorist of the latter. Mansfield admires Locke for the confusions and tensions his arguments contain (*ACS* 111; *SGPP* 41; *TP* 186, 192, 204–5, cf. 259, 276). They suit a free people better than the ineluctable logic of rationalist principles. Both kinds of liberalism make simplifying assumptions and are therefore ideological, or partial and imperfect (*SL* 93), but the second type better conduces to the development of the moral and intellectual virtues, although with no guarantees (*ACS* 148; *TP* 263). Human excellence cannot be engineered and still remain human or excellent. According to Sharon Krause, Mansfield "reminds us of the ennobling potential of individual rights and more generally the ennobling potential of a liberal political order," since "it treats us as if we had noble souls and it summons a kind of nobility from us." Hudson, "Arts of Rule." Mansfield himself notes that liberalism itself is not noble (*SL* 38; *Man* 188–89; *TP* 197f), and it forbids recognition of a class of noblemen, but it leaves space for the cultivation of some nobility in some of its citizens (*DA* xxxvi, xlviii; *NE* 1180a30). He reminds us that "freedom exists for the sake of virtue" (*TP* 37). And as Tocqueville argues, "the collective force of citizens will always be more powerful to produce social well-being than the authority of government" (*DA* 86). It is worth acknowledging that the free society also produces more stuff. The psychology of leftist liberalism is hedonistic, but as luck would have it, its policies compound want. Placing the two kinds of liberalism on a simple spectrum is nevertheless tricky. Historically speaking, the Lockean turn looks like a detour from what could have otherwise been a straight line from Hobbes to Marx (cf. *DA* lxix, 52; *Man* 244; *TP* 209–10, 224ff; *Fed*

No.48 313; *Pol* 1318b40–19a1, 1328b35). Modern liberalism has from the get-go sought to bring into being the rational state that controls man and nature, Mansfield contends (*Man* 230).

62. "How to Understand Politics: What the Humanities Can Say to Science," Jefferson Lecture in the Humanities, May 8, 2007.

63. Concerned with production, not action, *techne* does not tell us what we should and should not make, nor the right way to use what we have made. To value technological knowledge most is inherently irresponsible. Cf. *Man* 35, 41, 170, 224f; *SGPP* 50.

64. Mansfield proposes America as an exception to the rule that in all societies the many are poor (*SL* 2; cf. *Pol* 1279b35, 1290b1, 1293a1-10, 1295a25-97a10). In America, the middling element is largest and many of the poor are relatively well off in comparison with what constitutes poverty elsewhere and elsewhen (*2T* §41). The idea that the poor comprise 99% of America is un-American, and false, though it may preoccupy con-men and conned men. "When the government declares war on poverty," however, "everyone wants to be poor," Mansfield remarks (*ACS* 75). Tocqueville envisioned a society in which "The poor man, deprived of enlightenment and freedom, would not even conceive the idea of raising himself toward wealth" (*DA* 430, cf. 641).

65. Natural aristocracy may be approximated only where men have the opportunity to prove themselves, where "actual virtue... is tested in service" and "presumptive virtue" does not rule unchallenged and unaided by it (*SPG* 204; cf. *ACS* 214-16). As democracy advances, presumptive virtue is increasingly held by the multitude, holding back those who aim high, not bequeathed upon undeservingly privileged elites who would hold them down (*DA* 180). Liberal democracy, the very society that opens up to more people than ever before the possibility of living and doing well (*DA* xxii), relatively speaking, also produces legions who undervalue and squander their opportunities and resent and restrict those who would not (*TP* 226), spreading cynicism regarding the moral justification for inequality, its assurance that the successes of particular persons yield widespread benefits indirectly. In any circumstance, he who would live well must take responsibility for himself, letting neither pretenders nor prodigals get him down, envying neither people's champions nor the sons of tyrants.

66. Mansfield recommends contrasting Hamilton and Madison on the truth of the Presidency (*TP* 159, 276–78, 336n57).

67. "Political liberty is not the enemy of unity and order but, on the contrary, their necessary condition," writes Mansfield, "The false unity imposed by one at the top, characteristic of democratic big government as much as of absolute monarchy, is open to revolution and deserves to be so" (*TVSI* 97; cf. *ACS* 45; *TP* 185; *2T* §§232, 239).

68. It falls to philosophers to excavate the grounds of man's pride (*Man* 223–24, cf. 205; *MNMO* 276; *TVSI* 113).

69. See *Commentary*, November 2011, 38–39, cf. "Experts." He pledges, "I'm not going to make any bets against my country." "Booknotes" and "In Depth"; cf. *NE* 1116a1; *Rep* 560a.

70. "Experts"; cf. *Man* 202ff, 215–16; *TP* 98, 117, 236, 287.

71. See Mansfield's Introduction to Raymond Aron, *The Opium of the Intellectuals* (New Brunswick, NJ: Transaction, 2001), xiv. Some liberal theories are inaptly named, presuming the consent of and thus imposing it on hypothetical rational men to sidestep the inconvenience of persuading actual men, who are neither so rational nor agreeable (*ACS* 95–96; *SL* 48; *TP* 116). For more on the failings of well-intentioned rational control, see Mansfield's critique of modern science, especially empirical, quantitative social science, in his Jefferson Lecture and elsewhere, e.g., *DA* lxv–vi; *Man* 36–41; "Democracy and Greatness" *The Weekly Standard*, December 11, 2006; "Rational Control, or

Life Without Virtue" *The New Criterion*, September 2006; cf. *NE* 1094b10–25, 1098a25. Modern society has laid a trap for itself, in that it requires for the success of its mission political scientists that do not and cannot exist. Leo Strauss, *What is Political Philosophy?* (Chicago: University of Chicago Press, 1959), 15.

72. Luckily, America had neither a demigod nor prophet legislator, meaning that it takes only ordinary statesmen, like Lincoln, to set America aright. While conservatives usually disapprove of reading rights and powers into the Constitution, there is good reason to interpret the Thirteenth Amendment, embodying the spirit of the Emancipation Proclamation, not as a departure from the old Constitution but instead as the culmination of the proposition on which it was built and the fulfillment of a purpose foretold and invoked by, if providentially concealed within, its venerable script.

73. Mansfield links nihilism and egalitarianism, observing, "equality is prized not because equality is good, but because nothing is [held to be] good." "Principles."

74. "Responsibility, in order to be reasonable, must be limited to objects within the power of the responsible party, and in order to be effectual, must relate to operations of that power, of which a ready and proper judgment can be formed by the constituents," explains Madison (*Fed* No.63 383; cf. *ACS* 143). That limited government "do[es] not attempt to make everyone happy" is reason for commendation not condemnation (*ACS* 94, cf. 42, 95–97; *DA* liii; *Man* 165; *SPG* 218).

75. So habituated to ingratitude, modern men and women are scarcely appreciative of whatever benefits governments (i.e., the taxpayers of the present, future, and distant future) bestow (*MV* 239–40).

76. It is particularly comical when people claim that "justice" is but a social construct and then pertinaciously catalog, positively castigate and piously chastise injustices, postulating cures with perfect clarity (cf. *SGPP* 10–12).

77. "In Depth"; cf. *MNMO* 350.

78. Cf. *TP* 112. That Mansfield admixes his arguments with wit aggravates the outrage. Radicals are motivated by anger they confuse for reason (*SL* 24–25). The man who is reconciled to the imperfectability of man and the world is freed to find humor in mankind's folly, to the chagrin of—and often at the expense of (*NE* 1128a20-30)—our secular analogues to Jorge de Burgos (the blind monk from Umberto Eco's *The Name of the Rose*), men and women who need to and need us to feel insecure so that we retain our faith in their power to fix the world. They would forbid laughter because it betrays a lack of conviction and determination. Instead of agitating for more ambitious policies and technologies to avert natural catastrophes, Hurricane Katrina provided Mansfield with an opportunity to ponder which American cities would not be worth rebuilding were they destroyed. "In Depth."

79. At the center of the central paragraph of the central chapter of *Manliness*.

80. "The ancients tried to consider things from all points of view…they aimed for wisdom…But the moderns produce theories; they have a project and aim for change or reform…Their theories single out a single factor…on the basis of which they fashion a 'system'…that is intended to effect a reform in human affairs… Modern theories are deliberately incomplete" (*SGPP* 35f). Modern theories typically do not start with an open and honest consideration of all that is and was in order to determine what could be, for better or for worse, and what would be best or least bad. They affirm inflexible principles from which to promote policies derivative of a willful determination to attain final victory for a partisan view of what should be (cf. *SPG* 227). They apply force and fraud in the interpretation of what is, has been, and might be, so as to cook up an account of things with which to cajole others into sharing their fantasies and committing the necessary sacrifices (*TVSI* 109). Mansfield coronates feminism king of schemes like these. The

term "feminist philosopher" is redundant insofar as feminism recognizes the truth of any-thing that reason would discover, and self-contradictory in as much as it posits its prem-ises and plots its purposes out of anger and perceived interests. That aggressive feminists tend to be statists attests to the natural difference they try to deny (cf. *Man* 78). It takes philosophical courage to "always follow the logos, the argument, and not try to bend it to suit one's purposes" (*Man* 223, cf. 219–224; cf. *DA* 408).

81. For Mansfield's criticism of the emerging empirical research on happiness, see "Good and Happy," *The New Republic*, July 3, 2006, 30–33.

82. Confidence "that the best regime can be made actual" is arguably the most deci-sive error in human history, even though the American Revolution was complicit in it. "Experts"; cf. *DA* lxii.

83. "If carried to its logical conclusion, autonomy means tyranny, the will alto-gether unchecked" (*Man* 239, cf. 153, 156, 262n79). See also "Rational Control."

84. Just as tyrants cannot explain why there is any glory in oppressing the weak, one must wonder what makes meat machines worthy of moral consideration or possible objects of liberation (*Man* 138; *MV* 52, 238; *TP* 293; *DA* 11, 519–20).

85. "Rational control is afraid of exposing itself and thereby being compelled to take responsibility for its rule," observes Mansfield (*Man* 232; cf. *TP* 29, 282).

86. Rawls had the advantage of possessing Robert Nozick as his foil. For Mans-field's generous reading of Rawls, see "Cucumber Liberalism" in *SL*. Mansfield puts forward Rawls as an example of someone who hoped to be a latter-day Solon. "In Depth"; cf. *SL* 97. The premise behind Rawls's system is that cowardice is rational. Not that all men are cowardly, but they should be. Injustice exists mainly because jerks and dolts consider themselves important or courageous and dare to bet on themselves. The right thing to do, therefore, is rearrange everything so that cowards make good. I do not read Rawls regularly, but I contemplate him daily, whenever my five-year-old cries "it's not fair."

87. See Mansfield's Foreword to Pierre Manent, *Tocqueville and the Nature of De-mocracy* (Lanham, MD: Rowman & Littlefield, 1996), viii.

88. Cf. *DA* xxxvii. Mansfield has even less to say about love. See Patrick Deneen's letter in *First Things*, December 2007, and Mansfield's reply. Mansfield asserts that "rea-son and love are not consistent" (*Man* 103), a statement with some subtext (cf. *MV* 26; *TP* 133). Among progressive Christians, prostrate before earthly powers, filled with righteous anger (cf. *SL* 61) and mindful of bread alone, working to make trillions of loaves appear by means of Machiavellian liberality construed as charity (*P* XVI 64), love is conflated with "social justice," sanctified by compassion but begetting covetousness and poured from a cup that runneth dry.

89. Cf. *TP* 32; *DA* 611. His affirmation of "the fact of aristocracy" (*SL* 38; cf. *DA* 51) is more scandalous. Among Mansfield's other favorite facts is that a just republic cannot avoid imperial entanglements. It is the nature of men who uphold justice to com-bat injustice, not just stand on guard against it. "Their very goodness, when it is responsi-ble, compels them to compel others so as to make them good too," he discerns (*Man* 217, cf. 77; *MNMO* 198; *TP* 136). Moderation is needed to temper this tendency, since self-government requires self-sufficiency (*DA* lxxxii; *Man* 218; *TP* 215, 229; *NE* 1134a25; *Pol* 1252b25–30). Another fact: there is no bloodless revolution (*TVSI* 100; cf. *SL* 34, 44). For yet another striking fact, see *Man* 42, cf. 59, 75, 145, 155, 203, 212.

90. "Democratic equality is possible because democratic public opinion says it is," quips Mansfield (*TVSI* 73).

91. Every anarchist is a traitor to his own cause, as (with a hat tip to Dr. Horrible) the effectual truth of what he wants is *"Anarchy that I run!"* Cf. *Man* 186; *SGPP* 20; *TP* 30.

92. Bryan Garsten, "Seeing 'Not Differently, but Further, than the Parties'," in *The Arts of Rule*, 374.

93. Seeing neither differently nor further than the parties is the business of C-SPAN, which Mansfield appreciates for its unvarnished presentation of American partisan politics. "The Virtues of C-SPAN," *The American Enterprise*, September-October 1997.

94. People who complain that the modern regime features more inequality than equality expose their lack of historical depth and theoretical breadth. That the clamor today is for more equality in matters of wealth, sex, and health is telling (cf. *DA* 509). Basically, we remain unequal only in what is lowest in us. The reigning viewpoint refuses to rank soul over body, if it tolerates soul talk at all (*ACS* 103; cf. *Man* 193). It rejects the existence or significance of inequalities in matters of wisdom, godliness, character, honor, age, rank, caste, or occupation. Even armed service is open and voluntary. We relativize truth claims, cultures, "life-plans," values, tastes, and choices. Tolerance became indifference before becoming principled nonjudgmentalism on the way to gooey acceptance and out-and-out celebration. We show neither deference nor reverence. We respect only those authorities we consent to, and then we deny consenting to any of them. The theme song that goes, *"You're not the boss of me now"* may as well be the national anthem.

95. Oligarchs, actual and presumptive, tend to contribute to their own undoing (*Rep* 555b–56e, 565b–c). At the same time that he deprecates the left Mansfield gently reproaches and coaxes more ideologically inclined right-wingers. He describes Ayn Rand as someone who appeals to "young people," epitomizing "someone to start with" and "move on from." "In Depth." See chapter 6 of *ACS* for a critical treatment of several strains within American conservatism. Cf. *ACS* 44, 79; *SL* 93; *SPG* 218–19; *TP* 36; *Pol* 1280b30. Critics who mistook *Manliness* for an ideological apology for the domination of women by men frankly do not know how to read. See *Man* 70, 81, 143, 210, 214f. I suspect that *Manliness* cannot be fully understood until the reader has found something funny on every page. Cf. interview by Elizabeth Gilbert, "It's a Guy Thing," *O: The Oprah Magazine*, April 2006, 230.

96. Fun fact: Mansfield's commentary on *D* III 6 in *MNMO* runs from line 35 of page 317 to line 34 of page 343.

97. NEH, "Translating Politics."

98. In his Jefferson Lecture, Mansfield defines politics by identifying seven dimensions of what it is essentially about, the fourth of which is "change, or to speak frankly, let us say revolution—large or small, active or latent."

99. Tocqueville argued that because democracy is here to stay it must be educated so that it turns out relatively well rather than worse (*DA* xlviii, li, 12). Likewise, if we ever found ourselves stuck with despotism at home and empire abroad, an Aristotelian political scientist would have to wonder how to make the best of it, ameliorate the situation responsibly, and ward off worse alternatives (cf. *TP* 255; *Pol* 1313a40–14a40). But let's not end on a dour note.

Authors' Biographies

Leah Bradshaw is an Associate Professor of Political Science at Brock University. She has published several articles and book chapters and is author of *Acting and Thinking: The Political Thought of Hannah Arendt* (Toronto Press, 1989).

Charles R. Embry is Professor Emeritus of Political Science at Texas A & M University at Commerce. He is author of *The Philosopher and the Storyteller: Eric Voegelin and the Twentieth Century* (Missouri Press, 2008) and editor of *Voegelinian Readings of Modern Literature* (Missouri Press, 2011), *Robert B. Heilman and Eric Vogelin* (Missouri Press, 2004), and co-editor with Barry Cooper, *Philosophy, Literature, and Politics* (Missouri Press, 2005).

Molly Brigid Flynn is an Associate Professor of Philosophy at Assumption College. She has published several articles on Edmund Husserl, Robert Sokolowski, and Phenomenology.

Bryan-Paul Frost is the James A. and Kaye L. Crocker Endowed Professor of Political Science at the University of Louisiana at Lafayette. He is editor and co-translator with Robert Howse of Alexandre Kojève's *Outline of a Phenomenology of Right* (Rowman and Littlefield, 2000); co-editor with Jeffrey Sikkenga of *History of American Political Thought* (Lexington Books, 2003); and co-editor with Daniel J. Mahoney of *Political Reason in the Age of Ideology: Essays in Honor of Raymond Aron* (Transaction Publishers, 2007).

Lance M. Grigg is an Associate Professor of Education at the University of Lethbridge. He is the author of several articles with a focus on Bernard Lonergan.

Michael Henry is a Professor of Philosophy at St. John's University. He is series editor of *The Library of Conservative Thought* for Transaction Publishers and co-editor with John A. Gueguen and James Rhodes of *The Good Man in Society: Active Contemplation—Essays in Honor of Gerhart Niemeyer* (Rowman and Littlefield, 1989) and editor of *The Loss and Recovery of Truth: Selected Writings of Gerhart Niemeyer* (St. Augustine Press, 2012).

John von Heyking is an Associate Professor of Political Science at the University of Lethbridge. He is author of *Augustine and Politics as Longing in the World* (Missouri Press, 2001) as well as co-editor with Richard Avramenko of *Friendship and Politics: Essays in Political Thought* (Notre Dame Press, 2008), with Ronald Weed of *Civil Religion in Political Thought: Its Perennial Questions and Enduring Relevance in North America* (Catholic University Press, 2010), and with Thomas W. Heilke two volumes of the *Collected Works of Eric Voegelin* (Missouri Press, 2003).

Tim Hoye is a Professor of Government at Texas Woman's University. He specializes in political theory, American politics, and Asian politics and is author of the textbook on modern Japan entitled *Japanese Politics: Fixed and Floating Worlds* (Prentice Hall, 1998).

Nalin Ranasinghe is Professor of Philosophy at Assumption College. He is author *Soul of Socrates* (Cornell Press, 2000), *Logos and Eros* (St. Augustine's Press, 2008), *Socrates in the Underworld* (St. Augustine's Press, 2008), and *Socrates and the Gods* (St. Augustine Press, 2011).

Travis D. Smith is an Associate Professor of Political Science at Concordia University. He is the author of several articles on Francis Bacon and Thomas Hobbes.

Lee Trepanier is an Associate Professor of Political Science at Saginaw Valley State University. He is the author of *Political Symbols in Russian History* (Lexington Books, 2007), co-author with Lynita Newswander of *LDS in the USA: Mormonism and the Making of American Culture* (Baylor Press, 2011), and editor of several volumes, the most recent being *Eric Voegelin and the Continental Tradition* (with Steven F. McGuire, Missouri Press, 2011), *Cosmopolitanism in the Age of Globalization* (with Khalil Habib, Kentucky Press, 2011), and *Saul Bellow's Political Thought* (with Gloria Cronin, Kentucky Press, forthcoming).

Michael Zuckert is the Nancy R. Dreux Professor of Political Science at the University of Notre Dame. He is the author with Catherine H. Zuckert of *The Truth about Leo Strauss: Political Philosophy and American Democracy* (Chicago Press, 2008); *Launching Liberalism: John Locke and the Liberal Tradition* (University Press of Kansas, 2002); *Natural Rights and New Republicanism* (Princeton Press, 1998); and *The Natural Rights Republic* (Notre Dame Press, 1996).

INDEX